Television and New Media

Television is now online as much as it is "on-air." We watch TV on computers, phones, and other mobile devices. And, increasingly, we go online to follow additional storylines for shows in "webisodes," to play games centered around the show's characters, to remix and post video content from episodes, and to chat with other fans about our favorite programs.

Television and New Media introduces readers to the ways that new media technologies have transformed contemporary broadcast television production, scheduling, distribution, and reception practices. Drawing upon recent examples including *Lost, 24*, and *Heroes*, this book closely examines the ways that television programming has changed with the influx of new media—transforming nearly every TV series into a franchise, whose on-air, online, and on-mobile elements are created simultaneously and held together through a combination of transmedia marketing and storytelling. Television studios strive to keep their audiences in constant interaction with new media elements of the show franchise in between airings not only to boost ratings for the show itself, but also to move viewers through the many different divisions of a media conglomerate while in the same fictional world.

Organized around key industrial terms—platforming, networking, tracking, timeshifting, placeshifting, schedule-shifting, micro-segmenting, and channel branding—this book is essential for understanding how creative and industrial forces have worked together in the new media age to transform the way we watch TV.

Jennifer Gillan is Associate Professor of English at Bentley University. She co-edited four award-winning anthologies, *Unsettling America, Growing Up Ethnic in America,* and *Identity Lessons* (Penguin), and *Italian American Writers on New Jersey* (Rutgers University Press).

Television and New Media

Must-Click TV

Jennifer Gillan

Routledge
Taylor & Francis Group

NEW YORK AND LONDON

First published 2011
by Routledge
270 Madison Avenue, New York, NY 10016

Simultaneously published in the UK
by Routledge
711 Third Avenue, New York, NY 10017

Routledge is an imprint of the Taylor & Francis Group, an informa business

Typeset in Perpetua by Taylor & Francis Books

Library of Congress Cataloging in Publication Data
Gillan, Jennifer.
   Television & new media: must-click tv / Jennifer Gillan.
     p. cm.
   Includes bibliographical references and index.
   1. Television programs – United States. 2. Television programs –
United States – Rating. 3. Television broadcasting – Technological
innovations – United States. 4. Convergence (Telecommunication)
5. Television viewers – United States. I. Title. II. Title: Television and
new media.
   PN1992.3.U5G55 2010
   791.45'750973–dc22   2010001331

ISBN13: 978-0-415-80237-6 (hbk)
ISBN13: 978-0-415-80238-3 (pbk)
ISBN13: 978-0-203-87503-2 (ebk)

To PBC
for encouraging me to watch more TV

Contents

Acknowledgments

This research was made possible by scholarly grants and the generous support of the English Department, Dean Kate Davy, Dean Lynn Durkin, and the Faculty Affairs Committee at Bentley University. Invaluable assistance was provided by Kathy Sheehan to whom I am very grateful. For access to industry events and materials, I thank: Joyce Tudryn and the International Radio and Television Society Foundation as well as Frank Gonzalez and Bob Mendez of Disney ABC for funding to attend the Disney Impact Summit; Greg Pitts and the National Association of Television Program Executives Educational Foundation; Henry Jenkins, Sam Ford and Josh Green, Futures of Entertainment, MIT Convergence Culture Consortium; and Mark Quigley and the University of California, Los Angeles Film and Television Archive for access to its excellent collection of 1950s television transfers. Special thanks to Matt Byrnie and his team at Routledge for their commitment to this project and to my long-suffering family and friends for putting up with my obsessive commitment to it.

Earlier versions of parts of Chapter 2 have previously appeared as "Fashion Sleuths and Aerie Girls: *Veronica Mars*' Fan Forums and Network Strategies of Fan Address." In *Teen Television: Essays on Programming and Fandom*, ed. Sharon Marie Ross and Louisa Ellen Stein. Jefferson, NC and London: McFarland, 2008. The discussion of the fan campaigns in *Grey's Anatomy* in the conclusion are developed from parts of an earlier version of my analysis, "On the Job 24/7: The *Grey's Anatomy* Writers' Blogs and Fan Boards at abc.go.com." In *Grace Under Pressure: Grey's Anatomy Uncovered*, ed. Cynthia Burkhead and Hillary Robson. Cambridge, U.K.: Cambridge Scholars Press, 2008.

Introduction

It's network TV

It's about time. This deceptively simple sentence connotes many of the challenges facing broadcast television in the United States, especially during the first decade of the twenty-first century when the "Big Four" networks had to adjust their programming, scheduling, advertising, promotion, and distribution strategies in relation to the evolution of media technologies and viewer practices.[1]

It's about time was also the Summer 2009 promotional tagline for *The Jay Leno Show*, the short-lived variety program NBC scheduled for 10 p.m. every weeknight starting that fall.[2] Known as stripping, this scheduling decision to put a late night show in primetime sparked controversy, which eventually led to its cancellation four months later.[3] Stripping the program across the weeknight schedule, as opposed to giving it a single hour, was also viewed by critics as the displacement of five potential dramas that had come to be standard fare at 10 p.m.[4] and had provided lead-out audiences for the local newscasts of NBC affiliate stations. The irony is that NBC's marketing of its "quality drama series" had shaped expectations about the kind of shows that could be offered by a broadcast network in the time slot. NBC built its late twentieth-century brand reputation on having the most highly rated primetime schedule composed of a block of smart sitcoms followed by a signature drama such as *Hill Street Blues* in the 1980s or *E.R.* in the 1990s.

Those decades were dominated by programming power blocks like NBC's Thursday Must-See TV, which relied on strong lead-ins to carry weaker shows and encouraged viewers to stay with the network for the evening's programming flow, including the spots for sponsor and network products that ran between story segments. The first decade of the twenty-first century was characterized by an attempt to create power blocks through Must-Click TV, the term I use to describe new media-influenced network programming, marketing, broadcasting, and distribution strategies and audience reception practices.[5] Each Must-Click TV series utilizes standard notions of televisual flow between its broadcast network's programs and across its scheduling grid and capitalizes on emergent modes of overflow—from TV text to website, from a single network to a media conglomerate's other divisions and new media platforms.[6]

A useful shorthand, the term "new media," as this book demonstrates, is a problematic one that is akin to the advertising oxymoron "new and improved" given

the actualities of how a seemingly new medium usually evolves out of its predecessors and retains many of the features of the original.[7] Similarly, many audience
and industry practices that appear to be millennial inventions are more accurately
modifications of midcentury media industry practices.[8] Whether they are characterized as evolutionary or revolutionary, "new" technologies and devices as well as
the viewer behaviors and practices they enable have certainly impacted the way
television is watched and measured, distributed and followed, financed and promoted.[9]

    This book charts the collision of U.S. broadcast television and new media which
led to the transformation of TV series first into platforms for the promotion of
other media (e.g., *Dawson's Creek*'s promotion of featured artists' CDs) and then into
a multiplatform series of networked texts (e.g., *24*, the broadcast series, the interactive website, the mobisode and mobile game, the Playstation game, the interactive
DVD-ROM, the DVD box set). Websites transformed as well, starting out
as electronic billboards for TV series and morphing into immersive spaces in which
to continue to engage viewers (viewers/users)[10] through in-character and in-
storyworld TV series content. In a testament to the way established and emergent
media practices combine, traditional ancillary texts for TV series (e.g., *24*, the
board game, the companion volume, the novelizations, the tie-in books, the fanzine,
the trading card game) are still generated, but they are now accompanied by new
modes of tracking since they have their own websites and often extra content for
registered users. Requiring site registration in exchange for content is a way for
sponsors to track and target viewers. Sponsors have taken advantage of new media
platforms as spaces in which to attract and engage viewers, offering series-related
sponsor content such as "sneak peeks" or exclusive content available on a tech
device (e.g., mobile phone or iPod). They also license the rights to create themed
content that is produced in conjunction with, not just as an ancillary to, the original
on-air text.[11] The latter often has its own media presence on mobile devices,
in games, on-air, and/or online (e.g., Unilever's Degree Men antiperspirant/
deodorant's *The Rookie* series of *24*-related shorts). Even the repurposing of
the broadcast on a cable affiliate might be part of the networked text (e.g.,
"FOXweekends" had its own site and ads in the DVD box set). Conceptualizing a
new TV product as a series of networked texts encourages fan tracking of characters and stories across multiple media platforms. The presence of these networked texts on these various platforms also allows networks and sponsors to track
viewers' consumer habits more closely and, thus, to target them more effectively,
often through narrowcasting or microcasting that would not be possible in relation
to the broad-based audience address of broadcast TV.[12] Given the dual audience
address allowed by multiplatform content, networks can produce a "narrowcast-
broadcast" series, one that has a more narrowcast address on its alternate
platforms. Consuming the content available on those platforms, however, is not
necessary for understanding or enjoying the on-air text, which maintains its
broadcast address. Advertisers are also adopting this approach, buying into multiplatform elements through branded entertainment deals, while still buying time on

the broadcast platform. Both networks and sponsors hope that the viewers they do attract will become brand advocates who then form fan networks by copying links to or content from the series' multiplatform elements onto their social networking sites (e.g., MySpace and Facebook) or social utilities (e.g., Twitter and LiveJournal).

These changes are more about evolution than revolution in TV programming. Must-Click TV existed prior to the 2000s, but it was fans not the networks that were encouraging the clicking.[13] Soon production teams were positioning their creative texts to plug in to pre-formed fandoms and pre-established online cultures and communities. Deliberately produced with fans in mind, network-generated Must-Click TV marked an adjustment in networks' attitudes toward fans and the new media through which much of their interaction takes place.[14] Formerly directed toward curtailing online fan practices that were seen as running counter to industry interests, network energies soon concentrated on channeling them into their revenue streams. Realizing they could monetize fan activities if they hosted them on their sites, networks moved from an embargo to an embrace of fan activities. Instead of sending cease and desist letters, as FOX did to *The X-Files* fan webmasters whose elaborate sites seemed like infringement of intellectual property,[15] networks now issue invitations to superfans. A significant moment in this transition occurred when the writers on ABC's *Alias* (2001–6) decided to create a fan-style website. By the time members of that production team signed on to NBC's *Heroes* (2006–), their ventures into fan-centered web address would no longer be impromptu or informal.[16] They became carefully strategized aspects of the planning that went into a network's and a creator's conceptualizing of a new TV product— no longer a broadcast series with some ancillary web products, but a TV franchise that had on-air, online, and on-mobile incarnations.[17] Practices that used to be engaged in only by the most dedicated fans in the early 1990s were expected of regular viewers of the WB and later of ABC and then, during the next decade, were mainstreamed to all broadcast viewers via content and experiences made available on the networks' websites. Matt Hills is right to conclude that *Dawson's Creek* (1998–2003) became a mainstream cult text, as the immersive web experience associated with the WB series inspired broadcast networks to adopt niche network strategies and, as Will Brooker has demonstrated, to encourage their regular viewers to engage in what were formerly considered cult fan activities.[18] The transformation of *Heroes* into a series of networked texts called *Heroes Evolutions*, winner of the 2008 Creative Arts Emmy for Interactive Media Programming, represents the evolution of the process.

Multiplatform content invites viewers to become site visitors who, with just a click of a mouse or a tap on a keypad, can immerse themselves in the wonderful worlds to which they were first introduced on TV. Broadcast series like *Heroes* are treated as franchises, with on-air, online, and on-mobile elements that are created simultaneously so that all the content remains consistent and contributes some layer of meaning to the story as a whole. The content is held together through transmedia storytelling, a term Henry Jenkins uses to describe the way one story unfolds "across multiple media platforms, with each medium making distinctive contributions to our understanding of the [fictional] world."[19] The Must-Click TV programming model assumes that the franchise content available through different mediums must click together seamlessly to form part of interlocking pieces of a whole experience (e.g., *Heroes Evolutions*), one that is structured to encourage viewers to make emotional investments that will ideally lead to economic investments. This kind of transmedia storytelling approach, as Jenkins points out, replaces franchise models based on "urtexts and ancillary products."[20] Savvy showrunners[21] realize that all the divisions of the franchise need to be created simultaneously and click together in an interlocking gear model; in this way, the on-air, online, and on-mobile content make the product move (as well as "move" sponsor products and encourage viewers to move across the divisions of a media conglomerate). The key is to keep the TV franchise always in circulation and the audience always interacting with the show before and after its initial and subsequent broadcast airings.

Their investment in multiplatform entertainment and marketing does not mean that U.S. broadcast networks stopped investing in\ on-air promotion between story segments. They still try to get domestic viewers to start watching a series on TV and stay with the network through the rest of the evening's other programming. When British scholar Raymond Williams first experienced the U.S. broadcast television model in action in the early 1970s, a decade when CBS, NBC, and ABC were the three commercial networks, he was amazed by the commercial context in which series were embedded. He concluded that it wasn't individual series content that viewers were encouraged to watch, but an entire evening's flow of programming, complete with commercials and promotions between story segments.[22] Williams' original concept of televisual flow, which focused on the Big Three broadcast network model[23] and explained how it elevated the importance of a stream of programming over individual shows has been updated and challenged as the channel spectrum expanded and strategies were adjusted accordingly.[24] Many of Williams' insights about televisual flow still apply to aspects of broadcast network strategies, as the network promos, feature film previews, and short-form interstitial programming that still air between story segments indicate. Today's networks have had to adapt their models to adjust for the way some viewers switch from channel-surfing to web-surfing. To redirect this online activity toward their television texts, networks offer constant on-air reminders of the way television programming and even sponsor advertising continues online, where viewers can extend their engagement with a TV series, its sponsors, the network, and the media conglomerate of which it is a part. Also on the rise is product integration into story segments, a response to the fear that timeshifting technology allows on-air viewers to skip commercials. As the promos are skipped as well, networks also are finding ways to integrate their brand identities into the storylines and even into the DVD box set featurettes, webisodes, and mobisodes.[25] The Must-Click TV model emphasizes continual circulation of the interconnected parts of a TV franchise in a network's (and media conglomerate's) revenue stream. This kind of circulation is necessary in a media environment in which it is no longer clear where viewer demand for content will be met; where and how and even from which country viewers will access a TV show; or at which point in the circle they will begin to interact with the franchise. The hope is that wherever viewers interact with the franchise, they will continue to circle through its other elements.[26]

Must-See TV was premised on appealing to loyal and casual viewers as well as the elusive third category often called surfers or zappers. Today, those viewers are clickers because they are the distracted viewers who wield a remote control device that now allows them not only to click or scroll through an ever-expanding channel spectrum, but also to click on program titles on a digital TV guide.[27] For an increasing number of viewers that TV guide is linked to a digital video recorder (DVR) capable of storing at least forty hours of programming, although with each year the amount of storage capacity rises. Whether provided as part of a cable company package or purchased as a stand-alone device, DVRs make it easy for viewers to watch programs when they want and not as they air. During playback viewers have the capability to fast forward through commercials and, with more advanced models, even the capability to skip ahead in increments timed to match the length of commercials or commercial breaks.[28] Viewers are also often users of other clickable devices, including the computer mouse for web surfing and the console control for game playing on a TV monitor; such devices enable them to expand their at home entertainment possibilities far beyond the programs airing on television channels or their companion websites. The Must-Click TV model seemed like a way for broadcast television to stay viable in an environment in which viewers could choose not only from a channel spectrum full of original hour and half-hour scripted series, but also from a variety of web-, gaming- and mobile-based entertainment content. In this new environment the ideal viewers are the ones with multiple browser windows open as they watch or re-watch the show and simultaneously access its other franchise elements or sponsor websites.[29]

This book looks at this new model, focusing on its origins in the 1990s in the web address for series, such as FOX's The X-Files, NBC's Homicide: Life on the Street, and WB's Dawson's Creek, as well as later innovations, including the linked mobile phone content that was part of the development of a multiplatform address for Smallville. That WB series debuted in 2001, the same year the Must-Click TV model graduated to the Big Four with FOX's 24 and ABC's Alias. The latter series was a more literal graduate from the WB to ABC as creator J. J. Abrams imagined it as Felicity joins the CIA, referring to the title character from his college life TV show that had aired for four years on the netlet.[30] While both series developed innovative multiplatform content, Alias made more missteps than 24 in its attempt to create a mainstream cult series. The Alias team had the added burden of Big Three ratings expectations that the series could never meet, but the difficulties they encountered gave members of its production valuable experience, especially in creating a narrowcast-broadcast series and linking it to an Alternate Reality Game (ARG) that functioned as transmedia marketing and immersive web and mobile address. Some went on to apply that knowledge to help create and extend ABC's Lost (2004–10) and NBC's Heroes (2006–). The success of the advertiser-sponsored multiplatform content for *Heroes* (e.g., Sprint mobisodes and product integrations) inspired NBC in the final seasons of the decade to translate multiplatform storytelling and continuous circulation of content into multiplatform promotion and continuous network, sponsor, and media conglomerate brand circulation.[31]

Throughout its chapters this book also considers the problems with the multiplatform model, especially as it depends upon a concept of televisual time at odds with the time-structure of the Must-See TV era. Long-standing participating sponsorship arrangements naturalized the "magazine style" flow of advertisements that viewers would watch in exchange for free programming broadcast into their homes, or so broadcasters promised those "buying time" on television.[32] With the advent of TiVo, a brand name digital video recorder, and the popularization of DVRs more generally after they could be acquired along with a cable package, that promise was harder to make and even harder to believe than it had been when VHS players first enabled the recording of on-air programming.

Network executives prepared multiplatform marketing campaigns to promote series that were often structured as long-arc serials (as opposed to closed-arc, stand-alone episodes) in the hopes that viewers would become intrigued enough to "tune in" to their premieres and then become engrossed enough in their serial storylines not to click away during commercials.[33] As these series could become addictive and viewers would need to come back each week to get another detail about the mystery, programmers hoped that they would become "appointment television" and blockbuster ratings-generators that would translate into blockbuster advertising rates. These series are addictive, but they also require a time commitment and a high tolerance for delayed gratification, especially if watched on-air as they aired.

It takes time to build an audience for such shows, but broadcast networks contend that they don't have the luxury of time. They need top ten or at least top twenty ratings numbers out of the gate to keep one of these shows going. Given its variant structure as a network that only programs two hours of primetime a night, FOX has a higher tolerance than the Big Three for growing a series over time. It did just that for *24*, which was not an immediate hit when it premiered in 2001, but became a steady climber in the ratings. It had its successful on-air seasons, but it was a blockbuster hit on DVD and international markets. ABC's *Lost* was not only a megahit in those platforms, but also a top ten hit in its first season. In its second it achieved even higher ratings, sometimes coming in at number one or at least the top five. By the end of its third season, its audience had steadily declined. The season was a bit convoluted and some fans were less willing to indulge the creative team's drawn out timeline for resolving the serial mysteries, especially if further frustrated by the delays inherent in the network's scheduling timeline for the series (e.g., weaving in repeats). The ratings decline was also attributable to the fact that people turned to other platforms to watch the series. *24* had the same problem, but at least it offered mostly self-contained seasons, so that viewers had to watch episodes in order, but they did not necessarily have to watch the seasons in order. People hearing the buzz about *24* could begin watching on-air as a new season began. As *Lost* had to be watched in order from season one, episode one forward, it is hardly surprising that it lost on-air viewers over time, but that it continues to be a blockbuster series on DVD and download. These two series are considered in depth as case studies in this book in order to illuminate the programming and distribution challenges FOX and ABC faced and the ways they innovated the Must-Click TV model in response.

Lost, *24*, and other series like them are not well suited to the time-based structure of broadcast television. Their creators carefully construct serial mysteries and extend the on-air storylines into online and on-mobile platforms, doling out clues and revelations over time. Developments unfold over whole seasons or even multiple seasons. Viewers track these developments and speculate on outcomes. They carefully deconstruct these series and invest time in following their mysteries and searching for embedded clues to their solutions both in the on-air series and in their multiplatform extensions. These series also demand of on-air viewers a time commitment of watching episodes every week and demand patience between airings because the 22+ episodes that had been the recent standard broadcast full season order are typically scheduled into twice that many weeks to accommodate holiday breaks, special event programming, and some reruns. These series demand indulgence from their networks in initial seasons as they build their fan bases and indulgence again in later seasons when the ratings decline because casual viewers choose to access episodes via an alternate platform such as DVD or download.[34]

It's about time. Considering how demanding a long-arc, serial mystery can be, especially in contrast to a series composed of stand-alone episodes that contain a completed story arc, the waning support of NBC, along with the other networks, for long-arc serial mystery format is hardly surprising. The *Leno Show* decision was connected to NBC's increasing frustration with *Heroes*, which had been steadily hemorrhaging on-air viewers and had reached a new low in its third season in 2008–9, the one in which Leno's 10 p.m. series was greenlit.[35] In contrast to *Heroes*, NBC's smart comedies *The Office* (March 2005–) and *30 Rock* (2006–) had been underperformers in their initial seasons, but were slowly gaining viewers and racking up Emmy wins and nominations. By 2009, the network was turning its attention toward them as its way out of fourth place, especially as it calculated (or more precisely, miscalculated) that it could leverage them, along with Leno's variety show and NBC's new late night line-up of Conan O'Brien on *The Tonight Show* and Jimmy Fallon on *Late Night*, to re-establish the network as the destination for smart comedy. NBC had already moved in the all-comedy direction in 2008 with its renewed attention to scheduling blocks of scripted half-hours on Thursdays, the model with which it had risen to Must-See TV ratings dominance. Such series had potential to be ratings-generators as they could attract viewers beyond the loyal core audience because they could be understood by a casual viewer who started watching a random episode.

NBC branded the Thursday primetime blocks *comedy night done right*, a tagline that implied that the quantity of viewers ratings-leader CBS could offer was less significant than the quality of those viewers NBC said were attracted to its self-proclaimed smart comedies. NBC was repeating the argument it had made several times over the course of its historical rivalry with CBS: advertisers should view NBC series as more valuable because of the high quality of its target demographic of upscale viewers, those with more distinguished palates and discretionary income to spend on consumer goods.[36] NBC effaced the fact that this demographic also bought the kinds of devices that enabled them to watch TV on commercial-skipping DVRs or on iPods or other alternate delivery platforms.

Even though its comedies were never in the top twenty and often not in the top fifty in the ratings, NBC was hoping to undercut CBS's Monday evening comedy schedule, which included the highest-rated sitcom, *Two and a Half Men*, and its breakout returning series *The Big Bang Theory*. With several of its reality series and its procedural crime dramas, including Monday's 10 p.m. drama *CSI Miami*, often placing in the top ten and its other sitcoms often placing at least in the top twenty, CBS could easily proclaim itself *America's Most Watched Network*. With that brand tagline CBS was highlighting a significant distinction in the broadcast arena: it was the network that had the most eyes actually looking at its programming (including top-rated procedurals *NCIS*, *CSI*, and *The Mentalist*) as it aired and, hence, the most potential eyes on the commercials that supported it. Viewers accessing television programming via other platforms were not "watching TV," CBS was implying, or at least were not doing so in a way that is valuable to advertisers whose financial support was still central to the broadcast revenue model.

It's not TV: we know drama

While CBS was picked on by critics for the predictability of its procedural dramas, NBC was lambasted for turning its back on drama as a programming category in favor of cheap unscripted fare. Given its adoption of a yearlong schedule, as opposed to the once-standard September to May broadcast schedule, NBC countered that even with Leno taking up the week's 10 p.m. slots, the network could still offer a slate of drama series comparable to that of the other broadcast networks. The argument did not sway NBC's critics who viewed the move as a rejection of quality dramas (with a long shelf life) in favor of quick-fix unscripted programming (with no shelf life). More to the point, critics wondered if the fall 2009 stripping of *The Jay Leno Show* across primetime signaled a turning back of the clock on the decade's advancements in broadcast programming. Showrunners, the industry term for the executive producers in charge of daily operations of a television series that have increasingly large production teams, including a legion of executive producers, were especially vocal about the controversial scheduling decision. Peter Tolan of *Rescue Me*, the highly acclaimed FX series about the traumatized crew of a post-September 11 New York City firehouse, decried the NBC decision: "They should take down the American flag from in front of [the NBC] building and put up a white one, because they've given up."[37] He said the move signaled they were giving up on looking for the next quality drama. His claim that NBC used to create drama that represented "elegance and creative spirit," was seconded by Shawn Ryan, the creator of *The Shield*, FX's 2002 breakout hit about a corrupt police squad that ran for seven critically acclaimed seasons; NBC "used to stand for something better," Ryan said. Its dramas, especially *Hill Street Blues* (NBC 1981–7), had inspired a generation of writers, he notes, who are out there creating series that now have less of a shot of making it on broadcast TV.[38] A few drama series, including *Heroes* and *Friday Night Lights*, a football/high school melodrama hybrid, did make it on the schedule in 2006, but that was when NBC had at its helm Kevin Reilly, the executive who had brought *The Shield* to FX when he was head of programming there and the one who would go on to give Joss Whedon's *Dollhouse* and J. J. Abrams' *Fringe* a home on FOX in 2008 when he moved over to the broadcast network. In what would be one of many executive shakeups at NBC, he was ousted in 2007 when the network brought in Ben Silverman, the producer who brought *The Office* and *The Biggest Loser* to NBC. Both the scripted office comedy and the unscripted gamedoc are formats, meaning that they are template shows sold to networks and producers in various nations so that they could then adapt them to click with local audiences and suit local markets (which Silverman did when he helped produce ABC's version of the Colombian televnovela *Ugly Betty*).

In addition to the fourth chapter's discussion of *The Office* and other scripted formats NBC purchased during the decade, this book also briefly addresses the purchase of global formats by American networks in its discussion of reality television formats in relation to ABC's initial programming of *Lost*. The network imagined *Lost* as a hybrid that, in part, offered a scripted take on the social dynamics that so intrigued the audiences of CBS's *Survivor*. Other studies have examined the global circulation of these unscripted and scripted formats and considered the workings of the global fandoms of U.S. blockbuster series, especially as they intersect local taste cultures.[39] This book focuses only on the adoption of the Must-Click TV model by U.S. broadcast networks, which were attempting to stop the loss of on-air audiences to the expanded new media entertainment options. It is significant to note, however, that the global footprint of Must-Click TV series is quite large. Their online and on-DVD circulation, along with the more standard licensing of international rights, gives them blockbuster international circulation. Series like *Lost* and *24* also command blockbuster licensing fees as stand-alone products or make a media conglomerate's packaging of its media content more desirable overall. Once they are acquired, however, U.S. broadcast series can run into regulatory or distribution problems. Domestic broadcast strategies often conflict with international models, such as when the BBC had to determine what to do about Ford's brand integration deals with *24*, in light of its own imperative to broadcast sponsor-free programming.[40] A different problem occurred in the subscription TV market in the U.K. when satellite provider Sky, which had become the exclusive provider of new episodes of American TV blockbusters (e.g., *24*, *Lost*, *Prison Break*) and holder of the rights to on-demand distribution of earlier seasons, would not renegotiate its cable package so that its competitor Virgin could continue to carry the shows. Capitalizing on this content exclusivity, Sky courted new subscribers with advertisements such as "Don't Lose Lost!" and "Get Jack Back!" This distribution problem, especially ironic in Virgin's case given its "Hate to Wait?" slogan, is just one of the many in the global marketplace that has affected the circulation of this programming.[41] While these issues are addressed in chapter three, they are complex subjects for in-depth discussion in another study. For the purposes of this one, it is intriguing to note that U.K. fans reported bypassing the TV distribution tug-of-war between Sky and Virgin by getting online copies, often by illegal downloading or piracy, or simply buying them via the increasingly available downloading services or on DVD once they were released. These modes of access speak to the ways new media has enabled Must-Click TV, keeping the networked texts in continuous circulation, even long after the original U.S. broadcast airing.

One of those global blockbusters, HBO's *The Sopranos* (1999–2007), a dysfunctional family/business, mobster/family melodrama hybrid, is also a significant series in relation to this book because it established the concept of the *It's not TV* series.[42] As its brand identifier, the premium network chose *It's not TV. It's HBO* to distinguish its offerings from everything else on the channel spectrum.[43] Having established its premium brand on making available to its subscribers a schedule that included the cable premiere of the previous year's Hollywood movies, HBO intended its brand tagline to indicate that its series were more cinematic in look as well as genre. Within the decade HBO found itself with competition from fellow premium provider Showtime and a host of basic cable channels including FX, TNT, and even AMC, all of which produced their own *It's not TV* series that tried to rival HBO with their cinematic style, their original characters, their Hollywood star casting, and/or their explicit language, violence, or sex scenes.[44]

This book is not about those cable series, but rather about the pressure they put on U.S. broadcast networks, both in terms of ratings competition and of the expectations they set among audiences, reviewers and even, as Tolan's and Ryan's comments suggest, production workers who do not always acknowledge that the explicit language, violence, and sexuality that are part of the appeal of these cable series cannot be matched in a broadcast series given standards and practices, regulatory norms, and cultural expectations. Still, cable series are positioned in primetime slots that drain broadcast viewers. More to the point, these series can be hits with much lower ratings numbers than are needed to stay in the broadcast top ten or even the top twenty. Those numbers are more essential to the broadcast networks given that advertising rates are calibrated in relation to ratings and revenue is generated on broadcast television through its sale of air time to advertisers, as opposed to the full subscription funding of premium cable and the hybrid subscription funding and advertising revenue model of basic cable. Despite all these hurdles, broadcast television did offer some series, including *24* and *Lost*, which managed competitive production values and the budgets needed to sustain them. Their *It's not TV* elements helped make them international blockbusters, but those same features are often what caused them problems in the domestic arena as on-air TV series.

Viewers don't necessarily make the distinction among the financing, content restrictions, and ratings expectations that make possible the different levels of explicitness and different measures of success on premium, basic, and broadcast television.[45] By a strict ratings measurement, *Hill Street Blues*, a show beloved by most television writers and critics, was not a broadcast success. By Ryan's and Tolan's accounts, this kind of series still benefits the network because it builds brand equity and is a series through which other network programming can be promoted.[46] As already noted, a prestige series today has an even bigger role to play in the long-term revenue stream because it stands to make huge profits in international rights and can be used to headline packaging deals that include less famous or lower quality series that would not otherwise find an international market.[47] Their international success has further established the *It's not TV* status of *Lost*, *Heroes*, and *24*. These long-arc serials are also especially popular in both domestic and international DVD format, another increasingly strong revenue window, and they also are major earners in other formats and platforms on which a television series or its related or extended content can appear and be monetized. Despite all this profit potential, the *It's not TV* series is a less-than-ideal product for broadcast TV, which is at a disadvantage in terms of financing and regulatory structures.

Midcentury and millennial rivalries and partnerships

CBS is the one network that did not spend the 2000s investing in the kind of quality dramas about which Tolan and Ryan are talking or in long-arc, multiplatform franchises like *24* and *Lost*. Although some of the producers of its series have turned them into multiplatform experiences (e.g., *Ghost Whisperer*), CBS as a network has dedicated its energies to developing the more standard kind of franchising—hit series that generate spinoffs. It began with *CSI* (*Crime Scene Investigation*), which led to *CSI Miami*, *CSI New York*, and indirectly to *NCIS*, which is actually a spinoff of earlier CBS series *JAG*. The naval criminal investigation procedural paved the way for 2009's *NCIS LA*, a spinoff of the spinoff. Together the two series solidified CBS's first place status, with NCIS often coming in at number one in the fall of 2009 and the new series placing even better than CBS's new 2008 procedural, the breakout newcomer *The Mentalist*. Earlier in the decade, NBC had embraced franchising in relation to its ten-year-old series *Law & Order*, which had already in the mid-1990s inspired parallel series *Homicide: Life on the Street*. NBC had some hits with the *Law & Order* franchise at first, but it soon over-saturated its schedule with spinoffs. *Law & Order: Special Victims Unit* was the most successful. *Law & Order: Criminal Intent* started out strong, but then its ratings flagged. While other less successful *Law & Order* series were cancelled, *Criminal Intent* was shifted to sister channel USA, a programming move that is indicative of the possibilities of the media conglomeration era. Even with *Law & Order* still making it into the top ten on NBC, once sitcom sensation *Friends* left the air in 2004, NBC not only lost its place as top-rated network, but it also often found itself in fourth place.[48]

The decade that ended with CBS proclaiming itself the *Most Watched Network* began with CBS greenlighting its future Must-See programs, the unscripted reality format that became known as the gamedoc, a millennial modification of the mid-century game show. While the other networks soon found their own reality series, CBS had the most critically acclaimed, *The Amazing Race* and the two blockbusters *Survivor* and *Big Brother*. CBS popularization of the gamedoc was also significant given that the unscripted reality series became testing grounds for other scheduling and marketing experiments.[49] They started as short-run replacement series airing in summer and then became January premieres. Those alternate premiere dates have since become industry standards. The gamedocs were also spaces for testing viewer tolerance for product placement and product integration. Those reality series given a second weekly spot are especially significant and controversial as they offer much more promotion than content. By editing footage from each week's stage of the gamedoc, producers have created a cliffhanger structure driving tune-in from a competition episode to a results episode that follows it the next night or sometimes later in the week. The results episode is designed to be a space in which sponsors are given increased time in which to associate their products with popular series. Using this two-block formula with some weeks even having a third special episode, *American Idol*, the musical talent competition series developed from the original UK format template *Pop Idol*, became the decade's ratings phenomenon and boosted FOX, which had been "the Fourth Network", often into first among the Big Four. Although NBC eventually acquired its own hit gamedoc, *The Apprentice*, it was no match for CBS's blockbusters. In a bold move, CBS challenged NBC's Thursday night dominance by moving *Survivor* to the 8 p.m. slot followed by franchise blockbuster *CSI* and NBC soon found itself mired in fourth place and dubbed Must Flee TV.

The recent ratings success of CBS has its parallel in the 1950s when CBS toppled NBC, which had been the long-time leader in radio and the leader in television's initial seasons. As it did with gamedocs, CBS took a risk on the star-helmed variety sitcom, a new format uniquely suited to television as a new medium. While NBC just tried to import what had worked on radio and relocate its radio programs and stars to television without change in format or star pay grade, CBS recognized that need for a new format and new financing strategies for a new medium, according to Douglas Gomery.[50] NBC had been THE place on the radio and then television dial for in-home entertainment, so it could not imagine that CBS, long a distant second, would challenge it. CBS's midcentury dominance was the product of raids on NBC's radio talent pool. CBS was able to pull off the coup because of its embrace of broadcast TV as a new medium deserving of a new format, which its newly created reality (star) sitcoms offered. To some extent, *30 Rock*, NBC's half-hour scripted comedy featuring former *Saturday Night Live* (SNL) head writer Tina Fey playing a put-upon producer of an NBC sketch comedy show, is a return to the reality (star) sitcom format[51] complete with millennial modifications that take into account the synergy needs of networks that now are single entertainment divisions within large media conglomerates. Fey, both in her role as creator of *30 Rock* and in her persona as fictional production worker Liz Lemon, rails against product place-ment and media conglomerate synergy. Fey joins a long line of creatives, including Jack Benny, as a reluctant pitchperson whose ironic stance on branded entertain-ment only makes it more effective. The Tina Fey-Jack Benny link is significant as he was one of the big stars that NBC lost to CBS.[52]

In the early 1950s, according to Mike Mashon, NBC was still conceptualizing television as a sponsor's platform in which the network sold "time franchises," which provided sponsors (e.g., Texaco) with an hour programming block and a star (e.g., Milton Berle) and creative control over content.[53] Gomery notes that, in contrast, CBS was purchasing packaged programming from stars who learned to incorporate themselves as brands.[54] At first the network found single sponsors to support the programs, then alternating sponsors, and finally gained control over programming through participating sponsorship, which is the magazine-style spot advertising with which we are familiar today.[55]

That 30 Rock has succeeded by borrowing from the 1950s reality (star) sitcom format may have inspired the idea of the Leno variety show concept and scheduling, which on Thursdays at least, guaranteed a likeminded programming flow that NBC believed had the greatest potential for keeping viewers on their couches for the entire menu of an evening's programming, and perhaps even enticing them to stick around through the local news for NBC's late night shows.[56] The decision also needs to be seen as part of NBC's brand-centric strategy of stacking its schedule with already-known comedy commodities. In addition to geenlighting a series for Leno and Fey, NBC picked up three sitcoms starring former SNLers Molly Shannon, Amy Poelher, and Chevy Chase and gave recent SNL Weekend Update veteran Jimmy Fallon the coveted hosting slot on Late Night. The misguided Jay Leno Show decision was also an attempt to maintain and leverage the long-time NBC host as a brand asset. The network certainly did not want to lose him to another network as it had lost its late show host David Letterman to CBS when it passed him over in 1992 in favor of Jay Leno for The Tonight Show. Letterman then created a show with CBS that soon posed a serious challenge to and sometimes bested NBC's once-untouchable late night talk show.

All of these issues are addressed in the final chapter and conclusion in order to discuss the questions with which this book started: what led to the stripping of The Jay Leno Show across the 2009 schedule and what might the decision say about NBC's game plan to reacquire its title as Must-See TV network? More generally, what might the network's embrace of a midcentury TV format and branded entertainment deals say about the Big Three's intention to return in the next decade to It is TV television series?

It is intriguing that despite all the controversy about its recent scheduling, NBC is the network that managed to keep quality drama on-air by coming up with new ways to maintain an advertiser-sponsored revenue model without depending solely on the 30-second spot. With its focus on a Texas high school football team and the teens and families whose futures and livelihoods are dependent upon it, Friday Night Lights (FNL) has an interesting series history in this regard. It was created and greenlit mid-decade when the other broadcast networks were trying to copycat WB-style programming and bring over its youth demographic. Also representative of the emergence of NBC's end of the decade brand-centric programming decisions, FNL got on the air, in part, because of its connections to NBC Universal. It was adapted from a feature film of the same name. FNL also had the potential to crosspromote NBC's 2006 acquisition of the National Football League's (NFL's) Sunday night games. FNL's football focus continued to be useful because it provided an effective complement to NBC's hosting of the Super Bowl in 2009, and of the Olympics in 2008 and 2010. The only problem it had was attracting viewers beyond its loyal core. While those coming to the series for the football elements and those coming for the melodrama were pleasantly surprised to find the interwoven genres quite effective, many viewers stayed away because they either weren't football fans or weren't melodrama fans. That led to pressure on the series to change its structuring dynamic, which in the first season was the weeklong preparation for the Friday night football game. What was truly groundbreaking about FNL, however, was the deal NBC made with DirecTV to let the satellite provider have the first distribution window for the fall series and let NBC be the second window starting after the Super Bowl. The network was able to keep FNL on the air despite its low ratings because NBC brokered this cost-sharing arrangement with DirecTV. The partnership was an especially surprising one because a satellite provider would have seemed like the enemy of broadcast network in the twentieth century.

The deal, like that of ABC and iTunes, demonstrated that a strategic alliance between media businesses was more effective than a competition in which both lost. Commenting on recent Disney strategies for its network and its other divisions, *The Economist* said that it was less akin to vertical or horizontal integration and more like a wheel, "with the brand at the hub and each of the spokes a means of exploiting it. Exploitation produces a stream of revenue and further strengthens the brand."[57] Must-Click TV adopts this kind of strategy, which has its foundations in the midcentury Disney deal with ABC for the studio to provide content for the fledgling network in exchange for loans and promotional space for its proposed theme park. As Christopher Anderson explains,

> "Disney's television texts were, from the outset, fragmented, propelled by a centrifugal force that guided the viewer away from the immediate textual experience toward a more pervasive sense of textuality, one that encouraged the consumption of further Disney texts, further Disney products, further Disney experiences."[58]

This description sounds much like today's Must-Click TV strategy. The Disney-ABC Television Group, whose current logo is a water droplet creating bands of ripples in a revenue stream in which content is assumed to be in constant circulation among platforms, has returned to this successful midcentury strategy as well.[59] Anderson's description demonstrates that long before the vocabulary existed,

Walt Disney championed corporate synergy and integrated multiplatform entertainment and marketing. He understood, according to Richard Schickel, "the exploitation of technological innovation."[60] When Disney used his program *Disneyland* to promote his classic cartoon "vault," feature films, serials, TV studio, and theme park, he blended storytelling and promotion on each hour-long show. He also, as Janet Wasko points out, used the television show to repurpose theatrical content.[61] The show referenced the feature films, which had linked attractions at the theme park, and those attractions were given "making-of" docutainment segments on the television show before and after theatrical releases. Watching the show also promoted the park even before the park existed; going to the park promoted the show, which always offered updates on the park. *Disneyland* was the first Must-See TV program and the theme park the first must-visit simulated world promoted by a media corporation's TV programming, all held together by the *start here* openness of entry point and platform inherent in that twenty-first-century tagline of Disney's ABC network. Today's multiplatform television franchises follow the Disney model in blurring the lines between content and promotion. Writers and producers conceptualize ways to extend story worlds onto new sites and those connected to them through click-on links, all in the hopes of feeding people back to the on-air platform to continue the story, and then back out to the web again. It is not surprising that Disney's claim about his entertainment empire, *It all started with a mouse,* applies to twenty-first-century TV franchises that have been transformed by the click of the computer mouse.

If they have internet access, and Must-Click TV discourse makes it seem natural that everyone does, viewers no longer have to wait until the morning to discuss a "watercooler" show with coworkers. In contrast, the Must-See TV publicity discourse was premised on the idea that viewers would (or should be) watching on-air programming simultaneously with millions of other Americans. That kind of simultaneity is no longer necessary in order to participate in a community around a TV show. Must-Click TV prompts its viewers to log on while they watch or immediately after a program ends and discuss it with the kinds of dedicated fans who may not be available to them in their immediate offline world. Viewers do not need to watch a series in its broadcast time slot to participate in these ongoing discussions or to stay up to date on the latest developments—concerning story arcs, production decisions, and cast and network news. All of that information is just a click or a text message away and it's available to an increasingly global audience. Viewers who miss or cannot receive the weekly on-air broadcast can now access episodes via alternate content delivery systems such as DVRs, iPods, or website streaming video. The different content development possibilities of these new delivery systems enable transmedia storytelling, allowing the production team to create or extend content in on-air, online, and on-mobile formats, with, for example, character backstories fleshed out in web-only storylines, games that allow interaction with characters and sometimes even influence over the storyline, and peripheral characters or plot points developed in shorts for mobile devices.

Given that the content is also transformed as it moves across these new channels, writers must adjust it to new formats, screen sizes, and delivery systems. With each new medium in which fans can engage with the TV franchise, sponsors are given another chance to interact with potential consumers, which translates into more sponsor dollars for the networks. When broadcast networks embraced the transmedia marketing model, they acknowledged that many viewers are accessing content in formats other than the on-air broadcast. Yet the networks were still categorizing the on-air text as the only creative content for which writers got credit. This compensation does not acknowledge the actuality that in the Must-Click TV model storytelling and promotion are imbricated; there are areas in which they are distinct and others in which they overlap, making it hard to say where storytelling begins and promotion ends. This blurred line was one of the issues that prompted the Writers' Guild to strike in the fall of 2007. Establishing a false dividing line between content and promotion of content not only contradicts the networks' claims and rhetoric surrounding their own programming, but also belies the complexity of the production process—that an on-air show exists in a transmedia environment in which the franchise is conceptualized from the outset as a multimedia text; that the speed and access of the internet allow viewers to register immediately, directly, and en masse their approval and disapproval of production choices, thereby putting increased demand for new content on showrunners and writers. In other words, even though this transmedia side of the business is dependent on the expansion of storytelling and brings in new revenues, the old compensation methods remain in place.

Networks also too often still calculate return on investment (ROI) through traditional broadcast methods and metrics, causing them to overlook (or perhaps making it financially prudent for them not to acknowledge) that one of the reasons for the success of their TV franchises is the emotional investment encouraged by transmedia programming.

Through the web and mobile interaction that the extension of storytelling experience enables, fans have begun to invest heavily in TV franchises despite the demands they place on their time, their intellect, and their creativity. Viewers feel compensated through the intimate interaction with the production team as well as the actors and the fictional characters they play. Their recent financial commitment to dedicated websites indicates that networks are aware of the importance of fan investment and, yet, fan expectation for an emotional ROI is not often considered in network decision-making. When focusing only on traditional formulations of ROI, networks often pressure showrunners to tailor content for the casual viewers that broadcast television has traditionally courted. Most often, when a series is marketed toward casuals, the loyals feel that their interests and needs are not being met. Part of the problem is that the way that networks determine if a TV show is successful is still through the overnight ratings calculated by Nielsen Media Research.[62] Many executive producers complain that these measurements are inaccurate.[63] Part of the problem is that this ratings structure is premised on a Must-See TV paradigm rather than the asynchronous viewing patterns and alternate points of entry that characterize audience engagement with a TV franchise.

In addition, networks can offer narrowcast-broadcast series that are designed to attract not only the broad spectrum of viewers needed to make them mainstream Must-See TV, but also the narrowcast viewers who act as brand advocates for the series. Through the online platform, these viewers can jump into virtual discussions on message boards and, if necessary, join fan advocacy movements when a network threatens cancellation of TV shows that seem unpopular when measured by traditional ratings systems. Changes in the content formats and content delivery systems should result in changes in the way market share is measured, and that measurement should move from an impression-based click-on (eyeballs-on-the-product) rate to an expression-based emotional "clicking" with viewers, who then integrate the brand into their lives. Audiences are still divided into clickers, casuals, and loyals, but it is now, this study contends, both the mouse and the remote to which the clicker-based metrics should refer.

Must-Click TV: chapter summaries

Focusing on the emergence of the Must-Click TV model in the first millennial decade and its development in the 1990s, this book offers textual and industrial analyses of these decades of change; it traces the transition from dedicated fandoms for network shows to dedicated network websites; from fan-sponsored content to network- and corporate-sponsored content; and from fan engagement with TV texts through labors of love to network and sponsor engagement with fans through marketing lovemarks (i.e., through strategies intended to translate the fans' emotional connections to the show into economic investments).[64] As the 2007–8 Writers' Strike demonstrated, the blurring of the lines between fan-produced and sponsor-produced content and interactions as well as between emotionally rewarding fan labor and economically uncompensated professional labor, in turn, makes evident the inaccuracy of current metrics for measuring new kinds of fan access to and engagement with media texts. It also highlighted the inadequacy of the compensation paradigms for dictating how to calculate and divide the profits networks and media conglomerates make through these new kinds of interactions, access points and content delivery systems.

The case studies that I offer to illustrate the Must-Click TV model make evident a number of conclusions we can draw from specific examples that pertain to media studies and American Studies more broadly. To that end, I organize the book around a consideration of the double meaning of those key concepts—platforming, networking, tracking, timeshifting, placeshifting, and micro-segmenting—that simultaneously reference technical features or practices associated with emergent media technologies and act as the rhetorical foundations upon which claims about their benefits are based. The terms seem merely descriptive, yet I demonstrate that they embed within them value claims that apply not only to new media, but also to American culture more generally. Analyzing how these terms function allows for a consideration of the implicit assumptions that frame the representations of new media technologies and of U.S. television and its viewers.

Chapter one charts the movement of narrowcasting strategies to the broadcast arena and provides a pre-history of multiplatform TV. It locates its roots in the online fan activity of the 1990s in relation to FOX's *The X-Files* and the WB's *Buffy the Vampire Slayer*. It details the translation of that fan activity into network-sponsored rollouts of immersive in-story and in-character websites for NBC's *Homicide: Life on the Street* and WB's *Dawson's Creek*. The immersive desktop environment built for the main character in the latter series and the web promotion of its franchise content and ancillary goods set the template for future "mainstream cult" broadcast television. The web address for the WB's 2001 series *Smallville* shared many features with the *Dawson's desktop* series of linked websites and added innovative in-character and in-storyworld content for mobile phones. Given that the producers of the Superman prequel TV series cast a former model for Abercrombie and Fitch as young Clark Kent, *Smallville* also effortlessly fulfilled its function as a display window for trendy teen wear from mall store retailers, albeit to a lesser extent than *Dawson's Creek*, which had crosspromotion deals with J. Crew and American Eagle. The WB pioneered another mutually beneficial deal when in the mid-1990s it began turning its series into platforms for promoting new music. While this platforming approach is now a familiar feature of many current series, especially those airing on the WB's successor, the CW, it was another co-produced Warner Brothers Series, FOX's *The O.C.*, that perfected the platform approach during its 2004–7 series run.

While the chapter ends with an analysis of CW's current strategies, it focuses in depth on the WB's method of platforming, a term which I use to explain both the re-imagining of a TV series as a promotional platform for lifestyle brands (such as trendy clothing, music, and tech devices) as well as the reimagining of the on-air series as a driving platform from which viewers can jump into one of the media conglomerates' other revenue streams. As it assumes that viewers start watching the broadcast text and then jump from it to other media platforms, a platforming strategy is a step in revising the standard broadcasting model in which the on-air TV product exists in a hierarchical relationship to its official programming tie-ins and other affiliated secondary content. Fan-generated content and activities occupied a tertiary level, not usually acknowledged unless they were deemed a threat to the official text. Through this platforming model, especially in the way that it approached its embrace of other media platforms, the WB destabilized industry models, fan relations, and modes of measurement and compensation, establishing a precedent for viewing new media as an opportunity rather than a threat. I position this period as what William Boddy describes as one of those "moments of improvisation, where the prospects of destabilizing technological innovation served to throw into relief prevailing industry models, regulatory rationales, and consumer practices."[65]

Chapter one ends with an analysis of the CW's *Gossip Girl* to consider how the new netlet expanded upon the WB's attitudes toward platforming and timeshifting.

It contrasts the CW's web address in relation to *Gossip Girl* to that for *Veronica Mars,* a series co-produced by Warner Brothers that the CW inherited in its third season in 2006 when the netlet was created out of the merger of the WB and UPN. An analysis of the online message board posts related to the CW's scheduling and promotion of its acquired series suggests that the CW's attempts to manufacture a narrowcast-broadcast series was more problematic when applied to a program with an alternative character at its center. Specifically, it examines the fan activity that bubbled up in relation to *Veronica Mars*' initial two UPN seasons, focusing on how the weakness of the network's fan site and fan address left room for fan creativity. It contrasts that analysis to one of the top-down fan activities that was encouraged by the CW website, most concerned with tracking the fan activities on social networking and fan sites in order to attract and monetize audiences organized around a fashion- and tech-savvy identity.[66] The CW inherited the WB's experience with creating dedicated websites and using them to channel and track fan activity, but it misunderstood the complexity of the kind of tracking in which *Veronica Mars* fans were already engaged on fan forum sites. This chapter looks closely at the tracking activities engaged in by fans on TelevisionWithoutPity and LiveJournal, as those are the kinds of viewer activities that networks now try to channel into their own sites and revenue streams.

This final analysis builds on Henry Jenkins' contention that we should not look at something like TelevisionWithoutPity as just an online message board or Bit Torrent as just a peer-to-peer file sharing technology through which TV series' episodes and related music tracks circulate, but, rather, we should view both as "disruptive cultural practices."[67] Focusing on audience/user circumvention and on its categorization by media conglomerates as piracy, this chapter uses the movement of the UPN series to the CW in order to examine the transition from user-oriented circumvention (associated with piracy and tracking by audiences in connection with TV fandom) to network-oriented circulation (associated with browser "cookies" and the tracking of audiences' activities and preferences).

Addressing circumvention of a different sort, chapter two considers how viewers use new media technologies and alternate content delivery platforms to circumvent the carefully strategized on-air flow in which FOX embeds its long-arc counterterrorism serial *24* (2001–2010). The chapter begins with a discussion of timeshifting, the industry term for the process whereby new media technologies allow viewers to watch programs in formats other than their broadcast timeslots. Timeshifting poses a challenge for networks given that through this technology viewers could now displace network programming from the sponsors' goods and network promotions with which it would be associated if watched live. To counterbalance this problem, a network can not only increase the integration of sponsor products into the story segments, but also integrate its brand identity into the on-air program. It can also blur the line between programming segments and the promotions that follow and precede them so that DVR viewers are compelled to stop fast forwarding and watch the promos to be sure they aren't missing part of the show.

FOX popularized timeshifting when it shuffled the typical season premier and DVD release dates for *24*. The difficulties of attracting and maintaining an audience for a long-arc serial compelled FOX to experiment with the idea of moving a show around on the traditional network schedule, adopting the year-long cable format with the series debuting in nontraditional months and then repurposed during its initial run (often during the same week as the original airing) on a cable channel. These decisions represented the network's attempt to use scheduling innovations as new approaches to attracting and maintaining an increasingly fragmented and distracted audience.

The internet phenomenon of FOX's *24*—how word of mouth and of mouse kept the buzz about the show circulating—combined with the subsequent purchase of the show on DVD, doubled the audience for season two, with that fan base then growing incrementally with each new scheduling, repurposing, and alternate content delivery and release cycle. The TV on DVD binge-viewing phenomenon was particularly interesting as it allowed not only for easier understanding of long-arc storylines and for maintenance of viewers (especially as viewers could watch at their own paces and on their own schedules), but also for the show to be disconnected from the FOX programming flow, thereby making it more palatable to those who do not share the FOX News' conservative politics. Timeshifting past the flow or accessing episodes in alternate content delivery platforms did not, it turns out, allow viewers to circumvent the FOX News' *fair and balanced* brand promise as it is now integrated into the story segments themselves as well as the DVD box set featurettes and mobisodes, platforms that also offer spaces in which to integrate sponsor brands. Comparing the treatment of the threat of bioterrorism and justifications of torture in the on-air series and the DVD featurettes, chapter two concludes with a consideration of how the alternate means for delivery of content enabled by new media has a political as well as technological dimension. *24*'s racially and politically diverse cast of characters in the on-air series and its diverse political perspectives represented in its DVD featurettes function as ways to circumvent resistance to FOX's conservative take on national security issues and shore up its news division's brand promise.

Chapter three builds on the previous chapters' discussion of platforming, tracking, and timeshifting and adds a focus on placeshifting and schedule-shifting, looking at network strategies for dealing with demanding long-arc serials through the lens of ABC's scheduling of *Lost* and *Alias*. The chapter begins with a focus on networks' and advertisers' anxieties about viewers' ability to bypass network scheduling and programming flow with the aid of technological placeshifting devices. Advertisers and the networks they financially supported were also concerned with the loss of broadcast viewers to cable and to off-television entertainment, especially gaming and web-surfing/social networking. In the early 2000s the programming type that had the most success in attracting and maintaining broadcast television viewers was the gamedoc as it incorporates elements of both in its multiplatform address. The appeal of the new reality format is not surprising as gamedocs encourage people to watch TV on TV and engage with TV on mobile, web, and other new media platforms. The problem was that the saturation of broadcast schedules with gamedocs also contributed to the migration to cable of the "quality drama series," a marketable programming category that had been commandeered by HBO since the debut season of *The Sopranos* in 1999. To combat this channel spectrum placeshifting, ABC, the network most enamored of and most burned by the reality TV boom years at the beginning of the decade, applied what it learned from reality TV to the development of two series with serial mystery elements, *Desperate Housewives* and *Lost*. Through their success, as well as a strong schedule more generally, ABC succeeded in shifting some viewers back to network television.

As much as they are now credited with the re-emergence of strong fictional TV on broadcast schedules that had previously been dominated by reality programming, it is important to re-contextualize these two series within the industrial concerns of the reality TV boom (and bust) era in which they were greenlit. The powerhouse performance of *Lost* in particular can be attributed as much to its response to and incorporation of gamedoc strategies and its related multiplatform viewer address as to its premium cable level *It's not TV* cast and crew as well as pilot/series budget and the production values that resulted from both.

Looking at *Lost*'s position on what had formerly been its successful Reality TV Wednesday reveals much about the network's understanding of the new series' appeals as well as ABC's scheduling logic prior to that breakout 2004–5 season, the one in which *Grey's Anatomy* and *Boston Legal* also debuted. In winter 2005 reality TV's place on the schedule shifted and *Lost* was paired with *Alias*, a long-arc series that had been airing on ABC since 2001, but had never managed to combine narrowcast and broadcast appeals. It remained a cult series, but it was a testing ground for how to launch and maintain a long-arc series on broadcast TV. Following *Alias*'s multiplatform franchise example and having the benefit of inheriting some of its experienced production team, *Lost* tapped into already established online fandoms and targeted new viewers through non-broadcast formats and content delivery systems. In creating the 2001 series, the production team kept in mind, for instance, that message board members are "an integral part of the process" of creating a TV show, as Abrams argued in 2002 in relation to *Alias*.[68] *Lost* followed its predecessor's example of incorporating fan-based web activities of tracking and speculation into producer-generated web and mobile content. Both of these platforms became places in which sponsors could also get involved, although that resulted in some frustrations for viewers who did not expect the multiplatform content on offer would turn out to be multiplatform marketing.

That marketing was deemed necessary by ABC since it was a way to keep product placement out of the series even though it had crept into many other scripted programs such as *Desperate Housewives* as a way to offset the perceived losses of viewers watching broadcast television in timeshifted formats via devices that allowed them to skip the 30-second spots. The multiplatform marketing was even more necessary in *Lost* as its ratings had declined from their blockbuster peak of season two. Nevertheless, ABC continued to support the production team's vision for the series by reducing its episode order, giving it a continuous compressed

January to May season, and fixing a series end date. All of these changes came in response to the concerns raised by viewers and producers in the third season that *Lost* would fall into the traps of other long-arc serials (e.g., *Twin Peaks*, *The X-Files*, and *Alias*) and decline as it tried to balance the needs of attracting casual viewers and offering a compelling and consistent core mythology, all over the course of a 22+ September to May season. Still committed to the linear scheduling logic of the Must-See TV era, ABC tried thereafter (with little success) to shift *Lost* around the schedule and pair it with various kinds of series in order to attract new viewers to *Lost* and to use it as a lead-in for new series. Unlike *Desperate Housewives*, *Lost* did not succeed in launching new series. It was not only ill suited to linear scheduling logic as many of its viewers were putting down the mouse or the game control or clicking over from cable only long enough to watch *Lost*, but it was also ill suited to broadcast logic that required that series leave spaces for casual viewers who might hear the buzz about a series and start watching midseason. By its third season, *Lost* had little hope of attracting new on-air viewers or retaining those who missed an episode or two because it was a series that needed to be watched in episode order from season one forward.

ABC recognized this problem and hoped it would be alleviated when in October 2005 the Disney ABC Television Group made a deal to make the iTunes Store an alternate content delivery platform for its shows. That spring many series were also made available as day-after downloads on its website video player. By spring 2008 ABC.com offered streaming video via the first HD video player and segmented the episodes with five to six 30-second spots, a strategy that had its initial trial in May 2006 when ABC streamed commercially supported primetime content on its player. These platforms helped viewers keep up between episodes and gave an alternate and/or additional platform for advertisers. The problem was that as the number of viewers with access to timeshifting and placeshifting devices increased and TV-on-DVD became normalized as a platform through which to "watch television," the on-air viewership of *Lost* and other long-arc serials like it decreased given that it was easier to watch it outside of the constraints and frustrations of network schedules and timetables.

NBC had many of the same problems with *Heroes*, the 2006 long-arc serial through which it challenged the dominance of *Lost* and tried to make the Must-Click TV paradigm more broadcast friendly. The production team included show-runner Jesse Alexander, the co-creator of *Alias*'s Alternate Reality Game who also worked on the multiplatform content for *Lost*, and transmedia producer Mark Warshaw, the multiplatform content creator and producer for *Smallville* and its transmedia experience and marketing. Together the two enabled the launch of *Heroes Evolutions*, the award-winning multiplatform experience that skillfully interconnects its online, on-mobile, and on-air content. While *Heroes* represents the most extensive network-generated Must-Click TV to date and comes complete with the most detailed multiplatform marketing campaign, Alexander still maintained his connection to fans through his own blog and his team remained dedicated to making the series as fan-centric as possible. NBC showed less dedication to the series, as well as to long-arc serials more generally, after *Heroes* hit its first series low in its third season.

Chapter four explores NBC's movement away from long-arc serials and its increasing commitment to brand TV. It considers NBC's application of the circulatory paradigm inherent in the Must-Click TV model to television series, positioning them as circulation platforms not only for sponsors' goods, but also for network brand assets. As this paradigm is most evident in NBC's Thursday prime-time blocks, which keep network, media conglomerate, and sponsors' products not only moving between story segments but also within them as well, this chapter focuses primarily on that programming, with particular emphasis on *The Office*, *Kath & Kim*, and *30 Rock*.

The brand-circulation imperative is at work in other series as well, of course. The 2006 series *Friday Night Lights*, for example, was used to promote NBC's acquisition of air rights of the Sunday night NFL games, while the 1970s series *Knight Rider* was taken out of the vault and retooled to be a product placement bonanza. The network clearly considered its comedians its most significant brand assets and began to greenlight series for a variety of current and former *Saturday Night Live* (SNL) cast members and then made the controversial move to offer a new series slot to Jay Leno, who had signed a deal years before to step down as host of *The Tonight Show* in 2009. Its obsession with control over its assets extended to the web and NBC became known for its low tolerance of fans posting SNL clips on YouTube and seemed down-right curmudgeonly when it refused to offer its series via iTunes. To maintain control of its assets, NBC entered into a partnership with FOX, a network also with a low-tolerance reputation from the era when it forced fan webmasters to take down their TV series tie-in sites; together they created Hulu, an online content delivery platform that went on to be a web award winner and a delivery platform with which the other networks soon had to make deals to host their content.

Hulu allowed NBC to promote some of those assets, specifically its library of classic series, to viewers who came to the general network site and the individual series sites looking for current episodes. The NBC sites were micro-segmented in relation to all the different divisions that fell under the umbrella NBC Universal so that they would appeal to the particular interests of different viewers who visit the sites to engage with or watch current or classic TV series. Sponsors, of course, could be integrated into the address as well. Such integration was happening across NBC on-air programming during the period as well. While it was controversial in relation to series such as *Knight Rider* and *Lipstick Jungle*, which seemed to get picked up because they would be the ideal respective vehicles for branded entertainment deals with Ford and Maybelline, the integrations for Under Armour and Applebee's were often more seamless and subtle in *Friday Night Lights*.

While every network embraced this kind of integration in its unscripted series, NBC was the one to put the most emphasis on the placement and integration of sponsor products and its network and media conglomerate brands in scripted series. As they chose to make comedy out of many of the integrations and placements, NBC's Thursday night ironicoms, as chapter four's analyses of *30 Rock* and *The Office* indicate, succeeded in entertaining as well as in promoting products, although not without some controversy. While *The Office* was skilled in humorous product integration, *Kath & Kim* was especially adept at complementing the unscripted series promoted within the NBC programming flow. *30 Rock* was the most effective promotional platform precisely because it made comedy out of mocking product integration and synergy, which distracted from its role as a platform for promoting the other divisions within the media conglomerate (feature films, electronics, cable channels).

Even *Heroes* has a branded connection built into it, both with the opening image of the Earth shrouded in a solar eclipse as a constant reminder of Universal's Globe, and through the series' multiplatform product integration deals with Nissan and Sprint. While NBC gave *Heroes* a fourth season, despite waning ratings in its third, in the hope that it would return to blockbuster status, the network did not seem to have the same faith anymore in the long-arc serial as a viable broadcast format. The conclusion discusses that change in attitude as it is reflected in the network's ambivalent treatment of *Day One*, 2010's potential *Heroes* successor from its co-executive producer Alexander. Throughout the pilot phase, he wisely used his blog and his Twitter feed to offer his own promotional campaign for the series. The conclusion compares this use of the social media with the flogs (fake blogs) the writers of *Grey's Anatomy* were contractually required to create for the ABC series. It contrasts Alexander's skillful use of Twitter as a PR platform with FOX's failed tweet-peat experiment during which it ran a Twitter feed on-screen in an attempt to conduct two live Q&A sessions among, respectively, viewers and producers and cast members of its returning series *Fringe* and its new series *Glee*.

Start here and chime in: network identification campaigns

The tweet-peat experiment is indicative of FOX's willingness to embrace new media, yet its channel identifier that airs repeatedly between story segments does not reference new media at all. That contrasts with the new media address inherent in the selection of graphics by NBC and ABC for their channel idents.[69] For its graphic ABC chose an arrow that looks like the play button familiar from online media players and a tagline *start here*. The choice is fitting for the first network to offer a media player on its website and the first to upgrade its player to high definition quality. ABC was also the network that made the initial deal with iTunes. That NBC refused to offer its content via iTunes and instead partnered with FOX to create Hulu, its own content delivery platform, might explain why NBC was slower than ABC to acknowledge the web in its graphic, but then chose a very effective brand-referential one. NBC transformed one of the feathers of its peacock logo into a mouse by adding a clicking sound as it moved about the screen. The graphic-audio combination made it seem as if the viewer were clicking on and activating new windows of content. While individual series on CBS have media-savvy production teams that create web-style promos, the network does not integrate that address into its idents. That changed slightly, albeit temporarily, in spring 2009 when CBS, which usually gets the highest on-air ratings, did briefly use its on-air network graphic to acknowledge other platforms. With the advent of touch screens on many mobile devices and the in-dashboard availability of touch screen global positioning systems in many cars making them familiar to even the least tech-aware viewers, it is not surprising that CBS referenced the touch screen by transforming its eye network logo into an icon which could be "activated" by its network stars. In the 2009 idents they touched the CBS logo to highlight the title of an upcoming series and to signal that it was about to begin "playing." CBS did little more to emphasize content available online and, for the most part, did not position that content as integrated with the TV series. Although individual production teams, such as those for the gamedocs, do offer extensive websites, they are not promoted heavily on-air by CBS. In contrast, the CW fully embraces a multiplatform approach. As the *for those who think young* network, to borrow the famous *Pepsi* tagline, it is hardly surprising that the CW, as the first chapter demonstrates, has the most multiplatform graphic as it features a constantly rotating cycle of a television, computer monitor, and mobile phone.

Fan tracking, targeting, and interaction from the web to the WB

The CW, the broadcast network formed in 2006 when the WB merged with former netlet competitor UPN, has embraced the circulatory paradigm of Must-Click TV. Its 2008 network identification campaign featured graphics of a laptop computer screen, mobile device, and television monitor, all interconnected and on a timed rotation that represented CW television content continually circulating among on-air, online, and on-mobile platforms. The network ID emphasized the CW's commitment to a feedback loop, one in which comments viewers make online or via a mobile device have fed back into the content of the network's series. It also referenced the centrality of both technological and cultural convergence, that is, the capacity of devices to work in sync and the synching of the social practices and behavior enabled by these technologies.[1] Through this network ID, the CW proclaimed its understanding of how these new devices and technologies allow viewers both to interact with or at least respond online to the content of a television series and to acquire content that they could then integrate into their everyday lives (such as music for ringtones or for MP3 players, screenshots for use on websites or for social networking icons).

Watching TV and talking about it is a social experience, one that is just as likely to take place online as in person. The on-air, online or on-mobile content the CW has on offer for each of its series continues to be represented as interconnected, especially given that the episodes themselves are available in the three platforms. Hopeful that viewers engage with content in these other platforms in coordination with the terrestrial broadcast, the CW makes full episodes available in multiple platforms because it also understands that people "watch TV" on devices other than television sets. The online and on-mobile platforms also feature extensions of the story world beyond, but always in coordination with, the on-air TV show. These developments in the ways in which viewers watch and follow television series have posed challenges and opportunities for broadcast networks, the biggest of which is that if viewers do not watch TV on TV, then advertisers start to wonder if they should continue to sponsor programming.

The CW's 2009 network identification campaign addressed that concern with its assertion that the CW creates *TV to talk about*. The longer version of that tagline was CW TV: *see it, hear it, blog it, live it*. A reminder followed that the cw.com offered enhanced streaming of episodes, the opportunity to network with other fans, and click-to-buy fashions. A mobile device appeared in the space signaling that you could also "get music sent straight your phone," a feature sponsored by Verizon Wireless's VCast service with the tagline: *get it now from Verizon and play it on VCast*. This campaign assured viewers (and promised sponsors) that the CW is well aware that its viewers have a relationship with the television content on the network. That relationship, in turn, is what the CW can sell to advertisers worried about a continued investment in broadcast television. CW series, the campaign suggested, generate buzz no matter where they are watched and sponsors can "get in" on that buzz in all the platforms. Buzz is the ideal form of marketing, the CW implies, as it indicates that viewers do not just see these series, they want to be seen as affiliated with them, or more precisely, with the lifestyles and lifestyle brands they put on display. The 2009 campaign built on the 2008 graphic of the trio of devices as they represent the spaces in which potential viewers are engaging in these activities—watching episodes or clips on the CW's streaming video player; talking with friends on social networks or cyber-chatting with their inner circles or expanding those circles through social utility applications; writing online journals or blogs; posting on a blog network like LiveJournal or a microblogging utility like Twitter; playing and downloading sponsored games and music; purchasing DVDs, books, and other series-related content or the CDs and lifestyle brands with which it is associated. The CW campaigns suggested that its television series offer viewers opportunities to do all that because the network has a presence in all these new media spaces. The CW brings its content to the spaces in which it hopes its viewers congregate and offers them ways in which to extend their interaction with series via the new media activities in which they are already engaged. It addresses them in the vernacular of each space and tries to sync its content with the feel and tone of the surroundings. The CW understands that savvy producers and networks make sure their content is part of viewers' everyday lives and activities even when they cease to be viewers (either in their non-TV-watching hours or because they never watch TV on TV).

Of course, these were also damage control campaigns as it is the phenomenon of watching TV off-TV that has networks worried because their advertising rates are dependent on the promise of their ability to deliver a certain number of viewers. The CW became especially attuned to this problem as a good portion of its 12–24 target demographic and some of its extended demographics have become culturally habituated to click to view media available online or on-mobile. To combat this problem, the CW arranged alternative sponsor deals that captured the on-air viewer's attention through a combination of "sponsored by" advertising cards, bumper spots, and interstitial programming along with traditional 30-second spots and offered parallel promotional content and advertising space on its website and within the series storyspace. Often its on-air advertising also encourages viewers to move online or on-mobile and then back on-air again, keeping sponsor as well as network products in circulation among the platforms.

This circulatory advertising paradigm makes sense, the 2008 and 2009 network campaigns suggested, because viewsers use multiple platforms to stay up to date with trends and friends as well as TV characters, especially those associated with immersive web and mobile content positioning them as friends. Online message boards also enable viewers to make contact with other viewers and share with them consumer advice as well as their speculations about plot and production developments. Among themselves they circulate breaking news and updates about the TV series and their characters as well as information about the trends they represent. Viewers might think of these recommendations as part of socializing, but networks hope they can double as word-of-mouse advertising. Since the popularization of MySpace and Facebook, among other social networking sites, viewsers are also likely to post a popular culture-inflected online profile. While site users may simply want an online location in which to stay connected to friends in between in-person meetings or to make new online friends, television networks see these sites as potential spaces for marketing, especially given that users' profiles often include images, videos clips, audio snippets, and hyperlinks as a form of self-presentation or simply as recommended content.[2]

To that end, many production teams create pages on MySpace and Facebook for fictional characters, locations, and/or companies associated with their television series. Similarly, the blog network LiveJournal, an online space in which viewers ostensibly construct narratives about their everyday lives in posts that can be read and commented on by others,[3] has also become a place for organizing online communities that revolve around fandom for a particular series.[4] Community members post and respond to other posts about their favorite TV shows and characters. The appeal of the site, as Kurt Lindemann explains, is that "users with little or no technological savvy can construct narratives using texts, personal photographs, icons, and images appropriated from popular culture."[5] Twitter, a social networking utility that ostensibly enables users to send out a short burst of 140 characters' worth of information in response to the question "where are you," is now a space for fans to follow fictional characters as well. Production teams also use it to send public relations bursts in the guise of friendly "tweets" that offer breaking news or a link to series-related content. The irony of the space is that early adopters got ahead of producers and began posting tweets in the names of fictional characters. Producers quickly realized that they had to establish Twitter feeds or at least to reserve them in their characters' names, at the same time they created new series and casts of characters. This dynamic of fan-related production preceding network production has its parallel in the creation of fan websites and other ways that fans followed and kept track of their favorite television series in the early to mid-1990s, as the subsequent discussion of early X-Files sites demonstrates.

Networks have learned to create web and mobile content that accommodates all the ways that fans make and seek contact points with their favorite television shows. Of course, the economic motivation for creating such content is that the new media spaces which invite fans to engage with series-related content also provide important contact points for sponsors frustrated with the ineffectiveness of the television commercials that viewers now have the technological means to bypass. Today's network-generated fan address strategies grew out of those pioneered in the 1990s by the CW's netlet predecessor, the WB, which, in turn, drew inspiration from earlier offline fan activities and online fan and fan-producer web content. Tracing some of the key developments in relation to new media content related to FOX's *The X-Files*, NBC's *Homicide: Life on the Street*, WB's *Dawson's Creek* and *Smallville* sets up an analysis of the CW's 2007 address for newly acquired series *Veronica Mars* and its 2008 address for its original series *Gossip Girl*. Charting this history suggests that the collision of the world wide web and broadcast television programming in the 1990s resulted in a recalibration of space including the space dedicated on the web for a television series; the on-air and online screen space dedicated to promoting sponsor, network, and media conglomerate products; and the spaces in which storytelling, promotion, or a hybrid of the two occur.

FOX's *The X-Files*: Inside the X

Twentieth Century FOX played a role in this evolution of televisual space with the 1993 FOX network debut of *The X-Files* (1993–2002) as it conceptualized the television series as a multiplatform entertainment from the outset. *The X-Files* franchising was enabled by media conglomeration that allowed various divisions of Twentieth Century FOX to create and profit from *X-Files* content.[6] Modeling its approach on Paramount's successful franchising of *Star Trek*, Twentieth Century FOX purposely set up *The X-Files* as a franchise and was able to anticipate the kinds of content and products in which fans would be emotionally and economically invested. It was less astute about the behaviors and expectations of a cult fandom.[7]

For the most part, early 1990s internet use was not mainstream activity in that most daily users were accessing the net through a computer connected to a mainframe usually at a university, hi-tech company or government agency. Given the role of the latter two in science, research, and development it is not surprising that the genre of choice for these users was science fiction. The result was that many of those posting online were middle- and upper-middle-class university students, employees, and graduates.[8] They were also the tech-savvy early adopters who would want to be the first to try out the latest technologies and were often those with the skill to create their own sites. It was not until the first decade of the twenty-first century that the online activities in which only dedicated fans engaged in the 1990s would be mainstreamed.

The internet-enabled fandom soon would alter the economic structure of television production, distribution, and promotion, especially once fans created electronic bulletin board web pages dedicated to their favorite series. Given that the world wide web hyperlink interface was newly introduced (in 1990–91) and was only slowly popularized, especially after the Netscape browser was introduced, it is hardly surprising that the early adopters would create websites prior to the ones created by production teams and networks, which sometimes didn't bother to create a series site at all.[9]

As it is a series about two FBI agents who investigate possibly paranormal events and then become embroiled in a long-arc mystery, it makes sense that *The X-Files* inspired hundreds of websites between the series premiere on FOX in 1993 and the 1995 debut of *Inside the X*, the official dedicated website for the series. During that time, FOX did not categorize these initial sites as a threat. In 1995 a Twentieth Century FOX attorney said, "these sites aren't stealing any revenue ... They might not obtain permission, but most are not attempting to attribute copyright ... Basically they are promoting our product."[10] Fans agreed, noting the role they played in spreading the word about the series and expanding its fan base. They argued that they kept the series on the air by helping it advance in the ratings from a Nielsen ranking of 102nd in the first season to 64th in the second, and into the top 20 by season five.[11] One commentator called these early fan sites the electronic equivalent "of taping posters of favorite actors to a bedroom wall."[12] When the sites merely featured static screen captures of images or even snippets of audio and video, no one seemed particularly threatened by them, especially given that the content lacked sound clarity and video resolution because of dial-up downloading speeds and unreliable connections.

In the absence of an official *X-Files* site in the first two seasons, fan sites often provided information to keep people interested in between episode airings. Some even took on the time-intensive task of writing transcripts of episodes and posting them for other viewers who missed the episode. In the era before TV-on-DVD, these transcripts were the only immediate way to catch up before the next episode other than borrowing someone's taped-off-air VHS. In contrast to fan sites that offered episode and character guides and various show-related lists of information, most network sites at the time functioned more as electronic billboards, a sort of "point and click promotion."[13]

When *Inside the X* (June 1995–98), the official website, did finally debut, it copied fan site formats and offered something that they could not, the production team members' episode commentaries and "tales from the production site" anecdotes that now come standard as part of the special features on DVDs. The original site related the story of the development, for example, of the trio of computer hackers who became known as "The Lone Gunmen," expert web trackers and conspiracy theorists who were introduced in an early season one episode. From the message board commentary, producers learned about the popularity of the trio and, consequently, expanded their on-air appearances.[14] A never-seen fourth character called "The Thinker" was, according to the account posted on *Inside the X*, modeled on a fan with whom writer Glen Morgan had a long-standing, thought-provoking email exchange. That kind of interaction with, as well as acknowledgment of, early fans is part of what made them so loyal to the show and prompted them to spread the word about the series across the net. By cultivating an "address to the viewer as insider," the site created an "illusion of proximity" with the production team.[15] Fans flocked to the official site because series creator Chris Carter and his team logged on after the Friday night episode concluded and interacted directly with fans. In this way, they established a direct relationship with fans who dubbed themselves the X-Philes.[16] Amanda Howell argues that

> "the interaction between writers and fans in the early years of the series suggest just how well-suited the Internet is to promoting the sort of personal connection—the imaginary bond—between viewers and texts that has long been the goal and mainstay of film and television promotion."[17]

Once *Inside the X* was a well-established site, FOX began to see fan sites as competitors and potential brand detractors and, consequently, to send them "cease and desist" letters. Despite the existence of the official websites, fan sites continued to proliferate. That proliferation coupled with advances in technology that would allow fan webmasters to post more proprietary audio and video made the sites more problematic, especially given their capacity for circulating confidential production information prior to its revelation on-air.[18] In October 1996 a "flame war" of exchanged online insults broke out between Twentieth Century FOX and viewers. They argued that the network only cracked down on fan sites once they had generated a hit for them, a valid complaint. Viewers imagined themselves to be protecting or increasing the value of the series, enabling it to reach a wider audience. Twentieth Century FOX saw them as infringing upon its official expansion of the series into other platforms.

Part of the reason why FOX was the network that became embroiled in these flame wars was that it was transforming *The X-Files* TV series into a multiplatform franchise, which eventually became an "industry worth more than half a billion dollars."[19] In addition to the series and the website, Twentieth Century FOX launched content on several of its platforms. It also hoped to build on the popularity of the series and its creator Chris Carter with *Millennium* (1996–99), his second long-arc mythology series. A fan site's pre-emption of the rollout of that series was the spark that set off the flame wars. At this point Twentieth Century FOX understood that a series website was an essential part of the franchise package and, thus, felt it was copyright infringement when a fan webmaster had gone ahead and erected his own site prior to the debut of the official *Millennium* site.

Since it had not yet recognized the necessity of launching an internet campaign prior to the existence of the series, Twentieth Century FOX timed the debut of the website to coincide with the October 1996 on-air premiere.[20] Twentieth Century FOX took action to shut down a fan site for the series after "a FOX-sponsored IRC chat for the cyberpremiere."[21] Fans came to the defense of the webmaster, a fellow X-Phile, and supposedly sent so many protest emails that the FOX site had to be shut down.[22] Media conglomeration had made the transformation possible since Rupert Murdoch owned a studio and a TV network as well as publishing divisions, all of which enabled the on-air and on-video series to lead to a 1998 *X-Files* feature film, companion soundtrack, and a host of other texts, including novelizations, episode guides, and companion books.[23] As the latter were the kinds of products produced by fans on websites and in hard copies, it makes sense that Twentieth Century FOX was particularly anxious about fan production.

With the controversial move to send many webmasters "cease and desist" orders in the late 1990s, Twentieth Century FOX established a precedent for "what not to do" when extending broadcast network content across multiple platforms. Twentieth Century FOX got itself into more trouble when it came time to sell syndication rights, typically the moment of the big payoff for broadcast series that are deficit financed for their first few years upon the assumption that they will make it to the point in which the network exclusivity rights run out (typically the fourth season or 100 episodes). Then they could be sold for handsome profits in the syndication market and allow the production company to pay off debt incurred from original production costs and turn an often substantial profit. In the case of *The X-Files*, produced in-house by Twentieth Century FOX, the deal that was struck with cable channel FX prompted two lawsuits. The suit brought in 1999 by series star David Duchovny charged Twentieth Century FOX with self-dealing, alleging that syndication rights were sold to a sister network at a below market price, thereby reducing the profits allowed to him by his contract. Although it was settled, the initial result of the lawsuit was that Duchovny soured on *The X-Files* and bowed out as a series regular after season seven.[24] The long-term effect on the controversy over the syndication rights deal was that it delayed the development of a follow-up to the 1998 feature film. Because of a second lawsuit which was filed by creator Chris Carter over syndication profits, *The X:Files: I Want To Believe* was not released until 2008, 10 years after the first feature and six years after the series ended unceremoniously in spring of 2002 after two less-than-stellar mostly Duchovny-less seasons.

The webmasters of sites dedicated to *Buffy The Vampire Slayer*, the series Twentieth Century FOX created for the WB, were subjected to the same treatment and Twentieth Century FOX's resistance to fan websites followed the same trajectory.[25] The fan websites began appearing immediately after the series' 1997 debut. They proliferated until the series had accrued a fan base and were challenged the year the spinoff *Angel* was launched.[26] One of those who received a cease and desist notice in 1999 was a webmaster named AleXander who said he created his *Buffy* website in July 1997 in order to provide information about the show's elaborate mythology as well as episode transcripts for fans who missed an episode or newcomers who might want to start viewing the show. He claimed the series needed "a well-written resource where new fans can go to get backstory, and thus become that much more involved in it." He was frustrated by Twentieth Century FOX's attitude and said, "Now new fans will have no place to go to catch up until syndication starts in two years." He felt especially annoyed at FOX because he felt that it did not have as clear an understanding of viewers' web activity as series creator Joss Whedon did. He met Whedon at "the first annual *BtVS* Posting Board Party, on February 14, 1998," and he said he approved of the site. Creators' understandings of series are not the same as those of a series' network or its parent company. The latter want to limit the pipeline of information and channel viewer activity through their sites. David Oakes, a Twentieth Century FOX attorney, explained the decision to pursue webmasters because their websites undercut FOX's offical site. He said: "They took our images; they took our logo. They are doing things that are against the wishes of the creators of the show."[27] Whedon is one of those fan producers who understands and supports the creative play central to fandom. He knows how important fan production is to that experience and shows respect for the creative work inspired by the series:

> "People writing each other and writing fiction, and writing, well, porn. All of these things that do what I always wanted *Buffy* to do, which was exist outside of the TV show. Enter people's own personal ethos. The Internet has been a big part in how that has happened."[28]

A big part of the appeal of Whedon and his series is that he always communicated directly with fans in various online spaces and acknowledged the significance of their contributions. He admitted that he was often frustrated by the ways the internet also made it impossible to keep plot and character developments secret. Yet, he recognized that this spoiling was also part of fans coming together as a community, even if it was to track down information that would help them "know what happens before it happens." Whedon famously described the internet as "The bitch goddess that I love and worship and hate," and explained that the ability of the internet to bring together fans and transform them into a community was "important to everything the show has been and everything the show has done."[29]

While the initial web-enabled interaction of viewers with production teams for *Buffy* and *The X-Files* positioned fans as co-creators who used the series as a springboard for their own productions, FOX had always intended the use of the web to target fans whose dedication to the on-air series could promote consumption of series extensions and products available on other platforms. FOX's attitude toward fans was reflected in its 1998 revamping of the official *X-Files* website. The informal online interaction with fans that had characterized the original *Inside the X* site was replaced by a more authoritative site that focused on facts rather than speculation about the series.[30] Usenet groups criticized the revised website, complaining especially about the sporadic way it was updated and the way that often made the site outdated in comparison to the up-to-the-minute style of many fan sites.[31] The new site also did not seem interested in providing a space for fans to come together to speculate about series outcomes or to engage them in any real interactivity. Instead "Big FOX" positioned it as a site of promotion not only for the multiplatform content available that year, most notably the feature film and a videogame, but also for its television network and its feature film division.

Windowing strategies: distribution windows and online advertising

One reason that Twentieth Century FOX supported the early sites is that it did not understand the potential reach of the new medium. That quickly changed when it recognized that a website could be used not only to drive to tune-in, but also to drive viewers to buy other elements of the franchise (movie tickets, CDs, games), and, eventually, even to make click to purchase transactions right on the site. The fact that fans wanted to track down details of upcoming seasons and find out about details before they aired destabilized the careful windowing strategy that had previously existed in the U.S. television system, with production companies and networks pacing product releases to drive viewers to tune-in to season premieres, and to purchase repurposed content in the form of ancillary goods. This windowing structure allowed networks and media conglomerates to control the flow of content to viewers in order to build anticipation for product releases. A staggered windowing strategy, FOX assumed, makes a product scarce enough to enable it to remain desirable. The networks and production companies feared that if fans disrupted this official flow of information and products then the series would be oversaturated by the time of syndication or later VHS release.

The interesting thing about the cease and desist controversy is that it demonstrated that the media conglomerate categorized online fan activity as a form of consumption, not of production or even a hybrid of the two. Twentieth Century FOX incorrectly interpreted fan construction of websites as reflective of fan desire to consume images related to *The X-Files*. They did not recognize the ways that fandom offered viewers a creative outlet for producing theories about the series or even for producing content inspired by it. In their contestation of copyright infringement charges inherent in the cease and desist orders, fans asserted their power as interpreters of the text. That did not change the fact that they had no power over its distribution. The conflict made it clear that the maintenance of a two-way interaction between fans and official media texts and their producers was dependent on the indulgence of the copyright owners. Even though the power of viewers in relation to the production of the on-air text is in the realm of interpretation, the web did give fans a distribution platform, one used not only by webmasters, but also by fan fiction writers, artists, and video producers.[32]

Smarter networks recognized that they could leverage the power of the fans, especially given that their online sites were often superior to the officially produced texts. Tony Krantz, then CEO of Imagine Television and producer of *Felicity*, the WB's college drama, said that producers should "embrace," not "quash" fans as their sites enhance the series. More to the point, the producing of such a site creates "a richer experience for that particular fan and the people who click onto that particular Web site. If we can encourage that … that's what we're going to do." Executives like Krantz understood that the actual return on investment desired by many of these webmasters was acknowledgment for their own creative productions inspired by the series. They often considered these productions as complementary to the source text in that meticulously constructed and carefully updated fan sites demonstrate the webmaster's expertise as a close reader of episodes, accurate speculator of outcomes, and thorough archivist of series history and, if applicable, mythology.[33]

Many network executives and the companies that sponsored their programming did not yet understand how to turn this kind of emotional investment in a series into an economic one. In 1997 ABC viewed its site as a promotional space, not one in which to generate new advertising revenue. Brent Petersen, vice-president of photography and new media for ABC, said, "It's a marketing and promotional tool for us to involve users with programs and encourage them to watch TV."[34] At the time advertising agencies were reluctant to invest in the new medium. Advertising executive John Lazarus explained that agencies saw the website as added value, but "the networks want it to be a line item from sales." He added that agencies and the companies they represented felt that until the web space was "more quantifiable and accountable" they would "have a hard time putting money on it."[35] Edmond Sanctis, senior vice-president of NBC's Digital Productions unit, saw more potential of this new environment: "It's important that as all these new technology platforms for distributing content develop, we find ways of extending our creative content, branding and fan base in a way that makes sense."[36] His team figured out ways to get advertisers involved. It got Toyota to sponsor the online site for *The Tonight Show*, while also making a deal with the automaker to use "licensed content from NBC for an on-line auto area on its own site."[37] It made deals with AT&T, General Motors, Visa, IBM and Nissan to run banner ads on NBC.com.

The most ambitious deal was a branded entertainment arrangement with Microsoft to create a webisodic series to complement *Homicide; Life on the Street*, the NBC series from Barry Levinson and Tom Fontana. Microsoft made a logical sponsor as NBC Digital created a site that could only be viewed by someone with Netscape Navigator 3.0 or Microsoft Internet Explorer 3.0 Web Browser.[38] For the 1999 version site visitors had to use the Windows Media Player to access the video, which meant that Macintosh users could only see a text-only version of the script.[39] The site had audio and graphics content that was best viewed at modem speeds of at least 28.8 Kb.[40] Choosing *Homicide* for its experiment in doing "something more than just a promotional site following a TV show" made sense, he said, given that many of its "fans already communicated to each other over the net about" the series and would be open to its "cross-platform development."[41] In 1997 it was not clear how much the internet would overtake television as a content provider. As NBC Entertainment President Warren Littlefield put it then, "We believe we've got to get in the game because we don't know where it's going."[42] He felt the network had already benefited from the digital development: "Right now we're fortunate where we've generated some substantial profits for NBC. We've got to take that money and experiment. We've got to find other ways to make connections with an audience."[43]

Homicide: Second Shift

Homicide: *Second Shift*, a web spin-off of NBC's *Homicide*: *Life on the Street*, premiered February 14, 1997. Composed of nine 25-minute episodes, it continued the story-line of the precinct by focusing on the shift that followed the one dramatized on-air.

The web series maintained the fiction that the work of the precinct continues 24 hours a day. The same squadroom served as the set and the same bosses, bureaucracy, and Baltimore-based cases supplied the tension. Not only could viewsers "watch and click their way through an investigation" and "listen in via real-time audio to dialogue between characters," but they could also "scan script pages, take in visuals from the *Homicide* set and examine crime-scene photos and clues."[44] *Second Shift* encouraged viewers to exercise their investigative skills to solve the cases alongside the detectives. Site visitors could explore crime scenes and find evidence and then check their results against those of the detectives. With equal access to case files and confidential documents, they might even beat them to the solution. Calling it a "webisodic," Tom Rogers, NBC Cable and Business Development President, justifiably described the series as "a significant step forward for NBC Interactive and NBC Entertainment."[45]

Homicide: *Second Shift* is emblematic of the movement from simple information-based promotional websites to in-character and in-storyworld immersive websites. It contrasted with the sites for other 1999 TV series, which were mostly "digital fan clubs where folks can buy T-shirts and read bios of the stars."[46] Instead of erecting an electronic billboard site to offer simple cast and plot information, *Homicide*: *Second Shift* emphasized content creation and viewer interaction so that viewers would feel as if they were part of "creating a new narrative."[47] NBC's Digital Productions unit conceptualized the webisodic as a way to "leverage" "an established fan base."[48] The digital division's production team was inspired by the web content creation in which *Homicide*'s web savvy "passionate base of fans" were already engaged and the interactions they had already initiated on Usenet message boards.[49] Initially, *Second Shift* paralleled the distribution of the on-air series with a new case posted at noon on the Friday the series aired. Then *Second Shift* kept going through the hiatus of the on-air series that began after its February 21st episode.[50] When the series returned, *Second Shift* continued with the final web episode of the season featuring a detective from the on-air series, "marking the first crossover of a regular TV series character to an online series."[51] This interplay between the online and on-air series became more elaborate in the 1998–99 season when some web characters and storylines made it on-air and some on-air characters and details cropped up online. The on-air February 5, 1999 episode was preceded by an online episode which set up the plot about a computer hacker the team has to chase through cyberspace. "The payoff comes in the television episode, where the images from the Web site become clues to solving the murder."[52] The sweeps week stunt was to have an episode that began online, continued on-air and concluded online.[53]

Of the interactive website approach, Tom Helm, director of interactive programming and executive producer for NBC Digital Productions, said in 1999: "NBC shows do not just begin and end with the television tube." Describing the origins of NBC digital division, he added: "In the early days, we were seen as a pretty alien bunch. But now I'd like to see an interactive writer or producer sitting down at the table when the shows are conceived."[54] NBC Digital Productions had its own production team creating and producing the storylines, but did so in consultation with *Homicide* co-creator and executive producer Tom Fontana throughout the development process. Fontana was happy to work with the interactive team, approving its concepts and checking for continuity. While acknowledging his own lack of web savvy, Fontana understood the significance of the online space. He said that his series was ideally suited for a companion web series: "The show has always been cutting edge, and it was conceived to be original. If people are really willing to watch *Homicide*, they're probably the same people who'd be attracted to new forms of entertainment."[55] The on-air series was critically acclaimed as an original, "quality" series because of its script caliber and its use of handheld camera and innovative editing as well as its gritty footage.[56] Fontana felt that the web series needed to be original as well. Fontana said. "If you're going to ask somebody to come to your Web page, it's more interesting to offer more than just actor bios and a program guide. You should give them the same reason to go to your Web site as to your show, which is to see things going on."[57] The key is to understand the new medium on its own terms and not just as a space in which to copy on-air content or erect promotional signs. Fontana understood that the web series had to offer something unique as it was important "to give people a different experience online than they get from TV, while also announcing what's coming."[58] There was even an online press conference inviting users to question a *Second Shift* lieutenant about a murder investigation. Fontana was impressed that those participating took on the role of reporters: "The people tapping into the Web site were playing the part of the reporters. It really told me a lot about the future of this whole thing. It's not just about watching. It's about participating and getting into the role playing of it. That's a whole different experience than turning on a television set."[59]

Fontana recognized even then that such web series could be competition in the future, wondering in 1997 if he was witnessing "the beginning of the thing that's going to put me out of business."[60] While web content in general did lure away eyeballs that might have been otherwise watching television, an immersive web series linked to an on-air series is not positioned as an alternative to television. It functions to generate more interest in the on-air series and maintain it during the inevitable interruptions and frustrations of the September to May broadcast schedule. It is significant that *Second Shift* was conceptualized to run during the *Homicide* hiatus during the spring of 1997. These unanticipated interruptions to a broadcast season, added to the usual ones for holiday and special event programming, can have a corrosive effect on a series' audience. The web series can be a place to manage audience frustration about the scheduling of the regular series and maintain the loyal core audience. Bolstering a cyber-savvy fan base had the added benefit of assuring that a loyal audience would use the strengths of web-enabled communication and organizing to lobby for a ratings-challenged on-air series to continue. The deal was made possible by the Fin-Syn repeal[61] as the network is both the producer and owner of the series, which means that "using material and making money from the characters is less of a legal tangle."[62] Given the technological limitations of the era in which it was created, the initial *Second Shift* series was composed of "comparatively primitive text and still pictures," which were lined in sequence so that "flipping through them gave the illusion of motion."[63] By 2000 the site could use streaming video, but, because most people had slow connections, it was jerky. NBC Digital Productions worked that characteristic of the medium into its *Second Shift* design. "Instead of the jerkiness being controlled by the computer, it was controlled by us," he said. "Until they figured out how to make streaming video look like a motion picture, this seemed like an artsy way to find a creative solution to a technical problem."[64]

While *Second Shift* was its most ambitious project, NBC's digital division was already involved in spring 1997 in creating an in-character web address for some of its series. It gave some of its fictional characters home pages, and introduced TV characters and plot details online prior to their on-air appearance. It made sure this content was not necessary for understanding the on-air text, while enhancing the viewing experience for those who sought it out. Sometimes it made storylines exclusive to the web. Exemplifying this point, a companion website for the serial killer from the 1997 season finale of *Profiler*, its forensics psychologist series, went up simultaneously with the appearance of the site in the Saturday night episode. The key, according to Sanctis, was to do "everything in character." The website didn't have any NBC branding or advertisements: "so you kind of continue the suspension of disbelief from the TV set to the Internet."[65] He claims that the maintaining of the fiction in the online space "seemed to resonate with fans."[66] Similarly, a new character for *The Pretender*, its series about a genius who identity-shifts, was introduced online that fall prior to becoming a regular character on the series that would premiere a few weeks later.[67] Sanctis said that this advanced the on-air and online interconnection as the digital production team was using the web to "develop and impact what's happening on TV." He saw it as indicative of the future of such interconnection: "You can see the future here is using the Web as a proving ground, really, for concepts and for characters that make their way to television."[68] Both *Second Shift* episodes and a web tie-in game called *The Pretender Adventure*, in which viewers had to track down the main character, gave their respective series an online presence over that summer.[69]

For Fontana, *Second Shift* was a proving ground as well. He also applied what he learned on *Homicide* and experimented with online elements for his next series, HBO's *Oz* (1997–2003). In 2000, he used streaming video in a series of web episodes intended to introduce a new *Oz* character over the summer. As the *New York Times* noted, "The online series provided greater depth to the character, a city police officer who goes undercover as an *Oz* prisoner to track down a drug smuggler."[70] In addition to the footage that they could watch, registered site visitors could receive the actual emails the character was sending to his boss and family from the warden's office. Fontana had learned from his experiences on *Homicide* and *Oz* that ideally the web components should develop concurrently with the initial conceptualization of a series. He imagined a format that would be especially well suited to episodes that did not resolve at the end of the hour. An open-ended conclusion of the weekly episodes would, he felt, send people to investigate further on the web and try to discover clues to the resolution, and then drive them back to tune in to see the resolution in the on-air episode. The idea to use the web to "make a lot of information available that enhances the TV show"[71] would be central to the elaborate immersive sites for long-arc serials *Alias*, *Lost*, and *Heroes*. Fontana was right when he predicted in 2000: "I can see a future where the two experiences of TV and the Internet will be constantly linked. To not be part of that is a little like being the guy who's happy making silent movies."[72]

A giant step toward that innovation happened between the 1997 and 2000 versions of *Homicide: Second Shift* when *Dawson's desktop* premiered in October 1998. The in-character and in-storyworld immersive site for the WB series *Dawson's Creek* (January 1998–May 2003) was created by a team at Columbia TriStar Interactive (CTI), the series' production company and a division of Sony Pictures Entertainment. Understanding that a new medium required new strategies, CTI created content for the forms of communication and interaction enabled by the web as a medium.

Dawson's desktop

The debut of *Dawson's desktop* and the expansion of its linked sites over the course of the series was a watershed event in online media. The extensive immersive website built upon the *Homicide: Second Shift* model and incorporated elements of fan sites. It also captured some of the appeal of *Inside the X* by offering elements that would allow viewers to interact directly with production team members. As with *Homicide: Second Shift*, the success of the site could be explained by the fact that the series was produced by a company with a digital division that already was cognizant of the potential for multiplatform entertainment. The 1998 self-description of the goals of Sony Pictures Digital Entertainment (SPDE) is telling:

> "to tap the entertainment conglomerate's libraries and its talent relationships to develop new forms of online content, games and interactive programming as well as to provide video-on-demand, interactive television and the distribution of other forms of digital content and services over emerging broadband networks."[73]

CTI producers used the internet to maintain the fiction that the storyworld continues between *Dawson's Creek* episodes. Immediately after the fall 1998 episodes ended, the *desktop* team would make available new emails and journal entries and show updates and revisions to Dawson's screenplay.[74] As Chris Pike, manager of development at CTI, explained: "This site creates a fictional world where the characters stay in character. On the regular 'Dawson's Creek' site, everything's based in reality, but on the *desktop* there are no actors. It's actually Dawson's computer."[75] While the ultimate goal was to drive tune-in for the on-air series, especially by having material from the *desktop* appear on the series, the site also allowed on-air viewers to extend their immersion in the storyworld. Andrew Schneider, CTI's director of marketing, said that the site was explicitly imagined in terms of story flow: "We want to complement the show, to flow in and out of it—to drive viewers to the show but also offer a continuity program between new episodes and during the off-season."[76] The subtle connection between characters and the products sponsored within the on-air flow continued online. Schneider noted that the web could aid in branded entertainment deals: "We've created a concept that we think can nicely integrate major brands into the entertainment."[77] Geri Lieberman, marketing director for the Dep line of haircare products, explained her company's decision to become a presenting sponsor on the site:

> "We're in the midst of a major relaunch of the brand. The main consumer of our product is the same young audience that watches 'Dawson's Creek.' In addition to new ads and a new look, we're looking to associate with key entertainment properties that mean something to our consumers."[78]

Dawson's desktop was a site that tried to transform emotional commitment to the characters and storyworld into an economic investment in products associated with the series. The site was emblematic of a movement toward impression-based marketing in which advertisers pay for the exposure of their products to a specific audience. It is a more targeted approach and is ideal for a dedicated website for a TV series as it is a space frequented by those most dedicated to the series. The advantage of web marketing is that advertisers can measure exactly who is "clicking on" the icons or advertising banners that redirect them to the websites dedicated to their products. In terms of a presenting sponsorship such as that with Dep, the advertiser wants to be associated with a series or a character who functions as a style icon for viewers.

While the fans' expectation of a return on their emotional investment in the series is often at odds with the network's demand for an economic return on theirs, the smartest marketing teams try to integrate the two. Jenkins categorizes this kind of dual goal as "affective economics": "A new discourse in marketing and brand research that emphasizes the emotional commitments consumers make in brands as a central motivation for their purchasing decisions."[79] Sponsors were integrated into the interface itself since an intermediate page between the main site and the *desktop* site housed the presenting sponsor's page and sponsors could be referenced in other spaces such as: in a right side tool bar; in ad banners rotating throughout the site; in a bookmark in Dawson's selection of favorite sites; in an email newsletter in Dawson's in-box; and/or via sponsorship of a sweepstakes promotion.[80] The latter was an especially popular method of integration as the sweepstakes prizes could be products from media conglomerate divisions or from sponsors. Dep, Epic Records, and Sony Consumer Electronics, for example, were all connected with content on the *Dawson's Creek* sites.[81] A presenting sponsor might get a specially created space on the site, as was the case with a link for the Dep Virtual Beauty Shop.[82]

Through such sites networks, production companies, and series sponsors could collect data on viewers given that they were encouraged to create a profile and required to register to participate in chats and message boards, and, often, to play games. Effacing its role in delivering audiences to advertisers and emphasizing instead its function as an alternate platform for delivering series content to viewers, CTI officially describes *Dawson's desktop* as "a programming platform that extends the themes, plots, and characters of 'Dawson's Creek' to the online arena and offers 'derivative and original content between episodes and over hiatus periods.'"[83]

The web platform is significant as it offered a revealing window not only into the characters, their inner lives and off-screen activities, but also into the production process itself. Pike and Schneider came up with the digital desktop concept and recruited writer's assistant Arika Mittman, moving her over from the on-air series, and had her create all the content for the site.[84] Taking on Dawson's persona, she drafted his emails, journal entries, IMs (instant messages transmitted electronically by an email account holder) and even documents for his trash bin. She also created a draft of his screenplay "Creek Daze," and posted the edits each week so that viewers could experience it as a working draft and follow his edits and progress.[85] Mittman said that each required a different kind of writing and tone: "I like the variety … There are different kinds of things in the trash bin than in the e-mail, for instance. Dawson talks to people differently than he does to himself in his journal." She notes that she especially enjoys writing the emails:

> "It's such an unusual medium to write and to read. Not something that writers generally get to do … It's different than writing for a screenplay or the stage. You can relate to the characters on a unique level. It's almost more personal, in a way."[86]

Dawson's desktop executive producer Paul Sutpin said, "The Web site gives us the ability to extend our creative process in a new way and further expand and explore Dawson's character."[87] The *desktop* content added depth to the character, but the information was not necessary for understanding the on-air series.

In order to be sure it was offering an effective complement to the on-air series, the *desktop* team coordinated storylines with the writers. Mittman says of the flow of content for a season two episode between the online and on-air series that the team worked "really hard to fill in the gaps in the show … For instance, when Dawson and the gang are going to Witch Island, we set that up on the desktop ahead of time."[88] The multiplatform concept relies on circularity, as is evident in Schneider's comments:

> "An audience flow loop is created between the television show and the site to create one integrated experience; always complementing and driving viewership to the show while offering engaging interactive content online. *Dawson's desktop* takes a step forward in programming across different media."[89]

The digital production team understood that the site needed to offer unique content to be effective in driving tune-in for the series and purchase of content on other platforms.

Will Brooker argues that the *Dawson's desktop* site and the other websites to which it was linked signaled a change in "what it means to engage with a television program, to 'follow' a specific show."[90] Out of his observations about the site, Brooker developed his theory of overflow, now central to fan studies. Building on Williams' theory of televisual flow and Jenkins' conceptualization of media convergence,[91] Brooker explains how this kind of *overflow*

> "transforms the audience relationship with the text from a limited, largely one-way engagement based around a proscribed time slot and single medium into a far more fluid, flexible affair which crosses media platforms—Internet, mobile phone, stereo systems, shopping mall—in a process of convergence."[92]

This results both in the viewer's experience of the show's "characters, situation, and plot" merging with his/her internet activity, and in his/her experience of the show becoming "integrated with the sites" to which s/he can jump from the dedicated website.[93] This kind of site is both a springboard for social interaction as well as for consumerism. They invite visitors to participate in forums, post on bulletin boards, take and share surveys, or send e-postcards. More to the point, viewers are given the opportunity to purchase tie-in merchandise; to download screensavers, wallpaper, and ringtones; to follow links to products characters use/wear on the show and to sponsor merchandise; to check out, download, or purchase the music to which characters listen; and to learn about the network's other programming. Through its linked sites, Brooker says, the WB created a lifestyle experience related to *Dawson's Creek*, one that was aimed at encouraging "'regular' teenage viewers, not just committed fans" to "seek out the music and clothes favoured by the characters and to participate in their lives on a daily basis through online questionnaires and interactive simulations."[94] Matt Hills continues this line of reasoning, arguing that *Dawson's Creek* should be considered a "mainstream cult" series for the kinds of cult behaviors it inspired in everyday viewers.[95] Although it did not have the mysteries that often inspired X-Philes to keep track of series content and debate online about series mythology, *Dawson's Creek* and the other WB coming of age dramedies that were modeled on it, still understood and appealed to the archival interests of fans. It helped that *Dawson's Creek* has at its center characters who are obsessive cataloguers of popular culture knowledge, something that was also a feature of the WB's *Gilmore Girls* (2000–2007).

Although often dismissed as a simple teen soap, *Dawson's Creek* is a significant U.S. series as it established a precedent for creating a mainstream cult text, making it seem that any series could extend itself onto the web and support an abundance of tie-in merchandise of the kind compiled on fan sites—episode guides, anthologies, and videos. The problem, of course, is that these more recent sites don't always have a fan-producer like Mittman creating the content. *Dawson's desktop* and its linked sites encouraged viewers to follow the story and characters as they spilled over into online sites that maintained and expanded the fictional lives of characters and the existence of fictional places and companies. The linked sites (e.g., for the town of Capeside and its high school) extend the fiction that the lives of the characters are ongoing between seasons and that the locations with which they are associated exist independently of the characters and series. Such features are intended to allow the viewer to stay immersed in the fictional world and interact with fictional characters and virtually experience the locations introduced on TV. In this model, TV series are posited as starting points for "further activity," according to Brooker, rather than as "isolated, self-contained cultural artefact(s)."[96] The websites also draw viewers deeper into the storyworld of the TV series, as should be evident in descriptions of how *Dawson's desktop* invited site visitors to take pleasure in what Brooker described as "the illusion of participating in [the char- acters'] lives and interacting with them as friends."[97] This kind of web address enhances the feeling of intimacy when it also encourages fans to interact with production teams as if they were friends. The interaction might take the form of reading their blogs, listening to their podcasts, or participating in an online chat.[98] The latter was a feature Mittman and her *Dawson's desktop* team eventually inte- grated into the site's address.

One of the reasons that *Dawson's desktop* worked so well was that Mittman engaged in viewing practices that mirrored those of dedicated fans of the series, which, in turn, impacted the kind of content she provided. This fan-producer position enabled her to understand the kind of information that might intrigue other fans.[99] The site was so successful that Mittman was promoted to Producer and Headwriter of *Dawson's desktop* and had a team to create the variety of content. She added a new feature, "The Summer Diaries," to chronicle the happenings in the characters' lives in between seasons. In the on-air series viewers knew that Pacey and Joey, Dawson's best male and female friend, spent the summer together sailing on a boat, but what happened during that time was only explored online in the Summer Diaries.[100] On the Capeside site, Mittman added a feature, "Pacey's Rant." The feeling of authentic interiority she achieves in this feature, as was the case with the desktops for Dawson and Joey, was made possible by careful reading of the episodes. That close reading enabled her, she said, to stay "in touch with where he is at that moment, as opposed to just his general character."[101] Her own immersion in the storyworld was essential, she felt, for the creation of its online extensions. Although she typically watched episodes at least twice, she paid even closer atten- tion when creating "Thursday Night Trivia," for season three. She wanted to "try to stump people" by picking out very minor details only the most careful viewers would know.[102] Loyal viewers likely responded to this popular feature because it validated their dedicated, close reading practices.

Mittman discussed her strategies in one of a series of live chats in which online fans could ask questions of production team members. In addition to Mittman, the *Dawson's Chat* series featured writers for the on-air and online series as well as the music supervisor and various producers.[103] During his appearance on *Dawson's Chat*, Executive Producer Greg Berlanti positioned the writers as fans who were in tune with those who posted on the message boards, noting that while the storylines were written in advance of what is released on the site, the message board commentary usually paralleled the same arguments that the writers had among themselves.[104] The chats could be a site for personal revelation, whether actual or part of the performance of intimacy central to such online spaces. Berlanti offered one such moment when he said that he got great satisfaction from writing the two-part episode "To Be or Not to Be ... That is the Question," and confided, "To be able to provide gay teens with the kind of character on television that I never had was very fulfilling."[105] In response to one participant's question about whether Berlanti was sometimes surprised by the passionate intensity of fans who debate every element of character and plot development, Berlanti again aligned himself with viewers: "No. I definitely have a similar intensity of interest in certain shows myself." He added that it is disconcerting, however, when the attacks on the writing get personal.

A glance at *Dawson's Chat* transcripts indicates that a key appeal of posting to the message board is the potential for interaction with production team members. Many of those who post on the boards also assume that writers do visit them and are, therefore, hearing fan concerns, something Berlanti confirmed. *Dawson's Chat*, along with other elements on the site to which the production team contributed content, often educated viewers about the production process. During his October 26, 2000 *Chat* appearance, for example, writer Tom Kapinos defined the role of a showrunner, "the person who is in charge of the day-to-day creative voice of the show." As he explained, the showrunner is responsible for "putting out every script, making sure it's up to his standards." He added, "he's the person the network and the studio will come down on in the event that they don't like something," which is precisely what happened on *Dawson's Creek* when, after creator Kevin Williamson left the series in season one, the studio sent over a showrunner who liked to boast that he was being paid $2 million a year to run the show, but he didn't like it or have any sense of its narrative trajectory. Consequently, he added characters that Kapinos and the original team felt did not fit and, therefore, took the story in the problematic direction. The moderator and the others on the chat were impressed with Kapinos' willingness to offer a "tale from the production site." It was a smart move to place blame and suggest that the problem had been addressed because the message board had been abuzz with complaints about some of the season three storylines. Part of the role of the live chat with the production team was to offer viewers a safety valve to let off steam. In that way they could get their complaints aired, but still feel committed to watching the series because they felt writers had responded both on the web and in the series' new storylines. Kapinos recognized this dynamic in his final comment in which he thanked fans, "for sticking with us through the stormy seas of Season 3. And I hope you enjoy Season 4, 'cause we're really proud of it!"[106] Kapinos' comments indicate the role a website can play in managing fan discontent, a necessary element for any series in a new media environment in which fans can rally against a series as much as they can for one.

Back in season one, there was no official safety valve for fans to vent their frustrations or a space in which producers could directly address fan concerns. In its absence, two fans Tara Ariano and Sarah Bunting, who met in 1997 on a *90210* bulletin board, created a site called *Dawson's Wrap* on which they, along with other *Dawson's Creek* viewers who heard about or surfed onto the website, congregated after the on-air broadcast each week.[107] They broke down the episodes, wrote snarky recaps, and discussed what they liked and didn't like about the series. The site often took the writers and producers to task for plot and character developments. Interested in demonstrating their expertise about, and their emotional commitment to, their favorite TV shows, Ariano and Bunting are emblematic of the dedicated fan site architects who challenge themselves to create character- and series-consistent content and task themselves with the job of making sure the official producers do the same. They were so good at providing snarky recaps for the series that the duo, along with David Cole, soon expanded the site to cover multiple TV series and renamed it Mighty Big TV. The site continued to grow and many others joined them as recappers for programs and moderators for the extensive message boards on which every aspect of each series was dissected and any story or character inconsistency received a detailed critique. The site underwent a name change to TelevisionWithoutPity (TWoP)—with the tagline *spare the snark, spoil the networks*—and grew exponentially from there.[108] By 2007, it had developed so much power and credibility as counterbalance to the networks' often self-serving sites that it became a target for acquisition by a big media company. In 2007 TWoP was acquired by the Bravo division of NBC Universal, a deal which exemplifies the positives and negatives emerging out of the blurring between owner-produced and fan-produced online spaces.[109]

When the trio of founders left the site a year after the acquisition many complained that it had lost its bite. The bigger issue was that the site had previously only recapped series like *Dawson's Creek* that the TWoP founders believed had the potential to be better than they were, or shows that were so bad, they were great subjects for recaps. When Bravo took over, every NBC Universal TV series got a recap and board. TWoP quickly became more of a big budget, glossy space with more official content, and with it more advertising, but it started to lack depth. Then the three cofounders left and their strong editorial control was gone and the site became less of a destination. As one commentator recalls of TWoP in its heyday:

> "The site was tightly run, the recaps well edited and mostly hilarious. The forums would entice undercover Hollywood players like Aaron Sorkin who would [post to the boards to] defend his show [*The West Wing*]. There were interviews with writers of TV shows, humble, well-written interviews in which you'd actually learn about a show. It was evident that those that worked for TWoP loved their job, even when they were assigned awful TV shows to recap."[110]

The difference between the original fan site and the new media conglomerate site is the degree of dedication of the content creators, which is also evident in the difference between the top-down online content mandated by many of today's networks and the bottom-up content produced by fans or even by fan producers like Mittman. Recall the difference between the content Chris Carter and his production team offered on *Inside the X* and the lack of content that Twentieth Century FOX's revised 1998 *X-Files* cross-platform promotional website offered. The latter was less interested in providing content in which fans might be interested and instead saw the website as a space that should reflect the network's or the media conglomerate's brand and promote the products of both entities as well as of any sponsoring companies.

As already suggested, one of the reasons why *Dawson's desktop* was so effective and became a template for others to follow, was that it was produced and managed by Mittman, who was a fan as well as a producer. The same is true for the role Mark Warshaw played in the web content he created for *Smallville*, the series that, starting in its 2001–2 premiere season, continued to innovate the ways in which interaction with a TV series could be extended beyond its broadcast timeslot.

Smallville: The Torch and *Chloe Chronicles*

Another WB series with an innovative web presence, *Smallville* (WB 2001–6; CW 2006–), is both a prequel and a reimagining of the Superman character of the feature films, midcentury television series, and comic books, which are all part of the Warner Brothers-controlled DC Comics superhero franchise.[111] During the series, nine seasons thus far, Clark Kent transitions from high school teen to young adult to the "Red and Blue Blur," the man who will become known as Superman. The superhero element was downplayed in publicity for the first season as Warner Brothers was not sure that would attract its viewers. Instead, the marketing campaign, as the WB's Suzanne Kolb summarized it, sold it as a series about "a cute boy who's tormented by his high school peers and has a deep, dark secret."[112] It also emphasized *Smallville's Dawson's Creek* elements, especially its love triangle featuring a high school girl (Chloe Sullivan) who harbors unexpressed romantic feelings for her male best friend (Clark Kent), who, in turn, has developed feelings for their high school classmate (Lana Lang). This love triangle has similarities to the one in *Dawson's Creek*. That appeal, according to writer Tom Kapinos, is its series-long story arc about the resolution of the Dawson and Joey relationship, which is much like the way *Friends*, the series Warner Brothers produced for NBC, has at its center the open-ended series-long story arc about Ross and Rachel's relationship: "The show is really about Dawson and Joey, these two friends who fell in love, but then life got in the way."[113] Viewers are invested in following the twists and turns of the relationship as they speculate about whether they "eventually find their way back to each other."[114] The series and the website encourage viewers to invest in these issues, which were often the topic of message board debates among "shippers" who supported different relationships (e.g. Dawson/Joey, Joey/Pacey). The same thing occurred among *Smallville's* shippers who were divided among supporting Clana (Clark/Lana), Clois (Clark/Lois), Chlark (Chloe/Clark), with some slash fans rooting for the same sex pairing Clex (Clark/Lex).[115]

In addition to message boards on which fans could advocate for these pairings, *Smallville*'s website offers a *Dawson's Creek*-style immersive experience in which the series' fictional characters and locations are represented by a variety of web content. The town in which they live, the places they frequent or in which they work, and the school they attend all get websites linked to the main site. Particularly interesting are the sites within sites. The one for the high school newspaper *The Torch* is especially significant as it acts as a portal to a secret site containing the case files that Editor-in-Chief Chloe Sullivan has compiled in her investigations into the mystery occurrences that began in Smallville after a meteor shower that occurred in her childhood. Signaling that it is a WB series, "the torch" can also apply to the other long-arc mystery at the heart of *Smallville*: the open question about the girl with whom Clark ends up coupled in the series finale. As an origin story in a franchise, *Smallville*'s struggle is how to reconcile the present of the television series with the past and future of the feature films. According to the existing Superman mythology, he should in the end be with or at least still "carrying a torch" for his *Daily Planet* coworker Lois Lane. The twist is that in the television series, Lois is revealed to be the cousin of Chloe Sullivan, who is secretly "carrying a torch" for Clark. To complicate matters, Clark thinks Lana Lang is his soulmate and the series often encourages viewers to invest in a Clark–Lana pairing, especially when it muddies the waters about his future with "Lois Lane" by revealing that some of the people we know from the feature films went by other names in the past. That also leaves hope for a surprise coupling of Clark and Chloe (Clark–Chlois), but the series often positions her more as a costar than love interest.

Even in later seasons when Chloe gets her own love story and it seems as if her soulmate is Jimmy Olsen, she is never allowed to be with him for very long, leaving open the question of whether she has ever really stopped pining for Clark. Clark and Lana become romantically involved as well, but circumstances always occur that keep them apart. On the other hand, when high school age Clark first meets Lois, he can't wait to get away from her. Their banter intensifies when Clark finally starts working with her at *The Daily Planet*. Of course, the banter is also a central trope of the classic Hollywood romantic comedy about enemies who become lovers. In any case, the introduction of a young Lois and her juxtaposition with Lana and Chloe adds layers of mystery to *Smallville*.[116]

In this way *Smallville*, like the WB's other supernatural series, interconnects an ongoing serial mystery with an ongoing serial love story. All of the WB's other "young people with supernatural powers" series focus on characters whose desires, anxieties, and angst are relatable, even if their origins are alien (*Smallville* and *Roswell*) or their skills are superhuman (for slaying vampires in *Buffy* and fighting demons in *Charmed* and *Supernatural*). It helps that these extraordinary characters who often just want to be ordinary are paired with ordinary people who discover their capacity to be extraordinary. With the WB's second grouping of series, those that are both student-focused dramedies and family melodramas (*Dawson's Creek*, *Felicity*, *Gilmore Girls*, *One Tree Hill*, and the CW's *Gossip Girl*), the supernatural series share a narrative interest in destiny—both about one's future role in the world and one's eventual mate. Both of these series groupings investigate if people really have destined soulmates and explore the question through their characters' ongoing struggles to choose between different love interests. Each series builds narrative tension and maintains audience interest by endlessly deferring the answer to the question of which couples will be the ones that are together in the series finale and beyond.

Whether she is a love interest for Clark or not, Chloe Sullivan certainly is an empowered figure in her own right. It is not surprising, therefore, that she is heavily featured in the series and gets her own webisode, *Chloe Chronicles*. Chloe is no superhero, but she is a super sleuth, and as editor of *The Torch*, has plenty of practice as an investigator, especially given that Smallville is a town in which strange things happen. Through her investigations, Chloe concludes that all the "weirdness" can be traced to the meteor shower that occurred when they were all children. The pilot explains the backstory about that event. Viewers learn that the strange green rocks are Kryptonite and that the shower was intended to disguise the landing of Clark's spaceship. People who came into contact with those "meteor rocks" exhibit strange behavior or develop superpowers. Chloe investigates the effects of those rocks on high schoolers as they wreak comic book-style havoc on their classmates. Taking a cue from *The X-Files*, on which *Smallville* pilot director David Nutter also worked, the first season has a monster-of-the-week structure in which Chloe and *The Torch*'s investigative team, which includes Clark and Lana, discover and contain one of these "meteor freaks."[117] Chloe hones her web-sleuthing skills during this time and Clark works by her side to stop the "meteor freaks," usually with the aid of his evolving supernatural powers that Chloe does not yet know he has. At the same time, he tries to thwart Chloe's larger investigation into the strange happenings in Smallville as he does not want her to discover his connection to the "meteor shower." To keep track of all of the strange occurrences in town, Chloe starts to compile the newspaper clippings that chronicle the events. Eventually, she posts them on the newspaper office's wall, which becomes known as the Wall of Weird. Clark is conducting a secret investigation of his own into the extent of his own powers and the complete story of his Kryptonian heritage. His search leads him to a cave, the walls of which are covered with hieroglyphics that provide clues and eventually a way to allow him to hear about his destiny directly from the disembodied voice of his dead father Jor-El. As he pieces together his own history Clark must also worry that Chloe is piecing together the story of his Earth landing and his true identity via her Wall of Weird.

Chloe is a particular favorite of those who visit the series message board. As editor of *The Torch*, Chloe has developed the kinds of story-tracking abilities expected of investigative reporters and web-savvy viewers of long-arc serial television programs. Chloe appeals to fan trackers likely because as she tracks down clues for her investigation, she offers online fans clues in their investigations of and speculation about upcoming plot developments. The details of Chloe's investigations exist in several forms online. The first is the site for *The Torch* itself, issues of which are created for the online space so that viewers can read the articles written by Chloe and her staff. These are extensions of the storyworld in that they offer extra details beyond what we learn in the episode. As mentioned earlier, *The Torch* site also acts as a portal to a secret site on which Chloe posts her theories. To access it, fans have to follow a trail of clues that begin in a *Smallville* comic book issue and locate the necessary username and password (csullivan/wallofweird). Then they have to return to *The Torch* site and figure out that the trick is to click on the crow's eye on the newspaper masthead to reach the password prompt that enables access to Starr-ware, Chloe's computer operating system. Chloe directly addresses viewers, telling them that she wants them to be able to look at her collection of research as she needs their help in her current investigation. On her desktop they will find the clickable folder that offers access to her Wall of Weird database. Tracking down these clues is not easy, but the fan sleuthing is part of the appeal of the site. Loyal multiplatform viewers are rewarded for their willingness to immerse themselves in the game as web producer Mark Warshaw and his team took great care in creating a plausible and intricately detailed secret site. Such details suggest that while the on-air series might be a mainstream cult text, the website is the space in which the more dedicated cult fans are engaged.[118] As the broadcast TV show plays to more mainstream audiences, it is not surprising that the on-air story privileges the more conventional, former cheerleader Lana Lang as Clark's love interest. The webisodes are used to develop the character arc of fan favorite Chloe Sullivan. To dedicate too much screen time to what Chloe does when she is not with Clark would derail the series focus on him as the main character. The web space, however, is ideal for giving Chloe a starring role. In the *Chloe Chronicles* the character can be given more attention and as, Warshaw says, her fans can get more of what they want: "Chloe being Chloe."[119]

The *Chloe Chronicles* are also an expansion of *The Torch*'s secret site in that the webisodes represent the title character as an investigative reporter in action compiling some of the information that ends up in her secret database. The multipart video series is structured as if her unseen cameraman is filming Chloe as she tracks down various people who seem to play a part in the strange occurrences in Smallville and who know how LuthorCorp is involved. The segments are shot with shaky camera and poor framing and editing to give the effect of an amateur breaking news documentary. Allison Mack, the actress playing Chloe, imagines her to be akin to paranormal investigators of *The X-Files* or the seen-it-all detectives of *NYPD Blue*: "The Chronicles are like a detective story, with Chloe following clues and interviewing people, going from spot to spot, figuring things out."[120] Even though Chloe has always been more than a sidekick and was added to the Superman mythology for the TV series storyworld so that the male superhero would be balanced by a strong, female costar, her on-air activities are still seen in the context of Clark's. As he does not appear in the webisodes, in that platform she can take center stage. *Chloe Chronicles* established a precedent for using the website to develop in-depth characterizations that would distract from the main story if put in the on-air series.

The addition of Chloe was just one of the effective changes that series co-creators Alfred Gough and Miles Millar made to the Superman mythology to make the TV series appealing in its own right, while still offering a consistent, but original entrant in the Superman franchise. The focus on Superman's origin story was a very effective way of finding a balance between the network and franchise brand expectations. As Gough and Millar point out in the documentary *Christopher Reeve: Man of Steel* on the *Smallville* Season 2 DVD, "In the film, Superman is the character and Clark Kent is the disguise. In our show, Clark Kent is the character and ultimately, down the road, Superman will be the disguise." Their point is an important one when thinking about brand differentiation within a franchise. Clark Kent of the TV series is an adopted kid from Kansas trying to learn more about his origins, while keeping his strange and evolving powers a secret from his friends and high school classmates. Superman of the feature films is a superhero hiding his true identity behind the pose of clumsy, bespectacled cub reporter for *The Daily Planet*. The former is more suitable to television as it has a domestic focus and can speak to concerns about adolescence and identity formation.[121]

The TV series links those concerns to the franchise as well by offering a series-long story arc about how Superman's arch enemy Lex Luthor starts out as Clark's friend. The Superman origins angle is made more compelling by paralleling the story of the high school years of the adopted son of the Kents of Kansas with that of Lex Luthor, son of a billionaire businessman. From the time Lex is introduced, it is clear he struggles with the destiny that his powerful father has mapped out for him. Over time, we learn along with Clark about his mysterious origins as Kal-El, an alien from Krypton, but also about the expectations of his biological father, Jor-El, who has a troubling roadmap for his son's destiny. That they are both young men who struggle not only with their fathers' expectations, but also with their own choices in relation to that future is just one of the ways that the series skillfully parallels Clark and Lex.[122] Their friendship is explained by the fact that Clark saves Lex after a car accident. During the DVD commentary track on the pilot episode, Millar says of the moment when Clark saves Lex by giving him mouth-to-mouth resuscitation: "I love the idea of them kissing." Gough, his series co-creator, remarks, "Why not!" The relationship is not ever pursued in the on-air series, but it is by fans creating Clark/Lex slash fiction or video (as in the slash between the names of two same sex characters to indicate their romantic pairing). The intention of such fan productions is to "queer" the text, by reading a series' subtext and fleshing out relationships that are not typically explored in the heteronormative on-air world of American broadcast TV.[123]

Lex's father, Lionel Luthor, does become suspicious of the circumstances of Clark's rescue of Lex, but not because of any physical relationship between the two young men. Rather, he wonders how Clark had the physical strength to rescue his son from the twisted wreckage of his car. Lex ponders the same question and even saves the wreckage of the sports car to continue his investigation of Clark, who, as the viewer knows, does have super strength. Those nagging suspicions eventually turn into the Luthors' obsessive investigation of Clark and his history. In addition to providing narrative tension by offering two more characters who are tracking down clues that might lead to the discovery of Clark's secret identity, the series also offers a long-arc relationship mystery about how the two friends will grow up to be enemies. In this way, the writers make what could have been a very dull hero and villain story into a nuanced one and add a WB-style message about how our choices as young people impact whom we become later in life.

With this coming of age focus the series definitely fits within the WB brand. In 1999 Lewis Goldstein, co-president of marketing, described the network's vision for "a set" of series: "You'll notice in our print ads and other areas—tonally—they take on the same impression. Even though they are different shows, they belong together."[124] His marketing strategy positioned the network's good looking stable of stars as a set as well, which is likely how they ended up on the cover of *Entertainment Weekly* and in stories such as "The Entertainers: the Women of the WB" and explains their appearance in WB Image Campaigns, including 1998–99's "Faces I Remember," 1998–99 and 2001's "The Night is Young."[125] Goldstein talked of bringing back studio system-style promotion at the WB: "We love to cross-promote the movies with our stars and the studios. In the old days you knew which stars were with which studios and we plan to carry on that tradition."[126] The strategy succeeded, as Valerie Wee demonstrates in her work about how the feature films in which the series stars appeared were carefully tied in to the series so that each crosspromoted the other.[127] The series were also re-establishing midcentury branded entertainment deals, with an MCIWorldCom link to *Buffy* and the original *for those who think young* company PepsiCo in a crosspromotion deal with *Dawson's Creek*.[128] Media conglomerate and sponsor crosspromotion come together in *Smallville*. All elements related to the TV series are a development of the superhero from Warner-owned DC Comics, which, in turn, developed the TV show into a series of new comics. While *Smallville* is an obvious choice to be extended in graphic novel format as it has its origins in comics, it also was quite effective for the sponsored webisode and mobisode format as they could be spaces in which to develop the origin stories of other characters and to offer sponsors another platform in which to reach potential consumers. As already noted, the series' first set of webisodes featured Chloe Sullivan, who is a character original to the TV series' expansion of the Superman mythology. With origins in a plot point from the season one episode "Jitters," the first series of *Chloe Chronicles* were two-to four-minute video segments first offered as AOL broadband subscriber exclusives that ran between April 29, 2003 and May 20, 2003, but were later repurposed on the website and featured on the DVD release.[129] The multiplatform extension was ideal for AOL-Time Warner as several divisions within the media conglomerate were contributing and monetizing content.

Effacing the webisode's role as a platform for promotion of sponsors or media conglomerate synergy, the WB described the online series simply as "a platform to promote" new *Smallville* episodes and to provide "extended plotlines that give fans further insights" into story and character arcs. The webisodes also have embedded within them clues to future on-air developments.[130] The marketing team at WB thought of the webisode as having a similar role to music videos as a content-based form of promotion. As Lisa Gregorian explained: "Our goal is to create companion programming that offers new and exciting ways to engage the audience, just as music videos did for record promotion."[131] Patricia Karpas, vice-president and general manager of AOL Television, addressed the potential mutual benefit of the partnership: "Finding new ways to promote television shows, while providing our members with unique and exclusive content, is really at the heart of AOL Television's mission."[132] Another AOL executive also emphasized the exclusivity of the content on AOL Broadband and argued that it once again proves that the service is "a fast-growing platform for producers and networks to create entirely new forms of video programming."[133] During this same 2002–3 season AOL was also offering a platform on which to view a missed episode of WB drama *Everwood*, so that people could catch up before the new episode aired the next week.[134] It was an interesting solution in the years before episode availability via the iTunes video store and network media players. AOL had a vested interest in this kind of content as it would make people want to subscribe to a broadband account. More generally, the hope in such a branded entertainment deal is that viewer loyalty to and fondness for the series will extend to the company that sponsored the extra content. From the standpoint of WB's marketing department, the webisodes are a way "to grow fan investment and loyalty," as Kolb explained.[135] The relationship is a symbiotic one emblematic of the Must-Click/Must-See paradigm as the webisodes are intended to drive tune-in of the episodes up to and including the season finale, while the offer of exclusive, members-only content is intended to drive log-on to AOL and upgrades to broadband service for members who do not yet subscribe.

That is the same goal of the content creators, but as fan-producers they are more concerned about story continuity. As Warshaw explains, "The idea is to try and click every single element of *Smallville* together, to give one great overall huge story just for *Smallville* fans" without making it necessary to see the multiplatform elements to understand the on-air series.[136] A balance needs to be maintained so that the extensions don't "give you too much information that the show needs to take care of for you."[137] After the first volume "far exceeded [the WB's] wildest expectations," Warshaw and his team created a second volume of *Chloe Chronicles*.[138] In this one, Chloe is joined in her sleuthing by a new cameraman, Pete Ross, Clark's best male friend in the first three seasons. Because the webisodes are intertwined with the *Smallville* comics, this volume is an even better example of the way the Must-Click TV paradigm gets viewers to cycle through the elements of a franchise: they can watch the series, read the comic book, click to view the AOL webisode, and then return to the comic book and the series. Gregorian described the series as a

> "wonderful example of cross-company promotion, the storyline of 'Chloe Chronicles' starts on the pages of DC Comics' *Smallville*, continues on AOL and wraps up back in the comic books. Not only does this offer added content for viewers of the 'Smallville' television show, readers of the comic book and to

members of AOL, but also drives exposure beyond the television screen, comic book, and computer, hopefully creating new viewers, readers, and online fans along the way."[139]

The content would then generate revenue for another platform when the webisodes for each season were repurposed on its respective DVD box set. All of the content becomes a form of "enhanced backstory," which makes for a richer viewing experience for anyone who consumes all three franchise elements but is not necessary for understanding the on-air series.[140] The comics are more dominant in the second series extension, animated mobisodes that focus on superheroes from *Smallville*'s version of the Justice League, a group familiar from earlier incarnations of the Superman franchise. This extension was made possible by the change in the series itself. The end of high school signaled the beginning of the movement of *Smallville* toward the feature film's and comics' focus on recurring villains and legions of supporting superheroes. Later seasons also saw a movement from the early primary color look and sunny setting of Smallville to episodes set primarily in the noir spaces of Metropolis, the city of dark alleys and dimly lit (and often rain-soaked) streets in which someone always finds him or herself in need of a superhero. By this point Lex Luthor has taken a course of action that almost destroyed him and put him squarely on the path to be Superman's enemy. To take the place of the character still torn between good and evil paths once Lex no longer appears in episodes, new characters are introduced, most notably Oliver Queen (aka the Green Arrow). Like Clark, he is a DC Comics superhero who keeps his identity secret and leads a double life, but, like Lex, he is also a young man struggling with a dark side. A compelling character, Oliver becomes the star of *Smallville Legends: The Oliver Queen Chronicles*. As the origin story of how Oliver becomes the Green Arrow is one that involves a plane crash and a tropical island upbringing, it would have been too expensive and distracting to be filmed as part of the series. For season six Warshaw came up with the idea of telling the story in an animated mobisode, with six installments, made in partnership with Sprint. After their initial exclusive run on Sprint, these mobisodes were repurposed as website content and later on the DVD. Warshaw explained that they chose the Green Arrow origin story because it is a backstory "not widely known by many casual, non-comic book readers," but one that would be significant for fully understanding Oliver, who had a big role in the on-air season. The story was especially suited to the medium, Warshaw said, as it could not be told "within the budgetary constraints of traditional live-action network TV. He's on a tropical island. There are plane crashes, million-dollar yachts, leopards, monkeys, boars and an entire tribe of natives." He added, "when Sprint allowed us the opportunity to tell an animated *Smallville* story, we jumped at the chance to tell Oliver Queen's in this medium."[141] Sprint stepped in to sponsor the Justice League animated mobisodes because it knew that it would then gain access to "a unique group of very highly engaged fans," and, as Sprint's Alisa Smith theorized, "get ingrained with them over time."[142] That was the CW's theory as well, as Alison Tarrant of CW marketing explained: "There are passionate fans who respond to content created just for them, and they respond to the ad partner who sponsors it."[143] It helped that anyone who can afford the data and multimedia packages in addition to the regular Sprint calling plans would likely be a consumer with disposable income to spend elsewhere as well.

Smallville's web and mobile team continued to develop the DC Comics superhero angle in 2007 with *Smallville Legends: Justice & Doom*, a five-part series of supplementary animated shorts following the off-screen adventures of *Smallville's* Justice League characters—Impulse, Aquaman, Green Arrow, and Cyborg. It appeared in multiple platforms—on-air at the mid-point of episodes in April 2007, on the web, and the whole series on DVD, as an extra on the *Smallville: Season Six* box set. Sponsored by Toyota to promote its new Yaris, these on-air comics were digital shorts that ran as content wraps—"advertiser-aligned content that takes the place of typical 30-second TV commercials during programming, targeted to appeal to specific demographic audiences."[144] The Toyota-CW branded entertainment deal was, according to *MediaWeek*, the first time "a fully integrated campaign has been developed around the content wraps."[145] The content wraps were intended to drive on-air viewers to the web for more content (and promotion). The content/promotion hybrid on the web took the form of an online game linked to plot points from previous *Smallville* episodes. The campaign also included clues distributed via mobile and "street-teams" in various cities as well as national sweepstakes with prizes including a 2007 Toyota Yaris.[146]

Smallville producers had previously embarked on a different kind of extension onto the mobile platform when, for its third season premiere in October 2003, WB partnered with Verizon Wireless for a multi-million dollar text messaging campaign that was described by *The New York Times* as the largest tie-in promotion to date.[147] Registered Verizon Wireless customers could sign up to receive exclusive breaking news plot updates created by the *Smallville* production team. They took the form of breaking news reports from *The Daily Planet* sent via text message. Those who registered would also receive weekly polls and quizzes.[148] The multimillion dollar campaign was indicative of the attempt by telecommunications companies to, as Verizon Wireless's Martin Davis put it, "expand the wireless experience beyond making calls."[149] The format was significant as text messaging was, by 2003, "becoming an advertising medium, particularly for polling and voting, as evidenced by the partnership between the series 'American Idol' and AT&T Wireless."[150] The campaign was part of Verizon Wireless's dramatic increase in the purchase of commercial time on the WB, a deal which also included on-air product integration, 30-second spots, and ad cards.[151] As was the case with the CW's partnership with Sprint, Verizon Wireless's mobile devices were also featured in the on-air series, integrated in a way that would show off their capabilities as well as their style.

It is interesting that at the beginning of this changeover to the Superman part of the story arc when *Smallville* was gearing up to graduate its characters from high school and separate *The Torch's* investigative team, Warner Brothers helped Silver Pictures produce *Veronica Mars* (UPN, 2004–6; CW 2006–7), a series about a web- and mobile-device-wielding female sleuth who, like Chloe Sullivan, is "very Nancy Drew, very mysterious," to borrow the words of Allison Mack about her character's star turn in *Chloe Chronicles*.[152] Unlike Chloe, Veronica is the central character in her own on-air series and is never without her T-Mobile Sidekick mobile device, but the series aired on UPN, the least watched network. That location impacted the extent of the series' web address since UPN did not invest as much as the WB in web and mobile content. Of course, *Smallville*'s multiplatform extensions were less a tribute to the WB's general strategies than to those of *Smallville*'s digital producer as is evident in the award-winning work Warshaw would go on to do as the digital producer of *Heroes Evolutions*, the "multiplatform experience" connected to the NBC series *Heroes* (2006–).

UPN's lackluster official site for *Veronica Mars* left room for some intriguing fan activity, as will be discussed below. Similar to the movement of TWoP from fan to corporate site, the movement of *Veronica Mars* in its third season to the newly created CW came with an upgrade to a glossier site, but also with the stipulation that the series tone down its noir style so the series would look like "a set" with *Gilmore Girls*, the sunnier WB series with which it was paired on the new network's Tuesday Night schedule. The official web address for the series paled in comparison to the elaborate and constantly updated fan site MarsInvestigations.net which captures the essence of *Veronica Mars* with its distinctively noir color palette. It is not surprising that series creator Rob Thomas often offered interviews on that site.[153] The fan-producer also was a frequent and enthusiastic visitor to the TWoP boards for *Veronica Mars*, even giving the site exclusive breaking news and interviews, a fan-friendly attitude which won him an even more dedicated fan following as well as the admiration of *Buffy the Vampire Slayer*'s fan-producer Joss Whedon. Calling *Veronica Mars* "Best. Show. Ever. ... Seriously."[154] Whedon even did a cameo on the series, which only increased its status with *Buffy* fans, many of whom finally found in Veronica Mars a worthy successor to their TV heroine Buffy Summers.

Veronica's Closet: TWoP & LiveJournal fashion sleuths

Described as an "MTV-age Nancy Drew," the title character of *Veronica Mars* is a twenty-first-century update of the chaste, upper class, and preppy American literary character. A lower middle class outcast in a class-stratified Southern California town, Veronica Mars might be blonde like the original Nancy Drew, but UPN's teen sleuth trades in a parent-pleasing demeanor and a friendly relationship with local law enforcement for a sassy style and an outlaw hero anti-establishment stance. Her single dad is a disgraced ex-sheriff turned low-budget private eye. After school she works cases from his seedy detective agency and during school hours she meets potential high school clients in a boys' bathroom she temporarily commandeers to use as her office. Veronica's best friend is Wallace, the African American transfer student at Neptune High just relocated from Cleveland with his widowed mom. Her sometimes allies are Weevil, a Latino motorcycle gang leader from an even worse neighborhood than that of the Mars' motel-like apartment complex, and Cindy "Mac" MacKenzie, a blue-haired computer hacker. We learn in flashbacks that Veronica's transformation from a cheerleader into a teen private investigator is motivated by her desire to solve the mystery of the circumstances surrounding the murder of her best friend Lilly Kane. The aftermath of the murder and its controversial investigation led to the ousting and ruined reputation of Veronica's town sheriff father, the alcoholism and eventual disappearance of her mother, and Veronica's abandonment by her social circle and her boyfriend (Lilly's brother Duncan). When she tried to prove she was above the gossip by attending a high school party, someone slipped a drug in her drink and then raped her while she was passed out. Her search for clues as to the identity of that person is her second ongoing investigation.

Viewers learn all this information through Veronica's voiceover and in flashbacks in which they can see the transformation of Veronica from "Sweet Valley High" cheerleader to sarcastic mystery solver. They also witness Veronica being ostracized by her high school classmates unless they need to hire her to do investigative work for them. Ostensibly a part-time receptionist at her dad's dingy detective agency, Veronica is usually also engaged in some full-fledged detective work. The weekly cases she solves are secondary to Veronica's secret investigation of Lilly's murder. Its blending of noir mystery with a sarcastic take on adolescence prompted the *Village Voice* to declare that *Veronica Mars* "might be the first television drama to attempt a fusion of *Chinatown* and *Heathers*." Others have noted that the show's humor and quirkiness make it more of a teen *Twin Peaks*. The description offered by Kristen Bell (aka Veronica Mars) of her series as a "cross between *Twin Peaks* and The *O.C.*" might be the most apt. It's a serial mystery with a darkly comic tone that it shares with the cult classic, but *Veronica Mars*' South Californian teen characters are still style icons who put on display the latest trendy music, tech devices, and fashions.

During the 2004 and 2005 seasons in which it aired on UPN, *Veronica Mars* did not have an official clothing crosspromotion deal like the ones the WB had arranged with American Eagle for *Dawson's Creek*, but it still inspired its viewers to shop at mall stores. The difference is that the WB specialized in drawing a "detailed map" from series to mall stores, whereas UPN, likely for budgetary rather than ideological reasons, left the process of identifying and then locating Veronica's style to its mystery-loving viewers. An analysis of the TelevisionWithoutPity "Veronica Mars: Outta the Closet" (TWoP-VC) fashion forum and the LiveJournal Veronica Mars Fashion Community (LJ-VM) through which participants exchange information about where they have bought or have sighted clothing from the series suggests that part of the pleasure of fan interaction with Veronica Mars is the feeling of active participation.[155]

The central activities of the TWoP fan forums are related to tracking. Fans track the consistency of the characters and story arcs as well as the consistency of the network's marketing and promotion. They look for content clues that they believe Thomas is embedding within the episodes. Those with access to the trade presses and other industry sources search for commentary by network executives or production team members that might provide clues about upcoming episodes.

They share this information with each other on blogs, fan sites, and message boards. The discussions suggest that viewers look at the fashion on *Veronica Mars* in the same way they look at the show's other mysteries: as clues that they need to follow. The mystery these fashion sleuths investigate is how to acquire and pull off the trendy teen identity the show puts on display. They understand that they can follow the clues within the series about the kinds of costuming, accessories, and decor required for others to recognize their desired affiliation with the trendy teen identity Veronica embodies. Summing up the attitude of many of her fellow participants on TWoP-VC, one fan remarks, "One of my friends said that her shopping motto is now 'What would Veronica wear?' And I have taken that to heart, as well" (TWoP, April 17, 2006). Others concur that the TV character has become their de facto stylist.

The comments posted on TWoP-VC demonstrate how closely fans follow Veronica's fashion clues in each episode. Because the murky noir lighting and the red and green filters make her outfits more difficult to see, it is not surprising that fans on TWoP-VC explain that they tape episodes so they can get a better look. Technology-savvy, the TWoP-VC participants also have little problem surfing the web for information, sometimes finding a production still or scene capture on an official or unofficial VM website and cross-matching it to the clothes available on the online shopping sites of trendy teen mall stores. Many of the regular participants clearly get pleasure from being the first to match the outfit with the mall store. This response is representative of the way that "recognizing marketplace interventions has become part of the 'game'"[156] for fans. That they feel savvy when they identify in which brands the characters are outfitted exemplifies the kind of fan pleasure that comes from "exercising their competencies."[157] The ultimate thrill for these fans, though, occurs when Veronica appears on-screen wearing the Abercrombie Dillon motorcross jacket or its Claudia faux fur down vest, the Banana Republic Scooter Jacket, the American Eagle Chocolate Messenger Bag, or the Lucky Brand t-shirts and jeans that they already own. Their style sense is validated when it is reflected on TV. The posts reveal that a primary source of their pleasure comes from proving they are like Veronica, both trendy teens and plucky mystery solvers. Like her, they are capable of following clues and solving a mystery—not just the season one mystery of the identity of the murderer of Veronica's best friend Lilly Kane, but also of the names of the stores that are the sources for Veronica's trendy outfits.

The boards feature discussion threads dedicated to identifying the brands hanging in Veronica's Closet and locating the online and offline sites at which to purchase them. To do all this tracking, fans pool areas of expertise and levels of knowledge in order to track down information. These activities would appear to suggest the pleasures of speculation are central motivators in fan activities. Taking a cue from Matt Hills and Jenkins, it may be that fans are attracted to the satisfaction inherent in shared problem-solving and the opportunity to demonstrate expertise and to find a community that may not be so readily available in the offline world.[158] Writing about *Survivor* fans who pool their knowledge in order to track down the location for each new season prior to its airing, Jenkins notes that they enjoy both the collective nature of their endeavor as well as the individual satisfaction of being the person who could emerge as an expert in a particular area.[159] They create an online knowledge community to trade information about where to buy the fashions in Veronica's Closet. It functions in terms of what Pierre Levy calls a "collective intelligence paradigm" in which it is assumed that all participants have "something to contribute, if they will only be called upon on an ad hoc basis."[160] Building on Levy's theories, Jenkins explains that the collective intelligence paradigm is held together by "the social process of acquiring knowledge—which is dynamic and participatory, continually testing and reaffirming the group's social ties."[161] A September 2005 TWoP-VC thread (April 17, 2006) epitomizes this social process. After someone posts a question about a particular jacket, several others speculate on where it is from until one confirms that it's from Lucky and proudly declares that she just "bought it and, on sale, nonetheless!" That prompts several to ask how she managed to get the jacket at 30% off, to which she responds that she just happened upon a sale at the Lucky store:

> "It's like walking in to Veronica's closet (haha). I wanted everything right then and there. But I restrained (ha) and only bought the jacket :) I actually wouldn't have even gone into the store if it weren't for this thread finding out where articles of clothing come from."

Here the viewser points to the way individuals in online communities become part of "virtual communities of consumption" in that they impact each other's decisions: "Online interactions and alignments increasingly affect their behavior as citizens, as community members and as consumers."[162]

The TWoP-VC forum also impacts consumer behavior because the participants use it to share tips for being savvy shoppers, alerting each other to eBay auctions, sales, and consignment stores as alternate places in which to buy the clothes. The source of pleasure here comes from the fans' perception that there is a subversive element to sale shopping. They do not address the fact that the prices of the products are inflated in the first place. More often, they convey a sense of pride in their Veronica-like savvy, as is evident in another thread (TWoP-VC, April 17, 2006) in which several participants trade information on a different jacket. One fan supplies its brand name and then admits that during an earlier forum discussion she withheld a brand name because she was trying to win the piece in an eBay auction. She adds, "I'm sure you all understand." The next month, she gleefully shares that she won the auction for the Andover Plaid J. Crew Peacoat that she "coveted" since she first saw Veronica wear it. Many other participants are similarly determined to find ways to acquire the clothes featured on the show even if they have limited fashion budgets. The Veronica Mars Fashion Community on LiveJournal (LJ-VM) is committed to this cause. As its original September 2005 profile describes, it is a community "dedicated to finding out just where the wardrobe people pick up Veronica's clothes and accessories and if they are available for us ordinary beings to purchase" (LJ-VM, February 20, 2007). These fans are invested in the idea of themselves as independently investigating the clues Veronica Mars offers about new styles, collectively working together to discover the identity of the brands with which Veronica is affiliated, and subversively bypassing mainstream culture by buying from eBay or at least on sale. One of the posts to LJ-VM, however, does acknowledge that sale shopping is sometimes less a fulfilling culturally subversive act than a demoralizing economic necessity: "If I had a lot of cash, I could just point at what I like and buy it, rather than searching for deals" (LJ-VM, February 20, 2007).

It is easy to read the ways UPN gets VM viewers to, as the TWoP participants put it, "covet everything Veronica owns," only in terms of cynical marketing strategies, but as Jenkins, Brooker, Hills, and Gwenllian-Jones have noted, audience response is more complex.[163] To some degree, of course, anything viewers do on any website, official or unofficial, connected to a television series plays into network overflow strategies as the activities keep them engaged after the weekly program ends. Of course, viewers are well aware of the way they are targeted as consumers. For them, fandom can also become an exploration in or a lesson about how identity is negotiated in American consumer culture. While producers are banking on emotional investment leading to consumer investment, some groups of fans, again exemplifying the collective intelligence paradigm, use their mutual participation in consumer culture as a way to create emotional connections with each other. As Susan Murray, Louisa Stein, Sharon Ross, and Jenkins have demonstrated, online fans often commandeer websites or message boards for their own purposes.[164] This behavior demonstrates how, as Jenkins explains, "groups of consumers form intense bonds with the product, and, through the product, with fellow consumers."[165] Murray has analyzed this kind of fan investment in relation to *My So Called Life* (ABC 1995). In the discussion threads and forums related to the teen melodrama, Murray discovered that the fans "following" the series online had moved beyond watching TV for "entertainment, education on social issues, or fantasy fulfillment," but came to see the activity of watching and talking about TV as an emotional "investment in an individual and communal understanding" of their identity.[166] Part of the appeal of this kind of interactive online space seems to be that viewers acknowledge the legitimacy of each other's experiences, take their identity crises seriously, and reassure each other that they share similar problems and anxieties. The ABC bulletin board evolved into "a meeting place/discussion group for fans who thought that their lives would be significantly altered if the show was taken off the air."[167] As often occurs online, fans altered the intended function of the bulletin board space and used it "to generate friendships, share experiences, and talk about themselves."[168]

VM-related forums also function as springboards for discussions among fans about their negotiation of a host of identity issues, often in relation to adolescence, peer pressure, cultural norms, and gender expectations or stereotypes. Reading the posts to various TWoP discussion threads, for example, one is struck by the frequency with which interpersonal interactions override the discussion of the show itself. The participants in the TWoP-VC threads engage in such off-topic discussions, confiding in each other about their body and identity anxieties as they share with each other the stumbling blocks they encountered in trying to acquire or pull off the VM trendy teen look. For some, it is a matter of financial access; for others, it is an issue of body type; and for a good number, it is the anxiety that they are already too old at 25 or 28 to get away with some of the teen styles. Although most of the respondents take pains to declare that VM fashions are democratic (because they are from the mall and not expensive boutiques and so technically available to all), they also acknowledge that they can't always contort their bodies or their hair in the ways that would enable them to fit within or bear any resemblance to the straight-haired, petite WASP teen ideal established on the show.

There is a liberating aspect to the way the message board allows everyone to try on Veronica's styles. The participants are free of "such visible markers as sex, 'race' and age which, in offline interactions," Don Slater explains, "fix identities in bodies."[169] The problem, to borrow from Judith Butler's famous formulation, is that bodies do matter[170] and become obstacles to some fans' ability to embody fully the Veronica Mars styles. One April 2006 TWoP thread addressed this issue. When a fan discloses, "I hate that I'm 25, though, and can't pull off some of the stuff she wears," she adds that she can't copy the hairstyles either because of her "super curly, frizzy hair." Another chimes in and laments her own stubbornly curly hair. She recounts how when she wakes up and her hair is a disaster, she gets exasperated and thinks, "no one has suffered as I have suffered." Then she apologizes for going off topic, but as she explains, "I hardly ever hear about someone else with the same hair. And I see VM's hair and I am sad." These postings reflect the ambivalence of viewers who understand that the ways their bodies are marked by race, ethnicity, and ancestry will frustrate their desire to adopt mainstream identities, leaving them feeling as if they are poor imitations of an ideal TV type.

Age is also a barrier to an easy adoption of the Veronica Mars look, as an earlier TWoP-VC post notes: "I love what they do with her hair on the show. Sadly it inspires me and I'm not a high school student." She wishes she could go to the office with her hair in pigtails like Veronica's. Two other fans cheer her on. They reveal that they are both 28 and also inspired by Veronica's hairdo. One reassures her, "I've just started wearing pigtails again for the first time since grade school due in large part to the fact that Veronica looked so dang cute in them." She admits that she was nervous about adopting the style, but she was secretly pleased that someone told her that she looked about 16 in them. Another shares, "I'm 24, and have been incorporating my Veronica Mars look into my wardrobe as well … My boss actually told me I looked cute, and wistfully said she wished her hair was long enough for pigtails" (TWoP, April 17, 2006). Although they are anxious that they might be too old for some of Veronica's outfits, they still follow her fashion lead and take great pleasure in being mistaken for trendy teenagers.

Veronica Mars extends the offer of participation in its lifestyle experience to anyone who wants to buy into the *for those who think young* lifestyle on display.

Like many programs with teenage main characters and adult followings, it addresses viewers who are still working through teen identities. Some use teen identities to reflect on their own concerns in a dramatized way. Others take pleasure in vicariously reliving high school as the sassy teen with the snappy comebacks who can mock mainstream high school hierarchies and sometimes challenge them. It helps that as a petite blonde bedecked in the latest mall fashions, Veronica looks so good fighting and talking back. True to what Susan Douglas says about the composite appeal of many female TV characters,[171] the fans posting comments on websites related to *Veronica Mars* admire the title character for both her investigative and fashion savvy, especially her ability to inflect mainstream trendy teen fashions with her own sassy style. Veronica Mars courts anyone who wants to participate in the trendy teen lifestyle that she represents. The analysis of its affiliated TWoP-VC forum demonstrates that while actual teens experience pleasure in seeing their culture represented and acknowledged, twenty- and thirty-something viewers experience pleasure in acquiring the kind of fashion and tech savvy that leads others to miscalculate their ages.

In addition to their politically charged discussions of hair texture and age-appropriate styles, the TWoP-VC fan forum also raises the question about what brands are inconsistent with Veronica's supposed anti-establishment stance. An August 2005 discussion thread about the fact that Veronica's wardrobe rotation includes separates from Abercrombie & Fitch and a debate about whether the choice of the brand emblematic of American teen in-crowd status were inconsistent with Veronica's characterization as a lower middle class crusader against conformity is interesting for the way it registers this class ambivalence at the heart of *Veronica Mars*. The discussion starts when one fan remarks that several of Veronica's jackets are from Abercrombie and another laments, "Somehow I'm vaguely disappointed that Veronica wears Abercrombie" (TWoP, April 17, 2006). The fact that Veronica still wears clothes from Abecrombie and Fitch, the current badge of belonging to the Mall of America middle class, feels problematic for others as well. As another fan puts it, "Abercrombie represents that elitist high school/college 09er values that I thought Veronica had left behind" (TWoP, April 17, 2006). After all, Veronica has supposedly totally remade herself after Lilly's murder. She cuts her hair and, as one reviewer put it, "chucks her Abercrombie wardrobe."[172] Once transformed into Alterna-Teen, her clothing and hair take on such "sharp edges" that she resembles "a DC Comics superhero."[173] It seems inconsistent for Veronica, who constantly mocks the Abercrombie-clad kids from Neptune's elite 90909 zip code, to wear anything from a store sued for only hiring 09er white preppy types.[174]

Some of the forum participants (TWoP, April 17, 2006) explain away the Abercrombie pieces as a matter of practicality (she doesn't have enough money to buy all new clothes for junior year). "Let's not forget that Veronica was an 09er herself," one post reminds everyone. "I sincerely doubt that Veronica wouldn't wear her old clothing for the sake of rebellion against 09er culture." Another adds, "Especially if she's cash-poor. I think the wardrobe department does a really good job of 'punk'-ing up Veronica's look while still making use of her preppy stuff, such as Abercrombie." A third takes the argument to the opposite extreme, implying that if Veronica didn't wear Abercrombie, it would be like reverse snobbery: "I think it is perfectly fitting that Veronica wears Abercrombie because she also wears like, a million other types of clothing. I don't think she'd be one to not go to a store because of who it is marketed to." Abercrombie has to be recuperated because many of the participants share with Veronica a combination of desire and disdain for the commodified identities promoted by mainstream middle class mall culture.

On the TWoP discussion board the uncomfortable topic is soon abandoned and the forum returns to a space for celebrating Veronica's fashion sense and its participants' shopping savvy. Several also praise the Veronica Mars wardrobe department for dressing the characters realistically in clothes that are available at the local mall stores (TWoP, April 17, 2006). A few complain that less realistic items, like Seven for All Mankind jeans, are starting to creep into Veronica's season two wardrobe. A similar critique is made on the LJ-VM during season three: "I've always found it so funny that even though Veronica and her dad are supposed to be lower middle class, She is always wearing Sevens and Citizens of Humanity Jeans" (LJ-VM, February 20, 2007). It is notable that these are the jeans worn by the ultra-rich Marissa from *The O.C.*, the 2003–7 series that Warner Brothers produced for FOX. *The O.C.* mainstreamed the idea that ordinary young women should be shelling out several hundred dollars for the high-fashion jeans. All the posts on the TWoP-VC thread about the jeans eventually prompted the outcry: "They should not change Veronica's style at all!! If I wanted to see clothes from The O.C. I would watch The O.C.!" (TWoP, April 17, 2006). The irony is that such starlet wear is not donned by the 09ers who could realistically afford those fashions. Even Logan, the son of a movie star, is outfitted in mid-level mall store clothes, as one thread about his suede jacket indicates (TWoP, April 17, 2006). Given that the fashion sleuths discover that the jacket comes from Wilson's Leather—an ordinary mall store and, thus, an unlikely place for a movie star's son to buy anything, if we can judge by the actions of LA's Robertson Drive celebrity kid shopaholics—something other than realism seems to be at work. Several fans note that the clothes the 09ers wear really don't fit their characterization as the "haves" in Neptune. By outfitting Neptune's truly rich kids in the same mall store fashions, *Veronica Mars*, like most American TV, flattens out class differences so that everyone is or is depicted as middle to upper middle class or aspiring to be.

With the toning down of 09er style, the show seems to be leveling the playing field. In doing so, it taps into that American fantasy perpetuated by the media that everyone in the United States is essentially from the same class—the mall-shopping middle class. Sure there are some gradations, but such a view promises that there is no real chasm separating the haves and the have-nots. In a credit card culture, everyone can at least look like a "have," the show seems to be saying. That is probably what one fan felt when she bought Logan's jacket for her husband and her teen daughter and then proudly posted a picture of the two of them wearing their matching jackets. That they are sitting astride a motorcycle reminiscent of those ridden by Neptune's mildly rebellious "PCHer" gang suggests that a rebel "have-not" identity is available for purchase as well (TWoP, April 17, 2006). It is ironic that Logan wears the jacket in an episode entitled "Weapons of Class Destruction" (1:18). The fact that Veronica, in contrast, is wearing super trendy and super pricey John Fluevos "Bondgirl" boots prompts the comment: "I think lower-middle-class in the fictional town of Neptune is a lot different than lower-middle-class in real life." Even more interesting is Keith Mars' comment after he secures a bounty hunter fee, "Tonight we eat like the lower-middle-class to which we aspire." In this moment, among others in the episode, there is a disconnect between the dialogue and fashion cues about class.

That Veronica's style gets read as an alternative to consumer culture is a testament to the "counterculture as an enduring commercial myth."[175] Veronica and her season one style are broadly appealing because she seems like one in a long line of rebel types who represent an anti-establishment stance at the same time that she does not veer too far from identifiable mainstream identities. While seeming to occupy an anti-establishment position, Veronica is actually a representative of what Thomas Frank calls "hip consumerism," which he defines as "a cultural perpetual motion machine in which disgust with the falseness, shoddiness, and everyday oppressions of consumer society could be enlisted to drive the accelerating wheels of consumption."[176] Frank contends that corporations since the 1960s have embraced an "anti-establishment sensibility being developed by the youthful revolutionaries."[177] Within the hip consumerism paradigm "no longer would Americans buy to fit in or impress the Joneses, but to demonstrate that they were wise to the game, to express their revulsion with the artifice and conformity of consumerism."[178] Yet, it is consumerism just the same. VM fans might pride themselves in following their own routes, but a reading of the TWoP-VC forum demonstrates that they still end up in the same place—the mall. Judging by the number of posts on season one and two VM web forums about coveting and acquiring the items in Veronica's Closet, UPN's overflow strategies might have been underdeveloped, but they still worked.

On the message boards fans sometimes acknowledge this simultaneity of Veronica as an alterna-teen who often sports mainstream clothing choices and of independent viewers not easily taken in by promises of consumer belonging who conform to Veronica's style parameters. More often, they work to efface it because they position Veronica in a binary in which she is the champion of the have-nots against the haves. In season one Veronica's Chrysler LeBaron convertible, a car that often breaks down in the Neptune High School parking lot, stands in for her outsider status. With the third season relocation to the CW the LeBaron disappears and Veronica no longer makes daily visits to the Mars Investigations office, a location that had contributed to the noir feel of the series. When Veronica trades up to a new Saturn VUE, the bland, sport utility vehicle seems at odds with her scrappy underdog status. Viewers posting on fan message boards complained about the car and other inconsistencies, but they were also savvy enough to understand the centrality of sponsors' product placement and integration, especially for a show that was constantly on the brink of cancellation. That the car switch occurred when the TV series moved from the defunct UPN to the new CW (the network created by the merger of CBS and Warner Brothers) makes it even more significant as it reveals much about TV programming in an era of media conglomerates, multiple media platforms, and mobilized media-savvy fan networks. Negotiating the complexity of this new environment, showrunners often have to meet demands of media conglomerates and sponsors that are at odds with their own and/or fans' visions for the show, sometimes resulting in contradictory or inconsistent characters or story arcs.

Some of this ambivalence was encoded in the series from the outset. The pilot establishes class divisions with a tracking shot of the high school parking lot filled with high end cars and SUVs that accompanies Veronica's voiceover: "This is my school. If you go here, your parents are either millionaires or your parents work for millionaires. Neptune, California, a town without a middle class." Although many episodes of *Veronica Mars* do critically explore outsider social and economic positions in the United States, the voiceover's claim is not an accurate reflection of the class gradations in the town. After all, season one is filled with seemingly middle class kids for whom Veronica investigates cases—often ones involving mistaken identity or some form of misrepresentation related to the technology to which all the non-09ers seem to have access. They are the "havenots" described in the rest of the pilot episode's voiceover: "If you're in the second group, you get a job; fast food, movie theatres, mini-marts." If these teens are indeed lower class, then many of them are trying to pass for middle- or upper-middle class by spending most of their paychecks on trendy clothing and technology.

Tech devices are everywhere in *Veronica Mars* starting in its pilot episode. The most common shots in season one involve Veronica's Apple PowerBook and feature either a centered medium shot of Veronica seated in front of her laptop tracking down information on the Web or an off-center medium shot of Veronica taken from the right to reveal the upper half of her trendy outfit, her laptop cover, and another character. Often this is her best friend Wallace, but sometimes her pal Mac or her father Keith, all of whom are looking along with Veronica at the information she has tracked down. The shots indicate the centrality of trendy technology to the hip teen's lifestyle as well as the centrality of product integration to twenty-first-century TV. At other times Veronica stares at the screen of her camera phone, although that does not play as much of a role until she trades in the T-Mobile flip phone for the Sidekick. She utilizes the Sidekick not only to keep track of her friends and emails, but also to send text messages, a form of communication that enables her to orchestrate her own rescue in the final episode of season two. The T-Mobile Sidekick is more easily read as character-consistent since the phone was already popular with teenagers given its IM (instant messaging) capabilities and the fact that T-Mobile offered one of the lower cost plans. The choice of the Sidekick is an innovative way of integrating story-consistent product placement and of offering a new media update to the more usual kind of sidekick since there is a long history of pairing American TV characters with sidekicks and with sponsors' products.

In *Veronica Mars* the two come together as the teen sleuth title character solves mysteries with a little help from both her T-Mobile Sidekick and her friends. If Wallace is the old-style media sidekick, that type of African American male buddy Edward Guerrero claims became popular in Hollywood films of the late twentieth century, Mac is the mew media alterna-sidekick, both the hip face of new technology (a blue-haired female hacker) and of alterna-consumerism (driving a gecko green New Beetle, she is representative of counterculture gone commercial).[179]

CW Style: circa 2007 & 2008

As it is a TV show about the scandalous reports posted on a gossip blog about students at an elite New York City prep school, *Gossip Girl*, the CW series that was greenlit in 2007, the year the CW canceled *Veronica Mars*, was the ideal vehicle for sponsorship by mobile device manufacturers and service providers. Veronica checks her phone often, but *Gossip Girl* gives even more minutes of screen time each episode over to mobile devices—usually shots of students checking their mobiles for breaking news text messages, followed by shots of them using the devices to call each other to talk about the gossip or to circulate the gossip via a text to someone else. *Gossip Girl* registers more generally how technology and new forms of communication have transformed the twenty-first-century American high school experience and extended it past school grounds and into virtual realms via 24–7 texting, blogging, and emailing.[180]

On the CW's website for *Gossip Girl*'s first season Verizon Wireless promotions occupied almost as much space as CW content. At the time, the company was showcasing its Chocolate phone, which was featured in a top banner: *Chocolate—the slide phone guilty pleasure.* Clicking on the phone connected the viewser to a Verizon Wireless corporate page that provided a variety of downloadable video clips and ringtones that were part of the carrier's VCast service. Clicking on "As Seen On" led the site visitor to the regular corporate website, which showcased the selection of phones "seen on *Gossip Girl*." The site encourages viewers to visit every week because Verizon Wireless promised to help them stay up to date with the latest mobile products as well as "all the latest" *Gossip Girl* tie-ins, which it makes available as "exclusive content" for its VCast subscribers. Recalling the general Verizon Wireless promotion "Get IN Now" for its IN network services, the site declared, *Getting in is easy, keeping up is the hard part.* The sentiment is also applicable to the series' less privileged prep schoolers (who, of course, are still very privileged) and the way they have to work hard to stay in fashion and not fall victim to a *Gossip Girl* blog post or text message blast.

The site also encouraged consuming media conglomerate products related to *Gossip Girl*. Indeed, the *Gossip Girl* website is all about franchise synergy. The TV show itself is "high concept" TV given its reliance on the "pre-sold property" of the book series on which it is based as well as on the producing team of Josh Schwartz and Stephanie Savage, who created *The O.C.*[181] The website offers less series-consistent content than the *Dawson's Creek* or *Smallville* sites and more promotion that looks like content. The blurring of the lines between the two begins in the on-air series. A screen capture of the *Gossip Girl* blog welcome page acts as the opening shot for the on-air series opening "as seen on" episode recap. The latest gossip is offered via voiceover by the unknown young woman who is creating the blog. The irony is that it is spoken as a voiceover by *Veronica Mars* star Kristin Bell. While the on-air version of the blog lists links—Gossip, Pics, Parties—it offers no real interactivity. On the website version of the blog, viewers can click on the links or scroll down and read it as a series of blog entries illustrated by a series of photographs.

The main *Gossip Girl* web interface is also an interactive space in which viewers can click to activate or to learn about the various ways to participate in the *Gossip Girl* experience. On a wall-mounted flat screen TV, episode recaps and sneak previews play and other special content can be clicked to activate. In the center of the room, there is a literal desktop with click-on objects, including a laptop and mobile device, representative of the various formats in which *Gossip Girl* exists: as video that can be streamed to a laptop; as a DVD; and as a novel. There are also references to other purchasable aspects of the *Gossip Girl* experience such as series soundtracks. Viewers can receive series-related content as well in the form of text messages, clips, and audio snippets—sent straight to their mobile devices.

As in *Veronica Mars*, the leveling of the playing field between the haves and the supposed have-nots is connected to the consumer promise that everyone has equal access to the same trendy tech devices and fashions of the kind on display on the *Gossip Girl* website. Sporting an aptly named LG EnV phone and a plan from Verizon Wireless, Blair Waldorf is the Queen Bee with whom Jenny Humphrey, *Gossip Girl*'s version of a have-not, has to compete. An aspiring designer, Jenny has the capacity to sew some cool original designs, but she also is often outfitted in designer fashions that far exceed her budget. The series accounts for that discrepancy in a shot of Jenny surfing a designer discount website. The over-the-shoulder shot reveals the screen of her laptop on which we see that she is on a site called Bluefly.com with the tagline: *the ultimate hook-up for the fashion obsessed.* When she is joined by her brother and some friends, she tilts the laptop so they (and we) can see the site, models online shopping for them (but really for us), and talks about the deals you can get on the site. The online discounter crosspromotes *Gossip Girl*, offering a separate space on its site to showcase its fashion,[182] complete with a cast photograph that, when clicked on, opens windows to separate sites for each character's closet. The tagline for the site within the site reads: *Haute Gossip: cause there's more than just skeletons in their closets.*

Since its inception the CW has been offering this kind of click-on closet feature on its own CW Style site within the site. For its 2007 series, like *Veronica Mars*, viewers could click on the image of one of the characters and the action would open another window in which the character's clothes appear as a page of thumbnail photos as would be typical of the virtual catalogue of popular retailers like American Eagle. The same thing happens on the *Gossip Girl* site, except that the clothes are a mix of the kinds of designers that might be in the upscale section of a mall department store, and designers that one could only buy in a boutique or a very upscale department store. The storefront associated with each character is even more intriguing for the way that the costume department outfits the series' "middle class" (which, on this series, refers to the children of a once famous rocker who now owns a Brooklyn Art Gallery). Often the have-nots are wearing more expensive clothes than the socialites. In contrast, the biggest dandy in New York has a pair of Gap pants available under his link that he would absolutely disdain. The trust fund trio, the super-rich Chuck Bass, Blair Waldorf, and Serena van der Woodsen, would never be wearing the Urban Outfitters and American Apparel items in their virtual closets, as they are emblematic of mass market "wannabe urban chic." They set trends; they don't follow them. This costuming inconsistency speaks again to the way broadcast TV series flatten out the class differences among characters, making it seem as if anyone can acquire the look of the elite and perhaps even work his/her way up to that status (Jenny, by becoming a fashion designer, and Dan, by becoming a novelist). In contrast to the dominance of Abercrombie & Fitch and American Eagle on the WB's *Dawson's Creek* and the CW's *Veronica Mars*, these characters are the ultra rich city sophisticates so it is not surprising that their closets are filled with designer clothes by Nanette Lepore, Marc Jacobs, Tory Burch, and Jimmy Choo, among others. It is more surprising that the supposedly middle class Jenny Humphrey has an $818 Goldenbleu purse and her brother Dan, supposedly an anti-status guy, wears a $188 Marc Jacobs button down. Of course, the link to Bluefly would be a way for them to find such designer clothes at a reduced price.

This feature is a corporate-sponsored version of the kinds of tracking down of discounted versions of fashions in which the online trackers engaged in relation to Veronica Mars. Even in this more controlled space the fashion sleuth pleasures may kick in again, however, as viewers willing to engage in some online fashion sleuthing would probably be able to find the item cheaper on some site on the web or to get it used through an eBay auction as the viewers did for *Veronica Mars*. The CW learned a good deal from the behavior of *Veronica Mars'* viewers, most significantly that those who congregate online to talk about TV also work together to track down the in-clothes, technologies, and music with which their favorite television characters are associated. It is in this latter activity that the CW copied for its CW Style site and its Bluefly partnerships.

The Bluefly strategy is a return to the signposting of fan activity that Brooker saw as a problematic feature of the *Dawson's Creek* web address, especially in relation to the series premiere promotion deal with J. Crew for its characters to appear in its catalogue and then to sport the clothes in the regular episodes.[183] For the next season the deal switched to American Eagle, an upstart brand that was trying to pick off the customers of higher end preppy retailers like J. Crew and Abercrombie & Fitch. Characters on *Dawson's Creek* were always carefully positioned in shots so that the retailer's eagle logo, well known to most teenagers in America, was clearly visible. Two characters once even had a conversation about why American Eagle was so much better than competitor Old Navy. It was these kinds of deals that Rob Thomas, a former writer for *Dawson's Creek*, wanted to avoid when he created *Veronica Mars*, which he had initially imagined as an edgy cable series when he included in the pilot episode a class critique about the ever-widening gap between the haves and the have-nots and the role that fashion plays in obscuring it.

The problem with the CW Style's signposting strategy—*Visit The CW Style* and *Get The Looks from Your Favorite CW Shows*—is that, like *The X-Files* webmasters in the early 1990s, *Veronica Mars*' fashion sleuths had two years of fan-generated activity and community formation prior to the network's attempts to build a community around its official site. The network and advertiser-sponsored fashion tracking associated with *Gossip Girl* represents the way the network tried to monetize the online tracking activity in which *Veronica Mars* fans were engaged. The *Gossip Girl* audience does not seem to mind, but when the CW partnered with American Eagle for its 2007 launch of *Veronica Mars*, then in its third season, as a CW show, it alienated many viewers.

CW's and American Eagle's Aerie Girls minisodes

When UPN was disbanded in the merger and the third season of *Veronica Mars* was inherited by CW, Thomas ended up back where he started: finding it more and more difficult to write alternative characters on a network that made a branded entertainment deal with clothing retailer American Eagle (AE). For its fall 2006 pairing of *Gilmore Girls* and *Veronica Mars*, CW partnered with AE, which was eager to promote its launch of Aerie, a "lifestyle brand" of Dormwear and intimates for young women. The presenting sponsorship, marketed as "Aerie Tuesdays," featured the claim that Aerie tank tops, camisoles, t-shirts, drawstring pants, and intimates were "fun and flirty" and "sweetly sexy."[184] While those descriptors might suit sincere Yale University student Rory Gilmore, Veronica Mars remained edgy and intense even after she underwent a makeover to tone down her rebellious style and attitude for her first year of college.

Even during the UPN run of *Veronica Mars*, Thomas had already discovered that his vision of offering alternatives to the *Dawson's Creek*-style mall store teen, not to mention his attempt to tackle edgier topics (rape, class immobility, childhood sexual abuse), frequently conflicted with broadcast network pressure for the integration of the kind of products and lifestyles that sponsors need to put on display to secure their Return On Investment (ROI). That pressure only increased with the move to the CW. On the other hand, the pilot episode set up expectations from fans who had invested in the alternative character and story arc and, consequently, expected a return on their emotional investments. In the second and third seasons both kinds of returns got harder to deliver since while the networks continued to request that Thomas make the characters and scenarios more mainstream so as to appeal to a broader market, the loyal fans were still demanding that the episodes maintain consistency and complexity in characterization and content as established in the series' initial episodes.

The TWoP message board forums were abuzz with complaints at the CW's handling of the promotion for the third season premiere of *Veronica Mars*. Many of the TWoP posts addressed the CW's use of an experimental form of hybrid advertising, one in which aspects of a TV show are incorporated into interstitial "minisodes" that tie in with the series content, but are intended to promote the presenting sponsor's product. The night of the premiere the CW and AE joined forces to present "Aerie Tuesday," an advertising campaign in which the retailer and the CW's Tuesday night series, *Gilmore Girls* and *Veronica Mars*, promoted each other. With this branded entertainment deal, the CW obscured the flow between commercials and episode segments as well as between costuming for character development and for marketing sponsors' products.

These interstitial "minisodes" were presented as if they were documenting a group of young, female fans of the CW shows who were at a viewing party. While the idea might have been that the girls had gathered to watch and discuss the television series in a sorority common room, the space looked more like it was filmed in a back corner of an Aerie store. The girls lounged on a floral sectional couch, which was surrounded by wall- and ceiling-mounted display racks filled with Aerie Dormwear, tops and lounge pants that blur the line between sleepwear and casual wear. These were the kinds of separates in which the girls were dressed. Likely picked for their ability to represent the teen consumer AE hoped to attract to its new lifestyle brand, these Aerie girls seemed to have very little in-depth knowledge about either show. The complaints posted on TWoP about the Aerie campaign began immediately with comments such as, "the girls are being prompted on what to say, possibly how to say it, and you can tell. That really annoys me." The actual *Veronica Mars* fans who, as the premiere was airing, were logging on to TWoP to post their reactions, attacked the whole concept of the advertisement disguised as content. Of the lack of care that went into making the interstitial commentary, one annoyed viewer said, "When the Aerie girls were on and saying those things, I was saying to the TV, have you watched the last 2 seasons. HELLO !!!!!" The representation of *Veronica Mars* fans as naïve young girls jarred many, both because *Veronica Mars* relies on sarcasm and cynicism and because its fandom is diverse and extends well beyond the 12–25 female demographic that AE is targeting. As is typical of some TWoP posts, several assumed that their complaints would be read by someone at the CW. "I'm hoping that someone somewhere is listening (and counting) and will cut this annoying sidebar," one said. Others warn CW executives to be aware that their audience is larger than the Aerie girls target demographic: "I certainly hope the suits are reading all of this … As anyone can tell reading these messages, the audience for Veronica Mars is made up of all ages and both genders."

The most intriguing comment was one that suggested that network executives still did not quite understand fan activity as their on-screen representation of it had little to do with reality: "Doesn't the CW know that cool people discuss whether Veronica and Logan will make it through their college years on their *computers* instead of sitting around on sectional couches?" The way the CW structured the on-air and online versions of the Aerie campaign suggests that executives were familiar with the active fan participation of the fashion sleuths, but they did not really understand the fan investment in the forum exchanges and investigations, especially that fans are "drawn toward the collaborative production and evaluation of knowledge."[185] Many respondents also registered their annoyance with the CW for underestimating viewers' intelligence. As Jenkins has pointed out, fans understand that marketing is part of the game, but they want it to participate in the "puzzle solving."[186] The TWoP fans seemed to have a much clearer understanding of network and sponsor strategies as is evident in the following exchange: "I emailed American Eagle with a big thanks ... any company that helps keep my favorite shows on the air is a friend of mine, no matter how many faux sleepovers they impose in my commercial space." Another proclaims that she is just happy that *Veronica Mars* has a major advertiser because she recognizes the importance of the crosspromotion in convincing the CW that *Veronica Mars* is a lucrative product. The best comments, as exemplified in the following, came from TWoP posts that echoed the kind of remarks Veronica would make if she had to sit through the Aerie Girls interstitial programming: "Did anyone else get a, mom can I ask you a personal question vibe from those little aerie segments? The coffee, the girl talk, the Always-maxi-pad-like-logo. I think someone needs to rethink their campaign." As a final note, another offers a Veronica-worthy suggestion for a thread title: "The Aerie Girls-Where's A Taser When You Need One," referencing one of Veronica's weapons of choice.

The TWoP fan forums epitomize the positive role tracking plays in audience-generated fan activity, whereas the CW Aerie campaign points to the more ambivalent role tracking plays in network-sponsored fan activity. This is because the CW is most concerned with tracking the fan activities on social networking and fan sites in order to attract and monetize audiences organized around a fashion- and tech-savvy identity. While viewers understand the economic imperative that drives a broadcast network to transform its series into consumable lifestyle experiences, networks would do well to recognize that fans are most engaged when they are given "spaces to apply their skills and new openings for their speculations."[187] Instead of allowing fans to find their own ways to the fashions featured on the show, the CW uses obvious on-air and online "signposts" to lead viewers there by hand.

When *Veronica Mars* moved to the CW, the network formalized the fashion sleuth link by including on its website a "CW style" section (www.cwtv.com/thecw/style-veronicamars, February 20, 2007) in which fans could browse—by brand, character, episode, or product—for the clothing that Veronica and the other characters wear in *Veronica Mars* episodes. That feature remains today for current CW series, including *Gossip Girl*. In addition to the virtual storefront and the link to the Bluefly site, CW Style is also referenced on the *Gossip Girl* site in a subtle way. On the right side of the virtual room is a clothes rack of ties, representative both of the series' preppy costuming in general and an allusion to the ties that Jenny tells her brother Dan he can get a discount at Bluefly. The top banner of the website has the usual network website links, with the signature *Gossip Girl* blog links—Welcome, Gossip, Pics, Parties. A banner also invites Facebook users to click on a link to integrate *Gossip Girl* content into their personal pages.

The most interesting link on this site, however, is to the music. Through a click on the mp3 player next to the laptop on the homepage, we learn that *Gossip Girl's* music supervisor is Alexandra Patsavas, the same supervisor from a good number of significant series, including *The O.C.* and ABC's megahit *Grey's Anatomy*, a show that, like *Gossip Girl*, uses a confiding opening voiceover and trendy music to draw in the viewer.[188] The *Gossip Girl* soundtrack is a mix of radio-ready and underground songs, which is typical of Patsavas' strategies, which date back to her work on the WB's *Roswell* in the late 1990s.

CW music: from band to brand integration

Patsavas made a name for herself on *The O.C.* (FOX 2003–7), another series Warner Brothers produced but did not broadcast on its netlet. The series is significant in that it mainstreamed the practice of the integration of music into the story space and the space formerly reserved for series credits. The practice has its roots in the WB's conceptualization of its 1990s TV series as platforms for launching new music.[189] Its producers wanted to integrate the latest music into their series to set a trendy tone, establish a mood, and appeal to consumers interested in youth culture lifestyle products. Without the deeper pockets of the Big Three, the netlet and its series' music supervisors came up with the idea to offer dedicated screen space at the close of the episode in which a CD could be promoted.

The WB mainstreamed the practice of music licensing partnerships in which the network offered album promotion in exchange for a reduction or a waiver of music licensing fees, which in the late 1990s were in the thousands and sometimes over $10,000 for a single song.[190] The arrangement would allow for the artists whose songs were featured in an episode to be promoted, usually via a bumper end-promo immediately after the final story segment. The ad card would show each CD cover accompanied by five seconds from one of the tracks.[191] When Eagle Eye Cherry's music was used on the WB's *Felicity*, for example, the network featured an "as played on" ad card at the end of the episode in exchange for a discount on the license rate.[192] Lewis Goldstein, then co-president of the WB's marketing department, said that his team recognized early on the potential of promoting the recording division's artists within its network series as well as of making cross-promotion and licensing deals with other recording companies. When the WB "started to reach an audience of people who buy the CDs, a little light bulb went off in our heads."[193] In 1998 *Rolling Stone* recognized that Warner Music Group had in the WB a unique promotional platform: "As the only record company with a pipeline to a U.S. network, Warner has weekly access to teen viewers."[194] *Dawson's Creek* was significant in establishing a precedent for these network deals with record labels or recording divisions as it offered synergy opportunities for both Warner Brothers, its network, and Sony, the media conglomerate of which its Columbia

TriStar production company was a part. Even though critics wondered if the networks and production companies would only use in-house music, music supervisors did vary their playlists with an eye to producing best-selling soundtracks to be sold as part of the franchising of the television series.

The cheapest method, one that would be perfected by *The O.C.*, the series Warner Brothers produced for FOX in 2003, was to make deals with unsigned bands. *Buffy the Vampire Slayer* was the first to take this route. As its music supervisor John King explained: "because we were a nobody show and we were usually denied (music) licenses ... we would go to the local music scene and use unsigned artists."[195] Often these kinds of bands were happy to have an even exchange of their songs for an "as played on" ad card at the end of the episode, but even if there were fees involved they would be much less than for an artist from a major label, even one that was a division of the network's parent company. By 2004 *The Washington Post* was declaring: "For alternative and indie bands, television has suddenly become the new radio—a crucial outlet for music ignored by commercial radio stations and video channels."[196] In addition to making famous Phantom Planet's "California (Here We Come)" when it chose it as the theme song, *The O.C.* boosted the profile, for example, of Death Cab for Cutie, Modest Mouse, and Rooney. The television exposure led to increased radio airplay, not to mention a sales spike and "increased attention from major labels," according to *The Washington Post*.[197]

With 2003's *The O.C.*, the TV series as music platform to sell CDs and introduce new artists was perfected. The series not only had a powerhouse indie soundtrack that was much cooler than the characters, but its second season creation of The Bait Shop also provided artists with an in-series music venue in which to perform. The end result is that *The O.C.* has a soundtrack that is elevated above the series itself and does little to reflect the taste of the characters, Ben Wener complains. In amazement he lists the bands that appeared in the initial episodes: the first included Mazzy Star, Joseph Arthur, Black Eyed Peas, and the All-American Rejects, while the second had Doves, Rufus Wainwright, Rooney, and Jeff Buckley (doing a version of Leonard Cohen's "Hallelujah").[198] O.C. creator Josh Schwartz claimed that he was often unable to write a scene until he found the right song to accompany it. Then he tried to fit as many songs as he could into every episode. Confirming Wener's observation, Schwartz said: "It wasn't 'music from O.C.' or music that was cool on the radio, because it wasn't [on the radio]. It spoke to me, and it spoke to the characters about what they were going through and feeling."[199] Clearly, music supervisors are reaching audiences that would not usually hear this variety of music and in that Ben Aslinger sees a degree of subversion.[200]

Wener displays a common viewer cynicism about media conglomeration when he says that he is well aware that the music is "intended to attract a demographic, one FOX also hopes to lure into AOL's 'The O.C. Music Showcase' after each episode." He adds that he is certain that if the series succeeds, the second season premiere will be preceded by a complication CD. He was correct. *Music From The*

O.C. Mix 1 was released on March 30, 2004.[201] The compressed windowing strategies adopted by networks made it logical, although surprising, that two more series-related CDs followed in October 2004. *Music from 'The O.C.': Mix 4* was then released on April 5, 2005 and even made it to No. 4 on the iTunes album-download chart. Warner Brothers Records claimed that in 2005 worldwide sales of the four compilations reached the 1 million mark.[202] By that point, bands had been accustomed to the TV release strategy because, as music supervisor Patsavas theorized, "they are reaching an audience in a way that radio doesn't."[203]

While no recent series has been as ambitious as *The O.C.*'s Bait Shop integrations, artists still do appear in series produced by Warner Brothers, especially those that air on the CW. For its sixth season *One Tree Hill*, for example, did make musician Kate Voegele a recurring role as herself and not only used her music, but had her perform in a club within the series. Whether or not they integrate a musical performance into an episode, all CW series end with tags promoting the purchase of the CD or downloaded tracks of the artists played during the episode. Those tags are now familiar parts of every series that the CW inherited when it was created out of the merger of the WB and UPN, as well as many of its new series, and the practice extends to music-centric Big Three series such as *Grey's Anatomy*.

This kind of promotional arrangement is particularly well suited to the circulation made possible by the internet. The music helps attract viewers to the series or draw viewers into the story. The series, in turn, helps sell the CDs of the chosen musicians. Later a song might also appear on the series' "as heard on" compilation CD, which then becomes part of the circulatory paradigm of each element selling another.[204] As Goldstein put it: "We're figuring out how to promote a show with music and sell a CD at the same time."[205] With the evolution of websites as virtual stores came the fulfillment of Joanne Ostrow's 2000 prediction about the streamlining of the process: "visit a show's Web site (like buffy.com) and a link to 'music and videos' to find a CD incorporated into the show. Watch, listen, point, click and purchase." Goldstein predicted the same future: "You click on your mp3 and download."[206]

The CD on TV promotion strategy has been modified more recently so that dedicated space after the final story segment is offered to any presenting sponsors for the series, often mobile device manufacturers or service plan providers whose products can be touted in the story segments as well. These presenting sponsors are paying for "bumper" advertising that flows right out of the opening and closing segments of the story. Usually it is signaled by an ad card, which, if it is part of the closing credits, sometimes takes more screen space given that the credits are compressed and limited to a small area. An in-credits ad that is attached to the end of the show might make viewers more likely to watch. The space is made available for other companies particularly interested in the CW's target demographic and interested in sponsoring some web content as well. Dove co-created *Gossip Girl* "real women of New York City" interstitials and webisodes, for example, and Dr. Pepper offered a "road to *90210*" campaign of content wraps and a road trip sweepstakes.

Giving sponsors a place prior to or immediately after the network ID campaign bumper is a way to make the ad card and its message less likely to be skipped by timeshifting viewers. They are usually interstitial and multiplatform deals as well. The combined on-air and online content wraps catch viewers wherever they were watching the series and entice them with original content. For its 2008–9 branded entertainment deal for the CW's new *90210*, for example, Dr. Pepper chose bumper-branded entertainment, product placement/integration, 30-second spots, on-air and online simultaneous address, and interstitials in which the lead character addresses the audience through a video blog and informs them about the countdown to the 90210 prom and the road to 90210 sweepstakes, all prominently sponsored by Dr. Pepper.

From its inception the CW planned to "strike alternative deals to deliver its content," to its tech-savvy demographic comfortable with the "increasingly time-shifted, multiplatform media world."[207] Those alternative deals are a lot easier to strike with the alterna-characters gone from the network roster. After all, *Veronica Mars'* political undercurrent about class did not make for the most hospitable environment for corporate sponsorship. Broadcast TV series with young casts, even those focused on alterna-teens, are expected to be display cases for sponsor products directed at a highly desirable youth culture demographic. Writers and producers do not always get to make casting, costuming, and setting choices with an eye toward character and storyline consistency; rather, they are expected to put on display the types of people, styles, and locations that will most easily become spokespersons, samples, and showcases for the consumer products on which the TV industry depends for its financial support.

Thomas and his writing team tried to play the game and accommodate more and more product integration in the CW's *Veronica Mars* through deals with Saturn, T-Mobile, and even Gillette's Venus razors. Viewers commenting on the random appearance of the latter were pleased that it was done in a self-reflexive manner that echoed the fan consensus on message boards that it was better to have "lame" product integration than no *Veronica Mars* (LiveJournal). The integration is done with snarky humor as Veronica tells Mac, who catches her shaving her leg in the sink, "I think I read in *Teen People* that a clean leg shave will make that special boy sit up and take notice" (3.19). The snarkiness continues, much to fans' delight, after what Roger Holland of *PopMatters* calls "the longest sequence of product placements ever seen outside a big budget Sci-Fi movie."[208] Following a discussion of the superiority of Veronica's Saturn VUE over other hybrids, Mac mentions a rumored Matchbox 20 reunion and Wallace's roommate Piz proclaims, "So? Rob Thomas is a whore" (3.19). Although ostensibly referring to the band's lead guitarist, the line is a wink to the industry-savvy fans who are well aware of why Thomas and his writing team include sequences that do nothing to move the story forward. NBC's *30 Rock* would pick up this winking product integration style, as will be discussed in the final chapter. Both the NBC and the CW series exemplify a return to the midcentury practice of branded entertainment deals, which are a response to the anxieties about timeshifting and placeshifting.

The CW remains savvy about targeting potential consumers via a TV show in an era in which they could timeshift past commercials and in which placeshifting has impacted where and how they watch and follow TV, consume and share media, shop, and interact with each other and socialize via TV talk. CW has figured out ways to respond because, as *Entertainment Weekly* declared: "The generation watching *Gossip Girl* doesn't do appointment television. They are masters at using the latest technology to watch TV when and how they want." It lauded the fact that the series has consistently held the top download spot on iTunes and gets a 30% hike in the 18–34 year olds when DVR viewings are figured in. Those numbers matter especially because, as EW's Jessica Shaw quipped in 2005, "the old-fashioned overnight ratings are about as relevant as last season's Balenciaga bag." The alternate platform successes affirm Josh Schwartz's point that his show is a bigger hit than the ratings indicate: "We're focused more on the idea of cultural permeation."[209]

The production team for FOX's *24* had much the same plan for cultural permeation, except its show debuted in 2001, prior to all these alternate content delivery platforms, so it had to come up with other strategies to keep its series in circulation. Its experiments in relation to *24* were so successful that they ended up being adopted industry-wide. As members of the production team from *The X-Files* turned up on the team producing *24* for FOX, they had already refined their multiplatform and franchising strategies and were ready to meet the challenges of the twenty-first-century mediasphere, especially the problems and possibilities that arose in relation to the increase in use of timeshifting technology to change what it means to watch and follow broadcast television.

Chapter Two

Timeshifting, circumvention, and flow on FOX

Circumvention and containment are key issues in the twenty-first-century U.S. television industry. Using timeshifting technology, broadcast TV viewers make TV programming conform to their schedules and subject it to the whims of their clickers, now equipped with the capability of fast forwarding through live as well as recorded programming. In doing so, they circumvent the carefully planned commercial flow in which U.S. networks place their broadcast TV products.[1] This challenges the decades-long practice of the linear segmentation of an evening's programming into timed increments with a specific logic that Williams famously described as flow—the way an evening of network programming flows from story segment to sponsor commercials with network promos, feature film previews, and network news previews included among them throughout the primetime blocks. This timed segmentation is the strategy, or so networks have traditionally assumed, that produced the kind of flow that would best deliver an audience to the sponsors who had paid for air time, and, hence, for the TV shows. A similar assumption was made about getting the audience caught up in a network's sponsor-oriented seasonal scheduling, with its family-oriented school-year TV cycle with September premieres and May sweeps, preceding the upfronts at which sponsors buy air time in advance of the new Fall season. While this paradigm can be thought of in linear and sequential terms, in today's Must-Click environment, programming and scheduling and windowing are often conceptualized in more concurrent terms. Today's flow is more circular, with one platform encouraging viewers to access another, which, hopefully, prompts them to return to the on-air text. That networks now invest in the continual circulation of their TV products on multiple platforms does not mean that flow no longer matters, as should be evident from all the material networks and their media conglomerates pack in between story segments.[2]

To contain the impact of timeshifting on their own branding strategies, networks do increasingly blur the line between programming segments and the promotions that follow and precede them so that DVR viewers are compelled to stop fast forwarding and watch the promos to be sure they are not missing part of the story. Networks have also reactivated the 1950s television concept of branded entertainment, partnering with single sponsors to create content, and have intensified product integration.[3] While the prevalence of product placement and integration in

TV shows is not surprising, the rise of what I term network identity placement and integration is striking.

The practice of network identity placement has become commonplace, with networks posting their network IDs in a corner of the frame and sometimes utilizing a scrolling format to rotate information about network promos, show previews, and web/mobile content. Talking about station IDs keyed or burned into films that were screened on 1980s–1990s television, John Caldwell marvels, "One cannot imagine this sort of stamp of ownership being allowed in other artforms—the signature of the purchaser rather than the maker stamped directly on the artform."[4] In recent years these intrusive network IDs have become so ubiquitous that they even made it into a Lewis Black comedy skit at the 2006 Academy Awards. As product placement always has the potential to alienate viewers, the more innovative approach is network identity integration. This point will be explained later in this chapter in an analysis of a DVD featurette in which it becomes clear that the fictional Los Angeles Counter Terrorism Unit (CTU), the main set for 24, FOX's "events happen in real-time" government agency/terrorism serial, shares a color scheme first with the FOX Sports set and then with the FOX News set. By season six the story segments include multiple HD TVs tuned to FOX News featured in the background of many shots, sometimes positioned in the space between characters in a two-shot.[5] This suggests that during later seasons of 24 FOX not only fine-tunes embedded network branding and brand differentiation, but also reconfigures the relationship between on-air story segments and the sponsor and network texts that come between them. This integration assures that whatever content delivery system through which viewers watch 24, they will get some degree of sponsor and network promotion.

This chapter focuses especially on FOX as it devised these intriguing ways to address audience fragmentation in a television environment characterized by viewers' access to an increasing number of cable channels as well as the technologies that allow them to timeshift and watch programs in formats other than their scheduled timeslots. Ever an innovator about what constitutes broadcast television, FOX piloted many of those practices that have since become industry standards. Indeed, circumvention has always been the FOX corporate policy. FOX employed circumvention strategies to become the fourth network. It circumvented the rules governing networks by programming just under the number of hours required for network status.[6] By narrowcasting to a niche population and subsequently dumping it once it got powerful enough to attract a broadcast audience, FOX circumvented standard broadcasting practices as well as the fair and balanced programming mandate that the government's finance and syndication (fin-syn) rules are supposed to guarantee. FOX bucked standard operating procedures of the Big Three to carve out a competitive position. It has long experimented with variations on the timing of the traditional broadcast schedule and more recently with the time between distribution windows.

This chapter looks in particular at 24 (2001–2010), in part because its plots pivot on circumvention and time is its thematic obsession. As its season-long arcs unfold in "real-time," with each of the 24 episodes representing one hour in the season's day-long story cycle, 24 provides a useful case study to examine how FOX's aesthetic and industrial experiments, especially in relation to its circumvention of accepted network practices governing scheduling, windowing, and programming as well as story pacing and structure, have shaped twenty-first-century programming and set the stage for today's Must-Click TV.

With 24, FOX has continually tried new approaches to scheduling. Reviewers often attribute 24's success to innovations in this area, such as the premiere in non-traditional months or in double or consecutive blocks. As Brian Lowry remarked in Variety, "FOX's clever scheduling ploy of launching the show with four hours over two nights should plant the hook deep based on a preview of those episodes, leading loyalists to hang on for the thrill ride."[7] FOX also offered 24 content on multiple platforms on a condensed distribution timetable. Part of this decrease in the time between distribution windows is enabled by the technological capacity to make shows available via alternate content delivery systems. The shifting of the time between distribution windows and the change to what is available both within and outside the bounds of the on-air "window" of a TV text has radically impacted the industry.

The case study is intended to point to an emerging Must-Click TV dynamic in which media conglomerates are increasingly thinking of ways to blur the boundaries between different mediums so that one media product could maintain a presence on multiple media platforms. The intermedial features (of one medium in the space of another) and the intra-referentiality (to other News Corp. products) work together to assure that 24 is a media product that can be extended across multiple platforms and that can each cross-promote the others.

Timetables of rapid release

Building on its history of experimenting with moving TV shows around on the traditional network schedule, FOX eventually adopted the year-long cable format for 24. Traditionally, a TV show would have its first run beginning in September; summer months would be dedicated to reruns, and then the show would not have a second run on another network until it reached the number of episodes needed for syndication. With media conglomeration, networks could now repurpose their programming on affiliated cable channels, as FOX did when it ran 24 on FX during the same season in which it first aired, often in the same week as the original broadcast.[8] FOX also shuffled the typical season premiere and DVD release dates. As noted in the Introduction, the producers of Alias, the ABC series that debuted in the same 2001–2 season as 24, adopted a platforming model that conceptual-ized the on-air series as a jumping off point for other entertainment platforms. Producers of 24 would eventually adopt the same strategy, offering a game and innovating webisode and mobisode formats. The mobisodes are particularly sig-nificant as they are connected to FOX's experiments with branded entertainment, specifically its partnering with Sprint to create mobile-ready "minisodes" that blur the lines between story and promotion.[9] Those kinds of innovations would develop over the life of the series as it became a cultural phenomenon and attracted more branded entertainment deals. FOX turned its 2001–2 premiere season to two inno- vative strategies for building an audience: repurposing on cable and releasing the DVD prior to the start of the second season.[10] Both strategies followed rapid release timetables that challenged network practices by decreasing the industry- accepted standard of the appropriate time between distribution windows.[11]

While the industrial implications of the way *24* plays with time are essential for understanding the show as a particularly twenty-first-century TV product that has come to embody a Must-Click TV paradigm, the narrative manipulations of time are taken up more fully in part two of this chapter. It will explore how *24*'s "events happen in real-time" brand promise often requires producers to sacrifice real-time accuracy for mythic-time appeal. Real Time is the problem *24* "tackles," to borrow phrasing from Homi Bhabha, "and the tool it uses in order to reconstruct dominant myths, which through repeated narration, can become normalized and, through the binaries they hinge on, encourage racism." Despite its surface representation of a "we" workplace, at its heart *24* still reinforces an "us-them" dynamic, both in terms of the American "we" and the U.S. in relation to other nations. This dynamic was present in most American media coverage after 9/11 when, according to Douglas Kellner, "the mainstream media privileged the 'clash of civilizations' model, estab- lished a binary dualism between Islamic terrorism and civilization, and largely circulated war fever and retaliatory feelings and discourses that called for and supported a form of military intervention."[12]

An analysis of the season four DVD featurette on BioTerrorism exemplifies how in *24*, mythic-time appeal trumps real-time accuracy, especially in its representa- tions of: the plausibility of the rapid response capabilities of U.S. agents and agencies; the ease of terrorist acquisition of weapons of mass destruction and the likelihood of an imminent attack on U.S. soil; and the efficacy of torture as a time-based necessity for rapid information gathering. These can be connected to troubling national policies during the era in which *24* was produced. Jack Bauer's policy of always prioritizing speed and access over protocol when looking for information from suspected terrorists or their collaborators has its parallel in the Bush Administration's circumvention of civil rights and Geneva Convention codes in relation to torture, wire tapping, and surveillance.[13] Commentators debate if "*24* is effectively an ad for torture," as David Danzig of Human Rights First charges.[14] One thing is certain: *24* garners support for a policy that privileges action over deliberation. Yet, for all of its connections to real world issues and its real-time claims, *24* is not a TV product fully rooted in the specific time of post-9/11 U.S. culture; upon closer examination its story and its main character are less inhabi- tants of this specific historical moment than they are a product of the mythic time in which Benedict Anderson and others claim national narratives exist.[15]

While commentary about *24* as a multi-season series explores its real-world cultural implications and positions the TV show within a post-9/11 paradigm, especially the way *24* functions as a "working-through," to borrow a term from

John Ellis, the aftershocks of 9/11, it is important to note that the series was conceptualized prior to that watershed date. In its first season, even though it premiered on November 6, 2001, the assaults to which the TV show is responding are technological and industrial: the threats posed by timeshifting technology and of cable, specifically HBO.

As stated earlier, increased viewer control over scheduling—both the ability to access TV programming in non-broadcast formats and to timeshift with ease through commercials when watching on-air and thereby disrupt networks' preplanned commercial flow—has thrown the advertiser-supported content structure of broadcast television into crisis. The impact of timeshifting devices on this flow was worried over in the press during 24's first season. By May 2002, the anxieties caused by timeshifting prompted Jamie Kellner, who was then the Turner Broadcasting CEO and previously FOX Network's first president, to make the much-mocked assertion that skipping commercials was akin to stealing: "Your contract with the network when you get the show is you're going to watch the spots. Otherwise you couldn't get the show on an ad-supported basis."[16] Kellner's reaction to the mainstreaming of a DVR device that "skips certain second increments" was no doubt an expression of pervasive industry-wide hysteria about this attack on the network system's status quo.[17]

In creating 24, FOX producers initially were concerned with the more immediate problem precipitated by the kind of schedule timeshifting offered on cable: premiering shows at any time during a year-long schedule and running them for consecutive weeks without interruption. Subscription-based cable networks were freed from the sponsor-friendly network scheduling timetable.[18] Throughout the series run of 24, FOX would experiment with traditional broadcast scheduling, compressing the time between distribution windows in season one and finally adopting the cable-style nontraditional start date when it premiered season four in January 2005 so it could run the series in consecutive weeks without interruption.

In its initial greenlighting of 24, FOX was trying to compete with the quality dramas on HBO, which as a cable station with a subscription-based financing model, had the advantage of being able to employ an uninterrupted and often long-arc serial narrative.[19] Kiefer Sutherland's 2002 Golden Globe win for his portrayal of Jack Bauer kicked off 24's awards race with The Sopranos, the HBO dysfunctional family/workplace hybrid that was garnering all the Emmy and Golden Globe attention. Although he'd have to wait for his Emmy until season five and watch as HBO added Best Actor and Actress awards to those it received since 1999, Sutherland's 2002 Golden Globe did generate quality TV buzz for his program and ensured a larger audience for season two.[20] The significant boost from an 8.60 to an 11.73 audience share during that season also was the result of both a time-tested and new network TV strategy: the first was to schedule a new show after a hit show, in the case of 24, moving it to the spot after American Idol, the 2002 Summer replacement that would eventually become the number one show on network TV. The duo succeeded so well that by November 2006 Preston Beckman, FOX's Executive VP for Entertainment, would call it "our little programming tsunami."[21] FOX's second strategy was to compress the time between distribution windows and offer *24* on News Corp.'s cable channel FX during the same season it was airing on FOX and to rush the DVD into production so that it could be released the month before season two aired. FOX had originated the TV on DVD box set in 2000 for *The X-Files* release on DVD and it was the first to broadcast a complete season in marathon format. Sandy Grushow, Chairman, FOX Television Entertainment Group, said, "This marathon is a great example of synergy, which is only a theory until you see it implemented effectively to increase ratings and revenues. FX is providing an exceptional platform to bring new viewers to *24*, a program created by Twentieth Century FOX Television for the FOX network." The marathon also built hype for the DVD release that same month. Patricia Wyatt, President of Twentieth Century FOX Home Entertainment, characterized the FX marathon as "an excellent way to broaden the fan universe for the show and also provide a sampling opportunity for the DVD coming just two weeks later."[22] Commenting on the circularity of the paradigm and the way each part of the media conglomerate can be part of the interlocking gear that keeps the product moving and revenue generating, Grushow noted, "It is a successful venture because it is being implemented in the best interest of the program. And, ultimately, what's good for 24 is good for FX, the studio, the network, affiliates, home entertainment and the corporation as a whole."[23]

These marathons were a necessary strategy to generate and maintain interest in the long-arc program because, although *24*'s format was innovative enough to make it a competitor for Best Dramatic series spot, it was still saddled with the limitations of the broadcast TV schedule. Many viewers complained and some lost interest, for instance, because of FOX's constant preemption of primetime programming for sporting events and its shifting of *24* off the schedule for other special event programming and during low ratings periods.

Making the viewing experience more of an uninterrupted one was something that FOX was finally able to adopt in season four when *24* premiered in double blocks and over two nights in January 2005 and then continued without hiatus until May.[24] FOX also made episodes available in 2006 via iTunes, which since 2005 has been offering networks a deal to provide a delivery platform through which to sell single episodes or season passes to site visitors. To maximize profits FOX partnered with NBC in March 2007 to create Hulu, their own streaming-video downloading platform. Before the availability of this kind of service, many people could not find the time to commit to a long-arc series or to watch it as it was scheduled. As one user of Hulu explains, "I never really got invested in TV shows until I got my first laptop ... because I couldn't be consistent with it."[25] In *24*'s first season such alternate platforms did not yet exist and FOX was just innovating the compressed distribution strategy through which it would release the season one DVD box set just prior to the start of season two, an industry practice that is now standard. David Kronke of *Daily News* (Los Angeles) claims, "'24' was the first series to exploit viewers' hunger to see serialized dramas' episodes back-to-back-to-back."[26]

Building an audience for *24* was made possible by the compressed timing of the DVD release, a scheduling decision that challenged the wisdom of leaving ample time between distribution windows. Matt Zoller Seitz, of *The Newark Star-Ledger*, explains this rapid release strategy: "When '24' was released so soon after its season ended, it was preparation for the following season, and ratings went up." They enabled people a quick way to catch up: "You get, say, 22 hours of TV for 30 bucks."[27] He claims that TV programming is now accommodating viewers' schedules: "They used to say of serialized TV, 'The train has left the station.' This is the equivalent of stopping the train and letting people get on. It's part of the TV evolution."[28] A review of the season one DVD (released on September 17, 2002) points to the significance of the format for attracting viewers who had heard the buzz during the first season, but too late to follow the latest episodes of the on-air broadcast: "I was one of those unfortunates that missed a few episodes early on, and even with promptings from the plot summaries on the Web, felt hopelessly lost and confused for the next several shows trying to catch up. So the DVD was eagerly anticipated."[29] As the Hulu user indicates, viewers have a hard enough time in their overscheduled lives to make time for appointment viewing. Add to that the real-time structure of *24* that makes missing an episode even more confusing and it is understandable that the show took some time to build an audience. Season one DVD reviewer Steven Horn addresses this problem:

> "I first became aware of *24* too late in the game. Of course I had heard about it (the buzz from the pilot alone was deafening) but for various reasons I had a hard time making the commitment of "appointment television" to watch the show. Much like *The Sopranos,* which unravels the story week after week, *24* is not the type of show you can just wander into the middle of and expect to get nearly as much enjoyment from than if you kept with it from the start."[30]

The same kinds of reviews of the DVDs were posted each season as the buzz more widely circulated. A season three review from November 30, 2004 encouraged first time viewers to catch up on all the seasons via DVD, but suggested they didn't necessarily have to watch them in order as FOX wisely chose to begin each season with a new story arc and often many new characters given that so many regulars are killed off within a season: "If you have never seen this show, I suggest renting it. Even if you didn't start from season one, there's no reason you can't start with this one. But the whole thing is worth checking out, regardless ... The DVD sets are always excellent."[31] So excellent, in fact, that another reviewer concludes, "Ironically, FOX has created a show where it is actually better to watch on DVD than it is to watch it on TV."[32] He is hesitant to put that in print, he notes, because he knows that FOX would prefer people watched on-air.

Watched on DVD, though, *24* is quite addictive. A season two DVD reviewer advises, "If you have never seen this show, I would tell you to seek this out and try it immediately. Warning, though: you will get addicted."[33] Many other DVD reviewers also highlight the addictive quality of the series, offering disclaimers such as, "Viewers will likely get hooked after the first few episodes and may spend half a day blowing through the first discs."[34] The format of the show lends itself to binge-viewing of multiple episodes at one sitting, as many message board posts note. At the TV-DVD conference held in October 2003 Joel Surnow acknowledged in his keynote address that the DVDs were tremendous in boosting the broadcast audience by 25% for season two and the DVD sales helped to justify "the kind of money we have to spend to make the show."[35] Paul Scheuring, creator of *Prison Break*, the FOX serial that became a hit in 2005, explains that his series was also made more viable because of the DVD release: "People love sitting down for a weekend and knocking down the whole season. They want to watch the larger narratives. The format offers a larger canvas; the story becomes epic."[36] Seitz adds that there is a long history for the appeal of dramas accessed immediately in installments or later as a complete text, citing the two formats in which Charles Dickens' novels were published.[37]

As a reception strategy, watching on DVD allows for easier understanding of long-arc storylines and for maintenance of an audience, especially as viewers can watch at their own pace and on their own schedule. Horn describes a common experience among those accessing the show on DVD. Binge-viewing the whole DVD box set, watching all six discs (24 episodes) in one weekend, transformed him into a loyal:

> "I am such a fan of the show that I will miss weddings, funerals, graduations, even meals to make sure I catch each episode of the second season. OK, maybe not meals. *24* is one of those television experiences that makes journalists write stories like 'TV is back!' and 'Cancel cable!' etc. The show has meat, style, and innovation to the extreme."

Judging by message board posts filled with similar stories, this binge-viewing was fairly common.

The purchase of the show on DVD combined with the internet phenomenon of FOX's *24*—how word of mouth and of mouse began immediately and intensified over time, keeping the buzz about the show circulating—dramatically expanded the on-air audience for season two. That fan base grew incrementally with each new season's scheduling, repurposing, and alternate content delivery and release cycle.

Horn credits the significance of the DVD as a format for the success of complicated TV shows like *24*:

> "if you ever needed another chance to marvel at the DVD format, ponder this: without the format, a show like *24* would wither on the vine and die, being relegated to re-runs shown out of order by sloppy network affiliates. *24*, it seems, came to the party at precisely the right time."[38]

And FOX had just the right timing down with its new compressed windowing strategy.

One March 2007 DVD review describes *24* as "the kind of show that you have to watch from the beginning and have some kind of investment in it."[39] One viewer who did, *San Francisco Chronicle* staffer Tim Goodman, describes season one as "a brilliant but forgivably flawed gem that burst onto the FOX schedule and captivated an audience. It was audacious on several fronts; it absolutely required you to watch all 24 hours without fail—quite a lot to ask from a nation not prone to appointment television."[40] That he makes this claim in a review of season four suggests that watching the show from the beginning could make it seem repetitive, especially in relation to the number of times 1) Kim, the daughter of the show's hero Jack Bauer, could be kidnapped, or 2) a mole could infiltrate the Los Angeles CTU with which Jack is affiliated, or 3) that Los Angeles could be targeted again by a weapon of mass destruction or that after these repeated attacks anyone would still be willing to live there. Goodman captures this frustration when he complains in his review of the premiere of season four:

> Quicker than you can say, 'Hey, look, more Middle Eastern sleeper cells,' trouble rears its pesky little head. But this is familiar trouble. Everything on "24" is now overly familiar. Jack even usurps command (he's got real issues with that) and does grievous bodily harm to a witness. Not as drastic as, say, cutting the guy's head off and sticking it in a duffel bag (ah, fond memories), but excessive. We've seen this side of Jack before … Familiarity in Season 4 does not just breed contempt (why is it that Jack always gets someone in CTU to help him do illegal things at their computer all the time?), but comedy.[41]

Although he also offers an overall good review in *The Boston Globe* of the premiere Matthew Gilbert predicts that season five will inevitably deteriorate "into redundancy and irrelevancy by the final weeks." But "until frustration sets in," it will be "very absorbing."[42]

Of course, this frustration does not prevent Gilbert and Goodman from being hooked by the show, or respectively proclaiming it, "an addictive amusement park ride of a show" and "a two-hour blast of adrenaline." Goodman explains the frustration–fascination balance in his January 2006 review of the premiere of season five:

> "'24' is five seasons into it. Most of the people who tune in are diehards. But the point here is to tell people who either watched the first season or never watched at all – forget the past. Yes, tuning in now may seem confusing and stupid and implausible, but ain't it always? Watch the two-hour premiere on Sunday. It's a rollercoaster. Cut the top of your head off and throw your hands in the air. There are worse things in the world than getting a rush from television."[43]

People must have listened to his advice or the many posts on sites scattered across the web that were declaring *24* Must-See TV as there was a jump from an 11.90 to a 13.78 ratings share between seasons four and five, an overall 60% increase in viewers between seasons one and five, and a 16% overall boost for season six, which attracted 15.7 million viewers for its season premiere and over its four-block run an average gain of 33 million viewers over the previous season. The availability of the show on iTunes as well as DVD contributed to making this increased audience possible. Although many people were first accessing the show via DVD, for example, a quick scan of online reviews and message boards reveals that after they caught up on DVD, they started watching on-air. One season two reviewer writing on March 13, 2007 (although that season's set was released in September 2003) discloses,

> "I had not seen a single episode of this show until I got this DVD to review and I now regret having missed it the first time around. I immediately wanted to find out when it was playing on FOX and start watching it religiously."

This review is echoed by others, suggesting that accessing the TV product on alternate platforms often induces viewers to watch the new season on air. This phenomenon evidences the circularity of the Must-Click TV distribution and reception practices.

While it is easier to follow the story arcs watching on these platforms on your own schedule, it can be more satisfying to participate in the original delayed gratification model as it keeps intact the cliffhangers typical of the serial form that made 24 lean-forward TV in the first place. As Albert Cheng of Disney-ABC Television Group says, "There is still a preference to sit in front of the television to watch it. And if viewers can't, they know that they can at least catch up with it online." He contends that network website video players are mostly used to watch missed episodes.[44] In any case, networks have found a way to profit more from these new technologies as the FOX-NBC Hulu partnership indicates. Online streaming video has been a site for a new advertising model in which a company can microtarget its products by being the single sponsor of an individual stream. For these unskippable embedded advertisements, they usually pay about 50% more than for an on-air ad, according to Forrester Research.[45] "The frenzied talk about the DVR killing the 30-second spot turned out to be premature," James McQuivey at Forrester contends, "All the DVR showed was that people want convenience."[46]

The clicker that comes with the DVR (which integrates within it the standard remote control device) allows viewers to skip the preplanned network flow, but it also enables them to pay even more attention to it as they can pause and fast forward through live as well as recorded programming. Networks often force viewers to pay close attention by adopting segmentation techniques that encourage rewinding and pausing. As they work to blur the line between story segments and commercials (both by allowing no time between the two and by offering branded entertainment and network branding within story segments), networks force viewers to rewind to distinguish between a story segment and a promo. The blurred line between programming and commercial, mise-en-scène related to character and story and to sponsors, does promote multiple clicks on the remote control for those watching on DVR. Fast forwarding at too rapid a speed results in rewinding, pausing, and fast forwarding again when the line is blurred between story segments and promotions. That means that viewers might be watching the commercials in a slower fast forward speed or at least rewinding and catching some of them. Networks also schedule their promos for their other shows or network news right before and after story segments so the viewer is most likely to catch them. These ways of addressing the fast-forwarding problem make it more likely that viewers will use the clicker more carefully.

Of course, many loyal fans of shows take it upon themselves to pay close attention to textual details. The ease provided by the clicker encourages the kind of obsessive viewing behaviors that turn casual viewers into loyals. Fans fill message boards with information garnered by rewinding and pausing recorded programming. These viewers often become the keepers of the archive for the show and the watchdogs for authenticity. Of course, the networks are still under pressure because of the various clicks viewers can make on their remotes. When viewers employ the rewind and the pause buttons to scrutinize plot details and production choices, for example, the production team feels pressure to improve special effects and production values. Any lapses will be fodder for online critiques.

Producers are now tailoring content and adding hidden "Easter eggs" within shows or on the web just for these fans. They are the ideal target audience as they follow on-air prompts to engage in online interaction with the show and to get clues from the various web and mobile phone promotions that the networks and the sponsors offer. In on-air and online *24* promos, for example, Sprint offered special content for their existing customers and likely generated some new ones eager to get this customers-only content.

Eventually, the imperative to visit FOX.com also was integrated into *24*'s on-air text as well as the flow, suggesting that the current architecture of TV programming is also about speed—it allows you to engage in immediate interactivity (the fans who log on to message boards the minute the show ends) or delayed interactivity given that the discussions are ongoing and continue even after a series is cancelled.[47] This commentary can happen with the speed that it does because viewers can also be users who have the ability to open multiple browser windows simultaneously at the same time that they are watching TV either in another window or on another screen. Indeed, simultaneity is the defining feature of twenty-first-century Must-Click TV.

All this suggests that timeshifting presents opportunities as well as challenges for networks in their attempts to attract viewers and create Must-Click TV products. If producers are lucky, access and active fan engagement in one platform often prompts viewers to access and actively engage the text (and fellow audience members) in another. Dedicated websites for a show are particularly important in this regard, as Will Brooker notes, because they encourage viewers to continue "engaging with characters and narrative of show" after the on-air program ends, thereby extending the "program beyond its broadcast time slot."[48] Brooker calls this phenomenon overflow, as it represents a deliberate overflowing of the "bounds of television," particularly as "the simulacrum of a website" then merges with "the diversity of the internet."[49] One site leads to another and another and more interactions both with the show and other viewers.

Despite the ease of viewing in a timeshifted format, one of the appeals of watching a show on-air as-it-airs is that those who watch in real-time can participate in immediate interaction with other fans on the web, a key reception practice of those who post on message boards and fan forums related to *24*. Humorist Dave Barry is one of those viewers who relish the pleasures of real-time interaction.[50] After he got hooked on the show, Barry mentioned *24* on his blog and was surprised by the popularity of those posts. Soon he started live-blogging during the show, offering "as-it-airs" commentary on the story segments and the FOX flow in between. That so many others now comment live on his blog indicates that other viewers share the desire for real-time interaction. On-air immediacy fits within the Must-Click imperative as people want to be the first to comment, to post immediate reactions and to interact with others who do the same. An analysis of the commentary on message boards suggests audiences are still getting pleasure from immediate interaction even though so much TV viewing is now time-delayed. Even those who do not watch on-air as it is being broadcast can still enjoy the pleasures of immediacy given that the message board is a place in which they can log their immediate reaction no matter how delayed it is from the original broadcast and still find others with whom to engage.[51]

Timetables of rapid response

Instead of examining the kinds of industrial issues connected to time discussed in the previous section, critical attention has mostly focused on the way *24* plays with time within its diegesis, with notable essays appearing in the incisive anthology *Reading 24*. For the most part, they focus on *24*'s distinctive style as the anthology grew out of a panel on its relationship to the concept of quality television. Michael Allen argues that the split screen is "designed to make *24* stand out from other quality television dramas as a distinctive product at the start of the new millennium."[52] Steven Peacock and several others in the anthology position their readings of *24* in contrast to reviews that claim that the visual techniques such as the split screen are "purely functional" or simply "subservient to the onward rush of the story," as Rob White says in *Sight and Sound*.[53] Like Peacock, Deborah Jermyn asserts that these innovative features are not just bells and whistles, but are instead an "integral part of the storytelling process."[54] Picking up on a similar argument, Daniel Chamberlain and Scott Ruston gesture toward an industrial analysis when they note that producers combine "the visual markers of live television with a real-time narrative structure" to "forge what might be called a 'reality effect'."[55] They refer to Caldwell's theory about videographic style in describing how *24* utilizes "the core elements of a style that employs videographic elements not only as a distinctive style flourish, but also directly in the service of the narrative structure."[56]

All this focus on stylistic innovations as aesthetic matters overlooks how these features are always also industrial. As Caldwell says, "stylistic designations foreground television's obsession with merchandising and consumerism."[57] Indicating that the split-screen effect gets less interesting over the course of the series, Peacock complains that it simply becomes a mechanism for phone calls. Commenting on the "ticking-clocks and split screens," Chamberlain and Ruston assume that they "found their way into the show primarily to emphasise the real-time structural conceit and to make the myriad telephone calls seem more interesting."[58] It is true that the more complex split screens employed in season one eventually disappear, likely because they demanded more work on the part of the production team and the audience. Yet, if the split screens only served a narrative function, when they started to be used primarily for phone calls they would no longer be necessary as the telephone call filmed in a series of cross cuts is already understood to signify characters connected in time when they are not connected in space. Of course, producers now have to maintain the split screen as it has become a feature of *24*'s brand. As Mark Lawson proclaims, *24* changes the rules of television by "making format central to drama."[59] Allen concurs, saying that these features are a skillful part of FOX's product differentiation strategy. Yet, as much as they make *24* "stand out," they also make it conform to FOX's brand.[60] Allen gestures toward this point when he references the use of this format in television news, but he does not develop the industrial or corporate connection.

The paring down of the split screens to phone calls also serves an industrial function: to connect the characters to sponsors and position them as subtle spokespeople for mobile products. Each of those phone calls becomes another potential moment for product integration, which is hardly surprising given that in the FOX flow between story segments the commercials for mobile phones and mobile service providers compete for dominance of the commercial time with those for high performance cars and heavy duty trucks. It is a bonus when Jack is making a call from his car and two sponsors can be integrated into a single shot sequence. Assuming that the time a character spends on the phone or in the car has significance only in terms of narrative ignores the commercial imperative of television programming.

24 affords ample opportunity for product integration as the prevalence of computer interfaces and screens, mobile phone and desktop phone displays on the show is striking. The screens and communication devices that dominate the mise-en-scène encourage one to take for granted the essential nature of these technologies and desirability of "Getting IN Now," to borrow phrasing from Verizon Wireless, by acquiring this technology and accessing these networks. The cell phone industry displays itself as a necessary feature of everyday life; people are mobile, but they can still stay in touch no matter where they are. The representation of new media takes on particular importance and sometimes Chloe or one of the other techie characters instructs viewers about the uses of cool new technologies. These products are not simply embedded within the mise-en-scène, but dominate it, offering an extended advertisement for the speed with which information can travel in this plugged in and wireless in-network world. Surow says that in Chloe's world, the cell phones are characters. He is joking around in the DVD commentary, but viewers do pick up on the centrality of those phones, especially to Jack. Sharing Dave Barry's mocking tone (as well as his addiction to a show that he likewise admits often gets silly), a blogger whose site is called "GOP in the City" pays tribute to Jack Bauer's cell phone:

> Alfonso from Silver Spoons, Scrappy Doo, and KITT from Knight Rider. None of these sidekicks garners as much awe as Jack Bauer's Cell Phone. If you packed in the genius of the Professor from Gilligan Island's, MacGyver's usefulness, the style of Crockett and Tubbs, and the lasting power of Ron Jeremy—you may come close to the mind-blowing power of Jack's cell phone … [it] has already helped ID terrorists, organize a raid … While Jack Bauer's gun usually gets the glory, without his cell phone I doubt Jack would have been able to save Los Angeles, Kim Bauer and President Palmer over and over again.

While the show gives the character some human sidekicks, including Chloe, Jack is in contact with her for the most part only through his Palm Treo, which never left his side in those seasons.

While it might seem like the split screens are used only to maintain the real-time format and to accommodate "uninteresting real-time tasks, such as Bauer driving from one side of Los Angeles to another,"[61] they become over the life of the series moments in which Jack's cell phone and other sponsor products are emphasized, particularly the omnipresent Ford SUVs, vans, and light trucks.[62] Indeed, television has recently seen an increase in narratively insignificant sequences involving characters driving from one place to another, the extreme being *Knight Rider* (NBC 2008) in which a majority of the scenes involve the camera capturing different angles of the title car in motion. This occurs as well in several moments in *24*, most obviously in the season three premiere in which the Ford F-150 hood logo and a Ford van's branded wheel covers get close-ups, in addition to countless Fords in motion shots. By season five the Ford logo close-ups and shots in which the logo appears alongside or behind a main character are as numerous as the tracking shots of Fords in motion. It's clear as well that Jack Bauer is the ideal Ford spokesman, as like them he is "Built Tough."

In the new world of branded entertainment, in which the "brought to you by" is increasingly followed by the name of an automobile company, it is hardly surprising that there now are not only countless car commercial-style shots within TV programs, but also actual commercials embedded within the story segments.[63] The best examples of brand integration are those that don't seem like plugs because they serve the storyline and are seamlessly integrated into it, something sponsors and their advertising agencies increasingly understand. The goal of Ford Global Brand Entertainment, for example, is to make sure that Fords are "as much a part of the story or the limelight as a movie's or a TV show's flesh-and-blood or digital star."[64] Their positioning of the driving sequences and phone calls as simple narrative devices is just one example of the way critics have overlooked the industrial aspects of the FOX series' treatment of time, especially as it represents the network's attempts to experiment with on-air segmentation of time (and the ways in which sponsors buy time on a TV program). That the digital clock keeps running in between 24's story segments suggests that the commercials and network promos are also a key aspect of 24's effect as an industrial product as well as an aesthetic creation. Peacock offers a valuable argument about how the digital clock and its continued running during commercials serves a narrative effect (reminding us that danger continues even when we are not watching): "The appearance and reappearance of the clock before and after the breaks shows us that the digits appear to change in accordance with the length of the commercials."[65] He does not develop the point into an industrial analysis. That the hour-long episode clock continues to tick off minutes during the commercials is significant because it calls attention to that which is typically effaced in a TV show: that its primary function is to attract advertisers to the commercial time for sale between its segments by offering timely and edgy programming to which viewers will stay tuned even through the commercials.

The ticking clock, perhaps the brand feature most associated with 24, also has a subtle connection to "Big FOX" brand identity. It is a brand identifier not just for the individual FOX series, but also for FOX News, as the cable channel makes the claim that it is "on the clock" 24 hours a day, keeping abreast of breaking news, even when we are not watching. When viewers tune in during the middle of one news story, the continually scrolling crawl at the bottom of the screen alerts them to all the other stories that have broken in between the segments viewed. FOX News also has as part of its brand the promise that it is vigilant about providing news that one would not find on what it claims are the more lax, liberal news programs of its competitors. Teasers for the local 10 o'clock version of FOX News are part of the flow of the original broadcast of 24 as are promotions for its other broadcast TV shows and for News Corp. products being released on other platforms (e.g., features, gaming, mobile).

Given anxieties about viewers' abilities to timeshift that flow, it is not surprising that network branding now occurs on-air, online, on-mobile, and anywhere else the product circulates. As those platforms, however, do not include the original broadcast flow, networks are returning to the classic TV approach of product integration. Although it plays a role in storytelling, the mise-en-scène is often even more important as a site of brand integration. This dynamic can create conflicts between the creators' vision of the storytelling potential of the mise-en-scène and the network's view of it as a site for sponsor integration. Hinting at these tensions, director/executive producer Jon Cassar notes that the desks at CTU are equipped with Cisco Systems telephones and Apple or Dell computers. "Those are not really show-related as much as they are FOX related," he explains. "Big FOX makes a deal, and we have to abide by their deal."[66] Of course, his comments are made for the carefully orchestrated FOX featurette, "Breaking Ground: Building the New CTU," one of the many examples of promotional documentaries that are offered as special features for a season's DVD box set.

Although not addressed in the featurette, the major role that product integration plays in *24* becomes apparent when closely examining the integration of Cisco Systems into the storyline itself, especially when the company has a new product to launch. During season six, for instance, in addition to the Cisco phone systems used throughout the office sets, "Cisco Tele Presence" is integrated into the White House set and featured in the storyline. One scene starts inside a White House conference room equipped with a bank of monitors. The camera pans over the curve of the three-screen set-up, revealing that each 1080p flat panel displays the advertisement, Cisco Tele Presence. An assistant then activates the technology, with an insert shot of the control unit offering a demonstration for viewers. In addition to the flat panels, the set-up includes special conference table, microphones, cameras, lighting and teleconferencing equipment. To link disparate people and separate spaces as if they were sitting at one oval conference table, a company would pay $249–79K for the Tele Presence 3000 set-up and about $3–5K for the minimum 10 gigabit/second bandwidth that would be needed, according to Paul Miller at engadet.com.[67] In *24*, a show with an "act now, pay later" approach consistent with consumer-oriented U.S. culture, the flat panel monitors get two more promotional shots prior to and after the assistant activates the devices. Then Acting President of the United States Noah Daniels is shown using them to negotiate with Russian President Suvarov.

This product integration is paired in the flow with a commercial for Cisco Systems, this time featuring its new Tele Presence 1000 technology, promising that "Being Here is Being There" through its virtual conference capacities that optimize video, voice, and data convergence. The premise in the spot is that the two sets of grade schoolers use the single flat panel Tele Presence system ($60–79K) to have a staring contest. The all-American boy, with his reddish hair, chubby face, and freckles, has behind him first a blonde boy and then an African American boy followed by an Asian American girl, signifying a classroom that is diverse, but with the assumed white majority still at the center. The Asian boy is in an all-Asian classroom, a space that is marked as not American by its regimented communal seating system and the uniforms the students wear. When he wins, his classmates cheer, but it is hard to tell if they are cheering in English. In any case, the implication is that it is an international contest, especially given the Cisco tagline, "the human network." The global unity promoted herein is one in which the United States, represented as the nation that values individuality and difference over conformity and uniformity, is still imagined as superior. It will lose its edge to competitors, however, if Americans do not keep up with technological advancements.[68] Also endorsed are the homogenization of global culture into one single network and the replacement of local systems (corporate and social as well as technological) with a unified global system based on an American model. In a domestic sense, the spot not only takes for granted the continuing centrality of the Anglo American male as the national representative, while also offering a politically correct multicultural classroom, but also assumes an upper middle class norm. After all, how would an ordinary public school afford such amazing technology? Despite its multicultural cast, *24* establishes the same racial and global dynamic and presents an unrealistic picture of the budgetary and technological capabilities of public institutions.

In an optimal use of network flow in which a subtle correlation exists between sponsor and story segments, Cisco piggybacks on the excitement *24* generates for the acquisition of the latest technologies and gadgets. With both product integration and an integral position in the network flow, Cisco can represent its technology as aiding international relations on a large scale (as in the *24* story segment with Cisco's role in maintaining good will between the United States and Russia) and on a small scale (as in the commercial in which Cisco helps foster good will between American and Asian children).

Like Cisco, with its combined product integration and traditional commercial spot strategy, many of the other FOX/*24* sponsors choose both to integrate products into the mise-en-scène and insert several commercials into the flow between a program's story segments. The most obvious are the auto makers and mobile service providers and phone companies (e.g., Ford and Sprint), as they are often the overt sponsors mentioned in the "promotional consideration provided by" line at the end of the credits. These examples suggest that instead of one strategy replacing the other, multiple strategies coexist in the Must-Click TV environment, as sponsors as well as networks try to find new ways to bypass the audience's attempts to skip the spots. It is ironic that in their quest for "new" approaches to combating timeshifting, they are turning increasingly to product integration, as the practice goes back to the early days of U.S. television programming. As Caldwell notes, "Television mise-en-scène is far from sacred or inviolable ground."[69] Referring to the station IDs burned into the feature films that stations pay to air, Caldwell claims that the story segments that come before commercials are, "Visual turf upon which stations erect promotional signs."[70] Now media conglomerates are erecting promotional signs within story segments of TV shows on other networks, such as when a 2008 segment from *How I Met Your Mother* featured not only the CBS logo, but also a graphic referencing the theatrical release of *Forgetting Sarah Marshall*, a film from NBC's media conglomerate affiliate Universal that would presumably appeal to the same target audience, especially as it features one of the members of the TV show's ensemble cast. The frame was also crowded with CBS's promotional signs appearing in the rotating box at the bottom. Networks still also promote themselves and their products between segments and often position their promos immediately before and after story segments to entice the fast forwarders to stop and watch the spots so as to not miss the start of the story segment.

Timing sponsor and network brand integration

Networks are turning to network brand integration as well because viewers are skipping their promotions and previews along with sponsor spots. FOX employs innovative strategies for integrating its network brand into the story segments in order to create brand recognition (and perhaps even consistency) in a cluttered environment. *24*'s split screen and its on-screen clock, among other visual features, can be read as carefully orchestrated parts of the branding of the show as a FOX program, given that they link the FOX television series with the signature brands FOX News and FOX Sports. The split screen might have been, as Allen argues, a way to make *24* "a distinctive product,"[71] but it also marks it as a familiar FOX product. In passing, Allen gestures toward this connection, but doesn't develop it, when he says, "24 could be seen to be explicitly mimicking the televisual format closest to its own subject matter: twenty-four-hour rolling news footage."[72] Allen's offhand remark positions the news connection as an aesthetic issue rather than one that is simultaneously industrial. Yet, it is more than an aesthetic issue that *24*'s on-screen clock is an "obvious stylistic marker associated with live sports programming,"[73] and that *24* shares the use of split screens with television news and live sports casts; both use the device, as Chamberlain and Ruston put it, "to emphasise simultaneity of experience, whether during a crucial point in the game, or to unite geographically distant guests of a news programme."[74] Their comments have industrial resonance given that news and sports are two programming types through which FOX began to compete with the Big Three networks.[75] It also goes beyond the aesthetics of televisual style to say, as Chamberlain and Ruston do, that *24* utilizes the "videographic presentation" that Caldwell famously associated with CNN, the 24-hour cable news network that first "demonstrated the pervasive possibilities of videographic presentation."[76] More to the point, Caldwell says, "CNN created and celebrated a consciousness of the televisual apparatus: an appreciation for multiple electronic feeds, image-text combinations, videographics, and studios with banks of monitors that evoked video installations."[77] The video-graphic style is always already enmeshed in industrial concerns. Televisual aesthetics and style, Caldwell says, "cannot be viewed apart from business conditions."[78]

That *24* subtly references the interconnectedness of News Corp. products becomes evident in an analysis of the season four DVD featurette, "Breaking Ground," which focuses on production designer Joseph Hodges and his revamping of the primary set of the series, the main floor of the CTU bullpen. The original set is directly modeled on the FOX Sports set at which the pilot was filmed, and the second subtly evokes the FOX News set, sharing its red, white, and blue color palette.[79] The original set design resembles a standard broadcasting approach— saving money during the pilot phase by using a studio-owned space. Matching the series set to that of the pilot maintains visual consistency and narrative logic. The concrete and steel look of that set is consistent with the fact that CTU is a government agency, while the oranges that are carried over from the FOX Sports set make a visual connection between the two FOX products. Given that its mission is security and surveillance, the presence of many high tech gadgets at CTU even remains somewhat story-consistent, while still providing spaces for high-tech product integration.

With its much more overt red, white, and blue color palette, the set redesign represents an interconnected brand platforms approach as that is the same color palette employed by FOX News and seen within the local FOX newsbreaks that occur in the *24* programming flow during a broadcast episode. In the featurette Hodges talks only about the aesthetic reasons for the color scheme, but the similarity to the news sets cannot be random. While the featurette does not address the network branding point, Cassar's comment about the media conglomerate and the tone with which he describes it as "Big FOX" makes clear that if FOX was adamant about turning the set into an optimal site for the integration of sponsors' brands, it would also be sure it would be an optimal space for network brand integration.

The vision for the new CTU set is clearly a double one—as it must be both a site of storytelling and a site of promotion. Hence, the design accommodates both metaphoric possibilities and practical concerns. The unspoken objective is to create a branded set as well as an ideal set for filming a complex, ensemble TV drama. For practical as well as aesthetic reasons Hodges wanted to capture the light and create optimal spaces for filming, so that the camera people could peer through spaces at characters and the sound and light crews could work from above the set. The set is designed to facilitate camera angles and to embed thematic metaphors in the mise-en-scène. Hodges explains that the windows are frosted with lines resembling barcodes, for example, to signify that things are at once exposed and hidden on *24*. In addition, they also highlight that FOX is selling a product to viewers and that the mise-en-scène has everything to do with the product that is being promoted. Of course, the expensive set is a tribute to the success of *24*. As Hodges comments, producers don't usually get a new set in the fourth season of a TV show.

The set redesign emphasizes brand consistency and marketing logic rather than story logic; the space resembles a flush dot.com-style loft rather than a government office, especially as it seems unlikely that the government would budget for chic red desktops or that its agents all would have matching blue binders, that, in turn, match the physical space. Story-inconsistent mise-en-scène is nothing new, of course. The CTU main floor is most remarkable, however, for the number of flat panel monitors, which by season six are enormous spaces on which to project faux FOX News broadcasts. This network brand integration is new, especially the number of shots in which the directors are sure to offer glimpses of the FOX News broadcasts on screens behind the characters' heads or between two characters in conversation. In these moments the mise-en-scène becomes a site in which such brand integration (whether network or sponsor or both) is privileged over "show-related concerns." In the season five premiere, for example, FOX News is almost immediately introduced with a shot of the HP monitor on which it is airing. Then a second shot in President Logan's office in his Camp David-style retreat features FOX News on one of three giant flat panel displays (Panasonic this time) and a FOX breaking news clip of the secret service sweeping the undercarriage of some Ford Trucks outside the compound. The season six premiere ratchets it up a notch as the establishing shot is of FOX News playing on a monitor near a bus stop just before a suicide bomber blows up a bus filled with commuters. Throughout the episode the various flat panel TVs and monitors—from Panasonic, Philips, and HP—become the first thing to which the camera cuts between scenes. Cisco gets a few close-ups and the Dells are still on the desks, but it is the flat panels that dominate the scene ("the clock is ticking on the end of analog so get an HD TV now," they seem to proclaim). More to the point, FOX News broadcasts play on the monitors throughout and make it into the background of a good number of the shots inside CTU. In one transition after we get the close-up of the Panasonic broadcasting FOX's breaking news, it is followed by a lingering shot of Chloe raptly watching the news and exuding the heightened state of alert that viewers share (both in watching *24* and the real FOX News). In another Chloe and her love interest Morris exchange glances while behind each FOX News plays, with his showing a montage of shots, the kind of "America Attacked" slideshow that played right after 9/11.

These flat panel displays and TVs sprouted like mushrooms on the new CTU set, which Big FOX eventually fully utilized as a promotional space to maintain its brand consistency. As viewers could not be counted on to watch the flow, and many were accessing the show in alternate content delivery platforms, FOX found ways to integrate its network (and media conglomerate's) brand into the mise-en-scène. The set redesign featurette also provides a second opportunity for integrating sponsor goods. While DVD box sets offer such featurettes to viewers as a "peek behind the scenes" of a TV show, they also represent an opportunity to reinforce brand identities. Since much of the extra material on the DVD includes repackaging of story content or commentary on story content as it plays, Barbara Klinger argues that a DVD box set offers a chance to combine the already proven (the story) with some supplemental material that seems to expand the story, but usually only reconfirms what was already known or recirculates the story the producers want to tell about the text.[80] On TV on DVD that story is a branded one as a TV show increasingly blurs the line between promotion and storytelling. Klinger writes about feature films, so she does not mention that with a TV box set the sponsors' material gets a second potential airing in the chosen clips and there are new opportunities for sponsors to be integrated into the featurette's original or previously unused footage.

Writing specifically about TV on DVD, Derek Kompare claims that the DVD box set represents a reconception of our relationship to TV. Noting that it is different from the licensed products that have a long history of being offered for purchase to TV fans, Kompare says the DVD box set concept transformed into mainstream practice the acquisition of copies of the actual texts themselves. It was originally a fan practice to exchange tapes that were really "captured flow broadcasts"[81] or to acquire officially distributed selected episodes first on VHS and then on DVD. It helps that DVD represents the compression of the time and space used on VHS as the new format allows a whole season, even a whole series, to be reduced to a manageable set.

The box set brings the TV industry more in line with the direct-to-consumer feature film DVD market and represents, according to Kompare, a publishing model that is different from the flow model in which "producers sell programming to broadcasters, who then sell access to potential viewers—that is, time within programming on their widely distributed channels—to advertisers."[82] While Kompare is right that overall TV on DVD represents the publishing rather than the flow model, in the Must-Click model DVDs do also utilize some degree of flow.

Networks invested heavily in TV on DVD at the start of the twenty-first century, both because it represented an alternate revenue stream based on the publishing model and because of concerns connected to timeshifting needs and capabilities. It is important to note that FOX was first out of the gate on the box set concept when in 2000 it released one for *The X-Files*. That series, like *24*, was ideal for the new format because it always faced difficulties in attracting and maintaining an audience among those increasingly large numbers of overscheduled viewers without the time to invest in a long-arc show intended to be watched in sequence. The box set also addressed anxieties about the loss of revenues related to timeshifting. If TV was readily available on DVD, viewers would be more likely to purchase a series than find some way to acquire an unlicensed copy.[83]

Although Kompare is right to note that some viewers are purchasing the box set as a collector's object, others are purchasing time—that in which to watch a TV show on their schedules, in a high quality format right on their televisions, but without broadcast TV's commercial interruption. That new media devices allow for the skipping of commercials is, of course, at the heart of the TV industry's anxiety about timeshifting. The box set can be seen as another response to that anxiety because, despite the perception that they are, box sets are not completely divorced from commercial flow. As already noted brand integration is a response to time-shifting and in a product that exists on multiple platforms, a sponsor can get a second plug when its product appears in a clip used on another platform.

The season three box set featurette, "Bio Threat: Beyond the Series," for exam-ple, continues the brand integration of Ford's new F-150 truck. The scene that includes the trucks does nothing to move the featurette's narrative forward or to illustrate a point; it does begin with a close up of the Ford logo on the hood followed by a tight tracking shot of the truck backing up to the spot where workers outside the exposure site have been loading up the contaminated materials into the clearly sturdy and spacious bed of the "Built Tough" Ford F-150s, clearly chosen by the L.A. Hazmat Unit for that purpose.

The DVD box set itself is also a branded object, giving producers an opportunity for product integration given the prevalence of computer interfaces and screens as well as mobile phones and desktop phone displays on the show. That becomes evident in an analysis of the season six companion booklet. The cover image is of an American flag superimposed on the half-shadowed face of Jack Bauer. His representation is consistent with the ravaged self-sacrificing man we meet in the on-air series, the platform represented in the booklet's cover tagline, "The Most Explosive Season Yet!" The booklet's interior pages then offer promos and advertisements of the kind that would be part of the broadcast flow following and preceding on-air story segments, even ending with a print ad for Vault, a Coca-Cola energy drink.[84] The inside cover page promotes "24 on 24," which is the site accessed when you load the DVD-ROM included in the box set into your computer. The page informs us that the content on that disc as well and the technology featurette on the set's final disc are "presented by" Cisco systems, whose ad and logo are incorporated into the page. Functioning as an advertisement for Cisco and calling attention to its general sponsorship of *24* and its particular sponsorship of one of the box set's featurettes, the page also serves as a promo for season seven and the *24* website. It urges fans to "Start Now!" with the DVD-ROM as it will provide exclusive access to the site. Once there, viewers/users can "Enjoy interviews and other features leading up to the January 13th premiere of Season 7. Then, on Monday nights immediately after each broadcast, get insights into the 'making of' each episode." That plug for the upcoming season continues on the facing page, which is a promo that reminds viewers again of the season premiere. On offer next are downloadable V Cast episodes from Verizon, pictured playing on an LG phone. Readers are told to "Watch Entire Episodes of your favorite FOX Shows on Verizon V Cast Mobile TV" and to log on to www.flotv.com for more information about FOXMobile, another division of Big FOX. Other mobile content is available from Jamster, the sponsor featured next in the flow on the adjacent page. These kinds of series/sponsor plug hybrids are the kind that also appear on-air in the broadcast flow in the hopes that viewers will be engaged with *24* on these other platforms.

The booklet pages that follow turn to the ancillary products that have long been associated with TV shows. Included are ads for the *24* magazine, the HarperCollins novelizations, and three tie-in books/guides. Although not in the season six booklet, previous box sets reference licensed gear, a board game, and the music of *24*. This box does include the Jack Bauer card from the new 24: Trading Card Game. All these traditional ancillary products are associated with websites and some with other new media features, making them available at the click of a mouse. New media technologies spurred the creation of new kinds of ancillary products, such as downloadable ringtones, screensavers, and wallpapers for computing and mobile devices. While the television industry has long been offering fans such products, in the twenty-first century these items are arguably more likely to be incorporated into the mainstream consumer's everyday life (e.g., on their mobiles and laptops that they access constantly throughout the day). Although not referenced in this booklet, those from other seasons advertise the brand extensions that are unique to twenty-first-century television—including video games from Sony Playstation and I-Play and more mobisodes—products representative of the other platforms on which *24* circulates and which together make up the networked text of the series as a whole.

Complementing the booklet's promotion of the online, on DVD-Rom, on DVD, on-air, and on-mobile *24*, the final two promos before the Coca-Cola ad on the back are for *24* in syndication and *24* as part of a library of TV on DVD on offer from Big FOX. The first ad references repurposing, which FOX has branded as "24: Weekends," urging readers to "log-on to www.24weekends.com for local Time and Channel." The penultimate page offers a promotion for the *something for everyone* – Twentieth Century FOX TV on DVD, mostly sets for government agent/police and legal series, some of which is testosterone TV like *24* (e.g., *The Shield*) and others more quirky fare. There is one oddity – *30 Days*, a series created and hosted by Morgan Spurlock, the director of *SuperSize Me*, an exposé documentary about the fast food industry; it is likely included to appeal to the college-educated progressive niche and "fulfill" the FOX fair and balanced brand promise. Then as noted earlier, the booklet concludes with a sponsor product made explicitly as a tie-in to *24*.

While the Cisco products alluded to on the first inside page of the booklet are obviously not made explicitly to tie in to *24*, the company did help co-create "24: Technology File," the season six featurette that is referenced in the booklet ad and characterized as a crosspromotion for Cisco and FOX. As the transformation of a DVD featurette into branded entertainment is a new concept, it is worth analyzing in detail. A closer look at "24: Technology File" on disc seven reinforces the point that on the DVD sets—as in the on-air broadcasts—sponsor, network, and media conglomerate brand integration can be simultaneously employed. The featurette starts with the same image that appears in Cisco Systems' "Welcome to the Human Network" television and print campaign. That is followed by a full screen close-up of one of the Cisco products used in the show: Cisco Security Response System. This introduction to the product is followed by the more typical featurette opening with a clip from the on-air series; in this case the screen is divided into three boxes, with Jack Bauer and his "personal" tech expert Chloe in the top two boxes, each ostensibly looking at a screen on which the Cisco product is in action; along the bottom in a third doublewide box is the screen shot of the Cisco Security Response System. That same shot will be used over and over in the rest of the featurette. The trio of on-screen boxes, a *24* brand feature, points to the way Cisco and other tech products are integrated into *24* and displayed for the viewer: via shots of characters looking at screens followed by a shot of the screens that often offer branded displays of sponsors' hardware or software. Later in another box a Dell computer also gets a close-up as do some Sprint phones, but Cisco usually gets a dual chance to display hardware and software. Of course, constant shots of Chloe sitting at her desk make it easy to integrate countless shots of her Cisco internet protocol phone, with its "voice, video, and integrated data capabilities."

That the DVD featurette offers a second platform for the same product integration that was featured in the on-air series is evidenced again when some clips from the show are used to re-promote the Cisco Unified Personal Communicator, a device that combines computer, video, and phone capabilities. Much of the storyline is edited out for the featurette so that all the attention is placed on the communication device, making it really seem like a commercial, especially given that in the shot sequence the product gets: a long shot, a medium shot, a close-up of its screen, an extreme close-up of its features and a second of its features in use. Cisco Telepresence is mentioned as well in the featurette and the scene I discussed earlier is shown again. Howard Gordon even says of the actors utilizing the technology, "they actually felt like they were in the same room," which is the same concept

Cisco uses in its advertisements. This product gets a good plug, but the featurette seems most interested in promoting the Cisco Security Response System, which is given even more shots, both single ones inserted throughout the featurette and a multiple shot sequence with several close-ups. It is even shown in split screen with writer/co-executive producer Michael Loceff, whose comments about technology on the show act as brand claims for Cisco. That brand message can also be read as well in the snippets of commentary that the editor extracts and runs at certain intervals as a blue text banner at the bottom of the screen. Although ostensibly used to offer sound-bite versions of the commentators' points, when seen together, the banner text reads like concepts Cisco wants to convey in promoting its brand: *The world has changed — Such things actually do exist — That's not unrealistic technology — People who are thinking futuristically.*

The editor even turns a *24* character into a brand advocate when he adds into the Cisco shot sequence a clip in which Morris, a tech expert like Chloe, says to her, "I know these guys; they write really good code," after which a screen shot of the Cisco product is inserted.

The banners make the commentators into brand spokespeople for Cisco, then switch in tone half-way through the featurette, to proclaiming the necessity of arming oneself with the latest high tech security devices in the post 9/11 world. The snippets in this section are: bombs, C4, gas—suitcase nuke—mechanical nuclear device—really smart bad guy—an unfortunate but a scarily real effect.

The last snippet comes from Loceff whose full comment is: "People who want to do destruction have access to really smart technology that can assist them. When bad guys get their hands on such technology, it's an unfortunate but a scarily real effect." At the end of his comments the editor inserts a shot of a nuclear detonation and mushroom cloud formation, the one featured in season six and replayed over and over again on the faux FOX News broadcasts running constantly on the screens that pepper *24* sets.

Prior to that image other production team members also comment on terrorists and their likely acquisition and use of a weapon of mass destruction (WMD) on U.S. soil. Director/executive producer Jon Cassar says, "Fighting terrorism these days really means being able to one up the enemy technologically." He later adds, "The way we take advantage of this new technology is exactly the same way that the terrorists are taking advantage of it." The point is echoed by writer/executive producer Manny Coto when he says, "Suitcase nukes have been talked about in terrorism circles and there's been a lot of talk about whether they can be built or exist in such a small capacity; we posited that they could." In addition to creating demand for Cisco security systems, their comments also offer support to the idea that a terrorist attack on an American city using WMDs is something imminent for which the United States needs to prepare, a point of view not supported by experts in the field but embraced anyhow by *24* co-creators Surnow and Bob Cochran, the Bush Administration, and FOX News.

The same point is made in another part of the networked text that is Series Six of 24: the "Debrief," mobisodes—mini content made expressly for mobile phones, in this instance by Sprint. The first mobisode begins, as do several episodes during the on-air series broadcast, with an establishing shot of someone watching a FOX breaking news broadcast, this one of the detonation of a nuclear device in Valencia, CA that occurred during the regular season. This initial over-the-shoulder shot of the FOX News image is followed by a reveal via split screen that it is indeed Jack Bauer watching FOX News Channel, which in the next shot gets its own box and still appears in the shot with Bauer in the box next to it. This focus on another arm of Big FOX and the fact that each episode of the mobisode series ends with two promos, one telling viewers to watch more mobisodes on Sprint/FOXMobile and a second urging them to get *24* on DVD, indicates that even though the mobile product exists on a separate platform the space is still one in which to integrate sponsor and network branding and to promote the series as a network of texts (on-air, on-mobile, on-DVD, and online, and more).

The continuity of FOX branding is emphasized as well in the content of the mini story line. The first episode includes a shot of Jack half in the shadows of the door frame as he speaks to two male agents—specifically a Latino and an African American from District. It replicates the look and pose of the images on the cover of the U.S. box sets, and reinforces the FOX fair and balanced claim as the ensemble cast is always diverse. As the series unfolds over four more installments we learn that the District agents are debating whether to use coercive interrogation techniques on Jack to discover if he really didn't break when he was tortured by the Chinese for 20 months. Jack frees himself from their restraints (with help from another agent who is on his side) and proclaims that he did not compromise a fellow agent and get him killed, as they were speculating. Leaving room for a variety of different story arc possibilities for season seven, the mobisodes have an open-ended conclusion so that it can still be debated if everyone, even a super agent, breaks under torture, if Jack Bauer could have compromised the agent, or if the investigations into his behavior in this or other incidents will continue into season seven.

The mobisodes are consistent with the on-air storyline and are clearly conceptualized at the same time, while still extending the story beyond the final episode of season six as well as the general parameters of when a *24* episode ends. In this way, they are an example of transmedia marketing, the extension of the promotion of one story over multiple platforms, with each adding some new content, while conforming to the rules of the story world, and with each becoming a space in which the other franchise elements can be promoted.[85]

The mobisodes also represent a more traditional repurposing. Originally a form of branded entertainment co-created by *24* and Sprint and appearing in one season, the mobisodes are repurposed as a special feature on the subsequent season's box set, a format that was promoted at the end of each mobisode during their original run. The cycle is repeatable for each season. The DVD then promotes the mobisodes as well as Sprint, FOXMobile Entertainment and whatever other new content they might now be offering on their websites. Too often what is labeled new content is really just repurposed. The special collector's edition of the *24* season one DVD that FOX released in 2008, for example, was really mostly a repurposing of the original box set even though this new edition promised to offer the kind of in-depth commentary on the season that was not possible due to the rapid release schedule of that first DVD and the fact that the show was not at the time of the DVD release the cultural phenomenon that it has since become. This type of collector's edition enables, Klinger says, "the kind of product differentiation so important to repurposing, that is, to the strategy of repeatedly reselling the same titles."[86] Often these DVDs are less additions to than repositionings of the original material, resulting in what Klinger calls, "built-in and changeable intertextual surround" that can enable viewers to think of the same product differently.[87] Sometimes it is just a matter of finding ways to monetize the same content by positioning the same product differently. The "24 on 24: Behind the Scenes," the Web Diaries that were available through a special website to purchasers of the season five DVD, were repurposed as extras for the season six DVD. At the end of the Web Diary, Cassar addresses the viewer who would have been watching online and then returning to the DVD or the on-air episodes: "After you watch each episode come back here for a new diary," a comment that is followed by an advertisement for buying DVD box sets. Again, evidencing the circularity of original and then repurposed content, the Web Diaries promote the DVDs, the on-air show, and, when repurposed on the next season's DVD box set as a featurette, the DVDs, in turn, promote the website on which the diaries originally appeared.

These examples should indicate that Must-Click TV is not about the replacement of old approaches by new ones, but is an intertwining of the two, always directed toward continual circulation of the series brand as well as those of the network/media conglomerate. At the same time, a DVD's special features are not really "extras" as they are part of the overall product being sold and are intended to draw viewers back to the text and deepen their reverence for it as an amazing product.

Unfortunately, instead of being seen as promotional discourse or just one interpretation of a text that should be considered critically, the commentaries included on the various platforms become fact.[88] This occurs, in part, Klinger says, because DVD extras address viewers as insiders, promise to grant them access to specialized areas of the industry and employ "the rhetoric of intimacy (i.e., 'secrets' of the cinema) and mastery (i.e., technological expertise or media knowledge)."[89] Yet, as Klinger claims, "Rather than inciting critical attitudes toward the industry, then, behind-the-scenes 'exposés' vividly confirm Hollywood as a place of marvels brought to the public by talented film professionals."[90] Viewers are presented not with "the unvarnished truth about the production," but rather the "'promotable' facts, behind-the-scenes information that supports and enhances" not only what Klinger calls "a sense of the 'movie-magic' associated with Hollywood production,"[91] but also, in the case of TV on DVD, the promotable aspects of the series, the network, media conglomerate and their sponsors.

The fair and balanced featurette

The season three box set featurette, "Bio Threat: Beyond the Series," offers a good example of the more subtle strategy of network brand integration, specifically of the FOX's brand promise of programming that is "fair and balanced," the tag line for which FOX News has become infamous.[92] Even though it has at its center a scientist and U.S. government "disease detectives" offering evidence that biological WMDs are not easy to acquire or handle, the WMD featurette leaves viewers with the impression that the weaponizing of a virus is not only possible, but probable. It does so by following the FOX News formula of pitting a conservative commentator against a liberal one, and weighting the commentary in favor of the conservative, undercutting the liberal's claim, or choosing commentators with questionable "liberal" credentials. Erica Iacono from *PR Week* says FOX News "has publicly disputed its conservative label and extolled the 'fair and balanced' nature of its reporting." Of course, "its beginnings were arguably very much rooted in the notion that it was serving an underserved audience—one that was looking for less liberal-infused news." Robert Thompson says that FOX has built its name and audience "on hammering home a bunch of assumptions ... that were out there," particularly the one that the news media was too liberal.[93] That charge is carefully discredited by Eric Alterman in *What Liberal Media? The Truth about BIAS and the News*. Both Lewis and NPR's David Folkenflik have confirmed through their research that the FOX news strategy "is predicated in some ways on delegitimating much of the rest of the media in terms of its perceived objectivity or neutrality."[94]

That delegitimation process is at work in the WMD featurette. Through the factual, scientific and experiential information they offer, the experts indicate that it is unlikely that there would or even could be a bioterrorist attack in the U.S. Yet, the editors cut the segments in a way that makes it seem as if such an attack is likely. As this idea is the central motivating assumption for *24*'s suspense, the featurette ostensibly offers background on how producers and their research team worked to find real world parallels so that the season three scenario could be as authentic as possible. When Anne Coffel, as head researcher (2001–5) for *24*, was asked to track down details about some fast-acting pulmonary immuno virus, she located two virologists: Dr. Gabor Racz, a Hungarian research scientist affiliated with the University of New Mexico, and Dr. Mitch Cohen, a physician working for the U.S. government as a director of a division of the Centers for Disease Control. Interviews with Coffel, the experts, and producers are intercut with clips from *24* story segments about the explanation of the nature of the virus and its threat potential.

In terms of the "fair and balanced" paradigm, Racz's position that WMDs are neither as easy to acquire nor to manufacture as people assume they are is juxtaposed with the more cautionary stance of Cohen. The staged environments in which the interviews are conducted convey messages about the differences between the two men. Driving an old pickup truck out to a snow- and ice-covered mountain research site, Racz is established as an academic scientist. The remoteness of the location combined with his accented English and foreign name makes it seem as if this research is being conducted in some faraway place. A passing comment by Racz indicates that the spot is actually the American Southwest, but the reference is so subtle that, combined with assumptions about who and what counts as American, it does little to undercut the impression that Racz, his research site and findings, and his commentary are foreign. In contrast, Cohen's environment seems like a familiar American medical office, as the introduction to him comes through a pointless scenario in which his secretary Diane answers his phone, "National Center for Infectious Diseases," and says to the caller, "Yes, Dr. Mitch Cohen is in the middle of an interview, may I take a message." A dissolve of Cohen, who shares the frame with an American flag, follows. This sequence is included ostensibly to establish Cohen's credentials and his name, but also positions him more as a typical American doctor than a research scientist. To punctuate the point, the producers continue to include the edge of the American flag within the initial sequence on Cohen who wears military lapel pins, thereby associating him with the trope of "The Patriot," which for some of FOX's core conservative viewers would likely make him the more significant authority.[95] The centrality of patriotism to the FOX brand is apparent in the tagline FOX News adopted after 9/11: "be accurate, be fair, be American."[96] Sylvio Waisbord would say that the brand message was emblematic of the contradictory nature of a post-9/11 news environment characterized by "journalism that opted for flag waving reporting over facticity."[97]

A self-professed conservative, 24 creator Joel Surnow repeatedly uses the term "Patriot" to describe Jack Bauer and his willingness to resort to extreme measures to contain and diffuse threats to national security. "There are not a lot of measures short of extreme measures that will get it done," he says in an interview with Jane Mayer in New Yorker. "America wants the war on terror fought by Jack Bauer. He's a patriot."[98] Surnow positions himself as a patriot, as Mayer demonstrates in her description of how his desk faces "a wall dominated by an American flag in a glass case. A small label reveals that the flag once flew over Baghdad, after the American invasion of Iraq, in 2003." The Army regiment stationed in Iraq that sent it to Surnow said that they shared some box sets of 24 until an enemy bomb destroyed them. Surnow tells Mayer, "The military loves our show," adding, "People in the Administration love the series, too ... It's a patriotic show. They should love it." With his clear embrace of "flag-waving," it's hardly surprising that Surnow employs rhetoric that complements the Bush Administration's appeal to patriotism to justify the War on Terror and the War with Iraq.[99] "Bush's insistence that Hussein had fostered al Qaeda rationalized the invasion in terms of the trope 'America attacked'," Eileen Meehan explains. The trope may have been appropriate in relation to the 9/11 attacks, but "it was ill suited to an invasion launched by the Bush administration against a secular dictator whose regime had no ties to Islamic fundamentalists." Even though it was misapplied, it "appealed to patriotism."[100] The trope of America attacked is referenced in multiple-insert shots of biohazard warning signs in the segments filmed in Cohen's office. Even though those kinds of signs are a mundane part of any medical office or lab, the featurette makes them seem ominous, especially given Cohen's comments on the threat potential.

Elements of the mise-en-scène in the office of Dr. Laurene Mascola of the Los Angeles County Communicable Disease Department are emphasized in a similarly ominous way. A close-up on a certificate that reads Epidemic Intelligence Service (EIS) establishes more than Mascola's credentials. It alerts viewers about EIS, whose existence seems to confirm that the U.S. government is concerned enough with the threat of bioterrorism to have created a special division to train agents who would act as disease detectives. One might assume that the EIS is a post-9/11 development, but it was founded in 1951. Its original objective at the start of the Korean War was to train agents to identify and deal with bioterrorism-related illnesses. Yet, most of its actual work has been on more familiar health concerns; while Ebola and Bird Flu are listed among its "health threats," so are obesity, diabetes, aging, tobacco and youth, autism, and birth defects.[101] Indeed, Mascola makes a comment in the featurette that suggests that she thinks more Americans will be impacted by the latter "health threats" than any hypothetical pandemic or weaponized virus attack. Yet, the final cut includes only one comment about her office's daily concerns with more immediate health threats, an editing issue that I argue later in this chapter is part of establishing her as leaning too much toward political correctness.

As the featurette is intended to parallel the season three plot line about terrorists striking L.A. with a weaponized virus, the editors intercut the disease detectives' comments about hypothetical preparedness and planned protocols for a bioterrorist attack with clips from the briefings offered by the fictional disease detectives dispatched to the scene in 24. After Cohen says that if such a virus were to spread it would result in "massive illness and death," the editor cuts in the scene in which his fictional counterpart offers a power point on the projected "infection rate" of a weaponized virus. It projects that at the end of a week 9% of the population would be infected. Michele Dessler and Tony Alimeda from CTU look horrified. Tony exclaims, "That's over a million people." A cut to Mascola follows. Although she says that such a rapid spread would be impossible, the images from 24 are compelling. Here and elsewhere, they have more power than Racz's and Mascola's statements of scientific fact.

Cofell says the challenge for her as 24's head researcher occurs when scientific facts are at odds with the public's "understanding of science." She uses as an example, the cyanide capsule, the one with which Hollywood has equipped government agents who would rather die instantly than compromise their mission or the safety of their colleagues and country. Although "it is widely understood" that agents have such a capsule, Cofell says, this now-standard plot point has little basis in science. She learned through her research that cyanide is not fast-acting and results in a very painful death. In terms of 24, that means that it is not helpful to equip the virus-stricken civilians with a cyanide capsule so that they can bypass the horrific effects of the virus. After being informed of these facts, the production team did not change its storyline, but rather just made it vague, saying that the infected are given the option of taking a "suicide drug." Instead of correcting the scientific inaccuracy, the accepted fiction that such a drug exists is maintained. Cofell says that the show, with an eye toward maximum entertainment, would often "just get rid of all of the research complexity and simplify it."

Through her research on viruses, Coffel discovered that there is no virus in nature, as Racz and Mascola make clear, that would work the way producers wanted, especially within the compressed time frame. "It was very challenging to find a virus with a '90% kill rate,'" Cofell says, given that it is not the way viruses function as they "want to live and be passed on." To make it seem more realistic, the production team decided to weaponize the season three virus so that they could claim terrorists had manipulated it to suit their needs. Even that would not work the way it does in *24*. "Dealing with viruses is actually very difficult," Racz explains, and "manipulating viruses for your own purposes" is even more so. Another misperception, Racz notes, is that viruses are assumed to be easily accessible given that they are found "everywhere in nature."

As he appears to be very credible, Racz's point of view should prevail and the featurette should convey his unambiguous point that weaponizing a virus would be very difficult and very unlikely for a number of reasons connected to their instability and the riskiness of handling them. Instead, the public perception that biological WMDs are a real threat is reinforced, aided in part by the vagueness of the commentary Cohen offers. Although he has an academic science background like Racz and the experiential knowledge of fellow disease detective Mascola, Cohen offers little in the way of actual information. He technically confirms Racz's points, especially about the instability of viruses, for instance, but Cohen then undercuts them by asserting, "There is a potential of course." It's that potential that Cohen picks up on in his comments about the threat potential for biological terrorism, as is evident when his statements are contrasted with Mascola's.

While Mascola addresses the likelihood of an actual attack, Cohen concentrates on the potential for a hypothetical attack. Mascola adds experiential evidence from her role as a disease detective to the detailed scientific background Racz provides on just how slowly an actual virus spreads and, hence, how it would not be effective for causing rapid fatalities. She notes that the representation of the virus on *24* has little basis in fact. "It's hard to think of a virus that would go in a person to person way, infecting hundreds of thousands; if there was something that was aerosolized over the environment, that perhaps would." Then she refers to the infamous SARS virus epidemic, saying that it supposedly spread from five to six people to eight thousand, but it took four months to do so. Given these facts, it is not surprising that instead of offering evidence of a virus that could have the rapid release and rapid fatality potential of the *24* virus, Cohen focuses on the compressed time between infection and death and offers as an example Meningococcal Meningitis; it is a health threat of which most people have heard, as there always seems to be a case involving a healthy student who is stricken and then dies within a weekend. Cohen implies that people are most troubled by Meningitis because of its association with "taking someone who is otherwise healthy and resulting in a quick death."

The editors imply that the virus on the show is as real a threat as Meningitis by punctuating Cohen's comment with a cut to a shot of the ravaged body of the first virus victim. His other comments act as the lead into the clip from the story segment in which the disease detective tells Tony, "the host is dead," and later to clips featuring the virus-ravaged corpse. The mention of Meningitis can be used to instill fear into viewers because it is a fast-acting and seemingly random killer, even though it is one that affects very few people and has no connection to or potential for use in a bioterrorist attack.

Cohen's commentary is a good example of what Justin Lewis calls "associational logic": the juxtaposition of two unrelated issues that leaves it to the audience to make a connection between them. Lewis contends that this technique characterizes much of the public debate today, both on the news and in political speeches. "Political elites" take their cue from advertisers, "who have long understood that you make claims not by argument, but by juxtaposition."[102] As an example, Lewis uses the rhetoric politicians used to garner support for what is now vaguely called the War in Iraq:

> "those making the case for the war with Iraq would juxtapose it—vaguely, intangibly, but repeatedly—with the war on terrorism. For a public with limited knowledge of geopolitics, these associations become the building blocks for making sense of the world."[103]

That logic is central to FOX News coverage, Meehan says: "FOX News repeatedly claimed that Saddam Hussein had aided and conspired with Al Qaeda; that Hussein had, and was ready to use, weapons of mass destruction; that world opinion supported President Bush's decision to invade Iraq."[104]

Employing the same kind of associational logic, Surnow makes a case for his position that bioterrorism is an imminent threat. He tells viewers that the featurette interview is being filmed on February 3, 2004 when the breaking news crawl reminded viewers all day of "the report of the ricin outbreak in the Senate building." The kind of all-day breaking news coverage of this event and the anthrax attacks before it exemplifies, according to Waisbord, "that the media have trouble reporting risk in a cautious and watchful manner." Indeed, "The 'press panic' at the height of the anthrax scare in late 2001 confirmed that the media are better at scaring than reassuring."[105] In contrast, Mascola claims the role of media should be to talk to people before they get panicked as "worried minds don't listen. In other words, once people get panicked, you can educate them all you want. I don't think people are going to listen." Cofell confirms the significance of education in alleviating fear, citing how her fears about bioterrorism were allayed by gathering research for the show, all of which suggested the implausibility of the kind of bioterrorist attack that happens on *24*: "Regarding bioterrorism, I feel that my fears have subsided, the more information I have about it, about quarantine and emergency procedures, that Dr. Mascola is very well-equipped to deal with an outbreak."

Viewers of the featurette are not getting the same kind of unmediated access to Mascola's explanations as Coffel would have. Instead her comments are interspersed with the more fear-including commentary of Surnow on bioterrorism. *24*'s Loceff reinforces that fear when he claims that writing for the show has had the effect of "making me believe that it is easier than I thought." In addition, the editors keep inserting shots of the ravaged body of the first virus victim, even beginning and ending the featurette with the respective sequences in which he is first discovered and when his body is taken away. The images of his corpse are juxtaposed with Surnow's reference to the ricin incident. Like the news reports that day, he implies that the ricin incident is an act of bioterrorism, but fails to mention that although ricin may be easy to obtain, it would not be effective for a large-scale attack. Waisbord recalls the impact of such commentary in relation to the anthrax scare on public perceptions about terrorism: "While the media hammered away at the idea that the anthrax attacks were connected to September 11, it was hardly surprising that opinion polls showed an overwhelming majority believed it to be true."[106] Without providing any actual background on the ricin incident, but rather tapping into fears about biological terrorism, Surnow's comments also contribute to misperceptions about the connections among the incidents.

Like the reporters covering the anthrax attacks, Surnow takes for granted that the culprits are foreign terrorists because that explanation fits best with the trope "America attacked." Waisbord argues that "Patriotism establishes that only external forces pose threats to the nation. It excludes the possibility of internal actors interested in disrupting a seemingly unified community."[107] The imperative to maintain "the discourse of 'the nation in danger' displaced values of democratic journalism such as dissent and fairness."[108] It also became viewed as unpatriotic to acknowledge the possibility of internal actors or to call into question the motives of the Bush Administration. The problem, of course, was that the administration's response to the 9/11 attacks was premised on the binary, Good Americans vs. Evildoers. Rather than attempt to explain the complex situation, the press, also borrowing from Hollywood binaries, "framed the story as Hussein armed with weapons of mass destruction and Bush ready to disarm him,"[109] a narrative well suited to the President's tendency to adopt a "bring it on" aggressive American cowboy stance. If the anthrax and ricin attacks had a domestic origin then "the media could no longer render an account that fitted, in Michel Foucault's sense, the 'regime of the truth' in place since September 11," Waisbord points out. "At a time when patriotism was still pervasive, indications that fellow members of the nation apparently sent anthrax-laced letters flew in the face of the 'united we stand' patriotism that the media helped to perpetuate."[110]

The truth that Surnow is helping to produce is that America is still under attack and in particular danger from a bioterrorist threat. His mention of ricin in the interview allows Surnow to uphold that truth, despite the overwhelming evidence to the contrary. It is significant that he does not make the connection explicit as that is how associational logic works, according to Lewis. Viewers have to make the links themselves so that FOX can maintain its promise to be both accurate and American by supporting the narrative that is aligned with the United States' self-professed identity without making explicitly untrue claims. Although post-9/11 news reports juxtapose a series of incidents connected to the trope of "America attacked" and never "assert a causal connection, *in the absence of any other explanation offered*, most people tend to assume one," Lewis contends.[111]

In addition to associational logic, the WMD featurette utilizes an even savvier technique to support its fair and balanced brand claim: offering a secondary explanation, but then undercutting it. This strategy fits the FOX truth claim about its commitment to a fair and balanced treatment of hot button issues. The structure is apparent in the way later comments by Racz and Mascola are used to invalidate their earlier explanations. The editing creates an argument by juxtaposition: offhand remarks by Racz and Mascola that seem to undermine their earlier more nuanced explanations are inserted into the featurette after Surnow and Cohen use associational logic, rather than any scientific or experiential evidence, to imply that bioterrorism is not only possible, but likely.

Surnow's truth is confirmed not only by the more conservative Cohen, but also by a quick sequence with Racz, even though he explicitly states the exact opposite point. When we hear the off-camera interviewer ask Racz how to weaponize a virus, his response is, "that's a difficult question because it's top secret how to weaponize viruses and that's not my main research." The interviewer picks up on the idea of it being top secret, which in the movies, usually means that someone will then steal the secret and hatch a plot for "world domination." Reinforcing this impression, when the interviewer cajoles, "come on, how do you do it," Racz offers only silence, and a slight smile, again making it seem like it is a real threat as opposed to a highly unlikely scenario. The exchange reinforces the assumption that, no matter what Racz claimed earlier, there are indeed legitimate fears about the dangers of the information "falling into the wrong hands," another movie convention.

As with this Racz segment, a similar one with Mascola has a movie parallel: the bureaucrat who denies the possibility of a specific threat right before it becomes an actuality. It takes just one offhand remark to make it seem as if she has been downplaying the dangers of bioterrorism. To her statement that viruses just do not spread as rapidly as implied on *24*, Mascola adds the afterthought that perhaps the only way a virus could be spread as quickly would be in a stadium release in which the thousands who were exposed would then go home and infect thousands of others. After she uses the example she pauses and says, "Perhaps something like that could happen … That actually is a sobering thought, when I think about that." The editor gives her remark emphasis by lingering on her and then cutting to Surnow who says, "Unfortunately what you can imagine is usually true. As outrageous as some of the stuff that we come up with, there is always something there to support it."

The juxtaposition of Mascola's and Surnow's comments is significant because it points to the tension in commentary about *24* between categorizing it as a farfetched, but compelling fantasy that taps into our self-admitted paranoia or as a remarkably prescient drama that is reality-based even when it does not conform to what Surnow terms "the procedural truth." Before turning to a reading of 24's outrageousness both as savvy in relation to effective branding and as problematic when Surnow and the 24 fans in the Bush Administration and the military make reality claims for the show or use its plots as the justification for policy, we need to look at the way editors use the final comments of Surnow and Mascola to come down on the side of Surnow's truth.[112]

In the stadium release segment, even more significance is given to Mascola's caveat when the editor adds a final comment from Surnow: "Biological warfare and biological threats will unfortunately become scarier when they start to happen on US soil." Indeed, bioterrorist plots are probably being hatched right now, as Surnow already implied with his references to the ricin incident in the Senate Office Building. The inclusion of an additional comment by Surnow makes the possibility seem like a probability.

Yet, as it is Mascola who is given the last word, the featurette might seem to privilege her point of view that all the focus on WMDs draws attention away from domestic crises. Instead of putting "a lot of emphasis on preparing for bioterrorism," she argues, people should concentrate on the "things that we can control: making sure that our children are raised in a healthy environment, not using drugs or alcohol, that people work out, and have exercise in their diet." She clearly implies here that there is no real way to prepare for a terrorist attack; yet, because it is so out of our control, we consequently become obsessed with it. When she develops her point about more pressing health threats, she uses as her example the obesity problem in the United States: "There's an epidemic of obesity but people would rather talk about Weapons of Mass Destruction." It strikes a false note, especially when she adds, "I think our fast food industry is a Weapon of Mass Destruction, you know, that we should look at it that way." That the editor then cuts one final time to the virus-ravaged corpse makes her claim seem trivial by association.

Mascola's comment is representative of the kind of remark that Surnow intended to lampoon on The Half Hour News Hour, his short-lived 2007 conservative comedy show that had a brief run on FOX News channel before it was canceled.[113] Discussing the topics he envisioned for that show, he explains, "There are so many targets, from global warming to banning tag on the playground. There's a lot of low-hanging fruit." In New Yorker Mayer describes Surnow as "a foe of political correctness," an umbrella term under which Surnow would group the Mascola comment and the revisionist history that Racz represents when he notes earlier that biological warfare has been used for thousands of years. His example of the Tartars using plague-infested clothes as weapons in a war is only one step removed from relating the fact that the U.S. government employed the same technique in its distribution of smallpox blankets to American Indian tribes. He might also have destabilized the "America under attack" trope by noting that it was the United States that experimented in World War I and II with weaponizing ricin before it weaponized saren instead. Instead the final comment from Racz is "There are examples when viruses, viruses are used for the good purposes," phrasing that reinforces his foreignness and sounds like the kind of "there are good and bad sides to everything" balance that conservatives claim liberal academia encourages.

The association of Racz and Mascola with remarks that Surnow would categorize as politically correct is a subtle way to undermine their credibility, while still making the featurette seem fair and balanced. The final question the featurette addresses is if each commentator sees bioterrorism as a threat; the final score is balanced two to two, with one expert and one from the 24 team representing each side. That leaves Mascola, and Surnow, who clearly believes it is. Giving Mascola the last word is the most effective part of this fair and balanced strategy, as it is a reversal of the subversive Hollywood melodrama structure perfected by 1950s director Douglas Sirk: adding a containment narrative in the final scene that returns the status quo that had been undercut in the middle segments, but making sure it seems contrived, so that the real subversion in the middle of the film is what the audience remembers.[114] The majority of the featurette provides scientific facts that establish the improbability of terrorists acquiring and using WMDs, but the weight is placed on Surnow's remarks in the middle of the narrative even as the last word is given to the moderate Mascola. Typically, the Sirkian move involves a subversive critique of capitalism at the center of a film with an ending that re-establishes the capitalist and consumerist status quo. On 24 there is a subversion of the subversive critique via a reassertion of the viability of the conservative capitalist national narrative (good Americans vs. foreign Evildoers) even though there is a reestablishment of the revisionist, liberal national narrative at the end (not-so-innocent America in need of reconsideration of its heroic self-assessment). That reassessment involved, the conservative critique of it argues, the replacement of the results-oriented man of action by a kinder, gentler, but often ineffective man. In its celebration of gruff and tough Jack Bauer, 24 reasserts traditional male values (of physical and mental strength and decision-making) that had supposedly been displaced in the 90s by revisionist male values (emotional nurturing and consensus building).[115]

With little tolerance for revisionist history, Surnow positions himself as one of those Lauren Berlant calls America's ex-icons, the disenfranchised white males who feel they have lost their unmarked status in a Liberal America that celebrates a multi-culture and condemns the oppression of various groups throughout U.S. history.[116] Surnow says jokingly, "Conservatives are the new oppressed class," adding, "Isn't it bizarre that in Hollywood it's easier to come out as gay than as conservative?" He might have said more specifically that conservative, heterosexual, white males are the new oppressed class. Surnow views Hollywood as part of the liberal establishment: "Right now, they have to be nice to me. But if the show tanks I'm sure they'll kill me."[117] Saying that it is a risk to express conservative ideas, he implies that all of Hollywood is marked by a liberal bias.

To return to Mascola's final comment, Surnow would argue that only in Liberal America could a Big Mac be categorized as a WMD. Even though it is hardly characteristic of her tone overall, using her obesity remark as her final comment makes her seem aligned with the zealous tag-banners that Surnow likes to mock. Not at all strident, Mascola is a good sport throughout the featurette. She clearly sees its purpose as entertainment, not public service, even chuckling when she says of some hypothetical, hapless terrorists handling viruses, "[They're] gonna have to be technically very savvy, otherwise people are going to be dying like flies handling the virus." Although she makes the remark to confirm Racz's point that viruses are not an effective biological weapon, she is clearly more entertained than worried by the lack of realism in the *24* scenario:

> "The first time we were sent the scripts, it was actually a little humorous to read it, I felt like saying, 'God, I want to hire these people; I wish I had that technology and the ability to act as swiftly as they acted.'"

She understands that as docutainment, the information the featurette provides is intended not as an actual consideration of the threat of bioterrorism,[118] but as a promotional element to sustain and generate more interest in the show; it also makes sense that the on-air series, in turn, is less interested in offering viewers fact-checked accuracy than pulse-pounding anxiety.

In mentioning the obesity epidemic, Mascola is just taking her own promotional opportunity to sell her agency's brand message about the variety of health threats. She is well aware that the obesity epidemic would not translate into good television drama.[119] Irrational fears and outrageous scenarios are much more riveting, as Racz acknowledges earlier in the featurette: "In reality to use viruses in a bioterrorist act, it would be very difficult. I can understand the fear." Even though most of what the experts say should calm such fears, the editing of the featurette complements the producers' successful strategy of creating story arcs that are "ripped out of the Zeitgeist of what people's fears are," as Surnow puts it to Mayer. When he says that he purposely plays on people's "paranoia that we're going to be attacked."[120] his choice of the word "paranoia" implies that he knows the threat of a bioterrorist attack is unlikely, but he understandably manipulates the fear because his job is to enthrall viewers enough that they do not grab for the clicker to switch channels or fast forward on the DVR.

It's to be expected that he and the other executive producers privilege narrative intensity over historical accuracy. Surnow explains that his creative team tells the researchers: "this is what we want to do: we want to have this virus show symptoms in people in two hours. Can you find research that supports that?" The process consists of first deciding on a story, finding research to support it, tweaking the story to fit the research, but only if minor modifications need to be made. If no research can be found to support the desired storyline, the research is thrown out. Cofell recalls that they would often tell her: "we want to listen to the reality, but we also need to really respect the story line and what we're trying to create." It's narrative consistency and flow that matters, Loceff explains: "if it is dramatic, a little technical inaccuracy or omission isn't going to hurt it." Still troubled by the inaccuracies, Cofell says, "It's very challenging juggling my responsibilities to a sort of reality and good research and necessities for the storyline." Yet, she also understands that the primary objective is to keep viewers in a state of anxiety so that they will not want to turn away from the set until the final minute of the episode clock runs out.

Surnow does mention trying to heighten reality to offer "maximum fright value," but he also makes truth claims about 24's scenarios. "How we balance the scientific reality versus the dramatic needs of the show is one that we get asked a lot," he says and then asserts, "We try to convey a very real sense of the world of terrorism on our show." To which, Coffel would respond, or a real sense of people's assumptions about terrorism. While he seems to support Coffel's point that the show necessarily cannot achieve scientific accuracy, Surnow actually calls into question the accuracy of science: "On TV you are seeing heightened reality or you are seeing something that resonates with an inner truth but not necessarily the procedural truth of the way things are." Surnow employs a coded binary that ends up downgrading to mere "procedural truth," the established scientific fact that the show discards. He contrasts that to his own capital T truth, which, in the case of bioterrorism, is that an attack is imminent and that extreme measures are necessary in response even if they go against established procedures. David Nevins, the former FOX executive responsible for greenlighting 24 and buying the pilot immediately after hearing a pitch from Surnow and co-creator Bob Cochran, explains that "Joel's politics suffuse the whole show." Nevins says, "the political message of the show is that 'extreme measures are sometimes necessary for the greater good.'" Nevins continues, "The show doesn't have much patience for the niceties of civil liberties or due process. It's clearly coming from somewhere."[121]

While co-executive producer/showrunner Howard Gordon says of the plotlines, "for the most part our imaginations are the source," Surnow never makes such an acknowledgement.[122] Recall his comment, "Unfortunately, what you can imagine is usually true and as outrageous as some of the stuff we come up with, there's always research there to support it," to which he adds, "especially in the theoretical." When he uses the word "outrageous" to describe 24's storylines and plot points, he intends it to mean "unbelievable, but true." In contrast, Gordon means outrageous in the style of the James Bond franchise to which he compares 24: "at a certain level, it was a wish fulfillment. It's a fantasy folks."[123] Sutherland also describes 24 as "a fantastical show" during appearances on Charlie Rose and NPR.[124] In the "it's a silly, but compelling fantasy" camp are Dave Barry and the message board participants on his 24 blog who mock the show and themselves for loving it.[125] As already noted many journalists and online commentators share this perspective, noting that they have to watch with a sense of suspended disbelief.

Then there are those who, when the argument requires, switch between "it's just a TV show" and "it reflects reality." When questioned by Mayer about the impact of 24's representation of torture on national policy and military behavior, Rush Limbaugh quipped: "Torture? It's just a television show! Get a grip." Yet, as moderator of a June 2006 symposium at the conservative think tank, the Heritage Foundation, he praised the show's creators and writers for such a realistic depiction of the War Against Terror, adding, "And most of them are conservative!" The symposium, entitled " '24' and America's Image in Fighting Terrorism: Fact, Fiction, or Does It Matter?" was organized by Virginia Thomas, wife of Supreme Court Justice Clarence Thomas. In attendance as well was Homeland Security Secretary Michael Chertoff, who says of 24, "Frankly, it reflects real life." As Mayer notes, "many prominent conservatives speak of '24' as if it were real," citing the following as an example:

> "John Yoo, the former Justice Department lawyer who helped frame the Bush Administration's 'torture memo'—which, in 2002, authorized the abusive treatment of detainees—invokes the show in his book 'War by Other Means.' He asks, 'What if, as the popular FOX television program "24" recently portrayed, a high-level terrorist leader is caught who knows the location of a nuclear weapon?'"

The disturbing element is not that Surnow makes reality claims for his show as representative of "a very real sense of the world of terrorism," but that it has been lauded by many in the Bush Administration for the same realism. Chertoff contends that the show reflects the reality of government officials and agents "trying to make the best choice with a series of bad options." After the Heritage Foundation event, Chertoff continued an email correspondence with Howard Gordon. In addition, Surnow and others from the show were invited to a private luncheon at the White House with Karl Rove, the deputy chief of staff; Tony Snow, the White House spokesman; Mary Cheney, the Vice-President's daughter; and Lynne Cheney, the Vice-President's wife. The latter is, according to Surnow, "an extreme '24' fan" and, like Surnow, a foe of political correctness, quite an extreme one as proven during her tenure as chairwoman for the National Endowment to the Humanities (1986–93) and by her founding of the American Council of Trustees and Alumni in 1995 to monitor the standards of what she, Limbaugh, and other conservatives categorize as "liberal academia."

When pressed by Mayer in the *New Yorker* interview, Limbaugh switched back to the FOX fair and balanced brand message: "People think that they've got a bunch of right-wing writers and producers at '24,' and they're subtly sending out a message," he said. "I don't think that's happening. They're businessmen, and they don't have an agenda." While his final comment might be simplistic, Meehan's argument suggests that he is right to recognize the important business concerns of television producers. "FOX News' preference for neoconservative opinion over news," for example, "should be recognized as a matter of corporate policy."[126] It's a business strategy to reach an underserved market. The strategy has political implications, as it has the troubling effect of keeping public misperceptions in circulation, Meehan explains:

> Decisions about resource allocation are reflected in news channels' programming. News Corporation uses its FOX News channel to run non-news programs focused on the opinions of such flamboyant hosts as Bill O' Reilly.

> News Corporation's decision to run opinion programs instead of news coverage means that it has allocated money to hire personalities, money that could have been used to hire journalists and fact checkers.[127]

NPR correspondent David Folkenflik claims, "FOX News has completely reshaped the cable news landscape. It brought a highly developed and carefully tended sense of grievance to viewers looking for something different."[128]

Addressing FOX's News' greenlighting of *The Half Hour News Hour*, Surnow's conservative challenge to Jon Stewart's and Comedy Central's fake news, political satire and sketch comedy program, one message board post poses the rhetorical question: "why is a news channel running a comedy show anyhow?" One argument is that it is just a continuation of the way the channel already has blurred the lines between news and entertainment. Pointing to FOX News branding and network strategy, Surnow says that every comedy show was using the "same talking points against George W. Bush and Dick Cheney." He saw an underserved market: "The other side hasn't been skewered in a fair and balanced way."[129] Perhaps *24* is also a way to repurpose FOX News content in another format and to reach viewers who would not tune into the news. After all, many viewers claim that *The Daily Show* is their only source for national news.

24's story arcs are certainly saturated with FOX News staples—the justified circumvention of due process; unwavering faith in the system even though bad individuals try to corrupt it; the importance of maintaining the prestige of the office of the president coupled with the caveat that the 25th amendment should be invoked to remove a president when necessary. *24* also reinforces the concept that it is acceptable to circumvent the constitution for the country's immediate well-being; to put progress ahead of protocol; and to do something unethical if it will save more than it will harm. It offers evidence of a government capable of protecting its citizens and agents who will willingly sacrifice themselves for them. More specifically in the character of Jack Bauer, it celebrates the field agent willing to sacrifice his body and life and the patriotic torturer willing to sacrifice his mental well-being. As the WMD featurette analysis should already have suggested the series as a whole offers evidence by the truckload (preferably Fords) of the threat of WMDs: seasons two and six centered on a nuclear attack (and a nuclear device in one story arc of season four) and seasons three and five dealt with other WMDs, respectively a weaponized virus and nerve gas.

Given its constant referencing of terrorism and WMDs, *24* is a TV show that clearly engages in what John Ellis describes as "working-through." Ellis contends that television functions as a "vast mechanism" for "working-through" and "processing the raw data of news reality into more narrativised, explained forms." Commenting on the televised coverage of the first strikes on Iraq in March 2003, Benjamin Svetkey speaks to Ellis's point: "Perhaps because the war has been so long anticipated, with hours of 'Showdown with Iraq' coverage clogging the cable channels, it somehow feels less urgent now that it's finally unspooling on TV." Ellis explains that working-through is "a process whereby material is not so much

processed into a finished product as continually worried over until it is exhausted."
Spanning the volatile first decade of the twenty-first century, marked as it has been
by 9/11, weaponized virus scares, the War with Iraq, Abu Ghraib prisoner abuse
and torture scandals, and soaring and then plummeting presidential approval
ratings, the series run of *24* has offered such a working-through—not only
by replicating the 24-hour FOX News visual and argumentation style, but also by
filtering FOX News content to those who would never watch it.[130]

With all its focus on impending threats, *24* parallels the FOX News audience
retention strategy of keeping viewers in a heightened state of alert and a constant
state of anxiety. Trained by events of the Fall of 2001, American viewers learned
to keep close tabs on the news because developments broke all the time. Although
that heightened state of alert was short-lived, cable news channels have retained the
continuous looping news crawl at the bottom of the screen, originally used post-9/11
so viewers could be kept abreast of multiple stories simultaneously. While this
format in general inculcates viewers with the feeling that they are "missing" something, FOX News is especially adept at using it to tap into widespread fears.[131]

Watching *24*'s multiple boxes crowding the screen has a similar anxiety-inducing
effect. As Jermyn says, "Rather than leading to a shortened attention span, the
subsequent sense of continually running the risk of 'missing' something in
this process arguably demands a *heightened* attention span from the audience."[132] As
the screen splits into quarters on the series as well as on the news, viewers become
aware of the simultaneity of threats in a post-9/11 world, but the promise is that
Jack Bauer and News Corp., of which he is a part, will be vigilant on the viewers'
behalf. Bill Shine, a FOX News Channel executive producer, said in 2003, "By now
the American public knows we're here 24/7."[133] *24*'s split screens along with its
stylized camerawork also suggest "a narrative point of view which is constantly
assessing, moving, vigilant," Jermyn says.[134] She positions this feature as an aesthetic
device:

> "Working in conjunction with one another, then, the programme's aesthetic
> devices, from real-time to quasi-documentary camera style to split-screen, lead
> the spectator to experience some of the urgency and anxiety felt by Bauer and
> those around him."[135]

Yet, it also has industrial implications as urgency and anxiety are also part of the
Big FOX brand and its signature style. That the combination of graphics and split
screen are a key feature of news programming creates brand consistency.

The consistency of viewpoint between Surnow and FOX News commentators is
also clear. Surnow's representation of Bauer as "the Patriot" responding with the
appropriate aggression and protocol-breaking to "American attacked" and his
assertion that another terrorist attack using WMDs is imminent is echoed by FOX
News commentators. John Gibson, host of FOX News' *The Big Story*, said after the
season six premiere, which featured the detonation of a "suitcase nuke" over Los
Angeles: "Well, it certainly may be fiction for now. But *24*'s Jack Bauer has it right.

People need to wake up to the possibility of nuclear attack." He characterizes *24* as an early warning signal of events that are imminent.[136]

Picking up on this kind of comment, Keith Olbermann, host of MSNBC's liberal-leaning *Countdown*, discussed on January 16, 2007 "the possibility that the show [*24*] was in part a device to get people thinking we were living in a country where a car bomb could go off at any moment." As demonstrated in the earlier analysis, the mobisodes and the DVD extras contribute to this effect as they are platforms that also keep FOX News assumptions in circulation. Olbermann's point is exemplified in a message board post on NewBusters.com offered in response to the *Charlie Rose* interview in which Kiefer Sutherland comments on the unrealistic aspects of *24*'s representation of torture. The post argues that the concept of impending terrorist attack is not a "theoretical whatif scenario. It is more than conceivable that terrorists are planning to detonate a small nuclear device in a US city." Then on his February 2 show, Olbermann noted that his concern about the impact of *24* on public perception "was pooh-poohed in some corners" by people who told him that *24* is "just entertainment." He countered,

> "But now our esteemed colleague Cal Thomas of FOX Noise has pretty much underscored this point in his latest newspaper column: 'Watch the TV drama *24* for what could be our prophetic and imminent future, with a nuclear device exploding in major cities.'"

Thomas, like fellow FOX employees Gibson and Surnow, asserts that *24* is prophetic. An attack will happen, he warns, if the United States pulls out of Iraq as called for by many "privileged and pampered" protestors: "Having concluded we don't have the stomach to fight them on their turf, they might understandably deduce we are even less willing to fight them on ours."[137] Getting tough is necessary, conservative talk radio host Laura Ingraham concurred when she appeared on FOX News' *The O'Reilly Factor*, saying to its host, the fact that the "average American" loves Jack Bauer is "as close to a national referendum that it's O.K. to use tough tactics against high-level Al Qaeda operatives as we're going to get."[138] When Olbermann's remarks were reprinted on the conservative blog *NewsBusters: Exposing and Combating Liberal Media* in an entry that Noel Sheppard says he wrote to enlighten and silence "those foaming about this program being a tool to promote Bush administration views," one of the posts in the commentary section applauds Sheppard and says, "I'm sure some left wing weirdo professor will do a book on '24''s deceptions and how dangerous it is for the public to see it, and the terrible influence it is having, that all the libs will implore is an empirical study."

Intoxicating timetables: ticking bombs and torture

The warning, in fact, came from a much more conservative source, U.S. Army Brigadier General Patrick Finnegan, the Dean of the United States Military

Academy at West Point, who did offer empirical evidence when he and a delegation of top military experts came to the *24* set to talk with producers about the blurring of the line between the fictional representation of torture on *24* and the way actual soldiers were beginning to think of it. David Danzig, a Human Rights First official, arranged the November 2006 meeting to give Finnegan and some high level interrogators an opportunity to voice their concerns about the negative impact of the show's representation of torture as "an effective and permissible use of our Nation's might."[139] The show's support of unethical and illegal intelligence-gathering and interrogation techniques has begun to influence future interrogators and even some of their instructors. Surnow begged out of the meeting to take a conference call with Roger Ailes, the chairman of FOX News Channel, to discuss *The Half Hour News Hour*. Co-creator Bob Cochran and Gordon, among others from the *24* production team, met with Finnegan and three very experienced military and government interrogators: Stuart Herrington (Army), Joe Navarro (FBI), and Tony Lagouranis (Army).

These experts contend that *24* has had a particular impact on the attitude of professionals in the field toward torture, especially given the show's availability in a timeshifted format; soldiers serving in Iraq and Afghanistan watch the DVDs and what they depict immediately influences their behavior. A former Army interrogator in the War in Iraq, Lagouranis explains that the DVDs are very popular with soldiers stationed there. "People watch the shows, and then walk into the interrogation booths and do the same things they've just seen."[140] To combat this problem the Army asked Herrington, who has over three decades of experience as an intelligence officer, to evaluate interrogation procedures at Guantanamo Bay and in Iraq and then "assist in training a new battalion of Iraq-bound interrogators in non-coercive techniques."[141] With the same goal in mind, Finnegan, a lawyer, teaches a course on the laws of war at West Point to seniors who will soon graduate to command posts in the battlefields of Iraq and Afghanistan. Morality is a key concern in the course, which has been structured around both ethical and legal questions. Herrington also wants his students to understand that to sanction the mistreatment of prisoners is not only illegal but also a "slippery moral slope."[142] It's that slipperiness that so disturbs Slavoj Zizek about *24* in which "The pressure of events is so overbearing, the stakes so high, that they necessitate a kind of suspension of ordinary moral concerns."[143] Finnegan says that it muddies what should be clear ethical issues: "The kids see it, and say, 'If torture is wrong, what about "24"?'"[144]

Reminiscent of his distinction between procedural truth and capital T truth in the featurette, Surnow effects a savvy reframing of the relationship between torture and morality and argues that the coercive interrogation techniques Jack employs are representative of "what is right" in the situation. As he explains to Mayer,

> "Isn't it obvious that if there was a nuke in New York City that was about to blow—or any other city in this country—that, even if you were going to go to jail, it would be the right thing to do?"[145]

In Surnow's paradigm, torture might be "procedurally" problematic, but it is representative of an actual truth: do more good than harm. He twists the issue so that Jack represents the moral courage to do what is right even if it is deemed wrong by the establishment.

The establishment here as in the featurette is "Liberal America" that has given more rights to the criminals than the cops, that has made it harder for the good guys to catch the bad guys. This point is echoed by one of the responses on the message board for *NewsBusters*: "Liberals are moral cowards," it proclaims. "The reason they pretend torture doesn't work is cover for that moral cowardice." Elaborating on the point, it continues, "They want to remove themselves from the moral dilemma of having to choose, for example, whether it is justifiable to torture a single individual to elicit information that could save the lives of hundreds of thousands." That Jack never removes himself from that moral dilemma is what makes him heroic, according to *24*. The negative moral impact that such choices have on Jack is, producers argue, part of their fair and balanced depiction of torture. Far from glorifying torture, as critics contend, *24* characterizes torture as a necessary evil.

In contrast, those who oppose torture are represented as too blindly committed to untested academic theories or bureaucratic procedures to recognize the situational necessity of torture. An exchange about the treatment of detainees in season six is emblematic. Arguing in support of the rights of detainees, a lawyer warns an aide to the President, "You continue to arrest innocent people, you're giving the terrorists exactly what they want." The aide dismisses her with sarcasm, "Well! You've got the makings of a splendid law-review article here. I'll pass it on to the President." The lawyer and others like her, *24* implies, do not live in the real world but dwell only in the theoretical realm of academia, always represented on FOX News as a bastion of liberalism that has little understanding of the "real world" with which the President and his administration must deal. In that reality sometimes one has to break the rules to do the right thing.

That's the justification on which the actual President of the United States relies in his September 2006 defense of the actions of the C.I.A in its use of "an alternative set of procedures" in order to "save innocent lives." Brigadier General David R. Irvine says, "I've listened to some of our current leaders say that we should use torture—what they call 'enhanced' interrogation techniques—to combat terrorism. Abandoning our principles is never the answer. An expert interrogator needs to be cleverer not inhuman."[146] Unfortunately, such top level support for the use of "enhanced techniques" has clearly influenced future interrogators, as became evident to Herrington when one posed the following to him:

> "that 'tender-loving-care approach' sounds all well and good, but it takes time. What do we do when the chain of command sends out a requirement and says they need the information by the end of the day, and that thousands of lives depend upon it?"

Herrington says that to combat such misperceptions commanders also need to be taught that "detainee interrogation is not like a water spigot." He worries, though, that the administration and the senior command have since 9/11 adopted the following assumption: "Give the inquisitors the freedom to push the envelope of brutality and good information will follow."[147] In fact, they seem to be saying, adopt the "tender-loving-care approach" at your peril as that softness will leave the United States vulnerable.

That message is clear in season five of *24*. In one episode a liberal white suburbanite becomes symptomatic of moral weakness by standing up for his neighbor, an American teenager of Middle Eastern descent. At first the act seems to be one of bravery as the nerdy weakling holds off two burly neighbors who are trying to attack the boy after the F.B.I. arrests his father as a suspected terrorist. When the teen is revealed to the viewer to be the one aiding the terrorists, the white suburbanite's position changes from that of little guy standing up to bullies to moral coward whose softness allows for terrorists to threaten U.S. security. Not only is he killed by the terrorists, but he also leaves his family and his fellow citizens in danger. The same fate is shared in season four when a white suburban teen, whom the narrative positions as foolish enough to date her Muslim classmate and accept him as a typical American like herself, is killed by his mother to protect the unfolding terrorist plot and the family's identity as a sleeper cell (living and preparing in the U.S. for four and a half years).

Opponents of torture are similarly depicted as endangering the nation through their commitment to liberal sentiments. Season six even includes a rhetorical debate between Jack and President Wayne Palmer about the subject. Countering the claim of a Human Rights lawyer that torturing an uncharged suspect is unconstitutional, Jack says, "I don't wanna bypass the Constitution, but these are extraordinary circumstances." He does bypass chain of command and takes his request to the President who asks for clarification: "You're talking about torturing this man?" To which Jack responds, "Duh!" Actually, that is the kind of comment Dave Barry would make in his blog because this moment of wooden dialogue is one in which Palmer is just there so that Jack can counter a liberal argument against torture. Jack actually says, "I'm talking about doing what's necessary to stop this warhead from being used against us." Note that Jack never acknowledges the act as torture, but instead frames it as self-defense in a ticking-bomb scenario. Still, the President is not ready to justify torture, or at least not willing to condone it officially even though Jack warns him, "If we want to procure any information from this suspect, we're going to have to do it behind closed doors." Irvine also rejects this kind of "tough on terrorists" argument, saying,

> "It's about what's in the strategic interests of the United States. Torture doesn't produce reliable information, but it does harden hearts and minds against us, and torture by any agency of our government puts our own troops at greater risk. It's time to stop playing semantic games about what torture is."[148]

Those semantic games apply as well to those designated as "private contractors" for the U.S. military. Following a similar logic, Jack avoids the issue of the accountability of the U.S. government by quitting CTU; then as a private citizen he tortures the suspect. The maneuver allows him to be accurate (a lawman shouldn't break the law) and American (a self-sacrificing patriot should be willing to do the right thing even if it means he will be punished for it by those following the letter of the law). After he breaks the suspect's fingers and puts a knife to his throat, Jack gets the suspect to talk. Jack THEN knocks him out, saying, "This will help you with the pain." Instead of seeing that as evidence that Jack is sadistic, as Mayer implies when she quotes from the scene, the audience is prompted by the rush of the story to see him as a moral hero and cheer for him as the good guy getting revenge against the bad guy.[149]

Jack always makes a compelling case and his colleagues and superiors who stand in his way seem shortsighted, weak, or cowardly. Indeed, establishing that is the whole point of including exchanges with the President, whose liberal inclinations are at odds with the pressures of the actual crisis as is proven by more wooden dialogue given to Palmer. When an advisor reminds the President that there is a precedent for suspension of rights during wartime, Palmer indignantly retorts, "And Roosevelt interned over 200,000 Japanese-Americans in what most historians consider a shameful mistake." Of this scene Alessandra Stanley says, "the debate can stiffen into a 10th-grade civics lesson" with dialogue that "makes it sound as if the scriptwriters couldn't agree on whether it was truly shameful, and threw in 'most historians' as a palliative."[150] The dialogue is included to fulfill the fair and balanced brand promise, which always tilts the balance toward mocking liberals as PC enforcers of skewed revisionist history. Stanley hints at the argument, but doesn't develop it when she notes of 24, "The series thrives on ideological red herrings—it leans Tom Clancy right, then suddenly will feint left and then back again" and "jukes to the far side of political correctness and even left-wing paranoia."[151] The liberal appears in such scenes so that the point of view can be invalidated.

The credibility of the liberal lawyer, whose fictional organization is modeled on Amnesty International, is more obviously undercut. Her weakness is confirmed when it is revealed that the anonymous tip she received had come from a terrorist; with that detail, the show further underscores what Adam Green in The New York Times concludes is the "moral of the episode: regardless of good intentions, those seeking to protect suspect's rights risk abetting terrorist activities, to catastrophic results."[152] Stanley concurs, "the meddlesome naiveté of civil rights purists is also a leitmotif on '24.'"[153]

Given the different viewpoints voiced in the exchanges in these scenes, it appears at first as if 24 is providing a fair and balanced portrayal of the issue. It does not offer an actual debate on the subject, however; it merely provides Jack two strawmen to knock down so that his knocking out of the suspect can be framed as heroic, even by those who would on paper agree with the lawyer and the president. This scene is one of the moments that occur throughout the series when, as Mayer puts it, "secondary characters raise moral objections to abusive interrogation tactics." This point of view is not the one that is privileged, as is evidenced, Mayer says, by the fact that "Nobody argues that torture doesn't work or that it undermines America's foreign-policy strategy,"[154] or impacts its international reputation, as Finnegan and Herrington say that it has.

Instead, this kind of scene creates situational support for Jack's behavior, always justified by the assumption that it takes moral courage to do what Jack does. Surnow would identify this scene as exemplifying *24*'s fair and balanced depiction of the tension between those who think torture is morally wrong and those who see the situational necessity of it and have the moral courage to inflict it, sacrificing their own mental well-being to save others. For his part in all this torture, Gordon reminded Mayer, "Jack is basically damned" and he knows it.[155] Surnow returns to his point about the heroic torturer (torturer as the cowboy knight) in his comments to Mayer about the delegation's visit to the set:

> We've had all of these torture experts come by recently, and they say, "You don't realize how many people are affected by this. Be careful." They say torture doesn't work. But I don't believe that. I don't think it's honest to say that if someone you love was being held, and you had five minutes to save them, you wouldn't do it. Tell me, what would you do? If someone had one of my children, or my wife, I would *hope* I'd do it. There is nothing—nothing—I wouldn't do.[156]

Surnow's argument begins with an assertion without evidence about the efficacy of torture, but quickly switches to the ethics of torture, appealing to the audience's sentimentality about "protecting innocents." Offering that protection is contingent upon time, specifically the constraining time frame in which interrogators are working to extract information before more harm is done, before more "innocent lives" are lost.

Jack's behavior is justified by the assumption that in a ticking clock scenario different standards apply. Cochran argues that torture can be acceptable "in narrow circumstances," a view he says, drawing on his own background as a lawyer, can be supported by the Constitution: "The Doctrine of Necessity says you can occasionally break the law to prevent greater harm … that could supersede the Convention Against Torture."[157] Although not a widely supported argument among legal scholars, there are a few important exceptions. Harvard Law Professor Alan Dershowitz accepted the concept of the "ticking bomb" case and argued that judges could issue torture warrants, although he later changed his position. Fellow law professor and federal judge Richard Poser offered a similar opinion, "If torture is the only means of obtaining information necessary to prevent the detonation of a nuclear bomb in Times Square, torture should be used."[158] Citing the *24* season two plotline, Supreme Court Justice Antonin Scalia makes an argument for the permissibility of torture in the ticking bomb scenario: "Jack Bauer saved Los Angeles … saved hundreds of thousands of lives." Even though he did so through extracting intelligence through coercive interrogation tactics, Scalia says he should not be charged with a criminal offense: "Are you going to convict Jack Bauer?"[159]

Herrington says that in his entire career he never encountered the ticking bomb scenario, so he is disturbed that it has "become the rallying cry of many well-intentioned but ethically challenged military and civilian personnel." Even more disturbing is that it gets official support: "it has been hawked by a large constituency of senior government officials, from the White House to the Department of Justice to Donald Rumsfeld's Pentagon, and is most recently evidenced in the surfacing of a January 2005 memo, written almost a year after Abu Ghraib, that characterizes face slapping and waterboarding as acceptable conduct."[160] The latter are justified by the ticking bomb defense that "it is necessary and acceptable to torture in the name of saving an American city from 'the next 9-11,'" Herrington says. "This has magnetic appeal for legions of Americans, among them future soldiers," many of them fans of *24*.[161] As Cynthia Fuchs puts it, the torturers on *24* "all feel pressured to get their work done now, and so torture is granted a harried and compelling rationale."[162] When I watch *24*, the speed makes me also root for Jack and, with my attention always drawn to that ticking clock, hastily concur with the compelling rationales he offers. In his *Boston Globe* review of the season five premiere episodes that ran in the compressed time frame of back-to-back two-hour time blocks on Sunday and Monday, Matthew Gilbert captures this feeling: "With the clock ticking in the background, we root for Jack and forgive him his trespasses—not to mention his shootings, wiretappings, and beheadings."[163] Indeed, time and speed are the central conceits of *24*, with most episodes hinging on moments when the demands of speed outweigh the necessity of pre-authorization. Such a compelling narrative structure is understandable for a TV show premised on the real-time conceit, but it becomes more problematic given that the Bush Administration uses such rationales to shape real world policy. *24*'s riveting narrative justifications for why speed is of the essence in defending the nation (and in interrogating witnesses to acquire information to aid in that defense) have striking parallels to what Elaine Scarry terms the "intoxicating timetables of 'rapid response'" that are connected to policy justifications for the War in Iraq. According to Scarry, "Speed has repeatedly been invoked to counter ethical, legal, or constitutional objections to the way our weapons policies and arrangements have slipped further and further beyond democratic structures of self-governance."[164] Scarry claims that, "The most frequent argument used to excuse the setting aside of the Constitution is that the pace of modern life simply does not allow time for obtaining the authorization of Congress, let alone the full citizenry." *24* constantly displays this dynamic, encouraging viewers to privilege the need for speed over the concern for rights and protocol.

Instead of reflecting real-time complexity, the scenarios to which *24*'s creators refer are always clear cut. In her review of the season six premiere Alessandra Stanley says,

> It's like a video game version of a John F. Kennedy School for Government model of presidential decision-making: presidents on "24" are confronted with

split-second choices and horrifying moral dilemmas, like choosing to sacrifice the life of a visiting head of state to save American lives. The Cuban missile crisis lasted 13 days; on "24," the life-or-death consequences of a decision become clear within three commercial breaks.

Torturing suspects is also presented on a timetable necessitating rapid response. Mayer notes,

> Frequently, the dilemma is stark: a resistant suspect can either be accorded due process—allowing a terrorist plot to proceed—or be tortured in pursuit of a lead. Bauer invariably chooses coercion. With unnerving efficiency, suspects are beaten, suffocated, electrocuted, drugged, assaulted with knives, or more exotically abused; almost without fail, these suspects divulge critical secrets.

If the producers really wanted to offer a balanced portrayal, Finnegan says, "They should do a show where torture backfires."[165]

Instead, Surnow and Cochran and the show they created take for granted the notion that coercive interrogation techniques are effective means for extracting intelligence. To reinforce Jack's core characterization as the patriot who gets results through aggression rather than compromise, 24 continually emphasizes the speed with which Jack acquires information from suspects he tortures. Experts argue that its representation of torture quickly yielding useful information is inaccurate. Lagouranis says, "In Iraq, I never saw pain produce intelligence." He admits, "I used severe hypothermia, dogs, and sleep deprivation. I saw suspects after soldiers had gone into their homes and broken their bones, or made them sit on a Humvee's hot exhaust pipes until they got third-degree burns."[166] In each case, "nothing happened," not even when a colleague resorted to waterboarding, the most controversial interrogation technique involving the repeated near-drowning of a suspect. There were some confessions, but, people "just told us what we already knew. It never opened up a stream of new information." From his experience he learned that causing physical pain usually just works to "strengthen the resolve to clam up."[167] The ticking bomb argument also has the same faultline, as Finnegan notes, because if the suspect "can simply hold out several hours, all the more glory—the ticking time bomb will go off!"[168]

As the ticking bomb and the ticking clock are such effective dramatic devices, however, it makes sense that TV producers would continue to employ them after they discovered that they have no basis in reality. Finnegan and his delegation understand why producers would put business before morality. Navarro, one of the F.B.I.'s top experts in questioning techniques, says of the production team, "They were receptive. But they have a format that works. They have won a lot of awards. Why would they want to play with a No. 1 show?" He concedes, "It shows they have a social conscience that they'd even meet with us at all." Lagouranis is less charitable, noting that "They were a bit prickly." Yet, he too understands why: "They have this money-making machine, and we were telling them it's immoral."[169]

Clearly feeling less comfortable with the charge of immorality, Kiefer Sutherland seems torn between asserting "it's just a television show" and worrying about his role in perpetuating misconceptions. Agreeing with the delegation, he says, "Torture is not a way of procuring information. The way of procuring information is actually—is in fact quite the opposite, and, unfortunately, that takes a lot of time." Sutherland tells Rose that the torture represents the urgency of the situation and the desperation of the characters "to solve this one specific thing" under extreme pressure from a ticking clock: "And so it is a dramatic device. It is not to be confused with what we think is right or wrong. And it's a television show." He also concurs with the experts who say that torture does not yield accurate intelligence: "it is widely known that torture—you can torture someone and they'll basically tell you exactly what you want to hear, whether it's true or not, if you put someone in enough pain."

What is effective in terms of real interrogation takes too much time and lacks the dramatic pacing necessary to maintain the tension of 24's real time conceit. In actuality, the U.S. military and the F.B.I. teach "rapport-building," the approach also favored by military interrogators. "Professional interrogation is a developmental process," Herrington says, that requires "extensive preparation. It requires in-depth assessment of the prisoner, all complemented by a healthy measure of guile, wits and patience." The notion that brute force would get better results has been understood as "uninformed and counterproductive, not to mention illegal." As a trainer of interrogators, Herrington conveyed to the chain of command that resorting to force might be tempting, but it would "result in bad information."[170] The influence of 24 is, the West Point delegation argues, making this lesson harder to convey.

Although intrigued by the ideas the delegation presented, the production team made the ticking-clock argument: a real-time TV show cannot afford to represent such time-consuming tactics. Not to mention that the techniques that do work do not make for dramatic TV. How much drama is there in one of the seventeen effective, but non-abusive techniques that Herrington offered producers? Posts to Dave Barry's 24 blog already complain that the CTU seems to want to bore the terrorists to death with "too much talking"; how silly would it seem if Jack Bauer gave his "suspects a postcard to send home in order to get their addresses." Instead Gordon was interested in what the West Point delegation could tell him about truth serums, not if they existed, but which one was the best. There must be a truth serum just like there must be a cyanide capsule.[171]

Similarly, although "the so-called ticking time bomb scenario is a Hollywood construct" that Herrington says he never encountered in his 30 years on the job, people now frequently cite it to "justify the Jack Bauer-like tormenting of a prisoner."[172] As with the representation of viruses in the featurette, 24's depiction of torture conforms to the audience's pop culture-influenced understanding of the necessities and results of interrogation—not only about the pressures on U.S. interrogators in the ticking bomb scenario, but also about the superior abilities both of the Special Forces to extract information from suspects and to withhold information from captors.

One post on *NewsBusters* exemplifies how *24* fans read its depiction of torture through their accumulated media knowledge; the show, therefore, often serves to confirm misperceptions they already had. The respondent signed in as "Jack Bauer" insists that torture does work, but given his reference to Chinese Water Torture, a stock Hollywood convention, he is not basing his claim on any empirical evidence: "Clearly there are certain individuals who have a greater capacity to withstand pain. Special Forces are trained to hold out. But virtually everyone does actually have a breaking point. That is an undeniable, absolute fact." Is it? Or has it just become a movie fact? Hollywood movies always refer to Special Forces and their miraculous skills, but as they are secret forces, what evidence does this commentator or any of us have of their skills except what Hollywood has taught us? Even if we concede that they have such skills, wouldn't it follow that every nation's Special Forces plausibly are trained to withstand interrogation? The logic in the post depends only on Hollywood evidence. It continues,

> "If the aim of the torture is to elicit a specific fact—like the location and names of his fellow terrorists, or a bomb, they will give it up, given the time and effort used to get the info. As it can be quickly verified, where's the upside to the person being tortured? It simply continues if he lied."

He likely gets this idea from *24*, which proposes just such scenarios. The logic is faulty though, Finnegan and Lagouranis would point out, given that the tortured are more likely to meet interrogation with silence or at least misdirection.

As in the virus featurette, *24*'s representation of the efficacy of torture reinforces the public misconception that torture works. A December 2006 report of an advisory panel to the U.S. intelligence community came to the same conclusion as the West Point delegation about the negative impact of the misperceptions *24* circulates: "most observers, even those within professional circles, have unfortunately been influenced by the media's colorful (and artificial) view of interrogation as almost always involving hostility." Mayer sees a clear reference to *24* in the following excerpt from the report:

> Prime-time television increasingly offers up plot lines involving the incineration of metropolitan Los Angeles by an atomic weapon or its depopulation by an aerosol nerve toxin. The characters do not have the time to reflect upon, much less to utilize, what real professionals know to be the "science and art" of "educing information." They want results. Now. The public thinks the same way. They want, and rightly expect, precisely the kind of "protection" that only a skilled intelligence professional can provide. Unfortunately, they have no idea how such a person is supposed to act "in real life."

There is a desire to believe that a Jack Bauer can exist in real life. Glenn Beck, host of CNN Headline News, said, "I want a Jack Bauer out there ... It's the tactics and programs we don't know about that make me sleep well at night."[173]

Matthew Gilbert of *The Boston Globe* understands that impulse as *24* is "a greatest hits of apocalyptic worry, from bombs in airports to chemical warfare. It's condensed dread." To which Jack Bauer is "condensed solace," as he "does anything and everything to save us from doomsday." That explains his appeal among liberals as well as conservatives. Gilbert says, "Many of us who might condemn the idea of his cowboy vigilantism still can't resist the entertainment value of his superheroism each week, what with him being fictional and all," pointing to the fact that the morally conflicted torturer is pure Hollywood fantasy.

Mayer notes how Finnegan and the other experts point out that in reality such a figure would not be a role model; after all, Jack is "coolly rational after committing barbarous acts, including the decapitation of a state's witness with a hacksaw." Navarro explains, "Only a psychopath can torture and be unaffected." But, he adds, "You don't want people like that in your organization. They are untrustworthy, and tend to have grotesque other problems." In contrast, on *24* Jack's actions, while technically sadistic, are represented as defensive and self-sacrificing.[174]

Re-circulating brand identities, circumventing brand resistance

Jack Bauer's appeal is that he is a lawbreaking lawman, the kind of composite character that Robert Ray claims a Hollywood staple. In "The Thematic Paradigm," Ray theorizes that the most popular cinematic characters are good bad boys, composite figures who embody both outlaw and official hero traits. According to Ray, there are two contradictory traditions in the United States which represent the dichotomy of individual and community. Hollywood's composite characters are those who embody diametrically opposed traits (e.g., pacifist soldiers). By having one person embody both heroic traditions, Ray says, these characters appeal to the American collective imagination because they personify the ideal of inclusiveness which is at the heart of the American tradition. In their actual lives Americans are torn between individualistic and communal values, Ray says, so they create mythic characters who magically embody both traditions.[175] I would argue that the Cowboy Knight—unorthodox, yet honest; unrefined, yet honorable; ordinary, yet extraordinary—is the composite figure that has represented the United States since the late nineteenth century.[176] This strong, clear, and appealing national brand representative effectively communicates the identity with which the United States wants to be associated.[177]

That it has such a Cowboy Knight at its center indicates that despite a surface layer of difference, things are essentially the same at the core of *24*: its narrative might play with time, but it still offers situations in which its main character can display the supposedly timeless core American values;[178] its characters might be played by a diverse ensemble cast, but its main character is still the standard Anglo American hero; it might seem critical of the U.S., but its insider outsider character is representative of the beneficence at the core of the American system and of the benevolence of America's intentions in relation to the world. In short, at its heart *24* is about heroic Americans who save the world from disaster; they are cowboy knights gallantly and roughly rescuing others with little thought for their own self-interest; in a bloated bureaucracy, these heroic individuals must follow what they know in their hearts to be right even if it means doing what is legally deemed wrong.

Described as "righteously defiant," Jack Bauer is the latest incarnation of "The Patriot," a positioning that, according to Finnegan, undercuts producers' claims that they are offering a fair and balanced portrayal of torture: "The disturbing thing is that although torture may cause Jack Bauer some angst, it is always the patriotic thing to do."[179] Indeed, as Jack is well aware that inflicting torture has a toxic effect on his mental state, the show implies that it is evidence of his moral superiority that he is willing to damn himself to save others. Zizek argues that on *24*, "if an honest person performs such an act as a grave duty, it confers on him a tragic-ethical grandeur."[180] A typical representation of Jack Bauer as the tortured torturer occurs in a scene from season five in which Audrey, the woman he loves, has to come to terms with his double role as torturer and savior. Her physical and verbal reaction to Jack's behavior both implies that torture works and that she cannot quite reconcile her attraction to Jack with her aversion to his role as torturer. Maybe the problem is, as one post on Dave Barry's *24* blog jokes, "Somehow, even when he's at his most romantic, Jack looks like he's ready to gouge someone's eyes out."[181] In the episode in question those eyes belong to Audrey's brother Richard, who manages to aid terrorists through a combination of his closeted homosexuality, pot-smoking, protesting, and his overall misguided commitment to liberal theories. Audrey warns him to disclose whatever information he has to Jack or he will torture him until he reveals it: "I saw him torture someone today. It's what he's trained to do. He won't stop hurting you until you tell him the truth." Citing this moment, Fuchs argues that the show demonstrates that torture takes its toll on Jack and his relationships. She says, "The truth throughout the season is compromised and undermined by torture." Yet, if the show really wanted to do that, then Audrey would have said instead, "until you tell him what he wants to hear," to emphasize the problem with torture: cause someone enough physical pain and he will say anything to make you stop. Audrey's revulsion makes the scene seem fair and balanced. Mayer argues that this kind of scene conveys the message that torture is troubling, but it works.

It is this scene to which Fuchs refers when she discusses how her own fascination with *24* is connected to its ambivalent representation. "Particularly admirable is *24*'s consistent complications of terror and righteousness." She adds, "... even as the series pitches from one freefalling moment to another, it repeatedly questions such action-movie-standard decisions, not only by the characters abused, but also by those who observe and perpetrate." Like Fuchs, when I watch these kinds of scenes I feel as if *24* is complicating its representation of torture (although upon closer analysis I don't think it is). Fuchs' comments are especially intriguing because like many fans of *24*, including myself, she is a liberal academic who would never be swayed by similar claims if they were made on FOX News. *24* is so effective in expanding its audience beyond core FOX viewers because it uses its "intoxicating timetables of 'rapid response'" to grab people who would be hostile to the FOX fair and balanced brand in other contexts.

Looking at the Audrey and Richard exchange again, this time in the context of an earlier scene in which Richard is pitted against Audrey and their father, the Secretary of Defense, it becomes clearer that Richard is only in the cast of characters so that he can be the liberal perspective against which to argue. The backstory is that Richard, always rebelling against his father, plans to speak at an anti-defense spending protest and his father tries to talk him out of it. Richard ineffectively voices the liberal critique of the conservative U.S government, labeling his father and the administration of which he is a part "liars" with "a psychotic need for power," the same argument Al Franken makes against the Bush Administration. Angered by what he feels is a baseless accusation, Heller snaps, "We serve the cause of freedom, what do you do?" The mise-en-scène and costuming position Richard as an aimless, pot-smoking protestor who talks about saving the environment, but would never actually make the effort to save anything. "Protesting is dangerous for national security," Heller warns. The world is not a "utopia" and, he tells his son, as the "United States has enemies," it needs to spend more on defense. Siding with her father, Audrey says that what makes her angriest is that her brother "doesn't even know the first thing about the politics of all this." Voicing the current conservative critique of the hippie baby boomers, Audrey adds, "He's acting like a spoiled child. He's going to have to grow up someday." Secretary Heller repeats the critique when he says to Richard, "Can't you ever think of anything beside yourself?" Then in a dig against the liberal more hated than Franken, Heller says to Richard that he should stop relying on "6th grade Michael Moore Logic." Even though the elder Hellers resort to all these FOX News staples in their arguments, in the context of the ticking clock scenario even liberal viewers will likely side with them against Richard because he manages to aid inadvertently in getting them kidnapped by terrorists and then withholds information that would have helped Jack quickly rescue them and stop the terrorists. Adding insult to injury, although Audrey understands why Jack has to torture Richard, she decides that she can no longer be in his life because of it.

In his review of the premiere of season five Chris Bersanti captures the way 24 manages to win over those who would not accept 24's logic if it were presented on FOX News. He says that his initial impression of 24 is always that its moral is "Nobody gets away clean" in relation to torture. Yet, he wonders if his feeling that this is the ultimate message of 24 might be

> "my attempt to rationalize my love of a show whose politics and morals I have good reason to suspect are quite at odds with my own. That is, I want to see that Bauer and his compatriots don't really *want* to do the things they have to do, and are spiritually wrecked by it afterward, as a means of justifying how thrilling I find the show, which is like an action-soap opera for the post-9/11 era."

This kind of ambivalence about *24* has increased over the series run. Howard Gordon says that viewer response was different in the first few seasons of *24*: "everybody's fear was more acute, people's tolerance for violence, their own rage, seemed to make Jack's tactics more acceptable."[182] After the prisoner abuse scandals and torture memo as well as the mishandling of the War in Iraq, *24* has seemed more problematic. At first, *24* tried to reflect that ambivalence, maybe even atone for its own misrepresentations. After that "feint left," it veers back to the right for season seven. Gordon says,

> "in the wake of our own abuses in prosecuting this so-called War on Terror, we feel Jack is getting a bum rap. So instead of selling out the entire show and its history and legacy and apologizing for it and ultimately invalidating it, we decided to defend it."[183]

It's not surprising that many online commentaries on *24* defend it as well; what is notable is that they do so by employing the idea that it is "fair and balanced," evidencing the penetration of the FOX brand message. Sheppard's *NewsBusters* blog, which offers extensive excerpts from the 2007 *Charlie Rose* interview with Sutherland, is a good example. Although he does not mention it overtly, Sheppard is a champion for the fair and balanced brand promise. He not only cites the *Charlie Rose* transcript, but he also highlights all the details that would support the claim that *24* is representative of the FOX fair and balanced brand promise. First, he states the most popular claim that *24* is clearly a fair and balanced text because it has both famous liberal as well as conservative fans: the Clintons and Barbra Streisand as well as the Cheneys and John McCain. Rose introduces the topic of fans from both sides of the political spectrum and notes that some like John McCain have even been guest stars. Sutherland confirms:

> "Yes, and Dick Cheney and various people that are huge fans of the show. **And then youve got the Clintons and youve got Barbra Streisand**, and I think one of the great testaments of the show is that the show is incredibly balanced as well."

Sticking to the fair and balanced brand promise, Sutherland remarks that if it weren't balanced, "I dont think you could have it embraced by members of the right and members of the left at the same time." Rose notes that the show has been "**used by people from Barbra Streisand to Rush Limbaugh to make a point**" relevant to the politics of each. Sutherland attributes the applicability of different aspects of *24* to different arguments to the political spectrum of the writing staff: "**There is a representative from the right, and there is a representative from the left**."[184] Although his highlighting of these passages calls attention to Sutherland's point that the writing staff is fair and balanced, Sheppard never offers balance in his comments by acknowledging Surnow's conservative politics. The omission is noticeable, especially given that in these days of the resurgence of auteurism, more weight is usually given to the creator's point of view (even though that is not consistent with the actual collaborative nature of television).[185]

Co-executive producer David Fury sticks to the fair and balanced message as well: "a couple members of our staff lean very heavily toward the right, as there are a couple members that lean very heavily toward the left. We have a wide diversity of different political viewpoints." Fury is cagey on the exact liberal credentials of the writing staff. Like Surnow, Manny Coto, a co-executive producer for seasons six and seven, is identified as a "staunch Republican" and Bob Cochran is a "more moderate" Republican. The closest Fury gets to defining someone on staff as a true liberal is his description of co-executive producer Evan Katz, whom he deems "leaning more toward the left." Of himself Fury says, "I'm a registered Democrat," but he hedges his bets: "I'm either a very liberal Republican or a very conservative Democrat, I'm not sure." Gordon is also "a registered Democrat," but only his wife is identified as "heavily involved with liberal causes".[186] Gordon describes himself as a "left-leaning centrist."[187]

Without any acknowledgment of how the remarks of someone associated with the show are always mediated through the network's expectation s/he will be a brand emissary as well as the power dynamics in the relationships among different members of the production team, Sheppard continues to point to Sutherland's statements as support for the FOX fair and balanced brand promise. He highlights another line from Sutherland who says, "the thing that I can look back to with pride is that **its that balanced, that the polarity of the audience is that diverse**."

In contrast, Sheppard complains that media coverage of *24* has not been fair and balanced, with *Time* and *Newsweek* as well as some TV commentators "carping" about "a perceived conservative slant to the series." He asks why, however, they did not talk to Sutherland, "the admittedly socialist star/executive producer to get his take."[188] The irony is that none of the posts that follow his *24* piece pick up on the fair and balanced brand promise being fulfilled through the casting of Sutherland, but instead decry Sutherland's "socialist" leanings. One does recuperate Sutherland, but only by claiming that he is just espousing liberal outrage at the representation of torture to be politically correct: "I don't think Keifer actually believes that himself, he's just mouthing it." The commentator is more aware than Sheppard of how Sutherland's comments need to be read as carefully crafted statements rather than some kind of unmediated truth:

> "He's an executive producer on 24. He has a lot of clout on the plot. Time after time, either he or others are shown torturing people who give it up. You think if Keifer really believed what he said, that would appear in the show? I think not."

James Cromwell might disagree as he pointed out to an interviewer who questioned him about how his appearance on the show seemed to suggest he condoned torture: "I'm just a guy trying to make a buck."

Other comments posted to the blog suggest an awareness of the complexity of the motivations of the cast and crew of *24*. After all, they are technically all brand spokespeople. None of the comments go so far as to acknowledge that *24* is a media product created by producers and actors whose commentary about the show is often shaped by what their network or the show's co-creators would want them to say. After all, Sutherland was appearing on the talk show two days before the season premiere of his show in order to promote it, likely a contractual obligation. The contradictory comments in these blog posts are duplicated in much of the web commentary about *24*, suggesting that the show performs its intended function: it appeals to multiple audience segments and has enough risky material to keep the bloggers writing about and fighting with each other. All the nasty comments about "Libs" on the *NewsBusters* message board are the same kind voiced about the "Neo-Cons" on liberal sites.

Both liberals and conservatives can watch *24* as elements of it can be seen as confirming the point of view of each. Fury remarks that because people like "to filter their viewing of '24' through their own viewpoint," the writers try to offer "a very diverse viewpoint on the show." He doesn't really offer an example, but he does acknowledge, "Republicans will certainly embrace some of the more right wing aspects of '24,' the take-no-prisoners approach to terrorism, and there are others who recognize that that doesn't work all the time."[189] He adds, "Our executive producer/co-creator, Joel Surnow, is very vocal about his conservative Republican leanings, and he has a lot of friends of his who do enjoy the show and do think it supports their agenda."[190] Fury implies that *24* appeals to a mainstream audience because at times it can seem to be supporting a more liberal point of view. Making that point as well, Sutherland remarks to Rose: "Me, I kind of see things from a left perspective, so I'm always amazed when I see it galvanized by someone on the right." This same point about *24* is made in the mock debate "*24*: Liberal or Conservative" that blogger Steve Silver staged for his site on March 1, 2005 after receiving commentary supporting both sides of the argument.[191] David Palmer, the African American candidate and then U.S. President in the early seasons of *24*, is claimed by "Mr. Liberal." That is, until "Mr. Conservative" counters that the show tells us nothing about Palmer's domestic policies and does not ever label him a Democrat. That Palmer's own VP and cabinet members stage a coup against him could be an argument that they were unhappy that he was either a liberal who became too conservative or a conservative who became too liberal. The liberal notes that during the coup season we learn not only about the egregious "misuse of government power," but that the manipulation is "carried out by a consortium of oil interests." Although that season also conveys a liberal opposition to the idea of "pre-emptive war," the conservative rebuts that *24* is ultimately conservative because all of its seasons have reinforced the idea that the U.S. is "at war with terrorism," offering unambiguous support for the notion of striking back at terrorists. In this effort, "torture is not the last resort, but the first." The last main point goes to the liberal side: that the show "takes pains to balance out the Muslim villains with the Muslim good guys." That final point does not actually prove that *24* is liberal, just that it takes pains to appear fair and balanced. His additional point that it is liberal because it featured a Public Service Announcement by Sutherland in which he offered a disclaimer about the show's misleading representations has also been cited elsewhere as evidence of the ways in its later seasons *24* has "bowed to political correctness," and was just "mouthing" these liberal sentiments to appease Liberal America. Confirming that conflict Fury recalls that Surnow was criticized by his friends for the season six storyline, especially the part about

> [President] Wayne Palmer's sister who was voicing sort of the liberal bent, and her boyfriend, who was incarcerated along with other Muslim prisoners, [whom] we suspected to be involved with terrorism and then weren't. I know Joel got a lot of criticism that, "What, is the show starting to lean toward the left? There are good Muslims that were over-reacting?" We're trying to say that there's no easy answers, basically, and some people look for answers in the show, and some people recognize that that's just not going to come.[192]

The ambivalence of this season was the topic of much debate on message boards and blogs across the web. Again, the way that aspects of *24* can be used for either side of the debate indicates that it has the kind of open-endedness that makes for a broadly appealing media text.

Indeed, *24* is such a striking text because through it FOX circumvents resistance to the FOX brand promise and wins an audience outside its core fans. This circumvention is often aided by the fact that many viewers watch *24* in timeshifted formats outside of the commercial flow that accompanies the original FOX broadcast. Watched as it is broadcast, *24* contains many cringe-worthy moments for liberal viewers because the local versions of FOX News become part of the *24* episode hour given that teasers for the 10 o'clock news run throughout the story breaks. The availability of *24* on alternate platforms expanded the audience to include those who would not normally consume FOX's products given its right wing reputation.

In season five Jack Bauer is given a bit of the fair and balanced treatment, so that he seems to be the "Built Tough" 1950s hero skillfully blended, at least on the surface, with the demographically appealing millennial type. His "sidekick" Chloe also finally gets some millennial accessories, a Mac and a Toyota hybrid, the car of choice in liberal Hollywood. More importantly, Jack Bauer starts to wear a hoodie, an outfit that associates him with a hip, urban sensibility and makes him seem more liberal than he is. The hoodie is a circumvention device—it makes literal the show's claim that Jack Bauer is not a suit-wearing Washington insider even though he is (so much so that he has a direct line to U.S. Presidents); it allows producers to broaden their audience by circumventing the fact that its character is not really alternative to the usual fare—in *24*'s case, alternative to FOX's usual conservative political point of view. Even more intriguing is that Jack wears the same kind of hoodie and carries the same kind of messenger bag as those worn by

Veronica Mars, the alterna teen title character from the UPN/CW series analyzed in the last chapter.

Jack Bauer and Veronica Mars might appear on very different shows in different genres, but in the end they are essentially the same character: the insider outsider, outlaw official hero of which Ray writes. They might even be representative of different politics, but the bottom line for each show is profit; hence, each character has a primary function as a hanger for sponsor goods. The composite heroes that are the prototypical Hollywood product are also ideal spokespeople, not only for a mythic America, but also for the products that yoke themselves to it. In the era of unauthorized wiretapping and coercive interrogation of uncharged "persons of interest" in the War on Terror, Jack Bauer's constant demands for immediate access have political implications, but the phrase "Get IN Now" has the most immediacy for a broadcast TV audience as the slogan for Verizon Wireless, a major sponsor of Must-Click TV programming. When its commercials appear as part of the broadcast flow of 24 or Veronica Mars, they reinforce the story segments' messages about the imperatives of time and speed. The show's other product integration confirms that viewers could "get in now" by having the latest technological gadgets.

Both Veronica Mars and Jack Bauer carry a trendy messenger bag stocked with a variety of cool gadgets to help them to circumvent laws and protocol. In these endeavors Jack, like Veronica, has a diverse group of sidekicks. The difference is that 24 accepts the integration of the formerly white male workplace as an already-accomplished fact that evidences the United States' achievements in democracy. In its better moments, Veronica Mars chips away at that narrative, indicating that gender and racial equality are certainly not already achieved, nor are they ever likely to be, given the systematic power of upper class white male privilege. As the last chapter indicates, that message is not always compatible with the abundance of Abercrombie and other "in" fashions hanging in Veronica's Closet, not to mention her series of rich, white, Abercrombie-wearing boyfriends, as both suggest a conservative core beneath the liberal surface. The posts on the message boards that called attention to these elements worried that they made the supposedly alterna-teen show sometimes seem "too O.C.," a reference to the FOX soap about the woes of the fabulously rich teens of Orange County, CA. By the hoodie season, many conservative fans dedicated to 24 complained that the show was becoming "too mainstream." For these FOX regulars, used to the fair and balanced news stylings of Hannity and Colmes, mainstream meant "too politically correct," a constant lament on sites such as NewsBusters and the rightway.com.

The worry that Jack is "too PC" or that Veronica is "too OC" demonstrates that fans do think of TV shows as having a commitment to a certain politics when their primary commitment always has to be, no matter what the creators or fans want or believe, to sell sponsor goods and consumer lifestyles to desirable demographics. Beneath whatever social and political commentary they offer, these TV shows are also standard Hollywood products, and the thing that matters most is that they inculcate in viewers the desire to attain the products and lifestyles represented as the key to getting in, and staying in, or at least looking like one is a part of some "in" clique. Jack Bauer's hoodie and Veronica Mars' Abercrombie outfits are ways to circumvent too fixed a political position for these characters and hence serve to broaden their appeal and to make sure that there is not a Blue State America watching *West Wing* and *Veronica Mars* and a Red State America watching *24* and *The O.C.*, but that there is one America watching Sprint commercials and accessing its mobisodes, and buying clothes at the mall and arranging via a Verizon Wireless family plan to meet up at a food court chain eatery.

As this chapter's analysis of *24* hopefully suggests, the FOX show is a particularly useful site for thinking about the political as well as the technological side of circumvention. After all, *24* is a TV show about circumvention created by a duo who supported the Bush Administration's troubling policies of circumvention, airing on a network that established itself through bypassing the established rules of broadcasting, one that later turned the circumvention technology available to viewers to its advantage: the availability of the show outside the FOX flow enabled it to gain an audience beyond the network's core market. The next chapter focuses on scheduling and placeshifting in relation to ABC's *Lost*, a long-arc serial that adopted many of the FOX strategies for courting and retaining a broadcast audience. It analyzes *Lost* in the context of the ABC primetime flow into which it was slotted and considers the network's scheduling decisions in relation to changing attitudes toward the series and to long-arc serial mysteries more generally. Given that its 2004–10 series timeline parallels a significant period of evolution not only of the Must-Click TV paradigm but also of new media, the series offers an effective case study through which to consider the impact of new media-enabled behaviors on broadcast television's programming and scheduling decisions.

Chapter Three

Placeshifting, schedule-shifting, and the long-arc serial on ABC

Placeshifting, a new media term that refers to the ability of viewers to shift programming off their television sets and onto hard drives and mobile devices, has multiple meanings in the current television industry.[1] The technological placeshifting that allows viewers to access their in-home devices from remote locations contributes to the ratings drain associated with timeshifted viewing, especially given that many of these placeshifters are accessing stored rather than live broadcasts and watching TV on their own schedules.[2] The networks inadvertently contributed to this phenomenon when they began offering complex dramas such as *Alias* and *Lost* with series-long plot and character arcs that were better suited to viewing off the broadcast TV platform. The Big Three scheduled these kinds of series, at least in part, to respond to the channel spectrum placeshifting that occurred in the late 1990s when HBO began airing its own original series.[3] During the next decade audiences started to view the premium channel as the home of the "quality drama series,"[4] a marketing term that had come to stand for series with "large ensemble casts in well-crafted multilayered narratives that explore a side of American society not found in more formulaic fare."[5] Through its original series, HBO displaced NBC, which had built its late twentieth-century brand reputation on broadcasting both hits like *ER* (1994–2009) and critically acclaimed, although underperforming, dramas including *Homicide: Life on the Street* (1993–99), a quirky cop series that experimented in structure and tone.[6] It was HBO, however, that greenlit the edgy prison drama *Oz* (July 1997–February 2003) from *Homicide*'s writer/producer Tom Fontana and, later, *The Wire* (June 2002–March 2008), from David Simon, the writer of the novel on which *Homicide* is based. As HBO's first weekly hour-long scripted drama, *Oz* generated critical buzz for the premium channel. That buzz intensified in 1999 when David Chase, who had been a producer on CBS's quality drama *Northern Exposure* (1990–95), created HBO's *The Sopranos* (January 1999–June 2007).[7] It quickly became the *It's not TV. It's HBO* signature series. Positioning its television dramas and comedies in relation to conceptions of distinction was a way for HBO to target consumers who prefer products that reinforce their self-conception that their tastes are more elite than everyone else's.[8] Among them are the viewers who, upon learning that Fontana is a television writer, would proudly proclaim, "I don't watch TV" and then recount in detail the latest episode of *Sex and the City*.[9] Fontana's anecdote indicates how in the late 1990s NBC's self-proclaimed status as the location on television for "quality TV" had already been undercut by HBO's skilled marketing and programming choices.[10] It did not help that during the next decade, broadcast networks contributed to the migration of the "quality drama" to cable by giving more primetime slots to reality programming.

Just when it seemed that the broadcast networks had given up on scripted dramas, ABC, the one most enamored of and most burned by its overdependence on the primetime gameshow and reality gamedocs and docusoaps, surprised everyone with its breakout 2004–5 scripted series,[11] especially *Lost*, a genre- and time-bending long-arc serial about plane crash survivors stranded on a mysterious island. For a brief time, *Lost* changed notions of what genres and formats could occupy the prime real estate on the Big Three.[12] With its serialized story, giant cast, and genre emphasis, *Lost* "did go against, what people believed was viable television," series co-creator J. J. Abrams said in a *Nightline* interview in 2006. As is typical in the television industry, all the networks, including ABC, immediately tried to copycat *Lost* without considering the impossible time demands following several of this kind of series simultaneously would make on audiences. For a time it seemed as if long-arc serial dramas would dominate broadcast television with some on the 2005–6 schedule and the bulk arriving in 2006–7. Unfortunately, NBC's *Surface*, ABC's *Invasion*, and CBS's *Threshold* only lasted the 2005–6 season, while NBC's *Kidnapped*, CBS's *Smith*, FOX's *Vanished*, and CW's *Runaway* did not make it through the 2006–7 season. CBS did gain a cult favorite with *Jericho* and NBC scored a surprise hit with *Heroes*, whose production team featured alums from *Alias*, *Smallville*, and *Lost*. ABC thought that it had two big winners for 2006 with *Six Degrees*, an interconnected strangers mystery from Abrams' Bad Robot production company, and *The Nine*, the reverse-timeline hostage situation mystery series for which *Lost* was the 2006 lead-in, but neither succeeded in the ratings. FOX's *Prison Break* debuted in 2005 and thereafter built off the buzz generated for *24* and was considered a hit for FOX although its ratings had steadily declined by the time of its series finale in 2009. With the 2006–7 schedule cluttered with too many dramas whose long-arcs required committed viewing, it is no wonder that most did not last beyond a single season.

They were fairly high quality series, but there were just too many for viewers to invest in them all. One programmer predicted the outcome when the network slates were announced at the May upfront presentations for advertisers: "If a person can only commit to two or three serials, how many can the schedule support?"[13] *Mediaweek* saw the problem in terms of scheduling: "Do you break up the season in blocks of six or eight, or 22 in a row for half a season, à la *24*? Are they repeatable?"[14] If not, people can't catch up if they miss episodes, but if they are repeated, loyal viewers get frustrated, which are precisely the two things that happened in the 2006 season. The failure of these new series to generate good ratings and the subsequent decline of *Lost*'s numbers caused networks to reevaluate the suitability of the long-arc serial for broadcast schedules. By the 2008 season they started to shift back to the fringes, with only FOX willing to take a risk on cult series *Dollhouse* from *Buffy the Vampire Slayer*'s creator Joss Whedon and the aptly named serial mystery *Fringe* from *Lost* co-creator J. J. Abrams and *Alias*'s Alex Kurtzman and Roberto Orci. During the decade CBS secured its place as a ratings leader through procedurals, but also tried to attract younger viewers with more fringe fare, offering in 2007 its own WB-inflected sexy vampire-themed series *Moonlight* and in spring 2009 the long-arc horror mystery *Harper's Island*. Neither made it on the next year's schedule. During those seasons NBC was growing more tentative about its long-arc series *Heroes*, which had lost viewers since its 2006–7 debut season. Nevertheless, NBC seemed as if it were still willing to take a risk on the form when it greenlit *Day One*, a long-arc alien invasion serial created by former *Heroes* co-executive producer Jesse Alexander. The series was originally scheduled to start its run in winter 2010, but in fall 2009 NBC re-categorized *Day One* as a miniseries and suggested its tentativeness by making no promises about producing the rest of the original thirteen-episode order if it achieved high ratings. By January 2010, it was downgraded again to a two-hour TV movie that the network said would act as a backdoor pilot, but its future as a series seemed more and more unlikely.[15] From its inception ABC's *V*, an alien invasion miniseries remake, was scheduled for fall 2009 as short-run special event programming, but ABC showed more faith in the serial mystery by pre-ordering nine follow-up episodes for its return in March. ABC also put its full September 2009 premiere resources behind its new long-arc serial entrant *Flash Forward* because the network hoped to build the series' audience prior to the January 2010 return of *Lost* for its final season and to pick up even more of its audience share after it ended in May. Although *Flash Forward* started out strong, its long-term prognosis remains uncertain as of this writing, an issue I address in the conclusion's discussion of whether networks are growing unwilling to invest in long-arc serials given that the format seems only to be able to generate high ratings for about two seasons before the numbers start to decline when more and more viewers choose to watch in placeshifted and timeshifted formats.

That cycle applies to every long-arc series thus far, including *Lost*. To combat the problem ABC adopted the scheduling and windowing strategies FOX pioneered for *24*.[16] ABC compressed the time between *Lost*'s distribution windows and utilized alternate content delivery systems to make the series available to those who needed to catch up in order to watch the next on-air episode. As with *24* before it, *Lost* saw a boost in its ratings between seasons one and two because of the release of the DVD immediately before the premiere of the new season. Over time it had more trouble attracting and maintaining the casual viewers needed for blockbuster ratings because it really required sequential viewing not only from the start of the season as did *24*, but from the start of the series itself. As the mysteries piled on top of mysteries, the only way for a casual viewer to catch up was via an alternate delivery platform. Watching it in blocks of episodes made the convolutions of the series less pronounced because viewers could keep watching episodes if they wanted to get to the answers each season finale provided to some of *Lost*'s mysteries. Eventually many viewers found it more satisfying to watch it in some placeshifted or timeshifted manner as the record DVD sales suggest.[17] New media modes of access do make it more plausible for a long-arc serial like *Lost* to maintain an audience by providing viewers with more ways to follow and keep up with it. The audience built in this way, however, is not a broadcast TV audience that counts toward ratings numbers, which is the fundamental problem with long-arc series. They are designed to combat channel spectrum placeshifting of broadcast viewers to cable by offering equally compelling programming. They succeed in attracting people to broadcast TV products, but not necessarily in encouraging them to watch these series on TV because their form is better suited to viewing via DVD, DVR or download.

Without a DVD available prior to its second season or any of the later multi-platform distribution and windowing strategies from which *Lost* benefited over its series run, *Alias* had even less of a chance of success of attracting and maintaining on-air viewers. The history of *Lost*'s long-arc predecessor at ABC demonstrates that the time demands of broadcast TV have a significant impact on its content. If *Alias* were not forced to accommodate casual viewers, for example, and abandon the cliffhanger structure that was one of its key appeals, it might have had several seasons as good as the first. Instead the constant attempts to transform the cult series into a blockbuster took their toll and it was canceled in 2006. From the outset *Alias* was an ambitious choice for ABC given that it brought the more fringe science fiction and fantastic genres to a Big Three network. Abrams said his intention with *Alias* was to do "a familiar genre done with intelligence." He added, "TV doesn't typically do that kind of thing. It does medical shows really well. It's great with police and courtroom genres. But you have to look to FOX and the WBs of the world to find more fringe, out-there stuff."[18] Abrams' comments about the place on the channel spectrum on which the *It's not TV* series are located are ironic given that these kinds of series were only briefly embraced by the Big Three.

Alias made it onto the schedule at a time when ABC was trying to copycat some of the WB's success and attract some of its narrowcast *for those who think young* demographic. When Abrams and some members of his *Felicity* production team moved over from the WB to create *Alias*, ABC hoped that they would bring with them some of the niche audience from the netlet on which the successful college-age melodrama had been running since 1998. In the third season of *Felicity* Abrams joked with his production team about what they could do "if Felicity were recruited by the CIA, because she could go on incredible missions and have kick-ass fights and stunts!"[19] Then he created the first season of *Alias*, which was about Sydney Bristow, "a grad student who lived a double life and had trouble with Dad," a characterization that enabled the writers to tell a "story about a family where there are secrets, and what happens when those truths emerge."[20] The fact that she quickly learns that her father is also a spy puts the series in the dysfunctional family/business hybrid category with *The Sopranos*. One second season premiere print advertisement that ran on the back cover of the September 22, 2002 *Entertainment Weekly* positioned *Alias* as a *Sopranos*-lite with the tagline, "Spying. Stealing. Murder. And you think your family has issues." A steely-eyed, leather-clad, and midriff-baring Sydney Bristow stands between and slightly in front of her father Jack (a "black ops" CIA agent) and her presumed-dead, but recently resurfaced mother "Laura" (aka Russian double agent Irina Derevko).[21]

Alias has similarities as well to *24* and *Smallville*, both premiering in the same 2001 season. Abrams compared Jennifer Garner's portrayal of Sydney Bristow to Clark Kent, saying "she has this quality of the girl next door, the girl you'd want to know, or date, or be. And then the surprise—she's lethal."[22] It helps that she puts on a series of sexy costumes to become, as *Entertainment Weekly* put it, "the international-action-accessorized-fashion-girl" who was "stirring things up on an otherwise unglam ABC."[23] The chance to play a sexy and lethal spy appealed to Garner, who won a Golden Globe for her portrayal. Yet, the way she describes her attraction to the character sounds as if she sees Sydney Bristow as a composite of Superman alter ego Clark Kent and his best friend investigative reporter Chloe Sullivan, the lead characters of *Smallville*. While she makes no mention of Chloe or the WB series, Garner does reveal that her favorite childhood book was *Harriet, the Spy* and that she imagined Sydney as having some of that character's investigative curiosity.[24]

Alias sounds like a series that would attract the WB audience, but it did not and *Alias* remained a cult series throughout its run.[25] Despite a premise that seemed to have mass appeal, Abrams was aware that his series "was probably not a mainstream show."[26] That did not stop the network from trying to transform *Alias* into a mainstream hit. As a result, the production team was under constant pressure from ABC to tone down its long-arc, serial mystery elements and offer more stand-alone closed story arc episodes to bring in new viewers each week. The writers made several changes, including scrapping its spy-agency-within-a-spy-agency premise and transforming the evil mastermind of season one into a more ambivalent figure.[27] The team kept tinkering with his character and with the series structure more generally, which did not help it maintain viewers and did little to attract new ones. With the availability of episodes on iTunes download and the network media players still several years in the future, *Alias* had a hard time picking up new viewers over the life of the series and never generated the ratings that would move it beyond cult status.

The long-arc serial mystery and broadcast time paradigms

When members of the *Alias* production team became part of the team on *Lost*, they brought with them the knowledge of what had not worked on *Alias*. For a while they seemed to perfect the balance and *Lost* had a brief run at the top of the ratings in its second season. *Lost*'s serial mystery structure, like *Alias*'s, is fundamentally at odds with the time-based economic model of broadcast television. It can only stay on the air if it remains a text some viewers will watch on-air and if its story segments are made to accommodate the timed commercial interruptions that define advertiser-supported broadcast television.[28] Given its thematic complexities, it is hardly surprising that the series constantly strained against the fact that it was necessarily fixed in broadcast time, which has traditionally been organized around: the segmentation of a series over a season; of an episode over an hour; of episodes interrupted by saleable commercial time and network self-promotional spots. *Lost* exemplifies the tension between the production team's preset series timeline and the fluctuations of industrial time—in that it is supposed to be a story that unfolds in certain increments—divided into story segments, weekly episodes, seasons—and yet it is neither aired nor consumed in that way.

While it generates revenue from the various commercial-free ways that viewers watch it, *Lost* is still most important to ABC as a drama that can be slotted into a one-hour block that allows for precisely timed breaks for commercials. Emmy categories might place premium cable series alongside broadcast series as if they are in an equal competition, but each is produced within a different time paradigm, with basic cable (e.g., TNT, FX) falling somewhere in between. Broadcast TV is not given the leisure to develop and broadcast at its own pace as was *The Sopranos*. Embedded in the HBO approach is the *auteur* system, the assumption that Chase is an artist who needs time to develop a high quality product in a process that cannot be rushed.[29] HBO was not thrilled with this arrangement, but it did like the results. The premium cable model allows for flexible time between seasons, with *The Sopranos* exemplifying the artistic creation that was aired when it was ready, often leaving over a year between seasons and allowing for variable length episode runs.

Given its revenue model, HBO has to convince subscribers to buy in to the idea that it airs the kind of premium content across the spectrum of its programming types, or even just in one category, that subscribers especially value, and thus, for which they are willing to pay a monthly fee. Subscribers need only to continue to think that HBO has the kinds of shows that they want to watch, but HBO gets the fee whether they watch them or not. It only has to maintain the reputation of having particular kinds of shows, in other words, to entice new viewers to subscribe and to keep the current ones from canceling. As a certain amount of turnover, or churn, is inevitable each month, HBO does have to keep circulating its brand identity and creating buzz for its shows to attract new viewers.

On ratings-driven broadcast TV, a series is doing only as well as its latest episode's numbers say it is because they set ad rates or determine if expected viewer projections are met. That episode, therefore, has to balance between keeping its loyal viewers engaged and offering appeal for casual viewers, while adding a few hooks to entice channel-surfers. The ratings numbers that determine its success are based on the viewing choices of a small, but supposedly representative group of people who watch each episode as it airs. When *Lost* premiered, the measurement of its ratings did not count any timeshifted viewing. Nielsen Media Research did later expand its measurement time frame to include same-night DVR playback within the overnights and overnights plus playback up to seven days. That *Lost* is watched in an extreme timeshifted format, months or even years after its original broadcast, might add to the overall revenue associated with *Lost* as a multiplatform product, but it has little impact on *Lost* as a broadcast series. It needs ratings points to generate the interest from advertisers that will keep the series on the air and make it viable broadcast television.

The content of *Lost*, particularly the way the story is paced and the characters are developed, also depends on the fact that a broadcast network expects a hit series to be on-air for an extended time (e.g., 24 episodes for *Lost*'s first season). Instead of having the leisure for the creative minds producing it to come back when they are ready with new episodes, the series is required to return for a new season at a fixed time increment dictated by its network and sometimes it must stay on the air after its creators feel as if the story should come to a natural close, as was the case with *The X-Files*.[30] ABC became flexible in its understanding of broadcast time in relation to *Lost* when it started to experiment with the times when the series would premiere. The network had already adopted the FOX January premiere strategy for the fourth season. The change was due, in part, to the 2007 Writers' Strike. Like many shows that season, *Lost* finished fewer episodes than intended. The season's thirteen episodes plus a two-hour season finale preceded by a clip show established a precedent for a reduced episode order for the future seasons. With fewer episodes to produce, the team could spend more time striking a careful balance between the development of characters and the long-arc mysteries. The episodes could be tighter as they did not have to stretch out the season's "reveals" over twenty-five episodes. More generally, the Writers' Strike allowed networks—much to the chagrin of some writers, actors, and production teams used to the long-standing broadcast model—to adopt a cable-style season structure of series with fewer episodes that ran consecutively and often premiered outside of the usual September–October period. *Lost* had already begun gravitating toward this model in season three, which was divided into fall and winter "chapters." The season was oddly split, however, with six episodes running until November followed by a block of sixteen that began in February when it aired at 10 p.m.[31] This split caused its own problems, but it did allow the writers the time to address the weaknesses that arose within the episode arcs in the fall. While season four premiered in January and ran until May, it was not until season five's late January to early May season structure that *Lost* had an almost uninterrupted consecutive episode season.

All of these changes represent modifications of networks' and viewers' expectations about typical broadcast TV time, which has for decades revolved around a fixed amount of time between seasons, separated by a summer hiatus. Formerly seen as a repeat period, summer has since become a time during which the "B"-level reality programming runs. Once basic cable networks began launching their new original series in the summer, they put pressure on the broadcast networks to offer a tiered premiere schedule, with the prime fall season followed by series premieres in winter, spring, and summer.[32] When *Lost* was coming on-air in 2004, reality series had moved into the prime fall premiere period and were increasingly each given two series cycles a year.

This adoption of an annual calendar for broadcast series premieres was not the only reflection of the impact of the cable structure on broadcast network practices.

In addition to having non-fall premiere dates and an uninterrupted weekly install-ment formula, premium cable offers multiple encore presentations, affording sub-scribers the chance to catch up anytime before the next installment airs. With the introduction of Video-On-Demand (VOD), a distribution platform with which it had been experimenting for its feature film offerings since the early 1990s, HBO offered its early twenty-first-century subscribers the premium perk of being able to watch episodes at the click of their remote.[33] The flexi-time of cable structure enables an audience to grow over the week whereas the fixed time of network TV makes it harder for a series to gain new viewers between weekly episodes.

ABC was the first network to offer its broadcast viewers a version of VOD exclusivity, albeit off the television platform. Disney made a deal with iTunes in October 2005 that allowed for some Disney-ABC Television Group series, includ-ing *Lost*, to be available on what would become the internet's premiere pay-per-download video site. The April–June 2006 trial run of ad-sponsored episodes available on demand via streaming video on abc.com followed and the feature eventually became permanent on ABC's site and the model was adopted by the other networks.[34] VOD availability gave *Lost* a way for viewers to keep up with the series during that second season so that it could still attract casual viewers and hopefully convert them into loyals. As seasons stacked up over time, it became harder and harder for new viewers to start to watch the on-air episodes as they aired. *24* offered more of a reboot each season, especially in season three when only a few cast members returned, so that each season was a different single 24-hour period in the main character's life. There were certainly things that a loyal viewer of the previous seasons would understand that a new viewer would not, but the structure was such that the new viewer could comfortably jump in at a new season of *24* and make sense of the day-to-day storyline. The same was not really true of *Lost*. To court potential viewers, producers had to offer longer and longer "previously on *Lost*" recaps. By the later seasons, they were necessary even for loyal on-air viewers because they pointed out the snippets of specific information from the course of all the seasons thus far that would be relevant to a basic under-standing of the new events unfolding in the episode.

The one aspect of the structure that made this dynamic a bit manageable was that each episode had flashback segments that focused in depth on the backstory of a single character. The recaps could draw from several seasons of character-specific clips to offer a broad idea of the character and the events leading to the develop-ment of the character arc within the new episode. These overviews enabled new viewers to be given most of the information they would need to make sense of that episode. Following the series-long arcs, however, was a different story. *Lost* was not a very broadcast-friendly TV show because its timeshifting structure and themes meant that it could not really accommodate casual viewers despite its continuing attempts to do so. With each successive season, the time it would take for viewers to watch all the previous episodes so that they could watch the new season of *Lost* as it aired was increasing. By its third season *Lost* was more likely to lose viewers than to gain new ones. Anyone who wanted to start viewing *Lost* might opt for a season-pass on a content delivery platform such as iTunes or Netflix's DVD delivery service. With these alternate platforms, viewers could let the unwatched episodes accumulate so that they could watch several seasons consecutively. It was always possible that these alternate platform viewers would catch up enough to watch the latest season on-air, which was the only way to avoid someone spoiling the season's big reveals.

The way each episode draws on details from a discontinuous set of episodes over the course of the series as a whole makes *Lost* a series that is particularly ill-suited to the broadcast platform. It is much easier to remember all these narrative details if you are watching multiple episodes or, even better, multiple seasons in a period of time much more compressed than the typical broadcast season schedule. Those watching each episode on the drawn out and often interrupted September to May network timetable would be more likely to get confused and lose interest over time. The compressed viewing made possible by DVD keeps in balance the fascination-frustration dynamic[35] that characterizes fandom of long-arc television because the answers that are doled out by the writers can be acquired as slowly or as quickly as the DVD viewer desires. Those with a low frustration threshold could simply wait to begin watching the series so that they could watch multiple seasons at once, which many preferred once the series adopted a January to May season and viewers had to wait the long stretch of time between the May finale and the January premiere to learn the fate of the characters.

While alternate platform availability transforms *Lost* into a much more manageable text by enabling viewers to make their own schedules and watch at their desired pace, broadcast television and the ratings it needs to generate still make scheduling one of the most important network practices. The day and time on which a television series airs impacts reception. Scheduling a series on a Thursday suggests the network has great faith in its potential as a blockbuster because it is the night for which Hollywood studios and other advertisers pay a premium rate to try to reach weekend filmgoers, diners, and shoppers. While *Alias*'s original Sunday time slot opposite *The X-Files* suggested its cult status, its shift off the schedule for fall 2004 and its shift back on in the Wednesday slot after *Lost* in spring 2005 suggest a changing attitude toward the potential of creating a narrowcast-broadcast series, that is, "a bona fide hit that has a cult following."[36] Concurring with that *Washington Post* description of *Lost* in its second season, *Time* called the series "an unapologetically knotty, mass-market commercial hit [that] demands commitment-and gets it."[37] When *Alias* was relocated to Thursdays for fall 2005, ABC may have been signaling its belief of its potential as a narrowcast-broadcast series. Up against *Survivor*, *Alias* failed to gain traction in its 8 p.m. slot and spent the rest of year being shifted off and then back on to the schedule. First, it landed on Wednesdays for a brief December run and then was taken off for a hiatus and when it returned it aired at odd times so that even the most dedicated viewer might not know where to find it. While there were certainly many factors leading to the cancellation of *Alias* after that season, scheduling played a role.

Fast forward to fall 2009 and *Fringe*, another Abrams-affiliated series, found itself shifted onto the competitive Thursday schedule, but as a 9 p.m. signature series for FOX, which had no 10 p.m. series and less steep ratings expectations than the three full-service networks. FOX Entertainment president Kevin Reilly explained the scheduling logic: "We're not looking to take down *CSI* or *Grey's Anatomy*." Instead, *Fringe*, whose mythology procedural hybrid structure *Entertainment Weekly* characterizes as *The X-Files* meets *CSI*, just needs "to get in there and remain consistent," because, as Reilly puts it, FOX "can make money, even at a more modest rating."[38]

Despite even higher quality content than in its freshman season, *Fringe* had a hard time holding its own given that the Thursday slots were the schedule's prime real estate occupied by each network's signature series: CBS's *Survivor* and *CSI*, NBC's smart comedy blocks including *The Office* and *30 Rock*, CW's *Vampire Diaries* and *Supernatural*, and ABC's *Flash Forward* and *Grey's Anatomy*. As *Flash Forward* had already been named the long-arc successor to *Lost*, perhaps FOX assumed that at the 9 p.m. hour its viewers would be more likely to switch over to *Fringe* than stay on ABC for *Grey's*. Of the scheduling move, Abrams says that it shows that FOX has faith in the series, but, as co-executive producer Jeff Pinkner points out, the night is filled with the series everybody wants to watch.[39] A dual-recording DVR could not even keep up with them all.

Schedule-shifting at ABC

John Ellis asserts that the "dynamic process of scheduling" is a primary shaping force of the reception and assumed meanings of a television program.[40] When analyzing its series, Ellis contends that attention needs to be paid to the "architecture of the entire output"[41] of a network. Looking at that architecture prior to and after the 2004 scheduling of *Lost* and that series' relationship to others on the schedule (e.g., the scripted series *Desperate Housewives*, *Alias*, and *Grey's Anatomy* and reality franchises *The Bachelor*, *The Mole*, and *Dancing with the Stars*), reveals how ABC was positioning its series and network brand, especially in relation to those of CBS, NBC, and HBO.

Prior to its breakout 2004–5 season, ABC's brand identity was in crisis, having been critiqued by the press for the foolishness of big gambles and losses with unscripted fare. It enjoyed a brief moment at the top of the rankings because of the way game show *Who Wants to Be a Millionaire?* became a national obsession, but ABC schedulers soon turned success into disaster by stripping it across four prime-time slots in 2000–1.[42] Like the rest of the networks, it then overinvested in reality programs and saturated its schedule with them. ABC was singled out for its excesses because it had both failed to develop any hit dramas or sitcoms and had greenlit some of the more controversial reality series, including *I'm a Celebrity … Get Me Out of Here!*, *Are You Hot*, and *Extreme Makeover* [the plastic surgery edition], all of which sounded to critics more like FOX fare. Some commentators theorized that ABC failed to generate distinctive hits because it was putting less energy into targeting suburbia's young families with kids, the demographics with which it first differentiated itself in the 1950s with *Disneyland* and *The Mickey Mouse Club*. In the *New York Times* Bill Carter noted that in its scripted series ABC strayed too far from its comedy brand, which had been rooted in "family-style shows with largely blue-collar characters."[43] Commenting in 2001, ABC co-chairman Stu Bloomberg located the problem in the attempts by his late 1990s predecessors "to change the sensibility of the network during those years, especially in comedy."[44] When he was hired as President of Touchstone Television (the television production division that would be renamed ABC Studios), Steve McPherson based his strategy on the idea that ABC needed to develop new "family-centric comedies."[45] When ABC moved away from the kinds of series with which it had been associated (e.g., *Home Improvement* and *Roseanne*) and made a play for the upscale, urban elite demographic attracted to NBC's self-proclaimed sophisticated sitcoms such as *Will & Grace*, it succeeded only in losing its differentiated position in the marketplace. Trying and failing to copycat NBC's ensemble comedies and dramas, ABC was also no longer producing series that gathered family audiences in front of a single television set.[46] Household television viewing practices had changed more generally once families had more than one television set in the house. The adults and children were increasingly watching different programming. When families did gather together in front of a single television set, it was for *American Idol*, which was a smash hit by 2004–5 when its Tuesday airing finished first with 27.31 million, followed by Wednesday's with 26.69 million viewers.[47] During each of its series cycles for the rest of the decade, *Idol* continued to rest comfortably at the top of the ratings, often garnering over 30 million viewers.[48]

Although none could catch up to *Idol*'s numbers, other reality series gathered audiences as well and each network eventually found its own ratings-generator.[49] CBS had been the network to popularize primetime reality TV in the U.S. with its original gamedoc *Survivor* and its imported format *Big Brother*.[50] It even had the critically acclaimed *The Amazing Race*, which established a prestige reality category that *Extreme Makeover Home Edition* would occupy at ABC after it quietly shelved the controversial plastic surgery edition.[51] NBC finally hit on a winning franchise with *The Apprentice*, which debuted in January 2004. By that point ABC was already offering *The Bachelorette*, a franchise iteration of its hit dating series *The Bachelor*.[52] These series enabled schedule flexibility as they had short runs and could be part of a new model in which premieres could be staggered on an annual calendar.[53] These shows usually gave broadcasters their largest audiences, but even if they had middling ratings, they were still cheaper to produce than scripted series given their financing model, product integration opportunities, production costs, non-union workers, and a host of other economic factors.[54] Critics might have complained about *Joe Millionaire* and the other controversial series on FOX, for example, but the network was thrilled with these new revenue- and ratings-generators. They could also point to the ratings and suggest that it was audience desires and not economics that were motivating their choices, as Sandy Grushow, the chairman of the FOX Entertainment Group, did when he indicated why he would continue to embrace reality television: "I am excited by the notion that this form of programming, over which there has been a lot of hand-wringing, can galvanize a huge audience to come back to network television."[55] ABC was hoping to find that series that could galvanize viewers in the way that *Survivor* had. An early attempt was *The Mole*, a series that required of contestants a combination of *Amazing Race* globe trekking and *Survivor* savvy strategizing. While the original version was most successful (and hosted by Anderson Cooper), ABC later offered two seasons of *Celebrity Mole*. It paired the first of those with its newcomer *I'm a Celebrity ... Get Me Out of Here!*, and both series performed well enough in the ratings to become franchises,[56] although they also brought criticism of the scheduling choices of ABC chairman Lloyd Braun.[57]

Braun continued his quest in the 2004 development season to try to find a series that could compete with *Survivor,* the appeal of which he attributed to its structure and not the fact that it was a new format. As he put it in 2001, "People don't watch a genre. They watch good television. 'Survivor' is really good television."[58] That Braun had been burned already by the reality boom might explain why he turned to scripted series development in search of his blockbuster when everyone else was still caught up in the reality boom. He knew from experience that over-investment in one area was a bad strategy, comparing reality TV speculation to the stock market: "Those who put all their money into this might end up looking foolish in the end."[59] He wisely changed course in search of good scripted series, albeit ones he thought would complement reality programming.

With its on-location filming, its marooned-somewhere-in-the-South-Pacific premise and a thematic link to Australia, the country from which Oceanic Airlines doomed flight 815 originates and the setting for many of the flashbacks, *Lost* was just the kind of compelling television series that could challenge Mark Burnett's reality franchise.[60] Braun's original idea was for a hybrid of *Survivor* and *Castaway*, the feature film that had recently performed well on ABC's schedule.[61] When he didn't like the first draft of the concept he received, he enlisted Abrams to generate a better version and then teamed him with Damon Lindelof.[62] Together they came up with an outline for a series that built on Abrams' mystery island premise.[63] Writing in *The Los Angeles Times* Maria Elena Fernandez attributes the show's core appeal to the casting and the writing, which really is what "sparked water-cooler chatter beyond the island's frightening man-eating monster, polar bears and other spooky human inhabitants."[64] Braun said he knew that it was "the best piece of television," he'd ever read and felt as if it would be a quality drama on the level of *ER*. "With its unmatched pan-demographic cast of characters who all defy stereotypical expectations," *Lost* moves beyond that NBC series, Fernandez argues.[65] The cast of characters includes a Korean couple Jin and Sun. Of his casting as Jin, Daniel Dae Kim says that the series demonstrates to "America and television executives and movie producers that you don't have to have a lily-white cast of twentysomethings to have a successful project. The story lines speak to America regardless of color and can even be enhanced by mixtures of race and gender."[66] Fernandez notes that the producers even dealt with the language barrier in an innovative way; when Jin and Sun are alone their Korean "conversations are subtitled; when the other castaways are nearby, there are no translations."[67]

Lindelof says that he and Abrams and Braun all believed that the show should be international in scope: "We really felt we weren't going to be telling an American story the way that most shows do. *CSI* is a show about crime scene investigators in Las Vegas but it is a much different animal—it is distinctly American. Although we are American storytellers, we bent over backwards to not infuse the show with a real degree of patriotism."[68]   That makes *Lost* stand out from the 2006 serial mystery entrant *Heroes*, which positions its two main Asian characters as *Star Trek* fans who love America, and *Flash Forward*, which features a Japanese office worker who leaves her cubicle and her country behind to pursue her dream of playing guitar like Jimmy Hendrix. These series do share, however, some of the features that Lindelof says distinguished the *Lost* pilot from typical U.S. network television of the time: "Large cast, serialised storytelling, non-linear storytelling and science fiction adventure elements for the island itself."[69] In terms of scheduling, Lindelof also understood that the series' originality of premise and structure would enable effective counterprogramming to the formulaic procedurals in which both NBC and CBS were heavily investing. When *Lost* debuted, Lindelof recalls, "the climate of television was made up of procedural dramas, which were great but at the same time you knew what was going to happen next week." *Lost* was structured to do the opposite, to go "into this territory where anything could happen. And that sort of started to create a buzz and make the audience perk up and say, 'Wow, I have to watch this thing.'"[70] Where they had to watch was another question. The long-arc serial was not as well suited as the procedural to the structure of broadcast television, which depended on casual viewers being able to drop in and watch episodes. By loading up its schedule with procedurals, while offering the "I have to watch this thing" element via its hit reality series, CBS surged into first place to become in its own words *America's Most Watched Network*.

Lost and ABC's reality TV

With all of the later attention paid to *Lost*'s role in the re-emergence of strong fictional TV on broadcast schedules, it is easy to forget that *Lost* got on the ABC schedule in the first place because Braun imagined it as having the addictive appeal of a gamedoc. Analyzing *Lost* within the context of the reality TV boom era during which it was first conceived and the reality series with which it was paired in its initial fall season makes evident that *Lost* borrowed features from reality TV. With gamedocs like *Survivor*, *Lost* shares a focus on the psychological and sociological impact of working in teams with strangers with whom one is supposed to be simultaneously a collaborator and competitor. It has an element of policing the boundaries of behavior expected in a civil society that characterizes behavior makeover docusoaps (e.g., *Wife Swap* and *Supernanny*).[71] Both gamedocs and docusoaps reveal the contradictory aspects of the demands of the team-oriented capitalist workplace and the gratification-centered suburban ideal before offering resolutions. Those ideals were also treated ambivalently in the scripted fare greenlit along with *Lost* for 2004–5. In its initial season the campy suburban dramedy/mystery hybrid *Desperate Housewives* was an edgier series than it would later become. Although it was eventually categorized as a humorous take on the nighttime soap, early reviewers thought that its humor came out of lives that seemed "funny and a bit pathetic."[72] The combination also categorized the early seasons of ABC's versions of the one-hour legal dramedy and hospital drama. James Spader and William Shatner and Sandra Oh and Ellen Pompano brought a troubling ambivalence to their respective *Boston Legal* and *Grey's Anatomy* characters in those series' early seasons. The procedural elements of these shows, like those of reality TV makeover programs, deemed that a case would be "solved" by the end of the hour. Before offering those resolutions, the scripted drama and unscripted docusoaps had to expose deep-rooted problems within American social systems and institutions.

ABC paired *Lost* in its first season with two kinds of ambivalent reality shows, scheduling it at 8 p.m. as the lead-in to its hit *The Bachelor* instead of its lead-out. The former quality adult drama slot at 10 p.m. went to *Wife Swap*. Despite a titillating title that evoked a different kind of "adult" fare, this new reality program was less about breaking the sexual rules of polite middle class suburbia than about reinforcing comportment norms and assumptions about parents' responsibilities to provide their children discipline and quality time. *Wife Swap* is comprised of stand-alone episodes that feature a pair of diametrically opposed families, each required to live for a week under the rules of the (usually unwelcome) mother from the other family in order to get a cash prize. The series shares with the first season of *Lost* a focus on people forced to live by rules dictated by a stranger to whom they are hostile or about whose leadership skills and lifestyle assumptions they are doubtful.

Contrasting conceptions of leadership are at the heart of *Survivor*, a gamedoc with which *Lost* shares several features: the stranding of strangers on an island premise; casting for conflict; embedded challenges that test ordinary people's capacity to navigate extraordinary circumstances; and the generation of suspense through the cultivation of uncertainty about which characters could be trusted and which would survive to appear in another episode. The fundamental difference is that *Lost* is more unpredictable as the stakes are higher for the characters; as Lindelof says, "every week you tune in and you don't know what going to happen."[73] Mark Burnett points out that the audience of *Survivor* is well aware that the premise is an artificial construct as the contestants aren't really stranded and aren't in real danger, especially as the whole production team is there with them. Instead, "the perceived reality of the show was in its depiction of interpersonal relationships."[74] Although *Lost* ups the ante on *Survivor* by having characters die during the challenges they face, its remote island setting, like that of its reality TV predecessor, is "a narrative hook designed to facilitate interest in the 'mundane'."[75] Burnett claims his show is "a reflection of life, and its outcome is rather close to workplace politics all over America."[76] Working through issues about styles of leadership and team work as well as acceptable behavior in a group environment are central aspects of both *Lost* and *Survivor*. Each puts on display different styles of leadership and invites the audience to evaluate the merits of each character who emerges as someone other characters start to follow. In relation to these leaders, alliances and schisms form resulting in conflict and friction.

These were dynamics familiar to most American office workers, including those at ABC, which according to anecdotal accounts was a corporate environment beset with divisive office politics during the controversial period in which Braun pushed through the *Lost* pilot even though upper management at Disney had little faith in its viability. Well aware that his bosses were not happy that he greenlit what turned out to be an over $10 million pilot on the basis of a 25-page outline, Braun pressed the *Lost* production team to finish everything on such a compressed timeline that they would be too far gone for the network to pull the plug.[77] He saw his role in shepherding the project through the pilot process as a matter of strategy so that he could outwit those in the ranks above him who were threatening to cut its funding. The strategy worked, except Braun found himself out of a job not only before he could bask in the success of its fall premiere, but also before he could shepherd the series through the May upfronts, the pre-premiere promotional event at which networks present the upcoming season's series to advertisers.

Some newspaper and trade press articles about the breakout success of *Lost* sided with Braun in recounting the fact that he had been the one who had taken the risk on the series that would inspire new broadcast programming models and help bring ABC out of its slump, and was fired for doing so.[78] Susan Lyne, ABC Entertainment President, was ousted along with him, an outcome of the shakeup that editorialist Maureen Dowd characterizes in one of her columns as the result of double dealing among Lyne's male colleagues.[79] In creating his gamedoc, Burnett wanted to tap in to this tendency to take sides in conflicts that are not our own. Viewers of gamedocs are outsiders looking in at an unfolding group dynamic in which they come to side with certain contestants over others, but can only watch as people make bad decisions or are treated shabbily by their team members. Whatever the actualities of the situation at ABC that spring, the network clearly had some workplace intrigue worthy of *Survivor*, whose tagline was *Outwit. Outlast. Outplay.*[80] Burnett intended the series to reflect the fact that workplaces all over America were characterized by complex office politics often connected to the ways in which team-building and individual competition are expected to coexist happily.

Working together toward a common goal, while also trying to outwit or undercut colleagues, is at the heart of *The Mole*, an ABC gamedoc with which *Lost* shares commonalities. Just prior to *Lost*'s debut the *Mole* franchise was rebooted as a celebrity edition set in Hawaii, but *The Mole* originated in 2001 as ABC's attempt to combine some elements of CBS's *The Amazing Race* and *Survivor*. The globe-spanning original challenged its contestants with tests of physical labor and brain teasers and rewarded winners with cash. The cash went into a common fund, which was awarded only to the overall winner. The twist was that, in order to triumph, a contestant had to figure out which of the others was the mole planted by the production team to sabotage the efforts of the rest and, thereby, decrease the amount of the final prize money. This element led to much conflict and mis-direction and allowed the audience at home to speculate on the identity of the mole and play along in the guessing game. Adding to the level of mistrust among the strangers-turned-teammates was the fact that sometimes producers misdirected the contestants and only made the actual mission known to one person or one subset of contestants. The difficulty level was thereby increased along with the level of suspicion; *trust no one*, the series tagline warned. In its initial seasons *Lost* also dramatized the distrust among the survivors and encouraged viewers to share those suspicions. Several characters did turn out to be moles who infiltrated the survivors' camps and there were plenty of other characters on whom doubt was cast. It was even possible that one of those "eliminated" in season two for suspicion of being a mole was, in actuality, just an innocent bystander. The same could be said of those voted off reality shows by their fellow contestants. Often the real threat goes undetected as all the attention focuses on someone whose behavior seems suspicious.

Suspicion is generated and speculation encouraged on *Lost* because it borrows from the time segmentation central to reality TV. Early episodes introduce a diverse cast of characters and offer first impressions of their personalities. There is a slow reveal over several episodes of the actualities of their personalities and the details of their backstories. Viewers learn about the cast of characters through their interactions with others and, more significantly, through details offered only to viewers. While these kinds of revelations are made on a gamedoc in direct-to-the-camera commentary of contestants, *Lost* offers them in the form of a lingering subjective shot of a character followed by his/her flashback. The way the gamedocs and *Lost* offer direct-to-viewers revelations gives the audience an advantage in pre-dicting behavior and outcomes, which is the way both gamedocs and *Lost* invite viewers to play along at home. As the characters on the series and the contestants on the gamedocs do not have this information, they remain distrustful of each other. The dramatic tension is enhanced by the fact that, despite their mistrust, they often have no choice but to work together to complete necessary tasks and meet challenges.

Lost viewers become less suspicious of some of the characters over time because the details of each core character's history are revealed in fragments over a season of intermittent flashbacks. The mystery surrounding other characters is prolonged as any "big reveals" about them are meted out over the course of several seasons' flashbacks. The biggest reveals are saved for the season finales and they always have the potential to complicate what has been revealed earlier, sometimes calling into question what viewers assumed were established facts. These flashbacks invite speculation as they encourage viewers to evaluate the difference between what the characters say about themselves and how they present themselves and what their past actions and histories indicate about them. The way in which the characters in *Lost* are developed over time is significant as each is given a backstory that remains compelling by being parceled out over time. The structure works most effectively in season one in that all the backstories are not yet known, which makes each one a surprise. Then with each instance another character's backstory is offered or added to by a follow-up episode, connections to those of the others are suggested. This structure also allows for multiple perspectives on a single block of time, which is detailed from the different physical positions and psychological perspectives of several characters. The dynamic changes with the accumulation of flashbacks for each character until the point at which viewers have more than enough information that they drop their suspicions. After the first season, *Lost* writers dealt with the resulting loss of mystery and, thus, of some of the compelling narrative tension, by expanding the story world beyond the survivors who became known in season one as the *Lost*aways. In subsequent seasons the writers revealed another group of survivors from the plane's tail section, a group of seemingly hostile island inhabitants dubbed "The Others," and island and off-island factions hostile to "The Others." These additions of characters and layers to the story were all attempts to keep the series as enigmatic as it was in its first season. Reality television producers do not have to engage in such gymnastics as the single season structure for the cast of each installment makes them stay compelling. Not long after viewers figure out what motivates each person, the series ends and then reboots again the next season as a new "series" with new contestants and the speculation game can begin again.

Competition programs including *Survivor* and *The Mole* also are structured so that their ensemble splits off into smaller coalitions that work together toward a goal or at least toward competing against other coalitions or thwarting their goals. These coalitions keep secrets from others and sometimes are working toward their own ends and sometimes for the good of the group.[81] They face challenges and are tested. As in gamedocs, the characters on *Lost* often form secret alliances even with those that they distrust in order to achieve a desired end. The alliances often end in betrayal or failure. In the more positive iterations of these alliances, unlikely friendships can form between people of radically different backgrounds and different ages, although the core cast is still twenty- and thirty-somethings. On *Lost*, as on *Survivor*, people who certainly would never have crossed paths off the island become friends, allies, or co-conspirators. On gamedocs, alliances can save contestants from "elimination" or lead them unwittingly to it. Alliances on *Lost* often lead to the death or disappearance of characters, although often they die during an attempt to keep fellow survivors safe. One "big reveal" on *Lost* is that it seems that someone can be voted off the island by the mysterious island itself.

Over time, many of the survivors at first positioned as hostile or at least unhelpful are transformed into loyal members of a coalition. Newcomers and outsiders can occupy this position as well, but often they appear to restart the cycle of suspicion about and revelation of true motives. This structure can only work for so long on *Lost*, so it is not surprising that beginning in season four the flashbacks give way to flashforwards—which again have a gamedoc equivalent; they share a function with the reunion specials that commonly follow the finale of a reality television series. The reunion ostensibly answers the questions: what happened after the transformative group experience? How did it translate into behavior in their regular lives? *Lost* gives glimpses of the post-island lives of some of the characters, but the flashforwards also can unravel much of what the earlier seasons established by making each character question his/her decisions and motivations. These flashforwards open new spaces for speculation, especially as the impact of past decisions on the future is revealed in the same fragmented way as the characters' backstories were in the first three seasons.

One structuring logic *Lost* does not share with gamedocs is the centrality of product integration, which is an embedded part of a gamedoc's financing model. Such deals have increased dramatically in scripted series as well in recent years, both in relation to concerns about ad-skipping and timeshifted viewing. As Mark Burnett explains,

> "*Survivor* is as much a marketing vehicle as it is a TV show. My shows create an interest, and people will look at them, but the endgame here is selling products in stores—a car, deodorant, running shoes. It's the future of television."[82]

Product integration is especially appealing as it assures that viewers watching the show in any platform will be exposed to the sponsor's messaging, as is the case with *24* and its Cisco Systems and Sprint integrations. *Lost* seemed to remain free of product integration, while other scripted series increasingly offered story space as part of hybrid deals with advertisers that gave them additional locations in which to promote their products as an incentive for them to continue buying the 30-second spots with which the integrations were usually paired. Such deals were a way to manage anxieties about the impact of DVRs on the attention paid to them.[83] *Lost* had the advantage over other scripted programming as it could argue that, in contrast to a series like *Desperate Housewives* (which featured a notorious Buick car show within one storyline), product integration would disrupt *Lost*'s ratings-generating fictional construct.

Even after the *Lost*aways encounter people or spaces in which products could logically be found (e.g., in the luggage hold of the downed airplane), the producers do not choose to have them find any name brand products. This choice is less about maintaining story- or character-consistency as much as it is about mythology-consistency. The producers seem only to ask themselves: what can introducing a new element do to move the mythology forward? A good example is that the canned and packaged food that the survivors find on the island has labeling and packaging from the Dharma Initiative, some kind of scientific research organization/corporation. To have the series' mystery organization controlling everything, even the food its workers consumed, makes it seem more sinister, especially if one considers that the "big reveal" about the Dharma stations found on the island is that it is not clear who was the observer and who was the observed. Like reality TV mind games, sometimes the people who think they are controlling the situation are being controlled.

It seems logical that a remote and seemingly unoccupied island is a particularly ineffective broadcast series setting as it does not seem like a space in which consumer goods could be logically introduced. The producers of *Survivor* solved this problem even though they set the series in various remote locales. Accompanying the reality show's castaways was a massive production crew, some of whom had a stockpile of consumer goods that would be doled out as prizes. The producers did not need to maintain the fiction that the survivors were cut off from the world because viewers and contestants were well aware of the presence of the camera crew and production team members. Indeed, the program's entire financing structure is premised on sponsorship, as its producers had to acquire sponsorships to secure the original episode order from CBS. With all the series' product placement deals, it is not surprising that the "survivors" were often given name brand products as rewards for winning "challenges." One infamous incident involved Doritos. It was a great advertisement for the product as someone living on whatever could be found to eat on a remote island would not have to fake enthusiasm for a bag of chips offered as prize.

While the story about the long-term survival of the *Lost*aways is not one well suited to product placement integration, especially in contrast to more typical scripted fare set in domestic spaces, offices, and hospitals, name brand products were not even integrated early on when the survivors still had the airplane food and luggage. *Lost* even had its potential Doritos moment when a very pregnant survivor named Claire says she is craving peanut butter. Charlie, the stranger who has started to fall in love with her, encourages her to fantasize that they are eating peanut butter. When food is discovered inside a bunker built by the Dharma Initiative, Charlie nabs the peanut butter for Claire. She is thrilled to get it and savors every mouthful. As all the food is simply labeled Dharma Initiative, Claire's ecstasy cannot be linked to a specific corporation. Instead, the sudden appearance of food from the bunker found inside a secret hatch in the jungle floor just contributes to the mystery about the Dharma Initiative's experiments and objectives. A broadcast-friendly decision would have been for the producers to stock that bunker with name brands, as it would be unlikely that a corporation interested in scientific development and exploration would waste time making peanut butter. It was mythology-consistent to have all the *Lost*aways eating food with Dharma labels, a fact that could later be used for comedy, especially when they found some Dharma beer.

This self-referential element is part of the circularity of *Lost* as it is a series with elements that mostly promote further immersion in its fictional world. While sponsor products were not being promoted affiliated merchandise could be, including a fake candy bar called the Apollo, which the characters do enjoy and was later available for purchase by fans along with Dharma Initiative branded products. More inventive is the episode in which resident-scavenger Sawyer is seen reading a manuscript called *Bad Twin*, which turns out to be written by one of the passengers killed in the crash. It was actually the name of a tie-in book commissioned by producers and available for sale on amazon.com.

Some of the other books Sawyer reads, including *Watership Down*, are inserted as allusions or commentary on the evolving *Lost* mystery. While *Lost* may have inspired some viewers to buy these books as well, it more likely prompted viewers to find a description of them on the web so they could decipher the intended allusion. The producers even threw in the Generation-X tween-address *Are You There God? It's Me Margaret*. The title may be linked in a philosophical sense to the other titles about doubt and faith. Given its focus on questions about budding sexuality, it is more likely a bit of humor about Sawyer, whose avid reading is an early clue that he may be just playing the callous outlaw. Co-executive producer Carlton Cuse admits to using such elements of the show as nod to the avid fanalysts or as a way to talk back to their theories. "We'll do things in the show that acknowledge people's theories about the show," often to disprove them. They decided to use the short story "An Occurrence at Owl Creek Bridge," for instance, as "a shout to people who are theorizing that this whole show was taking place in someone's mind in the last moments of their life."[84]

The ways that viewers turned to the web for information on the books referenced in the de facto "*Lost* book club"[85] is suggestive of how following TV shows has changed in the internet era.[86] The web provides easy access to sites in which allusions can be investigated or the books could be purchased. *Lost* is designed to encourage quick Google-enabled interpretations of the on-air text, but also rewards close reading and analysis. Fans can write blog posts or comment on message boards about their interpretations of the allusions. Some fans try to one up each other by producing sites on which they offer detailed analyses of the allusions, and others by spoiling outcomes.[87] Others trace the connections among characters and events and propose interpretations of why the characters have the names that they do. As was the case with the series produced by Warner Brothers and/or aired on the WB, the hyperlinked nature of the internet turns viewers into trackers and allows them to locate, share, and link each other to information. To facilitate just such a process the Lostpedia was created as a resource posting and finding information in the mode of Wikipedia.

The cultural penetration of broadband internet makes viewsers worth courting, so it is no surprise that series now have elaborate websites through which producers and the network can circulate information and on which they can host fan activities. Aware that a primary fan practice is to speculate about outcomes and test out theories, searching across the web for information from producers and networks to confirm them, *Lost* producers hosted their own fan board site The Fuselage. To entice viewsers to frequent the site and transform it into a hub for their online activities, producers offered podcasts and interacted on message boards. The hope was that this branded destination would become a gathering place for fans. It was a space in which producers could elaborate on controversial content decisions, provide updates, breaking news, and teasers, and keep an eye on viewer response, while providing more in-depth content that could not find a place in the on-air series. The existence of this producer-generated fan site is a testament to the changed attitude toward fans and the degree of producer interaction it offers is a tribute to the fact that the series was created and run by those who consider themselves fan-producers. There were plenty of loyal viewers who either had no awareness or interest in *Lost*'s web presence. They are representative of the more general splitting of the loyals into dedicated appointment TV viewers and dedicated viewsers, the latter being those who would seek out access to series content, casts, creators, and production teams on any platform in which the series appeared. These viewsers play an important role as amplifiers of series information and hype, spreading buzz and often press release information around the web. It is through this process that a series enters into wider circulation and has the chance of becoming a narrowcast-broadcast series.[88]

In short, the web is central to the on-air success of *Lost*. Cuse says, "I think that 'Lost' would never succeed in the pre-Internet era. It's the fact that the show is complicated and intentionally ambiguous; it allows the fans to become involved in its analysis."[89] *BusinessWeek* attributes *Lost*'s original success to its paratextual existence on the web via official and fan sites and information.[90] The summer between seasons one and two was also a period of intense fan activity fed by the production team's release of in-mythology websites and fan postings of user-generated content related to the circulation of official clues and content.[91] A space for interaction and debate, the web offers a variety of sites for sharing and finding information. It functions as safety valve where the pressures of serial mystery fandom are released. Viewsers can have their questions clarified before the next episode or catch up on what they missed. Writers can tell if fan frustration is setting in and about what. Although there is still the problem of the time lag between episode production and airing, they can justify the decisions on fan sites and work in future episodes to address the problems.

Reviewers were soon characterizing *Lost* as a new kind of web-enabled quality TV given these ways in which it transformed viewers into fanalysts and kept them busy tracking down philosophical, scientific, and literary allusions. The series is peppered with references to the kinds of philosophical and scientific thinkers to whom students taking a classic liberal arts core curriculum might be introduced.[92] Series including *Veronica Mars, Dawson's Creek*, and *Gilmore Girls* did the same thing with popular cultural references. That the references in *Lost* are to high culture makes *Lost* seem smarter and likely appeals to the audience's sense that *Lost* is more of a "quality" program. Some fans do spend time investigating these references, though, and they often comment on blogs and message boards that the connections fall apart if one looks too deeply at the philosophers' theories. That does not mean that viewers don't still enjoy that the references are there even if the allusions don't go much beyond the surface.

Fan tracking is entwined with speculative analysis—not only guesses as to the way the pieces of information fit together and their potential impact on future developments, but also theories about character motivation. *Lost* encourages its audience to speculate about larger philosophical questions, particularly about the impact of a new environment on a person's entrenched behaviors. Could people make themselves over in new environments, especially those in which they face new challenges and are presented with opportunities that would not have existed for them in their previous lives? Would their past selves inevitably re-emerge and make them revert to old patterns? Do people have fixed personalities that cannot be changed even in a new environment? While there is a degree of philosophical speculation in gamedocs like *Survivor* as well, *Lost* makes overt these kinds of philosophical concerns.

Lost as quality ensemble drama

As such philosophical speculation is typical of quality TV series, it is not surprising that *Lost*'s Wednesday scheduling and its move into the 9 p.m. spot in 2005, put it in direct competition with NBC's *The West Wing* (1999–2006). Although the NBC show held the outstanding drama series title from 2000 to 2003, *The Sopranos* put an end to *The West Wing*'s hopes for a fifth win and took home the Emmy in 2004.[93] The HBO series would return for a win in 2007, but in 2005 the Emmy went to ABC's *Lost* and so did the Wednesday ratings win over *West Wing*. Prior to its breakout 2004–5 season, ABC had already established itself on Wednesdays with its reality programming. Jeff Bader, an ABC vice president, pointed out in 2003 how the network changed the Wednesday "landscape completely … It went from 'West Wing' being by far the dominant show in the time period to 'Bachelor,' after the third week, beating it every time it was on."[94] When the ABC reality series that succeeded *The Bachelor* in the time slot also beat *West Wing*, ABC became associated with the time period. Given the failures all the networks were having with drama series at the time, it is not surprising that Bader tentatively added that ABC might try to use its strength on Wednesdays to introduce scripted programming.[95] While the network hoped to maintain some long-term reality TV properties, Bader noted in 2003 that advertisers were still "clamoring for" a scripted show that becomes a really big hit, one that is around "for seven, eight, nine, 10 years. Ultimately that is where we would like to be."[96]

ABC ended up making its bold move on Sundays and its 2004–5 success with its scripted fare laid the foundations for years of schedule-building, including the eventual bid for Thursday night dominance. ABC's scheduling strategy was to counterprogram Sundays using *Desperate Housewives* as it offered a lighter take on both HBO-style suburban desperation and dysfunctional families and the escapades of sexy female friends and their "frenemies." It added the twist of a serial mystery element, which made it more unique and linked it to the cliffhanger structure that characterizes *Lost*. *Desperate Housewives* offered a strong lead-in for quirky newcomer *Boston Legal*. Both would join Best Original Drama Series *Lost* as Emmy winners in 2005, with a lead actress in a comedy award for Felicity Huffman of *Desperate Housewives* and lead actor and supporting actor in a drama awards, respectively, for James Spader and William Shatner of *Boston Legal*. Rounding out the awards, *Extreme Makeover Home Edition*, ABC's socially conscious reality series that ran at 8 p.m. Sundays, took home the Emmy for Outstanding Reality Program.[97] After gaining traction at 10 p.m., *Boston Legal* was then shifted off the schedule in late

March to make room for the short run of newcomer *Grey's Anatomy*. *Boston Legal* found a home and steady ratings on Tuesdays in the fall of 2005, while the pairing of *Housewives* and *Grey's* proved unbeatable on Sundays.

The initial Sunday success emboldened ABC to try to colonize another night by relocating *Grey's Anatomy* to Thursdays. *Desperate Housewives* became the lead-in for a family business/relationships series *Brothers and Sisters*, a successful pairing that continued to the end of the decade. Switching *Grey's* to 9 p.m. Thursday seemed more dangerous as in that slot it was up against *CSI* and *Survivor* or other reality series, but ABC was hoping that *Grey's* would launch a successful run for the interconnected strangers debut series *Six Degrees* from Abrams' Bad Robot production company. While the series failed, along with many of the other much-hyped original dramas that fall season, *Grey's* became a blockbuster on Thursdays and eventually the core of a branding campaign called Choose Thursdays that was indicative of ABC's targeting of a broad range of female viewers 25–54 years old. The pairing exemplifies Ellis's point that scheduling is the attempt to create a "viewing experience" out of "demographic speculation."[98] During its subsequent seasons, *Grey's Anatomy* shared Thursdays with several different female target series, including *Ugly Betty, Men in Trees, Dancing with the Stars*, and *Private Practice*. The latter, a *Grey's Anatomy* spin-off featuring more sexy doctors, was never a big hit, but it was an effective schedule pairing for keeping viewers with the flow of the on-air programming between the 9 p.m. and 10 p.m. blocks, which was exactly the kind of scheduling that appealed to advertisers. *Ugly Betty*, a quirky serial dramedy with origins in a telenovela format, did well in the 8 p.m. Thursday slot and even garnered America Ferrera an Outstanding Lead Actress in a Comedy Emmy win in 2006. After a ratings slip in 2008 and new scheduling needs, ABC broke up the female-focused scheduling logic and shifted *Ugly Betty* to Fridays.[99] It did so to signal its faith that *Flash Forward*, its fall 2009 long-arc mystery, would be the new series, indeed the blockbuster, to replace *Lost* after its scheduled end date in May 2010.[100]

The fact that it was given a pre-planned end date in consideration of its long-arc narrative needs was one of the many things that made *Lost* unlike anything else on broadcast television. The series violated many accepted broadcast television practices, which Cuse explained on *Nightline*:

> "We have a large and sprawling cast, we have characters who are inherently unsympathetic—there are murderers—we have complicated story lines. Those are all things that intrigued us as storytellers, and I think made the show feel different than other things that have been on the air,"

at least on network TV.[101] *Lost* covers the same philosophical and psychological ground as *The Sopranos* and *Six Feet Under*, HBO's dysfunctional family/business hybrids that focus respectively on a family man/mob boss and a death-fearing mortician reluctantly co-managing the family business.[102] Characterized by the moral ambivalence of its ensemble, *Lost* has a flashback structure that, in HBO style, makes sympathetic and sometimes heroic characters out of a group that includes a conman, torturer, thug, and a fugitive, the latter being only one of many of the castaways who has murdered someone.

Abrams told *Nightline* that revealing the less-than-heroic pasts of many of these characters through the flashback structure was a way to "sneak in an anthology element" because each episode follows a different character and so "You don't know exactly who you are going to be following every week, and you have no idea where they are going to take you. The flashbacks are sort of a minipuzzle within each episode."[103] The way that it encases the story of the interconnections among these characters in a game-like structure and mixes in cult genres might explain why *Lost* was never quite accepted as a quality TV series and did not find itself again in contention at the Emmys until Michael Emerson, the actor who plays the most morally ambivalent of all the *Lost* characters, took home the Outstanding Supporting Actor in a Drama Series award in 2009. Given *Lost*'s reality television roots, it is not surprising that his character, known for his manipulation skills, would be right at home on a gamedoc.

Speculating about his motives is popular on message boards, but more often viewers go online to discuss *Lost*'s complexly interwoven game-like structure. *Time* magazine categorizes *Lost* as more an interactive game than a television series:

> "An elaborate fractal pattern of intersecting stories concerning plane survivors on a not-quite-deserted island, a secretive international organization and a monster made of smoke, *Lost* only begins with the 60 minutes you see on TV. Its mysteries, clues and literary-historical allusions demand research, repeat viewing, freeze-framing and endless online discussions."[104]

Lost taught viewers how to play its games; they soon learned, for instance, that a new character's name would correspond to a famous philosopher, scientist, or mathematician and that there would be some significance to the correspondence. Encouraging these kinds of investigations between episodes, *Lost* prompts viewers intellectually and creatively to engage with it.

The structuring dynamic of each episode even shares similarities to a web interface. Viewers are cued that *Lost* is intended as a series of characters' perspectives that only provide a partial view by the subjective shots in several scenes that begin with an extreme close-up of an eye opening. The image sets the present time of the story in motion in several episodes. A lingering close-up of a character who appears to be illuminated at the same time that the other characters recede into the background is the cue for the flashbacks. This parallels the way viewers find out about characters on an interactive website in which the picture of a character is actually an icon, which when clicked will pop up information or open a window to the page with the detailed information about him or her.

A web content parallel exists as well to the storytelling structure of *Lost*, in which each episode sets up an in-depth exploration of a single character's past and the way that past is contributing to his or her motivations and behavior in the present. The on-air flashbacks are compatible with a hypertextual web style in that they function as if you have clicked the character's icon and activated a link that takes you to the flashback in order to learn more information about him or her. After producers completed several seasons of episodes, it was also possible for a viewer to go back and watch only the episodes related to one character in order to understand the complexity of his or her involvement in the larger mysteries. Indeed, each new season of *Lost* invites re-watching the previous ones not just in order, but also in various selected episode configurations to look for clues to the current unfolding of its mysteries. The individual selection process creates a hypertext, that is, "a narrative form that does not exist until readers produce it through a series of choices made according to their desires and interests."[105] Their creation of such a text transforms viewers into narrative collaborators.[106]

Following the *Lost* storyline by watching only one character's key episodes in order would provide a viewer with the whole story so far for one character (albeit, still a story of fragments), but the larger story of all the survivors would remain fragmented.[107] Of course, creating a hypertextual link among the non-consecutive episodes featuring one character's flashbacks might then prompt interest in following the linked episodes for another. As with hypertext, viewers choose their own paths through *Lost*, looking deeper into the characters or storylines by which they are most intrigued.[108] While such decentered pleasure is common to art house cinema it does not play well on broadcast television, so it is no wonder that producers felt constant pressure to make everything add up to an interconnected whole. Viewers put that pressure on the production team as well with many discussions centering on the hope that producers intended to wrap up all the loose ends in the conclusion. Although he first expresses the same concern, Matthew Gilbert wonders in *The Boston Globe* if some "mind-blowingly tight ending—with every single knot tied up, every action explained," would be more of a letdown. After all, *Lost*'s pleasures came in fragments, perhaps its conclusion needs to be fragmented as well. Maybe it is enough, Gilbert muses, to have had the pleasure of "The hour-by-hour process of following '*Lost*' and its character development."[109]

The mythology series and alternate reality game

Such worries already started to be expressed in the middle of the first season when commentators wondered if *Lost* would disappoint in the same ways that most of broadcast television's long-arc serial mysteries had done before it. Viewers did not have to look far for an example since *Lost* was paired with *Alias* starting in winter 2005. The spy-fy serial had started out strong but by its third season in 2003–4, it was already showing signs of fraying from constant revisions made to its structure in an attempt to balance creative and industrial demands. The network's hopes of attracting and maintaining casual viewers to *Alias* conflicted with the production team's creative desire to offer loyal fans a slowly unfolding, complex serial mystery in the style of *The X-Files*, but wrapped in a Jane Bond spy adventure and extended via a series of hidden websites. Tinkering with the series to make it more accessible to casuals weakened its initial effective structure, especially after the writers got rid of the cliffhangers that had made the series have an addictive quality similar to some of the twice-weekly reality TV series as well as dramatic scripted serials. The changes did little to attract new viewers and ended up alienating core fans.

Lost fans were anxious that the same thing could happen over time to the new series. Its good reviews came with the caveat that the reviewer would not be surprised if the series encountered the same trouble as one of the long-arc serials that preceded it. Aware of these concerns, ABC Entertainment President Steve McPherson said that in the fall of 2004, he and the producers often discussed how to balance the mysteries with "the reveals." In terms of the pacing, McPherson said he was always concerned with "how much we're giving, how much we're not giving."[110] By April 2005 *Entertainment Weekly* fretted: "we all know how this can end, don't we? Marooned on a spit of frustration. Like Twin Peaks. Like X-Files. Shows that come dressed in alluring mystery, but eventually reveal themselves to be sporting emperor's clothes."[111] Yet, the slow reveals of backstories kept the series from becoming too mythology focused. In a long-arc mystery the trick is to keep audiences interested in solving the puzzle and playing along without becoming frustrated by the predictability of the twists or by the overly convoluted nature of the plotlines.

Like the characters in *Lost* who cyclically have and lose faith that there is indeed some larger plan for them in relation to the mysterious island on which they are stranded, the series' loyal viewers try to maintain their faith in a grand plan, despite moments such as "the reveal" of the workings of the hatch in season two when they became worried that perhaps producers had no grand plan after all. This anxiety stemmed from experience with earlier shows, including *Alias*. Fans are willing to put in the time to figure out the mysteries of this kind of series, but they expect a return on their investment in the form of a satisfying finale that is neither insulting to their intelligence, nor hopelessly mired in complexity.

Lost's 2005–6 second season demonstrated both the series' continuing capacity to excite viewers with serial mystery and the problems with such seriality. *Entertainment Weekly* captures the series' appeal, describing *Lost* as "an unfolding epic about damaged souls with tortured pasts stranded on a menacing, monster-inhabited island that's located on the same parallel as The Outer Limits, The Twilight Zone, Dark Shadows, and The Prisoner."[112] In *Time* James Poniewozik depicts the success of *Lost* as a challenge to executives who assume that "viewers will flee anything that remotely challenges them." He contends that "*Lost* proves that millions of people will support a difficult, intelligent, even frustrating story."[113] As those frustrations mounted by the middle of season two, reviewers expressed their concern that *Lost* would end up being "one big tease without any kind of payoff."[114]

Viewers have been taught to be cynical about long-arc TV mysteries and *Lost* writers are no exception. Lindelof positions himself as a fan-producer and counts himself among that group of TV viewers who have been taught that long-arc TV often just ends up mired in its own mysteries, never able to pull the story together for a satisfying finale: "I identify with that, because I was a fan of those shows too." He and fellow co-executive producer Cuse, along with their whole team, try to keep that from happening to *Lost*.[115] Well aware of the graveyard filled with hot shows gone cold and of viewers' fears that their current favorite show will end up betraying them, the writers tried to keep a balance and use the website to satisfy cult fans' hunger for more elaborate elements of the series mythology. *Twin Peaks* taught them, Cuse says, to provide answers to some mysteries before introducing new ones. During the *Nightline* interview, he points out, "If you were to go back to the pilot and look at what the mysteries were that were posed by the pilot, a lot of those questions have really been answered."[116] From the long run of *The X-Files*, he and the other producers learned how hard it can be to sustain a mystery over the years as well as the pressure that can be exerted by a network that wants to keep a highly rated series on-air even if it means stretching out the mysteries.[117] As Cuse notes, it was too hard for *The X-Files* team to sustain the mythology for nine years. Seeing how this show left audiences disappointed made his production team hyperaware that they need to have "a clear idea as to how the story will end."[118] Both he and Lindelof agree that long-arc mysteries only succeed when they have that kind of focus and are more about the people than the questions so that "the audience never gets bogged in the mire of 'mythology'."[119] To maintain this balance, the writers always make sure that an episode pivots around the character on whom the flashbacks focus and links whatever is emotionally "happening on the island" to that backstory.

Their success at interweaving the strands is due, in part, to the prior experience of Lindelof and Cuse when they worked together on the production team of the police procedural *Nash Bridges* and found inspiration in the seamless interplay between the personal and procedural in the best episodes of ABC's *NYPD Blue*. Lindelof describes the latter as similar to *Lost* in that it is also about "characters searching for redemption in the face of their flaws and struggles."[120] Michael Emerson (Ben) points to exactly this dynamic at the heart of *Lost's* structuring flashforwards that enable "these bittersweet notes of regret and missed opportunity." He continues, "To the extent the island was some crucible in which people could hope for redemption, maybe not everyone was redeemed, at least not happily."[121]

With the layering of flashforwards and flashbacks, *Lost* is able to maintain the complexity of structure that *Alias* writers were pressured to jettison in the search for casual viewers. That series is the one whose struggles with its serial mystery taught the *Lost* team the most lessons. Part of the reason *Lost* was better able to achieve the balance than its predecessors is that some of the production team had worked on *Alias* and had first-hand experience of the problems of having an overly complex mythology. At its core *Alias* had a mystery surrounding a figure named Rambaldi, a Michelangelo-esque scientist/artist/philosopher whose centuries-old predictions and inventions were not only impacting national security in the present, but were somehow entwined with the personal history of the main character. The Rambaldi mystery appealed to cult fans, but left little room for a wider audience.

The production team felt pressure from ABC to simplify and de-emphasize its long-arc mystery, as the network wanted a mainstream hit and not a cult favorite.[122] As Alexander recalls in the audio commentary for "Nocturne" on the season four DVD, "one of the mandates we had gotten from the network" was to produce more stand-alone episodes as "they were really concerned with the serialized nature of the show and the way we told stories; they felt that was off-putting to a general audience." The team agreed to make episodes "more self-contained, less cliffhanger-driven and thus more viewer-friendly." The problem was that many fans saw that as "dumbing down."[123] It is a difficult balance to achieve, Lindelof contends, but a mythology series must have access points for casual fans without losing the complexity and degree of involvement required for loyals to "feel like they're being fed," Cuse says.[124] As already noted, one way of keeping the cult fans happy is to utilize the web as a place in which to offer more depth to the mythology. At the same time message board commentary that urges producers to add more mythology to the on-air series can be misleading given that the comments come from dedicated viewers rather than the casual viewers who are needed to move a TV show from cult series to narrowcast-broadcast hit.

Although *Lost* was attracting fans who had become frustrated with the compromises *Alias* had made to leave spaces for casual viewers, the production team understood that *Lost* could easily turn into the long-arc series that a core fandom abandons upon the arrival of another series. After all, *Alias* initially attracted frustrated *X-Files* fans looking for a new series in which to invest and follow via the web. By 2000 the FOX cult series had begun to unravel, especially after star David Duchovny left and returned only for guest appearances. As one fan put it,

> "All of us were pretty disenchanted with XF at the time we started watching *Alias*, and since they happened to air opposite each other at the time, there was an even greater connection. For me, getting into *Alias* fandom helped lessen the sting somewhat of the disenchantment with XF."[125]

ABC's scheduling of *Alias* was no coincidence, of course, as it recognized its new series' potential to pick off *X-Files* viewers.

With the *Alias* cancellation fresh in viewers' minds, *Lost* producers knew in season three that in their marketing for *Lost* they would have to promise that at a fixed point in time there would be a resolution offered and that the story arcs were being constructed in relation to the pre-determined timeline. As they were under the same network pressure for timely resolutions of ongoing mysteries, the *Lost* producers managed to negotiate a 2010 end date for the series so that it could provide a resolution to the series mysteries before it began to fray and unravel on its own.[126] It is precisely because of the problems it faced that *Alias* is such a significant series, especially given that many of its production team members went on to work on *Lost, Heroes,* and *Fringe* and brought with them to those shows their experience with creating a multiplatform franchise. The *Alias* team paved the way for "The *Lost* Experience," the ARG that had at its core a series of interlinked hidden websites associated with the fictional organizations referenced in the on-air series and the actual corporations that were sponsoring it.[127] Working in consultation with Abrams, *Alias*'s producers Alexander and Orci created immersive web content at a time when such sites were not yet the norm and viewers had not yet broadly embraced web interaction in conjunction with TV viewing.[128] *Alias* had inherited the pre-existing *X-Files* fan base, which had a well-established online presence. Those were the viewers for whom the *Alias* production team constructed an immersive web experience.[129]

Ahead of the curve on what would become known as a transmedia experience in which a fictional world was extended across multiple entertainment platforms, *Alias*'s producers had imagined from the outset that *Alias* was a video game and a web experience as well as an on-air TV series.[130] With its web savvy audience in mind, the series was designed to have a web presence consisting of a series of hidden sites representative of people and organizations from the on-air series. In October 2001, Abrams described "an alternative secret Web presence" or an "engagement-based web alternative" intended to engage viewers through new media. Alexander and Orci were creating the content based on their own experiences and expectation as fans. Not yet ready to reveal the details, Abrams would only say, "There are certain things we're doing that, if I were a fan of the show, I would find to be as interesting and compelling as the series itself."[131]

Creating a series of interlinked websites that present the characters, locations, and institutions associated with a media text as if they were real came to public attention through the use of the technique in relation to *The Blair Witch Project*, the feature film that has come to exemplify the potential of the web as a word-of-mouse promotion engine through which independent films can be transformed into mainstream hits. By the time most viewers became acquainted with the *Blair Witch* web presence, it had become part of a commercial campaign that was backed by a film studio's marketing budget. The campaign was calculated and most definitely commercial, but just done, as Amorette Jones of the Artisan marketing campaign says, "in a non-commercial way."[132] One Sony executive pointed out that the web content created for *The Blair Witch Project* was just "another channel to deliver the message."[133] Detailing how this new media address was integrated with a more traditional approach of television previews, billboards, ads in college newspapers and *Rolling Stone*, J. P. Telotte claims that what was new, but certainly not unique to *The Blair Witch Project* campaign was that it went beyond the electronic poster approach or even the digital press kit.[134] It was a teaser site that positioned the film within a tradition of other like-minded films. As Marc Graser and Dade Hayes explain, the site "was designed as part of the film experience—part of the film's horror address and tapped into fans of the horror genre."[135] The popularity of this kind of in-fiction film site can be attributed to the way it can start in a niche fan community and then circulate outward. Such a site invites viewers "with a few simple mouse clicks" to alert friends to the existence of the fan site and to the film with which it is associated.[136]

Lost also has one of these "must click" and share web experiences that encourages viewers to share the links as well as to keep clicking on hyperlinks to access a series of interrelated sites. Mike Benson, senior vice president of marketing for ABC Entertainment, explains, "by creating additional content for this show, we could create a marketing tool that would have fans more invested in the program, and if it was cool they'd share with their friends."[137] Such a series of linked sites invites immersion in the fictional world and mythology, sometimes via role-playing, but certainly in terms of participating in the text in some way. It also gives site visitors the choice of which dimensions of the story they would explore and the degree to which they would immerse themselves.[138] This feature is particularly well suited to viewers of a TV series who are assumed to be divided into loyals, casuals, and clickers. The latter might just be clicking around and find themselves stopping to watch the on-air text, to follow the text online, to click on the various hyperlinks, or to click away to something else entirely. While the producers always hope to entice some of these kinds of viewers, Lindelof remarks that with the immersive web experience, the producers are mostly addressing loyal fans. The web becomes a safety valve of sorts for them as the on-air series cannot delve too deeply into mythology issues or it will lose any hope of courting casual viewers (as has been the case with *Alias*). As he explains during the *Nightline* interview,

> "all the details of the Hanso Foundation and Dharma Initiative would just basically cloud up the brains of most of the people who watch the show but there is a hard-core group of people who love a mythology of the show and they want to see that stuff."[139]

While the web can be a place in which to cater to the tastes and desires of the loyals, the on-air series has to balance the genre elements with the more generic drama (e.g., leadership anxieties) and nighttime serial elements (e.g., love triangles) that are assumed to have more mass appeal. Abrams explains,

> "You have to be careful you don't start serving the wrong master where it doesn't become about trying to sort of make a show that's all about hidden meaning. There's certain point that can become a distraction and sort of lead you down the wrong path."[140]

Those elements can be developed on other platforms.

Like those associated with *The Blair Witch Project*, *Lost*'s interlinked websites encourage viewers to embark on a circulatory "path of further investigation" "that leads away from" and "back to" the core media text.[141] In this immersive model, the relationship of TV series and website is a circulatory one in that the objective is to keep a series alive by keeping viewers ever moving from show to site and back again, all the while keeping the buzz in circulation on the internet. Benson describes *Lost* as "a candy store of marketing." In addition to the usual on-air marketing and popular press advertising, his team turned to other platforms all to keep people circulating through the loop of platforms and back to the series: "we thought, 'What about TiVo, DVDs, the iPod, and the Internet?' They are all huge opportunities to drive people back to TV."[142]

The TV tie-in ARG is part of this mix and, thus, differs from other kinds of ARGs given its primary function of addressing the economics of the TV industry in which the main commodity is audience attention, not individual products (such as movie tickets, various DVD editions, and tie-in merchandise in the case of a feature film-related franchise).[143] The TV series and the game are not entertainment content in and of themselves, but content given in exchange for attention to advertising.[144] TV tie-in ARGs are intriguing because they rely on click-based consent by which viewers click on a sponsor's site to find clues for the game. Once there, they have to give their attention to the marketing site in exchange for accessing the series content they desire. It is a new media version of the television paradigm in which viewers exchange attention to advertising in return for entertainment content. Given their anxieties about the DVR's impact on broadcasters' ability to deliver as much audience attention as they once promised in the past, advertisers are shoring up their on-air investments by sponsoring such web content or co-creating hybrid advertising content such as the on-air content wraps discussed in relation to the CW's strategies.[145]

Crossplatform television series and the ARGs with which they are associated are less about creative form—a breaking down of the boundaries between kinds of texts to "create a transmedia narrative" that may be a feature of other kinds of ARGs—than they are about creative marketing. Henrik Örenbring says that they exemplify new forms of hybrid promotion that involve "creating opportunities to market texts through other texts."[146] By blurring the lines between content and promotion, the TV tie-in ARG is marketing that does not register at first as marketing. In this paradigm viewers' opportunities for interaction (with content) are also opportunities for interaction of consumers with products and for product makers with potential consumers.

By hosting opportunities for interaction and participation for a series' most dedicated viewers, networks and corporations that sponsor their content hope to benefit from the "gratitude effect" associated with prestige sponsorship models in which nothing is sold within the series, but the corporate brand is elevated in consumers' minds by the connection to (and the company's support of) their favorite TV programming. It is easy to see how, as Örenbring says, *Alias*'s tie-in ARG and others like it "fit well with cultural industry goals and strategies of brand building and creating a loyal consumer base."[147] Even though such tie-ins reach a very small percentage of the audience, the assumption is that those viewers act as amplifiers who attract attention and draw in others. It is likely that ARGs function as a form of buzz marketing in which "encouraging the consumer to purchase is seen as secondary to generating talk about and recognition of the advertised brand."[148] The *Alias* ARG that launched alongside the first season's initial 2001 episodes had that effect and certainly attracted to the series the kind of tech-savvy early adopters that would be most likely to desire the kind of products on offer by Nokia, a cell phone company that used a web-based ARG as early as 1999 to market its own products. As Nokia sponsored the commercial-free first season premiere of *Alias* as part of its campaign to promote its new 3300 mobile phone series,[149] it is not surprising that the series had an extensive web presence. Nokia was involved in the interactive website set up by ABC and it co-sponsored a "code breaker sweepstakes." There was an interactive element to the site that linked the on-air, on-mobile, and online platforms as "'Alias Alert' messages would be sent to those who registered through their mobile messaging. These messages would require the receiver to unscramble a phrase from the pilot episode."[150]

Solving the tie-in ARG, known as "The *Alias* Web Puzzle,"[151] involved teamwork of the kind Levy and Jenkins describe in relation to the collective intelligence paradigm.[152] Jane McGonigal, an ARG designer, explains how ARGs are not played alone, but rather with "thousands of other people from all over the world" because "ARGs are not about individual fantasy, they're about collective engagement."[153] It is a very compelling form of consumer engagement, as ARG designer Joe DiNunzio notes, "The fact that ARG experiences evolve in real time and involve real people makes them compelling to be part of, on both sides of the fourth wall."[154] Succeeding at the scavenger hunt aspects of the *Alias* ARG required a group with different specialized knowledge sets such as familiarity with Russian or with de-stegging, that is, the extraction of a file that has been hidden by the process of steganography in which programmers use "software to digitally 'hide' documents inside (some prefer the term behind) JPEGs and GIFs."[155] Clues were planted around the web and viewers could find pieces of the puzzle or hints about the next clue by clicking on site guestbooks, mailboxes, and emails, interacting via chatbots, email, and AOL Instant Messenger, or listening to MP3 audio files, telephone voice mail, and conversations in Yahoo! chat rooms. These new media features acted as "vessels for passing along information" to fans intrigued by the idea of interacting in the online space with a television series. Cool as that seemed in 2001–2, viewers and those commenting on these games seem to forget that these kinds of TV tie-in ARGs are not simply ways to activate and reward the archival and investigative skills or predilections of dedicated viewers. They are also "vessels for passing along promotion" in that each click to activate an MP3, a chatbot, or an instant messaging system is also a potential consumer touch point for the network and its advertisers. This relationship is overt in the way a typical TV tie-in ARG is overtly sponsored by a single company or multiple companies (e.g., *The Lost Experience* brought to you by Verizon, DaimlerChrysler, and Coca-Cola). The ARG is also useful evidence of engagement to offer to advertisers involved with the series on any platform because the ARG provides a trail not only of the level of engagement of series' viewers, but also of the places to which they travel as they click around the web. The sponsors that get involved in the ARG benefit in other ways as well because the kinds of websites that companies build as part of the game, such as Sprite Sublymonal.com site and the Jeep Compass site, also exist independently of the game so that they can attract other unique users looking for product information.

The drawback is that sometimes dedicated viewers participate in these web experiences, but feel at the end that there was little return on their investment.[156] This was the case with many who participated in *The Lost Experience* ARG[157] and their disappointment might have had a negative effect on the reputation of the sponsoring companies or the networks with whom they made hybrid advertising deals. Suffice it to say that these viewers perceive these kinds of TV tie-in ARGS as less interactive than they are reactive in that participants are only following and reacting to a trail laid out by series' producers and marketers, all of which lead back to the on-air text, driving tune-in to the series or "buy in" to the franchise and its future pay-to-view installments. These kinds of ARGs are a disappointment when they do more to promote than provide content, especially that which would influence or deepen an understanding of the series' universe or mythology,[158] as would be the case in a more interactive or immersive ARG that was truly engaged in multiplatform storytelling.[159]

The *Alias* and *Lost* ARGs are technically transmedia content in that each extends the story beyond the parameters of one medium and brings the fiction into a series of others. Yet playing the game does little to impact our understanding of the content so the story is not really unfolding across multiple media even if the marketing is. The existence of these ARGs is evidence of the escalating promotional costs (tripled, by some estimates, since fall 2003)[160] that networks feel they must incur or the branded entertainment deals into which they must enter to promote series. They do so via multiplatform marketing because they have to "compete for attention amid a clutter of cable channels, the Internet, video games, iPods and other entertainment options."[161] ABC's Benson explained at the time the network supported the creation of the *Alias* ARG that his marketing team was looking for "innovative ways to increase awareness and tune-in." He described the free video game available online as both content and promotion. As he put it, "Alias is a signature show for our network, and Alias Underground is intended to complement on-air viewing while appealing to new audiences."[162]

The initial appeal of the *Alias* and *Lost* ARGs was that they promised to extend the fictional universe and viewers' interactions with it beyond the confines of the on-air series. They did more, however, to extend the on-air flow into overflow, which, as the term implies, is inherently a commercial practice.[163] The on-air flow model works according to the assumption that people are not watching discrete television products when they are watching TV; rather they are watching a flow of different, but interrelated elements of the broadcast TV schedule—story segments, network promotions, 30-second spots, feature film trailers, more 30-second spots, and story segments of the next series on the evening's schedule. The online overflow model in relation to the ARG has a similar structure given that to play the game viewers had to watch a fake commercial in the on-air series, access an in-game phone number, move through and around a mixture of content, network self-promotion, and sponsor advertising on the web, track back to the on-air flow in search of clues, and then follow the overflow again onto the web, and so on. *The Lost Experience* even encouraged viewers to attend live events associated with the series, such as the panel at Comic-Con comics convention.[164]

Perhaps it is a tribute to the seamless nature of the overflow strategies of these ARGs that when they begin viewers experience them as a game rather than as promotion. They get caught up in the novel experience of clicking around the web finding clues to and on a series of hidden websites. Only over time does the advertising and promotion feel as if it outweighs the appeal, or perhaps more importantly, the significance of the content when it seems as if nothing is revealed that leads to a different perspective on *Lost* or adds a new layer to its structure.[165] Given the ways these tie-in ARGs weave together content and promotion, it is easy to forget that these multiplatform experiences are created to find alternate promotional platforms in an environment in which DVR viewers can shift through network promotion as well as content. A Verizon spokesperson discussing its specially designed "Richer, Deeper, Broader" site that became part of *The Lost Experience* explains the changed environment: "As the consumer customer base becomes more and more segmented by personal interests, social networks and types of content, we have to find equally diverse and compelling new ways to reach everyone."[166] *Hollywood Reporter* uses the phrase "massively multiplayer marketing" to describe ARGs like *The Lost Experience* as a form of cross-media content that blends "everything from real-life treasure hunting to interactive storytelling, gaming and, increasingly, advertising."[167] Advertising is at the center not the periphery of *The Lost Experience*, which surprised people who seemed to forget for a moment that broadcast TV has always been structured around content offered in exchange for attention to advertising. The ARG's intended target is "a connected, generally hyperinformed Web community," although series like *Lost* are making the experiences more mainstream "blending the physical world with a fictional arc,"[168] such as when actors playing roles in the games performed their parts at Comic-Con or on *Jimmy Kimmel Live!*

The Jimmy Kimmel connection is an interesting one as he constantly references his *Lost* fandom during his self-titled late night ABC talk show. As a viewer I take at face value that Kimmel is an actual fan of the series given the number of mashups and bits he does in relation to his fandom. I would not be surprised to learn, however, that he is really just playing his part in a larger ABC crosspromotional imperative deemed necessary in the wake of one-off single episode, timeshifted and alternate platform TV watching that causes viewers to skip not only the 30-second spots, but also the network promotions for the rest of its schedule. If it is part of a promotional campaign, it is an effective one. Kimmel went so far as to become part of the official *The Lost Experience* ARG when he interviewed Hugh McIntyre, the supposed head of the real Dharma Initiative, but actually an actor hired by ABC.[169] Whether Kimmel was playing along because as a fan he wanted to be part of the willing suspension of disbelief essential to finding pleasure in the game or because he was required to do the segment, he boosted his profile with *Lost* viewers who would be more likely to watch future *Jimmy Kimmel Live!* episodes so as not to miss any of the other *Lost*-related content his team creates. He has conducted on-set visits and interviews and made fan videos, such as the one in which he inserts himself into a familiar *Lost* scene as one of the Dharma Initiative workers. Unlike the many guest star appearances by *Lost* cast members and producers, these comic bits are unannounced in the program guide synopses, so the only way to catch one is to watch the show regularly or hope the segment gets posted online. Whether his fandom is performed or contractual, Jimmy Kimmel's display of the pleasures and minor frustrations of TV fandom is an effective promotion for *Lost*. It is also an indicator of the changed representation of fans whose activities are increasingly seen as mainstream behavior engaged in by a good number of viewers (rather than a small fraction), at least on the consumption side (by watching *Lost* fan videos and mashups on YouTube, for example, rather than creating them).

Whatever the faults of the ARGs for *Alias* and *Lost*, they did represent a break-down of the distinction between the primary on-air text and the secondary online text. The collapse was complete by the time some of the *Alias* production team joined with former members of the *Smallville* web team to create NBC's *Heroes Evolutions*, representative of a transmedia approach to programming in which content appears simultaneously on multiple platforms, all of which together make up a TV product that is envisioned as a single networked text. In this model fan activities are not only acknowledged, but are also appropriated and integrated into the official text.[170] This approach has its drawbacks as executives concerned with maximum exposure to the broadcast market and using the web to promote a TV series and sponsor products can conflict with creators and fans interested in maximum exposure to all the aspects of the show's universe or mythology and the creation of and participation in ARGs that do contribute to and extend the viewer's understanding of the franchise's universe.

It is interesting to note that the official *Alias* ARG was budgeted for a short-run to build up to the premiere and to continue to drive tune-in during the series' first month. Once the official web puzzle came to an end a more full transmedia experience began because *Alias* producers and web content providers Alexander and Orci found ways to use the free resources of the web to keep the game going.[171] Alexander describes the experience of using their "own computers, and tools available to anybody" to launch a transmedia franchise and its marketing campaign.[172] Alexander became one of the main advocates both for transmedia storytelling and for the corresponding development of a new media compensation formula because he had first-hand experience of how labor-intensive creating a web presence was.[173] The sites may function to promote the series, but they were content-based pro-motions that required both content creation and new media expertise.[174]

Channel branding in international and domestic scheduling

TV tie-in ARGs represent the ways in which television shows are both one element of a larger network flow of content and promotion on a single U.S. network and one element of a stand-alone franchise with international circulation. The international reception of *The Lost Experience* is especially significant as it points to two shifting paradigms in the U.S. television industry: the shift in the place of importance of media savvy fans and of the international distribution platform,[175] as those fans can be courted globally via fan- and producer-created websites. Both shifts are related to the impact of the World Wide Web on U.S. television. Viewers are often now responsible for or influenced by the increasingly global and paratextual circulation of the series, that is, by the way the TV series exists online and a franchise is built prior to the official on-air premiere.[176] The network-determined premiere date had been the marker of the birth of a new series, but now it usually exists on the web from the moment its pilot is greenlit, if not from its conception.[177] Producers learned to leverage these paratextual sites to their advantage, having watched how much trouble Twentieth Century FOX caused for itself when it tried to curtail the fan practice of creating websites and other paratextual web content for upcoming series, hence bringing them into existence prior to the official launch of the series and/or its carefully constructed web presence.[178]

Such paratextual circulation is global and therefore can affect international circulation and reception as well. Bad reviews can spread around the globe and news of a series cancellation after a short U.S. run becomes especially damaging when the news circulates before the series even debuts in other markets.[179] Good internet buzz is a problem as well because non-U.S. viewers are often frustrated by the time lag between the American debut of a blockbuster and their home country premiere. Aware that the pacing of windows of distribution needed to be sped up so that there was less of a time delay, media conglomerates worked to reduce it.[180] Disney found a way, for example, to send the most recent *Lost* episode as a digital copy via an undersea fiber-optic line to BSkyB for broadcast on the U.K. pay-TV service's main satellite channel. It also built an elaborate digital and satellite delivery system in Burbank. Part of the reason for the development of this system is to discourage piracy because the gaps between the domestic and international windows prompt people to find other ways to acquire a copy of the latest episode. As the *Wall Street Journal* explained in 2007, this attention to the international circulation of their TV series reflects the pressure on U.S. networks "to make more money on their shows and increase their share of the $110 billion non-U.S. television market."[181]

With these concerns in mind during the creation of *The Lost Experience*, ABC made sure to partner with "19 other networks around the globe to relaunch the 'Hanso Foundation' site as part" of the ARG and made sure it was a coordinated global effort[182] so that its kickoff through an embedded phone number placed within an in-story world faux commercial that ran along with a May 2006 episode would happen on the same day. Time zone differences impacted that plan, of course, and producers were surprised to discover that although it was the middle of the night and the episode had not yet aired, many U.S. fans had found out about the ad and were calling the number. As one Australian programmer put it, "The television gossip world is global these days."[183] While simultaneity would never be possible because of time zones, the fact that producers would even try suggests a new level of attention to global audiences as well as global revenue. This kind of global awareness is part, of course, of the more general conglomerate-wide business imperative at Disney, which had been successfully expanding and solidifying its global brand presence during the decade.[184]

Once the rights to a series like *Lost* are acquired by an international channel or cable/satellite provider, it controls how the series is promoted and scheduled, once again demonstrating that scheduling is often the industrial factor that most dramatically shapes reception.[185] In the U.K. *Lost* was impacted positively by its season one and two acquisition by Channel 4 as it was scheduled alongside a roster of U.S. series, including *The Sopranos, Sex and the City, Friends, E.R.,* and *West Wing,* among others, that gave it a quality TV patina.[186] When the rights for season three were poached by satellite provider Sky,[187] which was in the midst of a brand war with its chief competitor Virgin, *Lost* was caught in the middle because Sky would not let Virgin carry it.[188] While that meant that households without Sky would no longer get the series, the war turned *Lost* into an even more desirable commodity because it was unattainable. Those without Sky service who were already aware of and hooked on *Lost* would likely buy it on download or DVD, an outcome that would only add to the Disney bottom line. Other series are less lucky in their scheduling, which was the case with FOX's Joss Whedon series *Buffy the Vampire Slayer* which was run in the 6–8 p.m. tea time slot on BBC2 and censored accordingly. Mirroring some of the license fee and scheduling problems related to the WB's loss of *Buffy* to UPN and the resulting uncoupling in the U.S. from its companion series *Angel*, the series were acquired by different channels in the U.K. so they also could not run as a pair.[189] Complicating matters was the fact that they also had a distribution window during which they appeared on subscription channel (British Sky Broadcasting's) Sky One, which was affiliated with the series' Twentieth Century FOX production company through News Corp. owner Rupert Murdoch.[190] Sky was able to carry *Buffy* and *Angel* within weeks not months or a year after their original U.S. airing and screen them in primetime and use the series along with others to make its own claim to being the home of "must have" US-TV.[191]

In the international arena series are positioned in relation to the brand of the channel on which they appear with its scheduling choices activating new meanings.[192] In order to stake out a brand position as the home of in-demand U.S. imports, for example, U.K. Channel 4 acquired a range of series that enabled it to build a schedule that reads like the ideal DVR playlist of recent American hits. Detached from its original network and channel associations that impacted reception, these series become on Channel 4 a stream of undifferentiated Must-See US-TV series, regardless of whether they originally appeared on NBC, ABC or HBO.

U.S. networks want to prevent just such a detachment, one that is more likely in an environment in which U.S. viewers are accessing network content via an alternative to the broadcast platform. Disney-ABC Television Group made its historic deal with iTunes, for instance, because its site allowed it to maintain a branded environment for its series. This attention to brand environments is most evident on ABC itself in the network's use of high concept customized channel identifiers featuring images that make indelible in viewers' minds the entwinement of ABC and each of its series. Several of these idents run during the flow between story segments and each series' custom identifier appears on-screen to signal that the episode is about to air. The ABC channel call letters are still enclosed in a circle. The difference is that now ABC shares the space in some way with an iconic image associated with each series. The ABC logo is stamped on the center of the screen over an image that also references the series in some way. In the case of *Ugly Betty*, there is a New York skyline backdrop and Betty's signature red glasses hang from the side of the ABC logo. That logo has an apple inside it for *Desperate Housewives* and is filled with water for *Lost*, specifically water from the ocean whose endlessness is contrasted in the custom ident to the deserted island seen off in the distance. This *Lost* themed channel ident seems particularly connected to the ABC brand given that the general brand identifier of the Disney-ABC Television Group[193] is a body of water into which one drop falls, causing ripples that expand ever outward as a symbol of how one product is seen as interconnected to the revenue stream. Each product is also a potential space for promotion for another from the Disney-ABC Television Group or some other Disney division.[194] The more general ABC channel idents that run between story segments pick up on this concept as well by featuring a streak or flourish of what can be read sometimes as water and other times as wand sparks moving, usually diagonally, across the screen although sometimes bouncing around or circulating in some way.[195] It is interesting to note that these idents, which also move off screen and then return as if referencing the web address inherent in the *start here* brand identifier, also point to ambivalence at the heart of the relationship of ABC to its series. By 2009 television series had become discrete products to be consumed individually (and internationally) either as episodes or seasons; yet episodes were still expected to function as non-detachable parts of an optimally performing primetime flow of television content on a U.S. broadcast network that had to attract audiences and the advertisers that paid for the potential of catching their attention.

These concerns about network branding and about series that have become detached from the network to take on a discrete life as a brand of their own are evident in the network's promotional flow during the May 29, 2008 *Lost* season four finale. Spring season finales have long been used to promote summer and fall schedules and this one was no exception. A comparison to 2004 promotions associated with *Lost* demonstrates the changes over the years in the network's positioning of the series and its conception of its relationship to the rest of the ABC schedule. In its first season *Lost* episodes and the promotional spots for them were still purposefully misdirecting attention toward suspicious survivors as the writers had not yet revealed many of the more surprising backstories or the depths of the island's series of mysteries. A 2004 promo makes *Lost* seem like a fictionalized *Survivor* given that it shows the beach dwellers in a darkness lit only by torches.

It offers heightened drama because these survivors are stranded with little hope of rescue. The footage and dialogue chosen throws suspicion on a character named John Locke, especially when he is shown with a trunk filled with hunting knives and we hear someone say, "Who is this guy." The promo ends: *now's the time to get Lost.*

The tone contrasts to the 2008 ABC campaign tagline: *the fun starts here.* The 2008 flow positions the fall schedule's scripted programming so that it seems compatible with *Lost* as well as the lighter tone of the upcoming summer 2008 ABC schedule. The breakout hits of 2004–5 are still on the schedule, but their tone is frothier. Gone is the searing black comedy of the sometimes truly desperate women of season one of *Desperate Housewives* and the rawness of early *Grey's Anatomy*, with its contentious mother and mentor relationship and its colleagues'/competitors' storylines. While the actual series might be a bit darker, the promotion for the new nighttime drama *Dirty Sexy Money* emphasized its frothy elements in the vignettes representing the series and in the teaser lines: "For them, life is just a game—get ready to play ... *Dirty Sexy Money* on ABC." A lighter take on *Lost*-style genre-mixing is inherent in the next promotion: "A touch of romance. A touch of mystery. A touch of fun. *Pushing Daisies*. Wednesday's this fall." The excerpts position the series as a stylized, surreal fairy tale. One vignette shows a man touching and waking a sleeping beauty in a coffin. He says "What if you didn't have to be dead?" The larger-than-life fairy tale quality continues when another vignette shows a tiny, wide-eyed woman inside a cartoonish diner booth. She leans forward and says half curiously and half conspiratorially, "How mysterious!" Clearly, we are in the realm of magical realism.

Most of the rest of the promotions are intended to get audiences excited about the "fun" of the upcoming summer season. Throughout the breaks during the *Lost* finale the lightweight summer reality shows are emphasized. They are positioned as silly competitions that are fun to watch because they are self-reflexive about their own silliness. The promotion for *Wipeout*, an obstacle course reality program, adopts a *Lost*-style serious tone and then gets silly. The text that is written over selected images and footage from the competition is also read earnestly by an announcer, complete with pauses for effect: "There comes a time ... when ordinary people face ... extraordinary obstacles." In this case, it is an obstacle course that includes three enormous red, rubber balls. Contestants, who are trying to move from ball to ball, smack into them instead and wipe out into the muddy water below. The cheeky promo then adds its self-aware commentary and corny tagline: *the summer's next big splash is here.* The mock-seriousness continues for the next summer programming promo: "Ten unsuspecting Americans ... *Lost* on an entirely different island," which a giggling contestant reveals to be Tokyo, Japan where she competes in the deliberately silly *I Survived a Japanese Game Show.* The big surprise was that ABC executives decided to revive *The Mole*, although they should have learned the lesson that Ned does in *Pushing Daisies*: raising the dead is almost never a good idea. With the core similarities between the gamedoc and *Lost*, it is not surprising that the latter's two-hour finale flow includes four promotions for

The Mole, with one in the first commercial pod and one as the bumper commercial at the end of the two-hour block. The other two are in the penultimate pods in each of the hours.

The Mole promotion that kicks off the first commercial pod is the longest. The announcer tells viewers: "One Mission will bring 12 people together. The mole will tear them apart. The summer's biggest adventure is back. It's one for all. One against all." The tone is similar to the other three promos, all of which also associate *The Mole* with sabotage, mind games, and a search for clues. In the series' excerpts we see contestants in the confessional or hear them via indirect sound saying into the camera: "I've got to keep my eye on her" and "There's no one I trust." All are things that could easily be said about *Lost*'s season four and, will, viewers watching the promos suspect, apply to season five. They already know that characters have made alliances with people who proved untrustworthy, so there is a likelihood of some traitorous behavior. Watching *Lost* as well as gamedocs has also taught viewers that calling attention to those assumed to be saboteurs is a method through which producers distract attention from those who actually are. Season five of *Lost* did not disappoint, as it cast suspicion on several characters and never quite revealed who can and cannot be trusted. As viewers had to wait until January 2009 to watch these intricate plots and subplots unfold, they once again had a long summer and fall in which to speculate. Programmers were likely hoping these fans might spend some of that time sharpening their speculation skills by watching *The Mole*. In a *Lost*-style pitch the announcer in the penultimate promo begins: "In 4 Days the summer's biggest mystery will begin. 12 people will be sent on an international mission. One will try to sabotage it." The accompanying excerpts include the footage of various contestants in the confessional. They all say they are not the mole and the announcer counters: "Too bad one of them is lying." Then he prompts potential viewers: "Follow the Clues. Question Everything. And Above All, Trust No One!" Such tracking and speculating activities are precisely those in which *Lost* fans have been known to engage.

This *Mole* promo is especially significant as it builds a bridge from the spring season of *Lost* across the summer of clues planted on *The Lost Experience*'s hyperlinked websites and continuing into the fall until the January premiere. Those already familiar with the *Lost Experience* will recognize that the commercial pod also includes a stealth promotion in the form of an odd advertisement for a company called Octagon Global Recruiting. The company is supposedly holding a recruiting fair for various positions including janitors and IVF specialists, both jobs which are associated with the *Lost* characters of season five. The date of the recruiting fair coincides with Comi-Con, which is the comics convention at which a panel of *Lost* stars and producers always offers fans some clues about and a sneak preview of some elements of the new season. More to the point, the Octagon ad is typical of the way *Lost* maintains the fiction that the Dharma Initiative and other entities and companies mentioned in *Lost* are real by never breaking out of the fiction.

The final fall drama promotion, which runs between the faux recruiting advertisement and *The Mole* promo, also offers some clues about *Lost*, but you would have to watch season five to know it. It is for ABC's format adaptation of the BBC's *Life on Mars* and images that reveal its 1970s setting are accompanied by the proclamation: "Welcome back to the '70s. It's going to be a trip!" *Lost* viewers watching its season finale already know that the group of characters called "the Oceanic Six" will have to travel back to the island from which they managed to escape, but they don't know yet that some of the characters will also be traveling in time and get stuck in the 1970s. *Life on Mars* starts in the present, but quickly jumps back to the 1970s in its fall 2008 pilot and the rest of the season's episodes continue to explore the long-arc mystery of whether the main character has really experienced time travel, is on a drug trip, has lost his mind, or is experiencing something completely different. A series that embeds its long-arc time-traveling mystery within an episodic police procedural, *Life on Mars* was shifted in January to be the 10 p.m. drama to follow *Lost*. The series did not prove to be a hit, but it was a more logical pairing with *Lost* than the other shows that had been tried previously. The best solution for *Lost* scheduling was to pair it with itself, as was the case in spring 2008, when each week had a repeat and an original.

While the connections made between *Lost* and other ABC programs during this promotional flow make sense, it is doubtful whether many *Lost* viewers were inspired to tune in to the other parts of the upcoming schedules being promoted. The linear flow-based scheduling and promotion model does not work that well with circularly oriented television series built with overflow as an essential feature of their storytelling. At the end of an hour of *Lost*, viewers want more *Lost*, and might go online to get it, re-watch parts of the episode that just aired, or think ahead to purchasing the DVD or some other franchise product to extend the pleasures of the consumption experience. At the end of *Desperate Housewives*' hour, in contrast, staying to watch *Brothers and Sisters* feels more like a continuation of the same spectatorial pleasures on offer in the previous hour. Its viewers are more likely to conform to the Must-See TV model of watching programming flow and sticking with an evening's network fare, as some did, judging by the ratings, in the case of the *Desperate Housewives*–*Brothers and Sisters* Sunday pairing. The same is true on Thursdays with *Grey's Anatomy* and the female-target series with which it was variously scheduled.

Just as broadcast television had relied for so long on the sitcom because it was thought to put people in the right frame of mind to consume, so do these ABC series put people in the right frame of mind to continue watching television. They are not structured so that upon an episode's conclusion viewers feel compelled to keep talking about the series instead of watching the next one. Neither are they likely to want to immediately engage in web-enabled activities, such as downloading songs, looking up allusions, or logging on to see how other viewers are predicting outcomes based on the most recent episodes. That *Desperate Housewives* has a multiplatform extension with Sprint mobisodes is not surprising as such hybrid advertising is now becoming a standard feature of many series, but the series is not one that is generally designed to attract viewers who prefer to entertain themselves via web- and mobile-enabled entertainment.

It is significant that *American Idol*, unbeatable in the ratings, was in May 2009 no better than *Lost* at providing a lead-in audience for a new series. *Idol* was the broadcast TV show that had done the seemingly impossible in the new media-sphere; it managed to attract to broadcast television people who spent more time entertaining themselves and engaging with others via new media. It did so by turning new media users and music downloaders back into TV watchers by enabling them to combine watching television, downloading music, and text messaging into a single entertainment experience. These early adopters modeled behavior for the rest of the audience, making text messaging and downloading music to portable devices something moms and grandmas across America can now do.[196] What it doesn't do is retain viewers for the block of network programming that follows it. It didn't need to, of course, since it was a blockbuster earner on its own and was sometimes even scheduled into double blocks, indicative of how the best lead-in for *Idol* was more *Idol*.

FOX thought its new series *Glee* would be the perfect schedule pairing for *American Idol*, but when the pilot aired after the *Idol* season finale in May 2009, *Glee* did not retain its viewers. On paper it must have looked like an unbeatable duo as *Glee* was designed to tap into the appeal of the singing competition gamedoc since it was centered on a high school show choir, which performed several full songs and routines in the course of each episode. It even offered series music on immediate iTunes download. The bold scheduling decision to offer the season premiere in May was part of a plan to offer a sneak peek of *Glee* and then use the summer to build buzz through Facebook sites, iTunes downloads, and a mini-"tour" of mall perfor-mances. The buzz did build over the summer and, coupled with rave reviews, helped *Glee* to perform well on Wednesdays at 9 p.m. when it came back in the fall with a repeat of the premiere followed by a new episode in its official premiere slot. Perhaps the *Idol–Glee* pairing would have worked better if the new series followed the first single hour of *Idol* in January as viewers are now conditioned to expect midseason premieres. It is just as likely to have done no better there, however, as programs primarily designed to attract new media viewers are not ideally suited for Must-See-TV-style linear scheduling and lead-in logic.

Disney-ABC 2009: linearity and circularity in multiplatform US-TV

Over the six seasons of *Lost*, ABC changed from a fourth place underdog to megahit generator and settled in at the end of the decade as a solid competitor with strengths across a micro-segmented twenty-first-century broadcast schedule filled with a variety of program types. In terms of long-arc mysteries, things had come full circle since *Alias*'s premiere in 2001 when Abrams said long-arc pro-gramming that had been relegated to the fringe networks (by which he meant FOX and WB) had found a home on the Big Three networks. By 2008, these kinds of programs were mostly pushed back to the fringes, as was signaled by the premiere of Abrams' *Fringe* on FOX's fall schedule and Whedon's *Dollhouse* joining it in winter 2009. *Lost* was still holding its own on ABC that year even though a good number of viewers were probably watching it via off-air formats. On the broadcast platform, *Lost* found itself on a micro-segmented schedule, with reality TV, sitcoms, nighttime dramedies and procedurals. The network's high achiever was *Dancing with the Stars*, a gamedoc that debuted in summer 2005. ABC seemed to be focusing on romance both in terms of relationships and in a more classic sense of texts with satisfying resolutions, if not full-blown happy endings. It is interesting to note that in the fall 2006 season when *Dancing with the Stars* was its 8 p.m. lead-in, *Lost* focused more on its love triangles. The infamous Kate and Sawyer love scene aired in the final episode of *Lost*'s short-run fall season, a week before the season finale of *Dancing with the Stars*.

Preparing for *Lost*'s series finale in 2010, ABC did greenlight *Flash Forward*, a possible replacement in the timeshifting long arc mystery. Its scheduling at 8 p.m. may have represented that ABC finally understood, after several years of trying to figure out the key to its magic, that *Lost*'s core appeal could be that it shares the focus of successful gamedocs on tracking the behavior and the backstories of members of an ensemble as they find themselves in a variety of out-of-the-ordinary situations. Also with a gamedoc element to its structure, *Flash Forward* follows *Lost* in the way it offers viewers the opportunity to judge whether the characters' behavior in the current predicament documented by the series' present-time action has impacted both their long-held behavioral patterns and their assumptions about their own leadership or heroic capabilities. Like *Lost*, *Flash Forward* adds a super-natural and/or pseudo-scientific twist about the characters' flash forwards of their future selves, the knowledge of which impacts their behavior in the present and raises many philosophical questions about free will and fate. As *Lost* did before it, *Flash Forward* has a complementary and simultaneously constructed series of linked sites (a parallel of the on-air Mosaic website set up by the series' FBI team) and a series of secret websites (Red Panda, Blue Hand, among others).

The series' production team has the advantage of *Lost*'s example, both in terms of what does and does not work for a long-arc serial mystery on broadcast TV. Intended to attract the *Lost* fan base, the premiere episode featured a few "Easter eggs" for them, including a Los Angeles skyscraper billboard for *Lost*'s Oceanic Airlines. *Flash Forward*'s own mysterious organization Red Panda was advertised on a bus ad in the background of a key shot. That reference to the series mythology was balanced by a reference to the ABC schedule when a bus ad for the season premiere of *Desperate Housewives* appeared in the background of two shots. Added to the link between the two ABC series is the fact that the character in the scene is associated with a picture perfect family life that is ripe for revelations of unex-pressed discontent. Clearly, ABC is hoping that *Flash Forward* attracts the fanalysts who use the fast forward and rewind buttons on their clickers to scrutinize such details in the background of shots. For them, producers insert a split second clue in every opening title sequence. The series tries to offer answers as well as questions so that casual viewers can still follow the series. Even more interesting is the fact that the characters are compiling a website for keeping track of and comparing all the flash forward glimpses of the future that people saw during the global blackout of consciousness that is the mysterious event that the series investigates. This fictional website has a corresponding actual website where the fan tracking of the series' mystery can parallel the characters' tracking.[197] With its neatly interlinked on-air and online elements and its integration of references to its own schedule, ABC clearly has tried, perhaps too hard, to construct this long-arc serial to replace *Lost*, but not to replicate its less broadcast-friendly elements. The fall part of *Flash Forward*'s split first season failed to match the appeal of *Lost*, while replicating its problems. It started strong, but soon posted ratings losses. Whether those ratings declines are due to the diminishing appeal of its content or its long-arc serial structure has yet to be determined.

By the final seasons of the decade, NBC already had concluded that there was a general problem with the long-arc serial as a broadcast form and embraced instead brand-centric comedies and dramas. It wanted to create programming that didn't just have the potential to insert the equivalent of one *Desperate Housewives* bus ad, but a whole fleet. NBC's brand-centric approach was not without controversy. As the next chapter details, the biggest critics were the producers of the network's Thursday night ironicoms who had to figure out ways to have their series promote NBC Universal and its sponsors, without detracting from series content. NBC's saturation of its schedule with brand-based TV seems like a miscalculation, but with new programmers in place at its start, the next decade may bring some game-changing scheduling for the currently fourth place network.

In contrast, ABC's final schedule of the decade had an appealing depth and breadth, balancing blockbusters and steady earners, scripted and unscripted series, and new formats with variations on classic television genres. It included signature gamedocs (*Dancing with the Stars* and *The Bachelor*); silly game shows (*Wipeout*); prestige reality series (*Extreme Makeover Home Edition*); docusoaps (such as behavior makeover series *Wife Swap* and *Supernanny*); serial dramedy (*Desperate Housewives*); nighttime serial hybrids (*Brothers and Sisters* and *Grey's Anatomy*); long-arc serial mysteries (*Lost* and *Flash Forward*); event genre miniseries (*V*); and news magazines (*20/20*). While it had a weak area in the procedural category in which other networks have succeeded, it found a possible contender in *Castle*, which had debuted in spring 2009 and experienced an unexpected ratings surge in fall 2009. More importantly, ABC finally found a workable slate of new sitcoms with standout *Modern Family* being supported by *The Middle* and *Cougar Town*. With only one failure among the four 2009 sitcoms branded as ABC Comedy Wednesdays, the network has a prime slot open for sitcom development in fall 2010. While the 2000s began with seasons in which broadcast schedules were overloaded with a single style of programming to the exclusion of others (game shows; gamedocs; procedurals; long-arc serials), it ended with ABC showcasing this micro-segmented schedule with something in every category and a programming slate representative of a range of tastes and demographics.

This list of programs, of course, only tells half the story given that each television series is now integrated both into a grid schedule for the on-air platform, which is defined by a limited network-determined set of choices, and into a content stream, where the series circulates among an immense array of content across a variety of delivery and access platforms. While many commentators celebrate the freedom of this new mediasphere, networks and media conglomerates still retain schedule control in relation to release dates and modes of access and determine when to start and stop releasing content. Of course, even that has become non-linear given that user-generated content, piracy, and continued content consumption can give the series a pre-release existence and a long afterlife.

All this is indicative of how the multiplatform landscape has given each television series a dual existence. It is a part of a whole evening's experience on a terrestrial channel, but it also is an individual product (often an interconnected set of products) detached from the network-determined scheduling grid. New media has enabled series to be put into wider circulation and liberated them from the bottleneck of a predetermined sequence of distribution windows. Television content is still released on a schedule determined by its owners, of course, but in some platforms it can now be consumed according to the schedule of its viewers. Increasingly, multiplatform schedulers have even adopted more compressed and sometimes near-simultaneous distribution windowing in order to put an official copy in circulation to deter unofficial modes of access to content.

All of these issues are captured within ABC's brand identifier *start here* and its accompanying graphic of a rush of effervescent liquid. Although in a few cases the substance glitters or flashes as if it were sparks released from a magic wand, it more often appears as if it is a stream of liquid surging out of a bottleneck. The latter image evokes linearity as it is a jet of water, circularity as the liquid seems to be moving around the space propelled by its own momentum, and containment as it may actually be bouncing off walls of a large, but ultimately contained space, or at least it hints at the latter since those boundaries exist somewhere outside the space of the television screen. The channel ident's accompanying message, *start here*, implies that despite its embrace of the circulation of its content and its viewers, ABC wants the on-air platform to remain primary and schedules its release of multiplatform content so that its circulation hopefully results in a return to it.

When read as wand sparks, the ABC channel ident graphics subtly establish that the broadcast network is one part of a revenue stream of the Disney-ABC Television Group, which is itself one part of the Disney conglomerate. The connection becomes explicit if one clicks over to the Disney Channel to see that its idents feature series stars waving wands around the screen to spread magic sparks and to signal, with a tap on the title, the start of the next program on the schedule. The wand sparks graphic evokes "Disney magic" as a brand identifier to signal to viewers that a media text is a Disney product and as such will be marked by certain Disney qualities. Having established itself as a multichannel, multiplatform, and global entertainment brand, Disney has inspired others to embrace branding and synergy, although not necessarily with the same results, as the next chapter on NBC Universal indicates.

Chapter Four

Branding, synergy, and product integration on NBC

Two guest star and cast member pairings in a November 20, 1999 broadcast of *Saturday Night Live* (SNL) speak to the difference a decade has made not only for NBC, but for broadcast television more generally. The opening skit featured SNL regular Darryl Hammond impersonating Donald Trump and announcing not only that he was running for president, but also that his running mate would be John Carpenter, the big winner of *Who Wants to Be a Millionaire?*, the ABC gameshow that was then a national obsession. An opening monologue followed in which guest host and NBC sitcom star Jennifer Aniston interacted with Tina Fey, just promoted to head writer of SNL, but almost nine years away from her infamous impersonation of Republican vice-presidential candidate Sarah Palin. Planted in the audience, a then-unknown Fey posed as a stalker of Aniston and her boyfriend Brad Pitt. In the decade since this episode aired the programming that is considered by viewers to be Must-See TV and the places and devices on which to watch it have changed dramatically.

The transformation of NBC programming and network strategies during this time and the changing perception of the network in the eyes of both viewers and the industry[1] enables a consideration of the impact of the network's movement away from long-arc serials and its embrace of a brand-centric paradigm resulting in a schedule stocked with programming featuring former SNL cast members. By the 2008 season NBC was also applying the circulatory paradigm inherent in the Must-Click TV model to transform television series into potential circulation platforms for network brand assets as well as sponsors' goods. This move was even more controversial, but NBC saw it as a necessary response to the impact of timeshifting on ratings and on the advertising rates linked to them.

During the decade NBC embraced the rise of format and franchise as well as sponsor and network brand-based TV programming mixed together on micro-segmented network schedules and official websites. This micro-segmentation was an attempt to compete with the variety of narrowcast programming available on cable. It was also a response to the challenge that the availability of content on alternate delivery platforms posed to the advertiser-dependent broadcast TV model. Series were transformed into franchises with web, mobile, social networking, and other extensions designed to follow viewers to whatever spaces in which they sought out content. The point, of course, was to monetize the content on offer in those spaces. Soon broadcast networks made deals with or created their own new media delivery platforms for the circulation of content and promotion. They also worked to reinvigorate the broadcast model through the recalibration of the balance between storytelling and promotion or between on-air and online content.

Much has changed for NBC and broadcast TV more generally since 1999. In that year NBC was still enjoying its ratings dominance and so it was only a little nervous about, but not yet threatened by, ABC's decision to strip *Who Wants to Be a Millionaire?* across its 1999–2000 schedule in August, March, January and to schedule it thereafter as a three-day-a-week program. SNL tapped into NBC's status through guest host Jennifer Aniston, one of the stars of *Friends*, the highest rated of the sitcoms running in the highest-rated primetime Thursday block of programming that NBC branded as Must-See TV. Dominating that weeknight is significant since it is viewed by Hollywood studios as the prime preview slot for the coming weekend's new films. Of course, previews are liberally dispersed throughout the weekly schedule, reflecting the fact that studios see television as a promotional platform. In addition to the usual rounds of primetime and daytime talk shows, actors sometimes acquire cool cachet by agreeing to host SNL when they have new movies to promote. As her own movie had come out earlier in the year, Aniston ended up promoting *Fight Club*, the movie in which her soon-to-be husband was starring. By 2005 Aniston would make the covers of all the entertainment magazines not as part of one of Hollywood most glamorous couples, but as part of one of its most infamous love triangles when husband Brad Pitt left her for his costar Angelina Jolie. At the time NBC also was making the headlines in the trade publications for its sudden reversal of fortunes.

Reality TV formats

While NBC was still grabbing the top ratings slots at the time, the 1999 SNL episode already presaged the network's fall. As star of the ensemble sitcom *Friends*, Aniston represented the 1990s dominance of NBC's Must-See TV schedule,[2] but the ABC gameshow referenced in the opening sketch was that year's actual Must-See TV. Unscripted programming like it would continue to knock the sitcoms out of the top spots and empower CBS and FOX, the networks that featured the most popular unscripted shows.[3]

By stripping *Who Wants to Be a Millionaire?* across its primetime schedule, ABC not only dominated ratings, but brought back a genre to primetime that the broadcast TV industry had proclaimed dead. It would be the scheduling move that would impact broadcast TV for the next decade.[4] At the end of May 2000 CBS took a risk on *Survivor*, from then unknown producer Mark Burnett who would become the decade's dominant force in format TV. Following on its heels in early July was the gamedoc *Big Brother*, a format that was already emerging as a global phenomenon.[5] When it added *The Amazing Race* in 2001, CBS secured THE powerhouse Reality TV lineup of shows that are still on as of this writing.

Although making light of *Millionaire* in 1999, NBC programmers soon took the threat seriously. NBC would try to top *Millionaire* with *Fear Factor*, its infamous bottom feeder stunt/dare gameshow that debuted on June 11, 2001, two months after the premiere of its format adaptation of the UK's *The Weakest Link*, a quiz show in which the loser was told: *you are the weakest link*. FOX bested the Big Three networks in June 2002 with its translation of the UK format *Pop Idol* into *American Idol*. The musical talent competition held onto the top spots whenever it ran, posting ratings well above the rest. The success of *American Idol* was aided by the decision to draw it out over at least two nights, so that there was a competition show and a separate results show on a subsequent night. FOX even aired the audition tapes for the early elimination rounds in which judge Simon Cowell found various insulting ways to tell contestants that they were talentless or that despite some skill they still didn't have what it would take to be the next American Idol. The show catapulted FOX out of "the Fourth Network" position and made it a true contender for one of the top three slots. Once FOX created what it called its "programming tsunami," of *24*, *House*, and *American Idol*, it even knocked NBC into fourth place, something that was unimaginable in 1999.[6] The network that once prided itself on being an oasis for quality dramas and smart sitcoms would continue to try to compete in the Reality programming arena with NBC shows such as *Average Joe*, *Dog Eat Dog*, *Meet My Folks*, *For Love or Money*, *Who Wants to Marry My Dad,* and *The Restaurant*.

The particular irony of the opening sketch of that 1999 SNL is that a few years later NBC's attempt to regain its status as the Must-See TV destination involved making a deal with Donald Trump to star in a gamedoc, the unscripted format that merged competition with documentary footage and melodramatic interactions between and backstories about the contestants. *The Apprentice,* created by Mark Burnett, has been on the NBC Thursday night schedule in one form or another since January 2004, its highest rated season to date with a #7 ranking.

Humiliation is to some degree at the center of *The Apprentice* and, even more so, of its spinoff *The Celebrity Apprentice* (January 2008), especially in the boardroom scenes in which aspiring entrepreneurs are berated for poor performance or bad behavior and dismissed by Trump with the catch-phrase: *you're fired*. Although it sounds like a humiliation-based gamedoc, NBC's *The Biggest Loser* (first premiering October 2004) emphasizes encouragement of its weight-loss contestants. Even those who don't make their weight and are voted off the show continue to compete for the prize for most at-home weight loss. Lighter in tone as well, *Deal or No Deal* is the *Let's Make a Deal*-style game show that premiered in December 2005 and features a bevy of bikini-clad models holding suitcases that may or may not contain the show's top prize. The show and several of NBC's other unscripted series such as *Dog Eat Dog* could count as "Jiggle TV," the insult NBC hurled at ABC when it became the top network in the late 1970s through beautiful-girls-in-bikinis programming such as *Charlie's Angels*.[7]

Although it scored a temporary ratings surge with *Deal or No Deal*, NBC still could not quite extricate itself from its ratings loser status, not even after snapping up *America's Got Talent*, adapted from the big UK format sensation. The problem is that RTV programs have a short shelf life, particularly because the ratings-challenged networks resort to stripping episodes across the schedule, or offering several episodes a week or creating special extended episodes. As was the case with *Millionaire*, the pattern is usually that audiences that are initially enthralled with a gamedoc or game show become less interested with each season. As the opposite is often true of sitcoms and they have the added benefit of a long half-life in syndication, it is not surprising that NBC acquired some format sitcoms, initially BBC's *Coupling* and *The Office*. At first the strategy seemed like a failure, with *Coupling* not lasting the 2003 season and *The Office* making a poor ratings showing in its initial six-episode run starting in March 2005. An ironicom set at the fictional Dunder Mifflin company, a paper supplier for a paperless world, *The Office* started to grow an audience, especially after it moved away from the template of the UK original. The series' mockumentary style of filming allows characters to register ironic reactions directly for the "cameraperson" and viewers, to speak directly to them in the one-on-one "confessionals," or to be the subject of a caught-on-video moment. All three elements characterize many gamedocs. Also similar to reality TV, the story segments are often spaces into which product pitches are integrated. While *The Office* has some infamous product integration episodes, as will be discussed later, most episodes have some element of product pitching. In "Email Surveillance," for example, unwelcome cyber-snooping boss Michael Scott wedges himself between his employees at their break room lunch table and starts talking about the joys of Cup-o-Noodles: "This is a meal in a cup, right here. Hot, tasty, reminds me of college. Lived on this stuff. Brain food" (2.9).

While *The Office* integrations work because of the mitigating humor of the scenes, the integration of products into the challenges contestants faced in *The Apprentice* just made those story segments play like thinly veiled commercials.[8] Although it builds product integration right into the structure of the program, reality TV is less often the target of complaints about such tactics as it is already assumed to be purely economically motivated programming. Scripted programming is subject to more critique. One of the most mocked examples is the single-sponsor deal NBC arranged for its talking super car series *Knight Rider*, which had a trial run as a 2007 made-for-TV movie that played like an endless Ford commercial.[9] As a reboot of a 1970s series, it was already a brand asset. As a car-centric series, it was ideally situated for the automobile commercials that dominate broadcast TV. It is not surprising that NBC went ahead and gave it a series order and that Ford signed on as one of the sponsors. The Ford placements were story-consistent, but the stories themselves started off weak and got worse. The end was near when the producers retooled the series, keeping only the younger cast members, and turning the car into something that resembled an autobot from *Transformers*, a feature film that was itself product placement excessive.[10] The barely-there story left plenty of time for car commercial-style footage of the Ford Mustang Shelby in motion.

With the addition of the autobot feature, the car could even transform into other Ford models. Better yet, car-centric story segments and autobot action sequences could easily segue into action movie previews, car commercials, and gamedoc promos and back to story segments without a sense of disruptive flow.

Relevant commercial pods: *The Biggest Loser* and *Kath & Kim*

Gamedoc promos as well as some commercial spots would seem to be more problematic for the seamlessness of the flow of primetime blocks of ironicoms, yet there was often less disconnect than one would assume. With its sentimental and melodramatic tone, *The Biggest Loser*, the gamedoc in which obese contestants are put through weight loss challenges all in the hopes of being rewarded the prize money for being the weight loss competition's biggest loser, seems as if it would be an especially problematic fit. It is the series obliquely mocked by *30 Rock*, a sketch-comedy show-within-a-show sitcom about Liz Lemon who is the put-upon producer of *The Girlie Show with Tracy Jordan* (TGS), through its repeated jokes about television's obsession with obesity. Yet, that disconnect was remedied to an extent in a few winter 2009 episodes of *Kath & Kim*, a sitcom format adaptation that offered an ironic send-up of a cookie-cutter Florida suburb characterized by housing developments, big box stores and malls, and chain and fast food restaurants.

In "Florida" Kath's boyfriend Phil, the owner of a mall food court sandwich shop, becomes an advocate for sensible eating and counting calories even though his business depends upon repeat customers consuming more food than they should. One day Phil decides to talk to one of his obese customers about weight loss because he feels as if he is "an enabler" who has been "loading a gun with meat and cheese and aiming it right at his heart" (1.10). After he announces to Kath, "I have half a mind to march right over there and put that man on a 2000 calorie diet with a good strong dose of rigorous, but safe, low-impact aerobic exercise," he does march over to talk to Roland. As he had once been 400 lbs, Phil feels as if he is living proof that dramatic weight loss is possible. Unfortunately, Roland takes offence at the intervention and gets a group to protest Phil's beloved Sandwich Island.

Phil's comments are contextualized within the commercial flow as the promo that airs right before the episode begins is for *The Biggest Loser*, which by 2009 had become a franchise with several variations. For 2009 it was *Biggest Loser: Couples* and it played even more on the melodramatic backstories about the relationships that prevent or aid in weight loss. As usual, the episodes stress how weight loss is hard for contestants, but necessary to improve their lives. The gamedoc's promotional spots pivot on sentimentality, often catching a tear running down a contestant's face, or emphasizing the feeling through the announcer's "captioning" of an image of a struggling contestant with something such as, "She's a young mother trying to make ends meet." Although an ironic comedy overall, the aforementioned *Kath & Kim* episode is resolved on a sentimental note when Phil stops the diet crusade because he tells Roland that he can only start when he's ready, which is one of the foundational premises of *The Biggest Loser* and is usually represented through the contestants' sharing of a melodramatic backstory. Now changed from his red uniform shirt to a yellow one matching *The Biggest Loser* color scheme, Phil shares his story: "My mother spent my entire childhood trying to keep me on a strict diet. She did everything from hiding food in a locked closet to putting me on some very aggressive and equally dangerous experimental diets." He concludes with *The Biggest Loser*-style message: "the point is none of them worked because I wasn't ready to change. And I was doing the same thing to you" (1.10).

Several spots within the commercial flow of the episode also focus on weight: Truvia is the "honestly sweet" zero calorie sweetener "born from nature"; Extra gum "helps reduce snack cravings"; and Progresso Light is a "zero points value" soup endorsed by Weight Watchers. Also included is another promo for *The Biggest Loser: Couples*, in which the announcer tells us: "Last Tuesday they captured our hearts ... We held our breaths when they got on that scale ... Then we witnessed a miracle ... This Tuesday, cheer them on when the journey to save their lives continues." While the weight loss theme carries over from the promo to the sitcom, the sentimental tone usually does not. *Kath & Kim* is mostly a send-up of beauty culture, pointing out the ironic contradictions of weight loss ads and makeover gamedocs that tell viewers that it is who you are that matters at the same time that they emphasize that what you look like also matters. In "Desire" Phil, who mentions again that he used to weigh 400 lbs before he started to "work on" himself, acknowledges this contradiction: "I changed on the outside, which is really the only type of change that matters. I mean, people are going to tell you different. It's a lie though" (1.15). One contradiction in the final commercial segment of "Florida" does suit the irony of *Kath & Kim*. A spot for Slim Fast meal replacements runs prior to one for Olive Garden, a chain restaurant that serves the kind of high-fat-content food and extra-large portions that contribute to the obesity epidemic in the United States The rest of the flow, however, is mostly carefully calibrated to have a weight-loss emphasis such as that found in the Alli weight-loss supplement spot. Country singer Wynonna Judd offers her personal story of motivation and talks about her life as a single mother and her struggles with weight and how Alli has helped. The pitch humanizes her and makes her seem ordinary like the viewer, reaffirming the stars in adversity appeal, what Ronald Marchand calls "the democracy of afflictions."[11] Kath is always talking about how celebrities are "just like us." As a single mother, she would likely find the weight loss spots appealing.

"Idols," two *Kath & Kim* episodes later, makes that identification overt because it actually features Wynonna Judd, the Alli spokesperson who "happens" to be Kath Day's favorite singer. After Kath tries and fails to win a contest to be named Wynonna's biggest fan, Kim decides to intervene and records a self-serving DVD trying to explain why Kath IS Wynonna's biggest fan. When Wynonna watches as Kim only talks about herself in the DVD pitch, she identifies with Kath. Given her empathy for how hard it must be to be a single mother to a child who is "a hot mess," Wynonna gives in to sentiment and goes to meet Kath anyhow (1.12). The humor in the episode is debatable, but the commercial effect isn't: Wynonna's guest star appearance gives resonance to the weight loss spots, especially the one that immediately follows a story segment.

Whether or not Alli actually paid for anything beyond the 30-second spots or if the connections are just sweeteners to sell less and less desirable broadcast commercial time, the commercial flow during this and other Thursday primetime blocks certainly resembles the new advertising strategy of "relevant commercial pods."[12] With these more story-relevant or thematically consistent spots, advertisers hope viewers are discouraged from clicking away or past the commercials. If nothing else, Wynonna's appearance in "Idols" and in the Alli spot activates the classic advertising hook, *celebrities are just like us*. Indeed every *Kath & Kim* episode affirms that idea in the series' signature final scene: a shot of Kath and Kim lounging on the patio, reading gossip magazines and sharing snippets of celebrity news. In "Idols" Wynonna joins them and is as engrossed in the celebrity news as they are. Kim even repeats the message explicitly in the final scene of "Desire": "Stars are just like us—they walk their dogs and they pick up their dry cleaning" (1.15). The viewer has to have read a tabloid to get the joke that there is actually a section with those captions given to often unflattering paparazzi candid snapshots of celebrities doing the above as well as pumping gas, sweating while jogging, or tripping in the parking lot. The line suggests that as much as the series is making fun of taking tabloids seriously, it leaves room for viewers to read them as a guilty pleasure.[13]

Product integration: *The Office* and *30 Rock*

The same dynamic of mocking the characters' tastes, but then recuperating them as a potential guilty pleasure also is at the heart of the representation of the predilection of *The Office*'s characters for high-calorie chain restaurant food and mixed drinks. In "The Client" Michael's New York-based boss is particularly disdainful of his suggestion to hold a client meeting at Chili's, but the chain restaurant is redeemed when Michael uses the appetizers and drinks served there to put a client in the mood to make a business deal. Michael even declares, "Chili's is the new golf course" (2.7). The scenes in the restaurant set turn into plugs for actual menu items. While his New Yorker boss keeps trying to talk about a deal, Michael ignores her and discusses the merits of the Awesome Blossom appetizer, which is also promoted on a sign on the wall. Every time Jan tries to talk business, Michael focuses the client's attention on the appetizers and giant margaritas. The client so enjoys the food and the atmosphere that he eventually agrees to sign a contract with Dunder Mifflin even though buying from an office supply superstore like Staples would be cheaper. Michael describes such places as lacking in personal service and in ethics. Given the commercial imperatives of broadcast TV, it is hardly surprising that the critique is dropped as quickly as it is raised. Staples, as one would expect, has product tie-ins with the workplace-based sitcom. Staples even becomes the setting for several scenes of a later episode in which it is represented both as the unfair competition and an affordable and super-convenient one-stop-shopping place. In "The Client" the Chili's location is also story-consistent, while creating no real disconnect with the Chili's commercials broadcast within flow.

In "The Dundies" episode of *The Office*, set almost entirely in Chili's, the deal that allowed for the product integration did lead to some script changes. Instead of having one of the characters ordering drink after drink until she vomits, the script was changed to be clear about Pam's own culpability by having her steal the drinks from other tables. Then instead of getting sick, she only falls off her stool so that it doesn't seem as if the food made her ill. Most remarkable of all is that an actual Chili's executive appears in the episode to add the disclaimer that the company's policy is never to over-serve patrons (2.7). The sequence is still funny, but it does exemplify the pressures product integration puts on writers to convey a positive corporate image. *Office* showrunner Greg Daniels said in fall 2007 that he was cutting down on these deals because he "found it pretty impossible to balance the desires of the ad agencies and their clients with the needs of the show."[14] Because of the writers' skill, the episode succeeds in balancing its usual goal of mocking the characters and their behavior, while maintaining a generally positive depiction of the restaurant.[15]

This kind of product integration exists across a range of programming, but, as a comparison of two Applebee's integrations below indicates, they have a different effect in the dramas (in which the products become part of the storyline and are taken seriously by the characters) than in the ironicoms (in which the products are treated humorously because of their association with characters whom viewers are not intended to admire). As the Dillon, Texas branch of the restaurant is an everyday destination for local high school students and parents, the Applebee's integration in NBC's drama in *Friday Night Lights* is represented without the degree of irony inherent in those associated with the comedies. That Tyra, one of the characters featured in the high school football/romantic and familial melodrama hybrid, works there allows for several scenes to be shot in the restaurant and makes plausible the transition shots that track past the roadside Applebee's marquee. Instead of thinking of it as a crappy job as a character on an ironicom might, Tyra represents it as her economic salvation and even tries to work a positive reference to it into her college application essay. Compared to The Landing Strip, where her sister pole dances, Applebee's is a wholesome and desirable establishment. No one needs to gush over the taste of the food as the scenes very quietly reinforce that Applebee's offers food and atmosphere that turn families and groups of friends into regulars.

Applebee's is also the favorite restaurant of Kim from *Kath & Kim*. The series technically mocks her for the fact that she wants to eat there every night, but in "Desire," the restaurant's food is represented positively when Kath takes her there for a special treat. They order the "chocolate volcano cake, with extra lava" and when it arrives they marvel over its gooey chocolateness (1.15). The comic effect of the scene is that it is clear that the whole exchange is meant to be an over-the-top plug for the chain restaurant and, in acknowledging it, the integration seems more acceptable. It is a good thing this dessert is not integrated into the *Kath & Kim* weight-loss episodes. A Chili's version of the same thing, minus extra lava, weighs in at 1,600 calories. The Chili's Awesome Blossom is even worse as the onion rings-style appetizer has 2,710 calories, 203 grams of fat, and 6,236 grams of sodium. Those numbers garnered it a number 2 slot on *Men's Health* magazine's list of "The 20 Worst Foods in America," while the dessert made it to number 9. The McFlurry that causes so much controversy as product placement in *30 Rock*, is a mere 570 calories.

Story integration vs. product placement: *30 Rock*

Michael Scott's enjoyment of Chili's Awesome Blossom and Kim's enthusiasm for the Applebee's dessert pale in comparison to the ecstasy produced by the McDonald's McFlurry in the 3.11 episode of *30 Rock*. Of course, the writers of "St. Valentine's Day" intend for the scene to be over-exaggerated to make good use of the guest star stint of super sexy Hollywood actress Salma Hayek playing the role of Elisa, the girlfriend of Jack Donaghy (Alec Baldwin). Elisa and Jack are lounging on his luxurious sofa each enjoying a McFlurry. Then Elisa crawls over and feeds some of hers to Jack. It is probably broadcast TV's most memorable moment of characters marveling over a fast food dessert. When they return to opposite sides of the couch to concentrate on enjoying the dessert, the conversation sounds like commercial-ready dialogue:

J: TheseMcFlurrys are amazing!
E: I know. The soft swirl of vanilla and the hard crunch of candy and cookies. You'd think they'd fight each other, but no. Together they are perfecto.
J: Some would say that describes us.
E: Who would say such a thing. We are us. Let a McFlurry be what it is: *the world's greatest dessert*.

The scene ends after Jack proposes that the world's greatest dessert is the $1,000 marvel served at Plunder, an exclusive New York restaurant. His claim hardly seems convincing as he is still devouring his $2.50 McFlurry when he says it. Beyond the excessiveness of its pricetag and description—Tahitian vanilla bean ice cream in a pool of cognac, topped with the world's most expensive chocolate, shaved truffles, and edible 25k gold leaf—the "Lover's Delight" is made less appealing later in the episode when Jack does not even eat it because Elisa fails to show for their Valentine's date. Their real romantic moment comes when they run into each other in a McDonald's, the location in which the final scene is shot. Jack is ordering alone and just as he says, "McFlurry please," Elisa pipes up from the back of the line and orders a McFlurry at the same time. As she found a coupon in the church collection plate, she wants Jack to admit their meeting is divine intervention. He tells her instead: "I believe that we were reunited by the most successful capitalist enterprise of the last 100 years despite the McLean Deluxe or the McEmu ... " Elisa cuts him off, "Whatever. Someone's trying to tell us that we belong together ... maybe it's God?" Jack says, "Maybe it's [McDonald's founder] Ray Crock?" She counters, "Maybe it's the Hamburglar?" With that, they each take a McFlurry from the counter and clearly look forward to eating them together as in the earlier scene. That Jack is converted to Elisa's point of view about the superiority of the McFlurry is both comic and a great endorsement for McDonald's.

While many assumed there was a product placement deal with McDonald's, Fey denies it and says that she and the writers just thought the McFlurry discussions would sound funny.[16] They were funny, but as that episode's commercial flow did feature a McDonald's commercial and the company had been purchasing time throughout NBC primetime, the line between content and promotion was hazy especially in an era when networks are trying to get companies to continue to buy such spots even though many people admit to ad skipping through DVRs. There are many ways in which an advertiser can be kept happy, and, thus, buying such 30-second spots. Commenting on creating an environment that was sponsor-friendly beyond paid product placement, Ozzie Nelson, 1950s producer/star of his sitcom fictionalization of his life, recalls giving preferential story treatment for sponsors who were paying only to have their products placed on set. He assumed that offering Hotpoint, for instance, as many chances to be on camera as possible would make the company eager to continue to sponsor the show. He explains:

> One of the great advantages of being the only sponsor or of being cosponsor was that it was possible for us, perfectly legitimately, to give them a great deal of subliminal advertising in addition to their paid commercial blurbs. For example, when we were sponsored by Hotpoint, they furnished the kitchen with all the latest Hotpoint appliances, and if we had the choice of where to play a scene we'd move to the kitchen where Harriet could be cooking dinner or be putting dishes in the dishwasher or taking clothes out of the dryer. Or even if we were eating dinner in the dining room the Hotpoint appliances could be seen in the background.[17]

As Hotpoint never asked him to do those shots, they are technically not paid insertions. Yet, the effect is the same as if they were. *Ozzie and Harriet* becomes a shop window in which to display Hotpoint's latest appliances. Ozzie felt it was a simple way he as a producer could keep sponsors happy even though they weren't paying for specific plugs within the story segments.

The commercial flow between the story segments of "St. Valentine's Day" does feature a 30-second spot for McDonald's. It begins from the point of view of an unseen person eating a burger and looking over at a prep school trio that is hanging out drinking coffee as if McDonald's is the new coffeehouse, an idea heavily pro-moted that year. A tie-wearing teen looks over at his counterpart, a single guy dressed in a t-shirt under an open shirt with unbuttoned sleeves. Trapped and bored between his two chattering female companions, the preppy guy looks longingly at the single guy who lingers over and enjoys every bite of his quarter pounder with cheese. The spot, and a few different vignettes, was part of that year's *I'm lovin' it* campaign that ran throughout all the networks' primetime programming flow. Other commercial spots, some of which were as explicitly targeting young women as the aforementioned commercial was young men, emphasized the new coffee selections, an affordable alternative to overpriced coffee house drinks. A third spot had a guy come in with a dollar to see what he could get on the McDonald's Dollar menu. The variety of spots was part of a scatter buy that associated McDonald's with TV programming more generally.[18] In the cash-strapped 2008–9 season when even the investment bankers were taking a hit, the McDonald's message about the affordability of its meals was more than ever targeted to a broad spectrum of consumers, all feeling the impact of the U.S. economic crisis. In her other starring role that year, her Emmy-winning SNL impression of Sarah Palin, Tina Fey did make a crack about this campaign by having Palin list the McDonald's value menu as one of the ways people are being helped in the economic downturn. The joke pokes fun at Palin's lack of real policy platforms, but does nothing to detract from McDonald's advertising pitch. *30 Rock* is an even more hospitable environment for McDonald's references, not only because most sitcoms are, but because Liz Lemon and the writers are depicted as constantly eating take-out and junk food.

After the McFlurry episode aired, a variety of TV commentators, both professional and amateur, chimed in about the appearance of the McDonald's dessert in the *30 Rock* episode. One particularly interesting exchange involved *New York* magazine's Mark Graham's online post "Did *30 Rock's* McFlurry Praise Cross the Line?"[19] The journalist, along with those who posted comments to his morning-after blog entry about product placement, got a direct response from Tina Fey. In his discussion of *30 Rock's* product placement, of which he assumes the McFlurry is an example, Graham remarks on whether the general feeling of respect for Tina Fey and her series, as well as its earlier ironic showcasing of product placement, has allowed her production team to avoid criticism that might be heaped on a less critically acclaimed series. He asks his online readers:

> "what if this were a highly rated show that critics turn their noses up at, a show like [CBS's] *Two and a Half Men*, for example? What would people say if they spent 113 seconds of their show (9 percent of the show's total run time, taking out the time spent advertising "real" commercials) talking about how satisfying a Frosty from Wendy's is on a hot summer day?"[20]

Several responded that the episode did seem to lack the subtlety of other *30 Rock* placements such as the infamous one in which participating sponsor Verizon Wireless gets an overt plug, which is followed by Fey stepping out of her persona as Liz Lemon and turning to the camera to say, "Can we have our money now?" (2.6). Another post noted that anything could be tolerated if it meant that the low-rated show would stay on the air. Responding to all those who thought the McDonald's insertion was an overt product placement, a third said,

"The genius is that they ARE blatantly shilling something, and that no other TV show can get away with it. I laughed during that segment, because McFlurries are in fact quite good, and the product worked as a counterpart to Jack's '25-carat' ice cream sundae."

Still, in contrast to the other ironic insertions, a fourth viewer found this one "kind of embarrassing, actually. (And, yes, Tina Fey, you are free to call me out by name at the next awards ceremony you attend.)" Fey does exactly that through an NBC spokesperson who gave an official response directly to Graham at *New York* magazine:

It gives me great pleasure to inform you that the references to McDonald's in last night's episode of 30 Rock were in no way product placement. (Nor were they an attempt at product placement that fell through.) We received no money from the McDonald's Corporation. We were actually a little worried they might sue us. That's just the kind of revenue-generating masterminds we are. Also, the upcoming story line where Liz Lemon starts dating Grimace is just based on a recurring dream I have. Seriously, though, it's not product placement.[21]

Fey's comments started circulating online wherever the original debate had taken place and then extended out from there; this ever-circulating commentary was made possible by hyperlinks and the way that one comment online can launch a thousand discussions. She probably felt that the reverse should be true: drop one official response and it should launch a thousand corrections. That did happen to an extent, but it didn't stop the discussions as new ones cropped up in response to the response. Such is the circulation loop online. Only Fey's clarification that McFlurry was not product placement made it onto *Entertainment Weekly*'s website (ew.com).[22] On its message board, in the middle of many affirmations of *30 Rock*'s humor and of the series' running product placement gag, one commentator notes: "They would still need legal clearance to go film at the McDonald's and show their products. She says they weren't paid, but she didn't say there wasn't another kind of compensation." Brian Steinberg of *Advertising Age* went out and investigated the matter and reported that, as per usual, the TV show's producers had to contact McDonald's executives to get permission to film in one of their restaurants and then they had to get the franchisee to agree and compensate him for the time that his store was closed.[23] McDonald's also read the script, corporate spokesperson Lane Landolt said: "If we felt that something disparaged the brand, we would have pushed back on what they did, but no, we didn't make any changes." A McDonald's 30-second spot that came at the ten-minute point was no different than those that run throughout NBC primetime. As Landolt put it, it was "part of our traditional media buy."[24] She is referring to a scatter buy across network schedules that affords a company's products maximum exposure. Steinberg wondered if there was a residual effect of the product placement ambiguity, making "pundits and viewers assume that any brand mention on the show is part of an elaborate shilling deal."[25]

He questions if that, in turn, will eventually cause a backlash against the show and any products mentioned therein whether part of a promotional deal or not.

Back on the *New York* magazine message board, one post gets to the heart of the matter, implying that placement by any other name still has the same effect of advertising the product: "For a non-advertisement, it was pretty effective. I couldn't stop thinking about having a McFlurry all day!" and then remarks upon all the iPhones that "kept popping all over the show." Several more noted that they had started craving a McFlurry, as is exemplified in the following: "I got my first McFlurry in years today and I believe it's because of *30 Rock* and I also have been drinking lots of Snapple thanks to that episode in season 1." Picking up on this effect, one ew.com post described it as "the best free advertising they could get," concluding, "I bet they had a spike in McFlurry sales afterwards and today." Advertisers who do buy time during the commercial flow are likely to feel gratitude toward the writers for giving them a sales bump through an in-show reference. That is no small matter in an era in which advertisers are wondering if they should bother to invest in broadcast TV anymore given how many people skip the commercial spots or watch TV off-TV.

The inadvertent bump is different, however, than some higher-up mandating that a writing staff offer such value-added content. Dick Van Dyke recalls such a moment from the early days of participating sponsorship, the now-standard magazine-style variety of commercials that run between story segments. Producers convinced him to work smoking into a comic story arc of his eponymous sitcom because they wanted to reward the cigarette company that had been purchasing time on the show. It was a one-time integration bonus for Kent's, however, as Van Dyke felt that his character should not smoke.[26]

Fey's original talking back to the electronic (mis)information circulation loop seems to have been inspired by a desire to make a distinction between decisions that are artistic and those that are business-oriented. Yet, as a twenty-first-century TV producer, she has to make decisions that consider both simultaneously. One *Advertising Age* post noted that the writers could not just have decided that the characters should be ecstatic over a competitor's product such as Burger King's "BK Broiler."[27] Another concurs, noting that,

> "A show can't feature a BK product integration and then have a McDonald's commercial at the same time because neither brand would stand for it. So perhaps 30 Rock [producers] can credibly deny that they received payment for a product placement, but considering how much money the network gets from McDonald's by way of traditional advertising, I find it very hard to believe that the decision was purely artistic."

It is the fact that the episode was well done that made the McFlurry scenes work as advertising, even if that is not what they technically are. The original commentator added to his BK broiler caveat that the McFlurry episode can be used "to both showcase that it doesn't 'ruin art' to work products into scripts, and that even when we're not being paid we can't legitimately say it's not an ad for the product." This same line of reasoning was pursued by a different post, arguing that the quality of the episode and the fact that so many people did feel the McFlurry scenes were read as advertisement even though they technically were not suggests that "if you leave the writers alone, they'll come up with better stuff than paid placement. If it wasn't paid for, is it an indication for future advertisers that if they buy in, they'll get an added-value storyline, too?"[28]

Fey is likely defensive about the message board episode summaries that categorize the McFlurry references not as jokes but as product integrations because that term is popularly associated with the inclusion of story-irrelevant product pitches. Such a pitch occurred in season two of NBC's *Heroes*. While producers did a good job in season one of turning the integration of a Nissan Versa into a likeable storyline, in season two Claire Bennett's father gives her a new Nissan Rogue SUV (2.1) and they discuss its merits for several minutes. It is time that does nothing to enhance or move the story forward. In contrast, most of the products integrated into *30 Rock*, whether they are there because of some economic exchange or not, are used in funny ways that make sense in the story arc. That is not the case in the very distracting integration of Dr. Pepper in episode 1.19 of the CW's new *90210*. At the time of the April 2009 episode, Dr. Pepper was paying for promotional consideration in the series, which had already redecorated the Peach Pit "malt shop" hangout so that all the tables had Dr. Pepper placards and the fountain only served the company's brands of soda. Dr. Pepper was also sponsoring a web-promotion about winning a road trip, interstitials for which were run during the commercial flow that also included its regular spots. Given all that paid time, it is hardly surprising that the writers include a scene in the episode "Okaeri, Donna" in which the main character and her brother embark on a road trip and take along a Dr. Pepper-filled cooler. As Annie reaches back to get a soda, the shot lingers on the open cooler filled with cans. She grabs for a high-calorie regular Dr. Pepper that the very thin girl would probably never drink. They also have to keep stopping at bathrooms because she apparently is drinking soda after soda. Her brother Dixon points out her Dr. Pepper problem as he holds a can in his hand like a pitchperson and leans against the car during one of the bathroom breaks. She counters: "What's a road trip without Dr. Pepper. It's almost a requirement" (1.19). The heavy-handed scenes come across as forced, especially as they do little to move the story forward.

Not wanting to be associated with this kind of stilted strategy, Fey insists their product references are jokes; yet, that doesn't mean they don't also have the added benefit of product promotion for companies that are in some way paying to keep NBC shows on the air. As a participating sponsor of NBC primetime, McDonald's must love the "St. Valentine's Day" episode as it ends up mocking ridiculously overpriced Manhattan restaurants and contrasting them to the simple pleasures of an affordable, but delicious McDonald's dessert. The episode certainly has me wondering about what a McFlurry tastes like and, if nothing else, has made me aware of the brand.

Synergy and *30 Rock*

Still frustrated that people made a big deal over the McFlurry scenes, Fey stepped out of character as Liz Lemon to address the issue in "The Ones." Fey uses the episode to emphasize her point that products are most often used on the show simply to get a cheap laugh. The writers build "The Ones" around an as-seen-on-TV product called "The Slanket." When it is first introduced, it is worn by an infomercial-style hostess who has been hired to model potential anniversary gifts that the show-within-a-show TV star Tracy Jordan (former *SNL* player Tracy Morgan) might give his wife. After Tracy chooses something else, Liz snaps up the Slanket and then wears it in three scenes. When Tracy later comes to her office and finds her sitting there zipped into the Slanket, she says, "I'm just wearing it as a joke." Tracy doesn't seem to know what she is talking about. That happens again in a subsequent scene in which Jack finds her in the same state and Liz blurts out, "It's not product placement, I just like it." Jack just looks confused and says, "What?" because the comment makes little sense in the scene (3.19). There is no logic to Liz's statement as she is not on camera nor is she discussing the possibility of integrating the Slanket into a TGS episode. Instead, she seems to be speaking as Tina Fey and talking back to all those who had been misidentifying the use of McFlurry as product placement. The irony is that in both of these Slanket scenes, Liz is using a clearly displayed MacBook made by Apple, the company that did pay for promotional consideration in the episode.

The Slanket also becomes part of the Cartier paid promotional consideration in the third Slanket scene, this one in Liz's apartment.[29] Liz points out her own bodily flaws so that Elisa (Salma Hayek), looking gorgeous and flashing a Cartier engagement ring from Jack, will be dissuaded from her momentary belief that Liz and Jack are having an affair. Looking at Liz's "Body by Slanket," Elisa realizes the idea is crazy, so she wants to talk with Jack alone to try to explain why she is so paranoid. She dismisses Liz from the room: "Isn't there a Slanket somewhere you should be filling with your parts" (3.19). The whole episode has been about how Liz Lemon is as crazy about her Slanket as Elisa is about the Cartier engagement ring, which we watched Jack purchase in a pre-credits scene set inside the luxury jewelry store. Given its location around the corner from 30 Rockefeller Center, Cartier is a place in which an NBC executive might purchase an engagement ring. A sweatshirt-wearing Liz also looks appropriately out of place in the luxury showroom and is dismissed by the clerk once he realizes that she is just accompanying Jack on his ring shopping expedition and is not the intended recipient. Leaving Liz to crawl goofily around the floor looking for a diamond ring she accidentally dropped there, the clerk says conspiratorially to Jack that he will now take him to the "real showroom." The scene is funny and reinforces the series characterization of Liz Lemon as Average Jane. Fey and the writers probably came up with the scenario and then contacted Cartier (or perhaps even several of the area's luxury jewelers) and made a promotional deal in exchange for the ability to film in the store.

Fey would probably say, it is not really product integration because the point is to focus on humor, not Cartier.

Cartier is, nevertheless, still in a sponsorship relationship with the show, as well as with the NBC drama *Lipstick Jungle*, which also had a scene set inside the showroom. In both series Cartier is mentioned in the "promotional consideration by" line alongside Apple.[30] Through the sales associate's comments to Jack, along with the fact the character's fiancée is played by a glamorous movie star who is then associated with one of its rings, Cartier can maintain its luxury status, which is also the intention of the *Lipstick Jungle* integration. *30 Rock's* addition of the humorous bit connected to Liz gives the company the extra advantage of seeming more hip than stodgy as it is willing to make fun of itself. Fey's skill at goofy humor in this scene is also what makes the later Apple placement more effective because the scenes in which it is placed on the desk of Liz Lemon, who like Tina Fey is an Emmy-Award winning TV producer, reinforce the company's desired brand reputation as the laptop of choice for the industry's most successful creative workers. Liz and Jack are also, of course, equipped with Apple iPhones, which were integrated excessively into the McFlurry episode (3.11) among others.

"The Ones" is most fascinating for the way the calling of attention to the online debate about McDonald's product integration distracts attention from different examples of both product integration into the story and product placement on the set. As was the case in the McFlurry episode, the commercial flow between the story segments of "The Ones" includes a McDonald's commercial. This one makes a pitch for the company's new "snack wraps," which suits the in-episode discussion of the writers becoming upset that their snack table will no longer be stocked. They do get to keep the Snapple. Even if the McDonald's episode cannot be categorized as literal product integration, Snapple, the beverage integrated into the meta-commentary storyline of "Jack-tor" precisely to highlight the rise of product placement on network TV and the pressures put on producers to find ways to integrate sponsor products, is one of the actual sponsors in season one. Its paid "promotional consideration" leads to, for example, the writers drinking Snapple with their takeout food. These unremarked upon official Snapple placements do nothing to distract from the story, yet the writers decided to address the Snapple placements anyhow in "Jack-tor." In poking fun at the idea of network-decrees that writers and producers need to increase product placement, the episode becomes much more effective promotion for Snapple than those in which the beverage maker paid to be promoted. During a meeting at which the TGS writers each gush "casually" how they love Snapple, the camera lingers on sexy receptionist Cerie. She looks directly into the camera and says: "I only date guys who drink Snapple" (1.5). Liz and her co-producer Pete continue the "casual" discussion in the hall and are still there when the elevator opens to reveal someone in a giant Snapple costume. Liz and Pete then find themselves in a meeting in which Jack screens his industrial film on product placement methods.

The episode's humorous meta-commentary on sponsorship not only makes more of an impression than the ones in which Snapple paid for placement, but it also serves to make more effective the ones that would follow in subsequent episodes. The added value is that the company now seems smart and funny like Tina Fey. The "we know you are smarter than to be taken in by this" audience address is the kind of flattering and ironic advertising which suits the tone of the ironicom. As we have seen already, making fun of product placement is a way to make viewers more receptive to the practice, but it also makes them suspicious of any product that is mentioned in the series. The latter effect clearly annoys Fey and she and her writing team may be equally frustrated that any attempt to highlight the negatives of the practice only served to make it more effective and acceptable.

30 Rock and *The Office* are particularly adept at funny meta-product integration[31] and certainly plenty of products mentioned within the episodes of each are there for comic purposes only. According to Nielsen Media Research, however, they are also shows on which tons of ordinary product placement occurs: 142 product placements on *30 Rock* between October 4, 2007 and November 18, 2007 and 381 on *The Office* between that end date and September 27, 2007.[32] The most excessive product placement is usually associated with reality TV, a programming category that still always tops the list. Nielsen calculated that in the first half of 2007, for instance, *American Idol* did the most with 4,349 product pushes and the top ten was rounded out by other reality shows.[33] In the first month and a half of fall 2007 *30 Rock* did make it one time into Nielsen's Top 10 shows with product placement. In contrast, *The Office* made the list for four of the first five episodes of the 2007 season.[34] However many times they make the list, these series are not unique in their use of the strategy. According to Nielsen Media Research's product placement tracking service Place Views, placements on network primetime shows jumped almost 30% in 2005 (from 82,014 to 106,808). The duration rose 22% 157 hours in 2004 to 191 hours in 2005. Visual on-screen placements increased 33.5% from 64,920 to 86,668, while brand mentions rose 24% from 19,876 to 24,723.[35]

Placing comic emphasis on these new practices, even building a humorous story segment or episode around the integration, smoothes the way for the unremarked upon placements in later episodes, or, as in "The Ones," those included in the same episode. Fey's obvious disdain for the Dr. Pepper-style product integration and her desire not to be associated with it is precisely the stance that makes her such an effective product pitchperson. She joins some classic reluctant TV pitchpersons, including Alfred Hitchcock, Fred Allen, and Jack Benny whose mocking of product pitches made them more memorable. As *Television Magazine* explained in 1953, "the effective use of humor and ridicule involving the sponsor and his product can actually enhance the value of the testimonial."[36] Hitchcock mocked his sponsor Bristol-Myers and called attention in a humorous way to the fact that *Alfred Hitchcock Presents* was dependent on sponsors, but he didn't have to like it. *Time* magazine described his sarcastic pitchperson stance as "the equivalent of a fastidious man brushing a particularly repellant caterpillar off his lapel."[37] He segued to and from commercials with meta-commentary on them. Described by Lawrence R. Samuel as "the undisputed champion of integrated advertising," Benny brought the commercials into the show itself and developed an on-air persona as an ironic pitchman, making his product pitches for Lucky Strike and Pepsi, among others, more memorable.[38] *The Jack Benny Show* specialized in goofy product integration, but, as with *30 Rock*, at other times product placement went unremarked upon. The result is that Benny, like Fey, is associated in viewers' minds with comedy rather than commercialism.[39]

Like *30 Rock*, *The Jack Benny Show* is an entertainment industry series about putting on a variety/comedy show, albeit one with more traditional 1950s style acts that got more screen time than those of TGS. Jack Benny was a spendthrift in real life, but came to be thought of as a miser because of his on-air persona.[40] Liz Lemon is a "baby-crazy" singleton and beleaguered producer, whereas Tina Fey and husband Jeff Richmond are both empowered TV producers and parents of a toddler. Fey is also a well-known NBC TV writer/executive producer who is just playing an unknown and underappreciated NBC TV writer/executive producer. More significantly, Fey is perceived by fans as a crusader against media conglomerate synergy, when both the sitcom and the character she plays don't really put up much of a fight. Indeed, the joke in the season two opener is built around Liz receiving a GE award for "Followship." As Jack says, "When I think of the free-spirited Liz Lemon I met just one year ago, so resistant to product integration, cross promotion and adverlingus, it pleases me to learn how much she's followed" (2.4).

As the dialogue makes evident, *30 Rock* more often uses synergy scenarios for comedy and in the process becomes representative of the transformation of one of a media conglomerate's holdings into a circulation platform for its others. The series starts as an "us-against-them," working stiff sitcom that becomes a media-conglomer-com after fall 2007 when the network's new chairman Ben Silverman started making deals for high-wattage guest star stints.[41] Again, a *Jack Benny Show* comparison applies. Denise Mann claims that the structure of the variety show and the distinction it makes between a film star and a television personality enabled Benny to seem ordinary in contrast to the aura of the guest stars that appear in the sketch segments.[42]

30 Rock uses its guest stars to the same effect. The aura with which they are endowed reinforces Fey's ordinariness. Part of the joke of the Salma Hayek arc is that the sexy movie star is never fully believable as an ordinary person, which is lucky for McDonald's as she brings her star aura to the scene in which she is ecstatic over the McFlurry. Fey's comments on the McFlurry episode and the way she depicts product placement in other episodes as a practice forced on TV's creatives also help her establish an Average Jane against the monolithic corporation dynamic that is central to viewers' perceptions of *30 Rock* and Tina Fey as fighting against rather than being a part of media conglomeration and the increased commercialism that comes with it. Before the series moved in season three beyond the simplistic binary and had Jack and Liz become sometimes-allies and "bros," as Elisa describes the pair in "The Ones," its comic situations develop by pitting the ordinary creative worker Liz Lemon against bottom-line obsessed executive Jack Donaghy.

Viewers schooled in reality TV reception practices to "look for moments of authenticity in the performance environment," understand that *30 Rock* offers a broad comedic take on the kinds of people and corporate and production cultures within this famous city skyscraper.[43] Yet, they still often characterize the show as a subversive "peek behind the scenes" of a sketch comedy TV show and its struggles for creative integrity and respect in a market-driven media environment run by insensitive "suits" more willing to support copycat TV than original programming. Of course, the comedy of *30 Rock* is both original and derived from an existing franchise and yet, because of Fey's and Morgan's SNL history, viewers assume there is some degree of truth beneath the broad comedy and caricature. Part of the tendency to collapse Morgan and Jordan and Fey and Lemon is that the writers use fragments of personal experience or habit to create the two caricatures. "Tracy Jordan is a part of Tracy Morgan," the actor explains, but the resulting caricature is just a "figment of somebody's imagination."[44] Fey helps create this confusion, especially in relation to her own persona.

Because Fey is a writer/producer/actor on an NBC show and was one on SNL, viewers tend to assume that *30 Rock* offers real insight into the challenges facing broadcast television's creative workers.[45] More often than not, it elides the actualities of production work and reinforces the popular assumption that smart TV shows are the product of an isolated and inspired creative worker who is single-handedly responsible for the success of the show. It is the same claim at the center of the Tina Fey commercials for American Express, which ran more often than *30 Rock* episodes, prompting Bill Carter of the *New York Times* to remark in early October 2008:

> "With her three Emmy Awards, her ubiquitous American Express commercials, and especially her must-see Sarah Palin impersonations, Tina Fey is not just the hottest star on NBC; she is about the hottest star in show business at the moment. So where is '30 Rock?' The hugely praised but ratings-challenged comedy has yet to return to NBC."[46]

In both the commercial and in *30 Rock* viewers see Fey, albeit in the persona of Liz Lemon in the series, running around the corridors solving problems to make sure the show goes on. While the sitcom might more truthfully have been called *The Tina Fey Show* to draw attention to the persona/producer disconnect, that it is titled *30 Rock* effaces that difference and implies that the insider view on offer is of the media conglomerate with offices in that building, including the executives whose offices really are on the 52nd floor. It's not surprising that the series is often read as a subversive send-up of media conglomeration disguised as a sitcom. More often, it is a sitcom packaged as a subversive send-up. It effaces the actual workings of network and production cultures and in its place offers the standard little person against the world workplace sitcom dynamic.

The fiction of the lone creative struggling against business interests is a popular way production workers represent themselves on TV. It was the dynamic at the heart of the short-lived CBS music industry dramedy *Love Monkey*, which pits a mom and pop music establishment at which the main character works against the big label that fired him for saying it should be avoiding silly synergy deals. One episode calls into question the concept of "the suit" and just which kind of production worker qualifies. When someone labels him a "suit," the main character vehemently denies it. A suit is "a drone, an enemy, a hack," he declares. "I'm the anti-suit." Then he starts wondering: "Am I a suit?"

Jack Donaghy addresses the same issue in the episode guest-starring Carrie Fisher as Rosemary Howard, a sketch comedy writer from the golden years of late 1960s and early 1970s NBC satire, the era of *Laugh-In*. To Liz's claim that Rosemary is right that TGS should be "pushing the envelope!" Jack responds, "Push the envelope. You know who uses that phrase? People who don't have the guts or the brains to work inside the system." Liz insists that she got into comedy to be like Rosemary and "make people think." Jack calls her on the fantasy self-representation: "You got into this business because you're funny and you're weird and you're socially retarded ... And you also got into it because it pays well. Which means you are not like Rosemary. You are like me!" Liz is horrified: "No, I'm not. You are a suit! You feed off the creativity and the hard work of other people and turn it into commercials and pie charts and triangle graphs!" (2.4). Jack points out to Liz that she may want to imagine herself as being above crass commercialism, but she has to admit that she is working in a commercial medium and that her show is not an isolated artistic creation. He corrects her assumption that it even is her show: "This is my show. And once a week, I rent it out to the good people at the erectile dysfunction companies" (2.4).

The series' jokes about media conglomeration and jibes at various real life executives and personalities associated with NBC and then parent company GE are entertaining, but they don't prevent the series from being a site through which its conglomerate's products, even GE appliances, can circulate. Even a joke about the kind of eco-friendly campaigns in which corporations engage has a brand reference. In episode 2, Jack introduces a new GE Mascot Greenzo as "America's first non-judgmental, business-friendly environmental advocate." Even the bit about how GE's eco-friendly mascot goes rogue on *The Today Show* during a segment with Meredith Vieira on tips for protecting the environment still works as a GE plug. Instead of staying focused on the message that people should "buy a G.E. Front Loading Washing Machine to save water," he goes off script, saying: "Did you know that there are people out there with the power to heal Mother Gaia but they're paralyzed by greed? I'm talking about big companies and their two-faced, fat-cat executives." GE is not sponsoring *30 Rock*, but as the parent company that then owned an 80 percent share in NBC network, it is hardly surprising that a joke about a GE Tri-vection oven in the pilot episode is followed by a commercial in the flow for a similar product. *30 Rock*'s humor is not worrying GE executives, especially as mentions of the corporation usually start with Jack praising someone at GE when talking with Liz. Jack describes Jack Welch, GE's former chairman, as "the greatest leader since the pharaohs." Then his comments devolve into a tame critique when he praises Welch as a boss because "he held our hands during our triumphs and our Senate hearings." In a later episode Jack tries to write a tribute to him and ends up with the following: "Jack Welch has such unparalleled management skills they named Welch's grape juice after him because he squeezes the sweetest juice out of his workers' mind-grapes" (1.7). Instead of escalating into a critique the comments just become silly, making the scene more broad comedy than satire. Far from skewering them, the GE and NBC upper echelons are made to look like good sports who appreciate a bit of teasing. This dynamic is similar to the recent SNL impersonations of celebrity and political personalities, which lean more toward silly send-up than satire. *30 Rock* does not delve into some of the deeper issues at work in media conglomeration as much as it puts its possibilities on display.

Media conglomerate product placement and integration

Network identity placement is given the same kind of ironic treatment in the *30 Rock* episode "SeinfeldVision" as product placement is given in "Jack-tor." The premise is that Seinfeld, the king of NBC's recent Must-See sitcoms era, shows up at NBC after he finds out that Jack has begun digitally capturing and inserting Seinfeld's image into every primetime series as a way to boost their ratings. Of course, the meta-level is that *30 Rock* "inserts" Seinfeld into the episode to boost the ratings of *30 Rock*. The episode both mocks and employs the strategy of using an already-established network brand asset to enhance the status of a new one. The premise of "SeinfeldVision" allows for a mention of much of that season's primetime schedule—a plug which occurs when Jack lists the shows in which he has planned the digital insertion. The tactic is funnier than the more typical schedule or series reference in which a character's TV is tuned to a show as was the case in season one when Liz Lemon watched *Deal or No Deal*, the NBC gameshow that Kenneth the NBC Page later knocks off for an ill-fated spinoff pilot.[47]

Calling attention to the concept of the shameless plug, one scene has a clip from Seinfeld's forthcoming feature film *Bee Movie* running on Jack's laptop. It gets two more plugs when Seinfeld confronts Jack about the uncompensated use of his likeness within current network shows. Jack points out that NBC owns the rights to the footage and so is within its legal rights. Jack is willing to make a deal to avoid any bad feelings or bad press. He wants to let it run for a month more in exchange for a million dollars and "five free commercials for your animated film *Bee Movie*." Seinfeld counters that he wants two million dollars, donated to charity, and "ten free commercials for *Bee Movie*, opening Nov 2nd," a plug which he makes into the camera. They settle on one night of SeinfeldVision in exchange for the charity payment and "unlimited free promotions on the *Today Show*," during which co-host Al Roker will appear in a bee costume (2.1). The negotiation over the promotional deal is instructive for the kinds of exchanges that can be made. Seinfeld's movie was in need of promotion and reminding audiences of his blockbuster NBC series, which ended in 1998, was an effective way to activate the desire to see more Jerry Seinfeld comedy.[48] As "SeinfeldVision" was the first episode of *30 Rock's* sophomore season, the series was in need of promotion as well. Seinfeld's appearance did give a boost to the ratings-challenged show and the writing staff were very grateful.[49] The guest appearance also complemented the series of *Bee Movie* minisodes through which the feature film was promoted that fall on NBC.[50] In a circular paradigm the minisodes promote the movie and the TV show, which in turn promotes the movie and the minisodes. The strategy exemplifies how Hollywood studios have had to find creative ways to promote their upcoming releases in a cluttered environment. This kind of movie studio stunt is increasingly prevalent, according to *Advertising Age's* Andrew Hampp, who says that hybrid storytelling/advertising is valued by advertisers and the networks.[51]

If the film being advertised is one from the network's affiliated feature film division, then there is even more motivation for crosspromotion, as is evident in *30 Rock's* season three parallel to the *Bee Movie* reference. In the episode "Mamma Mia!," the guest appearance of another former NBC star is tied to a feature film promotion. Alan Alda, coming off a stint on the final seasons of NBC's *The West Wing*, is linked to *Mamma Mia!*, a more significant integration choice as it is a Universal feature film release. The episode puts Alda in a comic situation Liz terms a "Mamma Mia!" because he plays Milton Green, one of three men who might be Jack's biological father. Surprised that Jack has never heard of the film or its plot device, Liz says, it's "a madcap musical romp … fun … good," as if reading from the review excerpts printed on the DVD case. Not surprisingly, the final scene of *30 Rock's* "Mamma Mia!" episode segues into a promotion for the DVD release of the Universal feature.

The "Mamma Mia!" episode suggests that for all the attention paid to product integration on *30 Rock*, it is much more significant for its media conglomerate product integrations despite, or perhaps because of, its reputation for chiding NBC Universal for all its emphasis on brand synergy. From the outset *30 Rock* has been credited with offering meta-commentary on media conglomeration. Rob Owen of the *Pittsburgh Post-Gazette* deems it "TV comedy as cultural critique" and applauds the way the series "gleefully takes shots at NBC and broadcast network culture."[52] It works, he suggests, because of the show's "chipper" tone through which it then "excoriates NBC for craven attempts to use past success to win over viewers today." "Excoriates" is definitely an overstatement, especially given that in making fun of NBC Universal promotional strategies in the aforementioned guest star episodes, it puts them into effect. That results in *30 Rock* doing more to promote NBC Universal than to trash it. While hostility toward the "powers that be" is a staple of the workplace sitcom, the subgenre in which Fey categorizes hers, the creator/producer of *30 Rock* is more grateful than hostile to the network that has employed her for over a decade in a volatile industry and kept her sitcom on the air despite its low ratings. NBC Universal is probably grateful to her in return as she is fast becoming a significant brand asset, bringing the network critical praise with Emmy wins, especially given the hype surrounding the fact that *30 Rock* garnered the most 2009 Emmy nominations for a series (22). NBC's support of the series is representative of the balance networks are trying to strike between having shows that get high ratings and shows that get high praise. The ideal, of course, is to have a show that garners both.

Indeed, it seems that with all the brand building possible within the story segments of *30 Rock* as well as in its commercial flow, NBC Universal and GE are more than happy to take some mocking, especially as it is mostly gentle ribbing despite the series' categorization by various critics and bloggers as a "biting satire." *30 Rock* seems less concerned with fighting synergy than with pretending to get riled up about synergy to get laughs. Like the faux tours offered by Universal Studios in which media production is transformed into a consumable spectacle, the series stages media conglomeration for comedy. The show puts on display funny or awkward situations that arise with the push for synergy. Its comic stance against synergy ends up offering a primer for ways to make meeting the demand for synergy palatable to audiences. In a way *30 Rock* is the sitcom equivalent of Television Without Pity (TWoP), the fan commentary website acquired by the media conglomerate's Bravo division in 2007. Both the site and the series recognize that there are shows that, as Zalaznick puts it, "TV fans can't resist talking about, reading about and snarking about."[53] Both offer their commentary in a "forum that doesn't take itself too seriously—but which takes television itself seriously." Fey and her writers are like the TWoP creators, staff, and site visitors who are described as "smart, funny, sarcastic, incredibly knowledgeable about TV and essentially respectful of it as an art form."[54]

In short, for all its meta-commentary on synergy, *30 Rock* exemplifies the ways that a primetime schedule can be leveraged in the service of the circulation of a media conglomerate's varied content—in the case of *Mamma Mia!*, the features division, but in other cases GE Electronics or NBC's previous series. Many point to "SeinfeldVision" as a truly anti-synergy episode because although Seinfeld is there to boost interest in *30 Rock,* he ends up crying in dismay, "What's happened to this network!" in response to Jack's unscrupulous promotional schemes. Yet, he delivers the line badly and it sounds forced. That's the real irony of the episode: it reveals Baldwin's comic talents are superior to Seinfeld's, the king of NBC Must-See TV comedy. That might not be good for Seinfeld, whose *Bee Movie* was a flop, but it reaffirms NBC's then-current promotional push—that it offers *Comedy night done right*. Even if one takes Jerry Seinfeld's declaration at face value as a dig at the undeniable change in the status of the network since his sitcom left the air, the remark still positions NBC as the once and future home of cutting-edge comedy because he says it on a critically acclaimed smart sitcom. NBC was hoping that it would take off in the ratings if the casual viewers who tuned in to see Seinfeld would keep watching the season and turn the series into a ratings success.

Brand TV: coming to you from 30 Rockefeller Center

"SeinfeldVision" also positions *30 Rock* as Brand TV in that it is a show that keeps all kinds of brand assets in the public eye. Most basically, it offers constant references to other NBC on-air personalities, many of whom make cameos. Meredith Vieira and Matt Lauer appear in the context of faux segments of *The Today Show*, the morning show on which they are co-hosts. Newsman Brian Williams, on the other hand, is shown in his office, which is cleaned by Kenneth the Page. That unlikely connection leads to a few far-fetched characterizations and silly scenarios that technically portray Williams negatively, but actually make him come across as a funny guy willing to go along with a goofy gag. The lasting impression is positive, especially for Williams, who must adopt a somber persona as anchor of the top-rated *NBC Nightly News*.

Of course, the Jerry Seinfeld guest stint, along with the ones by Megan Mullally and Sean Hayes of *Will & Grace*, Janel Moloney and Alan Alda from *The West Wing*, among countless others, and the references to former NBC shows *Third Watch*, *Wings*, and *Night Court*, are a form of network brand placement, reminding viewers of earlier NBC comedy and drama series, now available on DVD or download. One November 2008 episode takes that referencing to the next level by linking an episode's A and B plots to different NBC sitcoms. The A plot features *Friends* star Jennifer Aniston playing a wacky former roommate of Liz Lemon's. In the B plot Tracy Jordan learns that Kenneth the Page is a fan of the 1980s show *Night Court* and that he was disappointed with the unresolved series finale. He stages a do-over in one of the production studios so that Kenneth can make the sitcom end the way he wanted it to. Guest stars Harry Anderson, Markie Post, and Charles Robinson reprise their sitcom roles and, in what could be read as a tribute to fan fiction, a fan remakes an official text to suit his own needs. The episode title, "The One with the Cast of 'Night Court'," brings the two plots together by borrowing the *Friends* title formula for the *30 Rock* episode. It serves a network brand function, both recalling NBC's "classic" comedies and generating new interest in them just as NBC began making them available for download on a segment of its website as well as on its content delivery platform Hulu. That is network multiplatform circulation at work.[55]

As Brand TV, *30 Rock* puts early or lesser-known Must-See TV dramas and comedies back into circulation. That is either an implicit or explicit corporate directive as the media conglomerate cable channel Universal HD also ran blocks of what it called "Rediscovered TV," something that is inherent in the way *30 Rock* encourages viewers to rewatch or get to know the series it references in its episodes. An on-air promo after a 2009 episode of *30 Rock* on NBC asks, "Miss your favorite TV classics? *Charles in Charge*, *Miami Vice* … Now they're back!" It then invites viewers to check out "Classic TV hits on nbc.com." At the very least, the series and its promotional flow offers viewers interested in doing so a sponsored platform on which to view the series. The section on the website dedicated to "classic" NBC series is just one of several different parts of the larger site. The website is micro-segmented so that viewers can continue to interact with whatever aspect of NBC or Universal content intrigues them. Different parts of the site are connected to different divisions. This micro-segmented website provides access to sites related to those divisions and reminds viewers of the various interconnected parts of NBC Universal.

Brand awareness is encouraged in the on-air series as well, especially when *30 Rock* directly acknowledges other media conglomerate holdings such as NBC's sister networks. The references are done in some humorous way such as when Telemundo takes over some of the TGS offices. The effect is to build brand awareness, in this case of the recent acquisition of Telemundo, the Spanish-Language network which is mentioned in multiple *30 Rock* episodes and even used as a memorable plot device in "Generalissimo" (3.10). Other affiliated cable channels get passing notations such as when John Lithgow, star of the 1990s NBC sitcom *3rd Rock from the Sun*, wanders around *30 Rock* looking for the SyFy channel. The channel gets a subtle shout out in several *Battlestar Galactica* references, most notably the character-inconsistent catch-phrase T-shirt worn by Jack's fiancée Elisa. Salma Hayek would make the "What the frak?!" T-shirt memorable just by standing there in it, but the writers give her a line to call attention to it. The T-shirt recalls an episode in which Liz mocks a network decree for more catch-phrases, but becomes secretly thrilled when she is associated with one. That phrase, "It's a deal breaker," is now used with a wink to promote *30 Rock*. Catch-phrase T-shirts as well as those that reference fictional *30 Rock* events such as the "Kidney Now!" benefit song, are on sale at the virtual and actual NBC stores. They sell branded merchandise as well such as a *Deal or No Deal* home game, which Jack holds up as a sweetener in an episode in which he is negotiating with network talent. Also on sale there are various peacock logo items, which have their parallel in the set design. Liz often walks past or stands near the hallway display of the progression of NBC logos from radio days to the variations on the present day's familiar peacock. The set design also accommodates media conglomerate logos as the building is the NBC Universal headquarters, a setting that makes it logical for Kenneth's reception desk to have behind it a wall-mounted NBC Universal name placard affixed to a large, elegant wood backing. Anyone who stops to talk with Kenneth shares the shot with that logo. Alternatively, characters often stand near one of the many HDTVs in the offices and hallways. Those can do double duty as network and product placement.

Comedy night done right: NBC 2009

30 Rock also shows its network loyalty by providing a platform from which to critique the competition and position the NBC brand in contrast to the other broadcast networks. In the May 7, 2009 "Mamma Mia!" episode (3.21) Liz implies that CBS only attracts geriatrics. Trying to guess Tracy's real age, Liz jokes that he might be seventy years old since his favorite TV series is *NCIS*, the long-running navy procedural that CBS developed from an earlier series called *JAG* crossed with elements of the already-franchised *CSI (Crime Scene Investigation)*. NBC claimed the same thing about CBS's ratings dominance that it did in the 1960s when the network's rural comedies were the top rated shows: CBS attracts the most viewers, but they do not represent the demographics that matter.[56] Countering CBS's assertion that it is the *Most Watched Network*, NBC resorts to the same desirable demographics logic it did in the 1960s. The episode also mocks the CW, in turn, with the logic that it might have a desirable demographic, but that it attracts no one beyond that (3.2).

Even what seems like mocking of NBC's own reality programming, such as in the episode 2.1 mention of three ridiculous faux NBC summer reality series, actually ends up being a critique of other networks' programs. The first faux series is *America's Next Top Pirate*, which mocks both the CW's *America's Next Top Model* and the features franchise *Pirates of the Caribbean* from ABC parent company Disney. The second faux series *Are You Smarter than a Dog?* sounds like FOX's *Are You Smarter Than a Fifth Grader?* The third, and most egregious, faux series is *MILF Island*, which references FOX's infamously outrageous reality dating show *Temptation Island*, but also takes the "hot mom" conceit and the "cougar" phenomenon that are topics for humor on SNL and *30 Rock* to the extreme in its tagline: "25 super-hot moms, 50 eighth-grade boys, no rules." The fact that in a later episode (2.11) the writers become engrossed in *MILF Island* even though they had been outraged by or mocked it earlier suggests that reality TV programs can be a guilty pleasure. Beneath the sophomoric humor, the sequence of references really doesn't satirize any current NBC programming, but it could be an insider jibe at the fact that the network would in fall 2008 introduce another in-bad-taste dating gamedoc called *Momma's Boys*. In the end these references have the effect of doing more to excuse than to critique NBC for its reality TV by implying that often the people that mock such shows are secretly watching them.

The rival network bashing continued in an actual interview *Fortune's* Patricia Seller conducted on the 52nd floor of 30 Rockefeller Center with real NBC Universal CEO Jeff Zucker and Alec Baldwin, who at the end takes on the persona of Jack Donaghy. Baldwin said he likes "the tone" of NBC series: "You know, on one other network, every show can be summed up with a certain one-line descriptive sentence, and then for the next six months, the shows are all about sexual relations between the main characters." Seller inserts her own ironic take on these press release-style answers, indicating that she knows that Baldwin's first comment is directed at ABC and the next one at CBS: "Another network has shows that are very loud. Driving! Thumping! Pulsing! They grab you by the lapels right through the commercials." Baldwin concludes that NBC is superior because "it leaves the viewer to make choices. The word is subtle. With comedies—like *The Office*—they're not banging you over the head. That's because of Jeff Zucker." Of course, Zucker is sitting next to him, which is especially funny when Baldwin morphs into Donaghy and proves himself more versed in synergy speak than the actual CEO.[57]

Baldwin's brand-booster stance fits right in with the network's new Thursday tagline, *Comedy Night Done Right*, with which it tried to woo viewers back to NBC, and take a swipe at CBS's Monday night of ratings-getting comedy. In previous seasons NBC's comedy night was sometimes cut short by a reality TV show such as *The Apprentice* swapped in for the usual 9 p.m. and 9.30 p.m. sitcoms. The tagline fit better with fall 2009's all-comedy Thursdays as the 10 p.m. block featured

Jay Leno's new variety program. Part of the scheduling logic for the series was that it is the kind of distracted viewing show that might pick off some of the broad-based CBS audience that NBC needs to win the night.[58] As discussed in the introduction, NBC's ill-fated decision to strip *The Jay Leno Show* across the weekly 10 p.m. slot not only displaced quality dramas that might have been programmed there, but also caused competition for *The Tonight Show with Conan O'Brien* and *Late Night with Jimmy Fallon*. The scheduling logic was that the latter two shows would appeal more to a younger crowd with their new 2009 hosts, whereas Leno would draw audiences who would not stay up for the late night shows anyhow. To the charges that it was cutting out quality dramas, NBC responded that it was not; rather, it was spreading them out over a micro-segmented season with a staggered schedule for premieres in September/October, January, March, or May/June. While the March premiere period has proven unsuccessful for actually launching new dramas, it has provided a slot in which NBC has been trying out new comedies including 2009's new ironicom *Parks and Recreation*. Billed as "from the producers of *The Office*" the series stars Amy Poehler, Tina Fey's SNL co-anchor on "Weekend Update." With a summer to work out the kinks of its initial run, the series returned much stronger for fall.

To cash in on Poehler's impression of Hillary Clinton and Tina Fey's of Sarah Palin, NBC offered several 2008 Thursday editions of SNL leading up to the U.S. presidential election. The strategy was repeated in fall 2009, but it was less successful without the election link. Each year the SNL franchise also rolls out several clip-based specials. In 2008 one was a collection of SNL shorts, a topic intended to build on the popularity of Andy Samberg's digital shorts that became internet sensations after their inclusion on *Saturday Night Live* episodes. The shorts continue to have long afterlives on the web, so much so that Samberg claims that more people have seen them than the late night show or at least more people recognized him after the shorts began to circulate online. Also recognizing the significance of web-based programming and interaction, Jimmy Fallon beta tested his *Late Night* with online viewers before premiering it on-air in March 2009. His segment *7th Floor West*, a send-up of reality shows such as MTV's *The Hills*, is always available on nbc.com. Although the shorts are really minisodes for the web, a medium for which they are ideally suited, one also runs every Monday on the TV show. The web life of the Fallon and Samberg content suggests a new model of doing business, one in which on-air content also circulates on the web, often as an extended online-only version. Samberg and Fallon understand the web as a medium suited to short-form content. Some of the other short-form content offered by NBC involves the extension of the storylines of minor, yet scene-stealing sitcom characters, such as *30 Rock*'s Kenneth the Page or *The Office*'s Accountants. Such features have become standard elements of the online extensions of TV shows.[59] Websites also include ways to extend viewer interaction with the series and their creators and casts such as *30 Rock*'s "Ask Tina" and "Dear Tracy" features, among other web elements. NBC was not immediate in its embrace of the new platform nor was it as comfortable with web content and its "free" circulation as have been

Fallon, Samberg, and other individual creators and producers at NBC (e.g., those working on *Heroes*). At the time of Samberg's breakout digital short "Lazy Sunday," NBC was still not comfortable with individual SNL skits circulating on YouTube and other fan video-sharing sites.[60] It co-created Hulu with FOX, in part, to control such circulation.

The 1999 SNL episode with which this chapter began included a sketch in which Jimmy Fallon plays Nick Burns, a tech support computer geek who comes and fixes the desktop computer of an office worker (played by Aniston). She froze her system by downloading a faulty screensaver, a rookie mistake for which the patronizing tech guy mocks her. The sketch is premised on the idea that at the time most people with computers could only do word processing and minimal web surfing. Everything else was the province of the tech geeks. The internet would soon become a space for amateurs as well as professionals, one in which people could do much more than download screensavers. People soon had the capability for gaining control of the content owned by studios, networks, and record companies and could not only distribute it to each other, but also manipulate it for their own uses. In addition to bypassing established corporate distribution channels and ignoring copyright, consumer-creators claimed ownership of media texts posting video mashups of existing content with their own edits and additions on YouTube and using blogs and message boards to create an immediate feedback loop with producers. It was not always appreciated or particularly constructive, which was part of the humor when Tina Fey, just having won the Golden Globe for Best Actress in a 2008 Comedy, turned her acceptance speech into a joke. "If you ever start to feel too good about yourself," she started and paused for effect, "They have this thing called the internet." Another pause. "You can find a lot of people there who don't like you." The voice she adopted had a hint of Sarah Palin and the persona was the put-upon producer that she played on TV, the Average Jane who stumbles into the spotlight probably for less than fifteen minutes of fame. It worked and allowed her to humorously call out specific people posting snarky comments like "Tina Fey has a smug smile" on the *Los Angeles Times* website. The live Golden Globes audience loved it when she continued, "And I'd like to address some of them now, 'BabsonLacrosse, "Suck It!"' ... CougarLetter, you can really 'suck it' 'cause you've been after me all year." The faux rant was a smart comedy way to deal with the problem.

Like it or not, message board commentary on TV shows is here to stay, but all the cheering for Fey's faux rant suggests that many producers and actors have had the same impulse to talk back to snarky posts. The most famous incident involved NBC producer Aaron Sorkin who tried and failed to interact with fans on the message boards for his series *West Wing*. He then turned the experience into a scene in the NBC drama and then used it again as the basis for a scene in his one-season series *Studio 60 on the Sunset Strip*, a behind-the-scenes drama about a sketch comedy show that premiered in the same fall as *30 Rock*. In a post-awards show interview, Fey told Tom O'Neil of the *L.A. Times*, "Once you register [to comment], then you know you're a crazy person." That comment got her a bunch more comments that she probably shouldn't read. Like Sorkin, who could never quite extricate himself from the endless feedback loop, the comments only caused more commentary. Fey won the round though despite the common refrain that "no one" is watching broadcast TV as that "no one" still translates into four or five million in *30 Rock*'s case and that is a lot more people than are reading the commentary board at the *L.A. Times*. Along with Fey and Sorkin many television producers probably prefer a more one-way content push and the slow and relatively private form of critical commentary via "fan" mail. The public forum that the internet creates is one in which media texts can be debated and critiqued while still on-the-air, after which a record of the exchange might circulate endlessly. One way to rein in the problem can be to set up talk back forums on official sites, which is what NBC did for *30 Rock*. Every NBC show now has a message board as well as various ways for fans to interact with producers.

NBC was not eager at first to embrace new media commentators and platforms. It was slow to make its content available online, and the network adopted a hostile stance to downloaders and constantly required YouTube to remove videos containing its branded content. It demonstrated that it did not understand clip culture or short-form and new media content. It was not the first time NBC dismissed new formats and tastes to its peril. It did a similar thing in the early 1950s by continuing to pursue business as usual, while the entire game had changed. It thought it could carry over practices from one medium into another unchanged, which in the 1950s meant importing what had worked on radio to television.[61] In the early twenty-first century NBC made the same mistake with the transition from television to web and back again. Instead of finding ways to circulate content online, especially in clip form or in ways that could result in user-generated mashups, it tried to block downloading and user-generated content creation. It was especially hostile to downloaders/users of SNL content, probably because the parts of that show have always been much stronger than whole episodes. The network did support the creation of a web series called *Quarterlife*, which had a video blogger as the main character and a vlog as a feature of the text. The network then imported it mostly unchanged to TV, not understanding the difference between the two mediums, and then cancelled the series after airing one episode.[62] NBC was also both anxious about monetizing its online content and unwilling to allow the iTunes store to become its distributor. NBC finally partnered with FOX to found Hulu, their own content delivery platform. With that deal, NBC had figured out the way to leverage the new media environment for its own interests via Hulu and the network's interconnected websites (both now winning web awards) as well as through arrangements with DirecTV and Comcast, among other partners.[63]

In terms of the changes to its TV programming style, that too mirrored its 1950s mistakes as in both eras CBS surged ahead of the once-unbeatable NBC and stayed there for several years by making deals for new kinds of content. In the 1950s they were often brokers with talent-agent-turned-producer Lew Wasserman who, as Gomery explains, was turning former NBC Radio personalities into millionaires by teaching them how to incorporate themselves into a brand and then turn that brand into a brand personality TV show.[64] The twenty-first-century association between NBC and Ben Silverman, talent-agent-turned-packager-and-producer, has some parallels. Eventually, NBC had to start working with format packagers like Silverman, not to gain back first place, which was lost, but to stay competitive. In the early 2000s CBS had already cornered the market on the strongest unscripted series and NBC was left scrambling for a hit. As noted earlier, a deal with Mark Burnett, producer of CBS's sensation *Survivor*, gave NBC a top ten finish with the Trump-helmed *The Apprentice*. NBC was also engaged in a series of deals with Reveille Productions, Silverman's company. Silverman had "a vision of the network business built around international co-productions and partnerships with advertisers to get their messages directly into the content."[65] He supplied the gamedoc *The Biggest Loser* and, more significantly, got the network involved in buying scripted formats, including March 2005's *The Office*.[66] The shows were greenlit by NBC President of Entertainment Kevin Reilly, who also got *Heroes* on the air that year and *30 Rock* in fall 2006. While *Heroes* helped it compete with ABC's *Lost* phenomenon, the *Office* acquisition was more pivotal in that thereafter NBC started to rebuild its comedy blocks. It was ABC that acquired *Ugly Betty*, the 2006 comic adaptation of a Colombian telenovela format, and that adaptation was viewed as the kind of bold programming decision that put Silverman in a position to become the new Co-Chairman of NBC Entertainment.[67] To make room for Silverman, NBC ousted Reilly, who moved over to FX. Silverman had a controversial tenure, lasting from May 2007 to July 2009. He greenlit more format adaptations such as *Kath & Kim*, which was one produced by Reveille, a company Silverman would divest himself of in February 2009 for an estimated $125 million to avoid the conflict of interest concerns.[68] Owning that company, however, had made him many contacts in the industry, which he used to get guest stars on NBC shows, including many of the high-profile guest stars for *30 Rock*. He even convinced his *Ugly Betty* co-producer Salma Hayek to do a multi-episode arc. Silverman also ushered in a string of flops and the network stayed in fourth place, a fact that was mocked in a spring 2009 *New York Times* article just before Silverman was replaced. Whether his successor has any better luck in getting NBC out of fourth, especially with controversial CEO of NBC Universal Jeff Zucker signing on for three more years as part of a deal with Comcast, the cable company hoping to take over controlling interest from GE in 2010, has yet to be determined as of this writing.

Whatever else the legacy of his association with NBC may turn out to be, the 2005 acquisition of *The Office* adaptation from Silverman's production company will continue to be a significant marker for the network as it established the foundation for the reassertion of NBC's smart comedy brand claim and enabled the network to roll out an all-comedy primetime Thursday for fall 2009.[69] After its success in 2008 as special event TV, *SNL Primetime* Thursday got an officially scheduled short run in early fall 2009 prior to the late fall premiere of *30 Rock* in the same slot. *The Office* kept its 9 p.m. slot, so that the new ironicoms could lead in to the two established ones. Comedy blocks traditionally come to an end at 10 p.m., but as already noted,

NBC bucked tradition and put *The Jay Leno Show* at 10 p.m. The comedy continued after the news with Conan O'Brien's *Tonight Show* followed by Jimmy Fallon's *Late Night*.

With all the attention being paid to the failures inherent in stripping of Jay Leno's 10 p.m. variety show across the fall 2009 primetime schedule, little notice has gone to how *Saturday Night Live*, its former cast members and its comic sensibility are now as central to NBC programming as *Law & Order* franchises have been.[70] In addition to Fallon's ascension to the *Late Night* spot, many former SNL cast members also took the helm of NBC shows in the last few years, with Molly Shannon starring in 2008's *Kath & Kim*, Amy Poehler in *Parks and Recreation*, which debuted in March 2009 like Fallon, and Chevy Chase in *Community* that fall. The biggest employer of former SNLers is, not surprisingly, the 2006 series created by Fey, who was Fallon's former co-anchor at "Weekend Update" and SNL's long-time head writer. Fey's *30 Rock* co-star Alec Baldwin is the movie star who is a contender for most stints as SNL guest host. In addition to co-star Tracy Morgan, who was on SNL when Fey was, other former SNL cast members, including Rachel Dratch, Chris Parnell, Fred Armisen, Will Forte, Kristen Wiig, Molly Shannon, and Jason Sudeikis, appear in a variety of recurring and guest roles on the show.

NBC is hoping that their combination of comedians formerly on SNL, Comedy Central's *The Daily Show*, E's snarky *The Soup* and *The Office*, not only bring success to the two new ironicoms *Parks and Recreation* and *Community*, but enable NBC to reassert itself as the Must-See comedy channel it was when Jennifer Aniston hosted SNL. 1999 was the same year in which Jon Stewart took over *The Daily Show* and Comedy Central started to prove a serious challenger to NBC as the network location on the channel spectrum for smart comedy. It secured the title when it gave *Daily Show* correspondent Stephen Colbert his own comedy platform with the spinoff *The Colbert Report*. NBC's move to reassert itself as the smart comedy destination may come from these talent raids, the most significant being casting *The Daily Show*'s Steve Carrell for *The Office* in 2005, the year of his star-making role in the Universal feature film *40-Year Old Virgin*. That was one year after NBC Universal was born. Whatever the outcome of its all-night comedy plan, NBC Universal has certainly embraced brand-based TV for the immediate future. The imperative seems to be to circulate its desired brand message—through its TV series; its schedule; its website; its collaborations; and, most significantly, the stealth PR it drops in the blogosphere, which then gets circulated as news rather than promotion by countless websites.

Prestige TV: the Super Bowl, the Olympics, and *Friday Night Lights*

Such brand-based scheduling continued in the winter with the Super Bowl in 2009 and the Winter Olympics in 2010 acting as a promotional platform for the return of NBC dramas, most notably the football-themed *Friday Night Lights*. The January 2009 promotions for the series, for example, were often linked in with those for

NBC's broadcast of the Super Bowl. The campaign was also connected to the reassertion of the NBC brand as the tagline was *NBC ... where dramas should be*. More generally the series history of *Friday Night Lights* (FNL) reflects developments in the broadcast TV industry in relation to distribution windowing, and multiplatform circulation and promotion. FNL's broadcast history is emblematic of the ways that texts are now able to move across a media conglomerate as the series circulates among NBC, Bravo, and Universal HD as well as on the co-owned alternate content delivery platform Hulu. During his tenure, Ben Silverman kept the quality drama on the air, despite its ratings troubles, through a unique deal with satellite provider DirecTV.[71] Season three was the first to be made available exclusively on DirecTV before it premiered on NBC. It was unheard of for a broadcast series not to have its first distribution window on broadcast, but it was also common for quality dramas with low ratings to become one season wonders. The deal was made so that the series, a fan favorite, was not totally dependent on advertising revenue, and, therefore, on selling commercial time. Silverman touted such deals as necessary "to drive the survival" of NBC's "content base." He concluded: "if we're still going to make the best programming in the world, we've got to find the funding for it."[72] Viability also required networks to find ways to drive viewers toward the content, often through new media approaches. As FNL is a WB-style show done Big Three, it is not surprising that it also took full advantage of web content, especially as it had the kind of indie music playlist for episodes that prompted viewers to want to download the songs immediately.

Executive producer/writer Jason Katims' prior shows include *My So Called Life* (ABC 1994–5), an early attempt to bring a narrowcast show to broadcast TV, and *Roswell* (WB/UPN 1999–2001), which the WB greenlit as part of its strategy of narrowcasting to a teen market to differentiate its brand from those of the other broadcast networks. Linking all three shows is Katims' preference for what he describes as character-driven drama. Adding Sci-Fi in *Roswell* and Sports in FNL is, he says, a method of brand differentiation. Yet, FNL goes beyond that hybrid strategy looked at in the previous chapter given that FNL is a drama series with great potential for network brand asset integration. Indicative of the changes to the TV industry even since 1999, that FNL is about football and that its storyline references the Beijing Olympics go beyond story differentiation. They allow for a link to NBC Sports, a division that began its coverage of the Olympics with the Tokyo Games in 1964 and continued through the Beijing Games in 2008, which were broadcast on NBC as well as on its media conglomerate's other networks and platforms. Even more significant was the return of the Sunday night games of the National Football League (NFL) to NBC in August 2006, a coup about which FNL could subtly remind viewers with the build-up to and premiere of its pilot. While there were some broadcast viewership problems with initially hyping the show only as a sports drama, the genre choice makes perfect sense in an environment in which timeshifting and alternate content delivery systems make it necessary to integrate promotion into storytelling segments.[73] Promotion is built into the sports genre, Gary Whannel contends: "Title sequences and video segments promote sporting events through constructing narrative conflicts between participants."[74] These conflicts are promised "to be resolved, at least temporarily, in the contest to follow."[75]

As with sports programming, reality TV docusoap also pivots on the editing of raw footage into narratives rich with multiple character conflicts, revealing individual backstories, and melodramatic and tension-filled story arcs. Thus, it is no surprise that FNL also relies on a docusoap for its filming style. The season one episodes, some of the series' best, exemplify this point. The "A" plot in the episodes centered on football, and the first season was quite smart in the way it made the countdown to the Friday game central to the structure of an episode, which gave it a "will the team be ready in time for the competition," docusoap element. The B plots were more melodramatic. One character arc followed Jason Street, the star quarterback paralyzed in the pilot episode, who later decides to train for a quadriplegic rugby team headed to the Paralympics. The docusoap element of melodramatic backstory has roots in the athlete backstory that was used to transform Olympic event coverage into Event Programming, complete with its own storylines and creative primetime scheduling for maximum effect.

In this first season in fall 2006, *Friday Night Lights* applied the relevant commercial pod approach to promotion in that it heavily emphasized football gameplay in the season that NBC acquired the NFL rights, and even worked in a storyline connected to the Olympics, the long-term rights to which NBC Universal had already secured. By supporting NBC's bid to be the network to host the Olympics and its affiliated cable channels as locations for more specialized Olympic content, then parent company GE got the added benefit of using the special event programming to run corporate image campaign spots. These kinds of spots and the single sponsorships with which they were associated were staples of 1950s TV. They were often called prestige sponsorships because the company got reflected prestige from hosting upscale or revered programming.[76] NBC's 2008 Beijing Olympics coverage was peppered with spots touting GE as the earth-friendly company with the "eco-imagination" needed for the global twenty-first century.

While corporate image campaigns are nothing new, it is interesting that NBC rolled out a twenty-first-century image campaign of its own to remind people of its prestigious brand history. In the network identifier promotions that began around January 2008, NBC stars hummed or otherwise performed some version of the NBC chimes aural signature—its G-E-C musical cue—while standing in front of an NBC radio microphone. The chimes date to radio when they were the audio identifier of the network. The chimes serve to locate NBC within its original esteemed radio history and that of its original owner RCA. Linking the current stars to the classic chimes implies an unbroken legacy stretching from NBC's millennial TV programming to its midcentury radio history, the era when NBC dominated the dial and CBS had not yet surged into first place with its investment in star sitcoms and variety shows.

While there is a nostalgia effect to seeing the old microphones, which likely has appeal to NBC's upscale urban viewers who go out and buy turntables, it still associates NBC with radio, which is a media industry in even worse shape than broadcast TV. This has some of the same irony of the smart comedy writers who made *The Office*'s Dunder Mifflin tagline "paper for a paperless world," characterized Liz Lemon's boyfriend as the beeper king of Manhattan, and had her boss Jack Donaghy fire the executive in charge of the boombox division. Acknowledging the significance of new media, a variation of the network ident, this one reading *chime in*, began around June 2008. It was sometimes part of the chimes promo above and sometimes featured alone. It invited on-air viewers to "chime in" on nbc.com. NBC's "chime in" does not have the inviting openness of ABC's "start here," especially given that NBC's ironicoms make fun of the kind of corporate "suggestion box" mentality in which people are asked to "chime in" so that they can be ignored or get in trouble (the subject of an *Office* episode, of course). One version of the 2009 NBC network ident chimes was quite telling: it was sold as commercial time to Orville Redenbacher's popcorn. The tagline was *TV is better popped* and it featured buttery popping corn morphing into the NBC peacock logo followed by: *chimes brought to you by Orville Redenbacher's*. That was the most honest depiction of the basic fact of broadcast television: it is a commercial medium. As Jack tells Liz, the story is there to give people something to look at between car commercials.

NBC's Television City: Rockefeller Center

NBC's recent embrace of product integration and brand synergy makes it harder to reinforce its association with an esteemed industry legacy that it was intending to convey through the original chimes network idents. For its part, Orville Redenbacher's sponsorship seems typical of branded entertainment deals in which a company hopes to elicit "the gratitude effect" from viewers who will purchase products made by the company that is keeping their favorite shows on-air despite their less-than-stellar ratings. As it is unique and, therefore, memorable, especially given that it is set up as a bumper to story segments, it is also likely to be watched by DVR viewers unsure when the story is about to begin again.

In recent years NBC has tried to retain its network associations with the historical landmarks and the Art Deco architecture and art in and around its location in Rockefeller Center in order to put distance between itself and synergy and commercialism for which Disney and Times Square are infamous. Times Square has been synonymous with "Disneyfication" since the company's cash infusion revitalized Broadway theaters and the whole area more generally, making it enough of a tourist-only zone that its stretch of Broadway has been transformed from city thoroughfare to pedestrian mall. From there tourists can walk up and over to Sixth Avenue to see the exterior of Radio City Music Hall and turn into the 50th Street entrance to Rockefeller Center. Once at the center of the Plaza, they can see the NBC Studios entrance, the bronze gilded Prometheus, and the concourse of international flags. After visiting the famous ice skating rink, they can travel across Rockefeller Plaza onto Fifth Avenue. After a stop at St. Patrick's Cathedral or at least a break on its steps, visitors often window shop in the luxury stores along the famous avenue, including Cartier, the jeweler that made those paid appearances on NBC shows in 2008–9. Its competitor, Tiffany and Company, is a few blocks north; its air rights are used by its neighbor, the massive Trump Tower, which boasts an indoor waterfall and public arcade. The building is familiar from the NBC gamedoc *The Apprentice*. Although it is associated with the weekly boardroom showdowns with the infamous toupee-wearing real estate magnate, those scenes are filmed on a set that apparently bears little resemblance to the actual space.

Given that Trump tore down the Art Deco building that used to occupy the location, the former home to the Old New York retail institution Bonwit Teller, NBC would likely prefer to play down that connection. If they continue to head north tourists will pass some more of Old New York's buildings such as *The Plaza* and the statuary associated with it and that entrance to Central Park. After a visit to the park, they can retrace their steps or head over to the subway at Columbus Circle, which is now presided over both by a Trump International Hotel and Towers, where *Celebrity Apprentice* contestants have occupied a suite, and the massive Time Warner Center, the street level of which has its own collection of luxury retailers. This entire Midtown Manhattan tourist zone is a space overwritten with the recent conglomeration of the media industries. Tracing this pedestrian route reveals that the actual New York address of NBC network headquarters in Manhattan might allow it to affiliate itself with Art Deco New York and Fifth Avenue luxury, but NBC is not so distant from mallstores and megaplexes or the chain, theme, and fast food restaurants that are associated with Disneyfication of Manhattan. As NBC's media conglomerate ties increased in the past decade, so did its on-air references to its association with Rockefeller Center.

Rockefeller Center and its ties to Old New York—the Rockefeller family has its offices on the 54th–56th floors—lends the broadcast network its prestige. To make sure that connection lasts indefinitely, NBC purchased the floors that it had only previously leased, when they were made available for sale in a condominium-style arrangement. The deal also involved a long-term lease on the studios at 10 Rockefeller Center, the studio location for *The Today Show*. The increase in on-the-Plaza *Today Show* segments has given NBC a branded presence there. Mentions of the association have increased as well on NBC and MSNBC news programs that are also broadcast from there. Together all of these shows frame Rockefeller Center as part of the NBC branded backdrop, most literally through *Today*'s studio window. Even if its morning show studio is located in a plaza whose buildings boast Art Deco adornments and statuary instead of a square crammed with massive electronic billboards and flashing marquees, NBC, which since 2004 has been NBC Universal, is as much a representative of media conglomeration as Disney-ABC.

NBC's increase in on-air references to its Rockefeller Center location try to ensure that these similarities are overshadowed by its claims to a brand legacy that dates back to its number one status in the radio era, embodied by the two classic marquees inside the plaza: NBC's on the entrance to 30 Rockefeller Center and the one for the music hall whose name was changed to reflect that the area had already by 1932 become known as NBC's Radio City. The NBC marquee is well known from its appearance in many network shows such as *Seinfeld*, but its most famous link is to the weekly broadcast of *Saturday Night Live*.

In the past few years NBC has reinforced the idea of Rockefeller Center as its site of television production, although the majority of series production is done in Los Angeles, by offering on-air references to the actual studios and offices within the building. The association is reaffirmed in the introductions to various programs throughout the day, including *The Today Show*, *NBC Nightly News with Brian Williams* and two late night shows. Viewers have long been told that SNL comes live from Studio 8H in Rockefeller Center and now they know that 6B is home to *Late Night with Jimmy Fallon* hosted by former SNLer Jimmy Fallon. Viewers are reminded of the location when the skits and contests to which Fallon challenges guest stars spill into a hallway that has a giant 6B painted on its wall. Fallon is also associated with the building's 7th Floor West because that is the title of his faux reality series segment. He offers snippets of it every Monday and makes it always available online. Fallon's embrace of new media has made his show NBC's most millennial yet, but it has midcentury brand history connections as well. Once home to *Texaco Star Theater*, the hit show hosted by Mr. Television, Milton Berle, Studio 6B is most famous for its association with *The Tonight Show*, first with Jack Parr and then with Johnny Carson until he relocated it to Burbank in 1972. In June 2009 when Conan O'Brien became the host of *The Tonight Show*, at least for seven months, production was relocated from Burbank to a brand new studio in Universal City, thereby representing the recently minted NBC Universal Media Studios.[77] As the end of *The Tonight Show* segues without a commercial into the credits for *Late Night*, the combination of the new Universal studio with the refurbished historical Rockefeller Center studio allows the back-to-back nightly late night broadcasts to link the West Coast's Universal (Studio) City with the East Coast's Television City.

Television production has been associated with "cities" organized around that purpose since announcers reminded viewers that their favorite programs were coming to them from "Television City in Hollywood" or, more flippantly, "from beautiful downtown Burbank." If fans visited the buildings featured in television series credit sequences famous for their tracking shots of Queens and Brooklyn neighborhoods, they would encounter, as scholars in Tourism Studies describe it, the incommensurability of "intrusive lifespace" in such locations.[78] Setting a television show at 30 Rockefeller Center is more complicated, however, as the building is an historical landmark, tourist attraction, media conglomerate and network headquarters, branded space, and a site of television production all at once. It is, therefore, actually a place in which some NBC executives work and some producers and talent have offices. It is not the site of the production of the television show that takes its name as that sitcom is actually filmed in a typically uninspired-looking studio space in Queens. Those who take the NBC tour at 30 Rockefeller Center with a real NBC page are unlikely to see much other production-in-progress unless they also have tickets for a taping of one of the late night shows. If they are really lucky, visitors might see Tina Fey the producer somewhere in the building or

Tina Fey the actress filming a street scene as Liz Lemon. More likely, after having seen very little that resembled actual television production, they will find themselves out on the Plaza and be left looking up at the towering building from the angle that is the same one given of the building in *30 Rock* transition shots. It is often the angle associated with Liz Lemon's perspective as the Average Jane. This similarity between her point-of-view and the ordinary audience member's goes a long way to explaining her appeal. Fans of the show who visit the site could Photoshop some pictures of themselves against its backdrop. *30 Rock's* credit sequence shares that mashed together, new media aesthetic, with its black and white live action footage of the characters digitally overlaid on photographs of the buildings and sites of Rockefeller Center. The photos advance as if in a digital flip photo album: the *Prometheus* and *Atlas* sculptures, the *Wisdom, Light and Sound* 30 Rock entrance art, and various buildings in the complex as well as the art associated with them, including gilded carvings and bas-relief. The effect is decidedly not seamless and gives the credit sequence a cartoony feel that signals that the stories have little correspondence to actuality, especially given that Liz Lemon's co-producer Pete looks paranoid and Jack Donaghy, the final character featured, looks like he might start maniacally laughing in that cartoon evil sort of way. Neither of these characterizations corresponds to story segment actuality.

A closer look at the credits confirms this exaggerated emphasis. The characters are associated not with their offices, the writers room, or the studio where the real series or even the show-within-the-show is filmed, but with exterior shots of Rockefeller Center. Exteriors and a few street scenes are mostly all that is filmed in Manhattan as the sets are in a typical warehouse studio space in Queens. The lines between real and actual locations and producers are blurred, of course, given that viewers are aware that *30 Rock's* star, creator, and executive producer Tina Fey worked on a production team for the late night sketch comedy show that does film in the complex. The branding continues in the transition shots. In the first season they are often low angle shots of the skyscraper as if to suggest the power dynamic of the lone creative fighting the floors of clueless executives above her. By the third season, the transition shots change to shots of the Art Deco embellishments on the building and Rockefeller Center's art more generally. Some of the same art and architecture of the credits appears as do newly added elements, including the stainless steel plaque, "News," over the entrance to the Associated Press Building and the new special entrance to the 30 Rock Observation Deck. They are not simple establishing location shots (as are typical of the buildings shown in transition shots of most sitcoms), rather they are brand establishing shots. The Atlas sculpture in front of the International Building facing Fifth Avenue is a frequent choice for transition shots. It still retains the hero of a workplace comedy image of Liz Lemon that positions her as the lone creative holding up the world of trouble everyone piles on her back. It can also reference the heroic perception of Tina Fey holding up NBC both through her Emmy-winning sitcom and her ratings-boosting simultaneous guest stint on the election year Primetime and Late Night SNLs. Finally, it can reference the blurred perception of Liz Lemon/Tina Fey as a creator-producer who is forced to shoulder the expectations for synergy that come with NBC's position beneath Universal within the media conglomerate. However they are read, it is clear that *30 Rock* and its credits and transition shots function less to offer insight into television production or to deconstruct a production culture and more to construct a platform from which to circulate branded messages about the network on which it airs and to familiarize viewers with the various sister networks that join NBC under the NBC Universal umbrella.

In contrast to *7th Floor West*, Fallon's faux minisodes, which clearly have nothing to do with actual staff members or relations on that floor or whichever one on which Fallon, his writers, and assistants actually occupy offices, viewers often assume that *30 Rock* is intended to be a broadly comic version of actual NBC production culture interactions.[79] Yet, the series not only empties production work from the production site, it also does less to expose the inner workings of production cultures, than it does to circulate a preferred narrative through which NBC's production cultures describe themselves.

NBC wants to be associated with an authentic New York inlaid with Art Deco design elements versus a manufactured New York overlaid with brand signifiers, but as is evident in the *30 Rock* credits sequence, the network also values iconic NYC sights as brand assets rather than for their historical or artistic significance and is just as involved as Disney in the transformation of city space into branded city space. Its website continues this branded encounter by providing opportunities for virtual interactions with the NBC series as well as encouraging visits to the steel and stone sites of Rockefeller Center.

NBC Nightly News and the Obama effect on broadcast TV

NBC's biggest brand coup of 2009 was the March 19th guest appearance of President Barack Obama on *The Tonight Show with Jay Leno*, the first time a sitting president had ever been a guest on such a show. While he did talk about policy, the President started on a lighter note and said of those criticizing his early decisions: "I do think in Washington, it's a bit like *American Idol*, except everybody is Simon Cowell." He was speaking directly to the broadcast television audience by referencing the snarky judge of the gamedoc that had managed to achieve on-air as-it-aired ratings numbers that most critics assumed were no longer possible in the multichannel environment of US-TV. For the rest of the appearance, the President talked extensively about serious policy issues and addressed very complex questions. The final segment turned to a lighter note, however, with Leno asking what it was like to fly on Air Force One. That gave the President the chance to tell a funny story about how his daughters, Malia and Sasha, were "just not as impressed" as he was with the presidential air fleet. During their first time on Marine One, for instance, the President tried to point out the Washington Monument and the other sites. The girls caught sight instead of some Starburst candies in the seat pocket. They got their attention. "So they're splitting up the Starbursts," the President recalled, and they never even looked up as the aircraft passed the Lincoln Memorial. President Obama's *Tonight Show* appearance ended with a discussion of the presidential puppy, with which the media had become obsessed. The dog would become a topic of interest as well when NBC scored a second prestige program a few months later when the Obamas and new puppy Bo welcomed *NBC Nightly News*' Brian Williams, along with "25 producers and 32 cameras" for a special entitled, *Inside the Obama White House*. The special event programming, described as a decades-old "great tradition at NBC News" to take its viewers behind the scenes at the real West Wing (and East Wing) of the White House a few months after a new president is inaugurated, was split into two NBC News Primetime Specials on June 2nd and 3rd. Both did well in the ratings, attracting 9+ million viewers and winning their timeslots.

After those appearances, President Obama held various 2009 primetime press conferences and a daytime address to school children, leading some critics to complain he had been overusing his presidential prerogative to preempt primetime programming for special addresses and press conferences. While quite reverential during the President's visit to his late night show, Leno joked on his new 10 p.m. show that Obama might be overdoing it. Of course, the jokes came after the President, eager to set the record straight about his health care reform proposals, went on CBS's *Late Show* helmed by Leno's old rival David Letterman, a booking that undercut the exclusivity of the President's 2009 NBC appearance. Whether or not the 44th President appears on TV too often is under debate, but the question is less interesting than the fact that in an era when TV is supposedly dying, President Obama clearly still sees it as the medium through which to reach the most people simultaneously. That is a significant endorsement coming from a president with a White House Twitter feed and an addiction to his web-enabled Blackberry.[80] Obama might have appeared on Leno's *Tonight Show*, but he is the digital generation's president, more likely to appreciate the web-savvy, if not the sophomoric humor, of the producers responsible for rolling out *Late Night* online before Jimmy Fallon's on-air debut as host in March 2009. After all, the Obama campaign was much more viable online, before it took off on the streets. As a candidate and as a president, Barack Obama understands that if you don't offer a message and shape it across all forms of media, then others will do it for you.

President Obama knows that so much is put into circulation about him and his administration in the blogosphere, that he needs to leverage the forums at his disposal and try to refocus Americans on the actual facts about national issues and policies. The hope is that at least some of the ubiquitous political blogs and political commentary sites will pick up and circulate his actual statements or, better yet, actual video snippets. He is well aware that the same channels through which he was able to spread his political message are those that also enable the rapid circulation of political snark and unsubstantiated claims. More troubling, is that the web allows demonstrated falsehoods to be circulated as fact, such as the continued movement around the world wide web of the falsehood that President Obama was not born in the United States. When the rumor surfaced again and gained power in the summer of 2009, Williams did a segment on the claim for *NBC Nightly News*. Given that the program is the number one broadcast newscast, the segment demonstrated that broadcast TV still has plenty of power to set the record straight in a few seconds of commentary coming simultaneously right into the homes of many viewers and onto the desktops, laptops and mobile devices of a good number of viewers. Of course, the dispersed and continuous power of new media circulation is evidenced by the fact that Williams had to address the issue at all. He noted that no matter how many times news professionals have detailed the evidence that the claim is baseless, it continues to circulate. The upside is that the Williams NBC news segment on the issue was repurposed on nbc.com, which, in turn, led to its circulation on video file-sharing sites, embedded video blogs, and blogs offering news transcripts and snippets. The long electronic afterlife of the NBC news segment, which has more power because of its longevity and less because it lacks the simultaneity of broadcast TV, is indicative of the current ambivalent relationship of broadcast TV and new media.

For the purposes of this chapter, *NBC Nightly News* more generally is most interesting for the way it also works to associate NBC with the prestige of Art Deco New York and NBC's branded presence in Rockefeller Center. The NBC announcer, Williams, and the NBC newscasters who sometimes report from the Observation Deck of 30 Rockefeller Center, are there not only to provide the news, but also to provide NBC brand claims about its capability as a broadcaster and its willingness to be a microcaster that offers enhanced content on nbc.com for web and mobile viewers.

It is interesting to note that like FOX's use of the story space in *24* to circulate reminders of its news division's fair and balanced brand promise, NBC News' *Inside the White House* reinforced NBC's status as the *most watched newscast* as it included footage of White House televisions tuned in to NBC news programs. The special, which was billed as television's "most accurate portrayal of what happens in the real West Wing," also made mention of NBC's recent hit series *The West Wing* (1999–2006). While that NBC drama series encouraged viewers to recall the promise of American political service as it might ideally be, President Obama reminded viewers, by exercising his right to preempt broadcast TV, of the promise of broadcast television as a public forum and a means through which to keep citizens aware of public issues. All the new media offered by the White House suggests that Americans like to feel as if the government is keeping them informed as citizens and that they find appealing the imagined simultaneity made possible by live feeds and updates on social networking sites and utilities. Yet, there is nothing like broadcast TV to create a sense of imagined community. A good number of Americans still are attracted to the idea of watching a live broadcast of the U.S. President talking to the American people who, in turn, feel as if they are expressing their collectivity as a nation by watching him on TV at the same time as they imagine millions of their fellow Americans are doing the same.

Broadcast TV still holds out the promise of imagined collectivity in which Americans come together not only as citizens to watch the Inauguration of the first

African American President or the funeral of the last of the Kennedy brothers, but also as collective participants in a nationalized entertainment event such as the *American Idol* final results show or the Super Bowl. That such shared broadcast TV experiences are still powerful and worth investing in is evident in all that NBC Universal and its then parent company General Electric did to secure long-term rights to the Olympics in order to brand it as an NBC event, a GE event, and, in its broadcast editing and airing, as an American-centric event.

The now common claim that we have entered an era of "post-network TV" is not quite accurate. Broadcast TV continues to exist and matter, but it has remained viable by partnering with professional web content creators, alternate content delivery platforms, social networking sites and utilities, rival TV content providers such as DirecTV, and, most importantly, viewsers. Not only do viewser websites offer free publicity for network series, but other forms of user-generated content can be aired on TV or posted online to enhance network content or, more typically, to make viewsers feel as if they are partners with the network and its production teams. Actual viewer video reports and video footage add an air of authenticity to news programs, for example. They also often reinforce the authority of the official newscasts given that the professionals typically offer more polished and objective-sounding comments than the amateurs. Perhaps these kinds of new media-enabled features demonstrate that people want to feel as if they are active participants in relation to television content even if they understand that being encouraged to "chime in" does not translate into having the power to make decisions. The conclusion addresses some of these partnerships and considers how broadcast networks and production teams have figured out ways to leverage multiple platforms for their own ends, while still making viewsers feel as if they are part of the production and decision-making process.

Conclusion

In the first millennial decade U.S. broadcast networks responded to the challenge they heard in HBO's *It's not TV* brand claim and created programming that was as compelling and smart as cable, which was the key to its failures as well as its successes. The problem, as the broadcast networks discovered, is that the kinds of dramas that have the most critical and audience buzz are those most ill suited for watching on-air as they are broadcast. That made it difficult for these series to get the ratings they needed to be declared a success by the Nielsen Media Research metrics. Despite the flaws of that system it was still firmly entrenched at the end of the decade and maintained its power over free-to-air, advertiser-supported broadcast television series.[1] By the decade's end, NBC was following CBS's lead in keeping broadcast TV viable by programming familiar rather than innovative programming.

By 2009, it became possible to "watch TV" in a variety of ways, as this book has demonstrated: by downloading a series from an alternate content delivery platform (e.g., iTunes, Hulu); streaming video on a network's media player; or purchasing it on DVD or renting it, often by mail through Netflix or via digital download. Finally, as CBS's overnight ratings prove, millions of people were still watching TV on television as it was broadcast and millions more watching on slight time delay that same evening via their DVRs, or, at least, within the seven-day playback period now part of the extended Nielsen's ratings charts.

U.S. viewers feel especially compelled to watch on-air as-they-air gamedocs like *American Idol,* major sporting events such as the Olympics or the Super Bowl, and other special event programming such as U.S. election coverage. As discussed in the last chapter, people are attracted to the general idea of participating in a national television event, but they are also motivated to watch Event TV as it airs to avoid having someone spoil the announcement of the results. The second category that commands decent ratings, by 2009's standards at least, is the episodic drama, especially case-based procedurals that track and resolve an investigation with a single episode. These series, as CBS's ratings indicate, are those with which broadcast TV can still draw in the clickers with their propensity for web- as well as channel-surfing. The kinds of traditional TV programs in which CBS traffics also do well with casual viewers who cannot quite make time for the regular viewing practices of the loyals, but still watch TV series when they can. As the networks learned in the 2000s, the casuals are harder to reach with long-arc serial programming because with each episode they miss, they are less and less likely to want to or be able to make the time to catch up so that they can watch the next episode on-air as it airs.

As this book has argued, time is at the center of the challenges and controversies surrounding today's primetime broadcast television programming, scheduling, and metrics. TV time has been affected by the broad adoption of technologies and the social behaviors they make possible. Before the popularization of the World Wide Web and the access it offered to TV content and information about it, broadcast television was a predictably timed and controlled commodity. Information on upcoming series would be released on a PR department's timeline calculated to build only positive buzz about a program before its traditional September premiere. That schedule would allow viewers the time to get familiar with a series, to be encouraged to watch it by other people they knew, or to happen upon it on their own prior to the first Nielsen measurement time—the November sweeps. A television show would have a fixed time on the schedule to encourage repetitive viewing. Once the sweeps period passed, then it was hit or miss when a program would appear again because it might be displaced by holiday and special event programming. It would resume a somewhat regular schedule, but viewers who made an appointment to be in front of the set each week at the scheduled time were sometimes dismayed to discover a rerun played instead. Reruns are essential for stretching the 22+ episodes out over the September to May season and for providing viewers time to catch up on missed episodes prior to the May season finale. This primetime schedule presumed an episodic drama or sitcom, one which did not have an episode-to-episode timeline requiring it to be viewed in order for optimum continuity. Increasingly broadcast programs have adopted more serial features, which make this kind of haphazard timing of episodes less suitable. *Lost*'s long-arc serial mystery and *24*'s "events happen in real time" season-long storyline, for example, require episodes to be watched in order or, better yet, watched several episodes at a time and not on a broadcast schedule, especially one that creates gaps between episodes. The popularization of this kind of story format coincided with the rise of alternate platforms—DVRs, DVD, download, pay-per-view—on which to watch the programming, that better suited them. The problem, of course, is that watching television in this fashion is at odds with the other essential element to TV time—the timed breaks for the promotion of products not only from series' sponsors, but also from networks, and, increasingly, the media conglomerates of which they are a part.

With their fast-forwarding capabilities DVRs allow viewers to spend less time watching a TV series, but studies have shown that their time-saving capabilities actually increase viewers' dedication to a series and their willingness to spend more time interacting with a series in other platforms.[2] Alternate platform availability allows casual viewers to watch a series when their schedules allow, while the ongoing and archived structure of online message boards makes it possible for casual viewers to jump in to discussions that in the past would have only been for dedicated fans.

Grey Matter: From the Writers of Grey's Anatomy

The 2000s saw the public's broad adoption of these behaviors and their eventual co-optation by broadcast television. The networks embraced fan practices as they figured out ways to leverage them to their advantage and to use them to monetize content. Content available in new media spaces helps to keep a series "fresh in fans' minds between episodes" and to "nurture the loyalty" to the show by assuring viewers that networks are catering to their choices and responsive to their needs.[3] Picking up on some of the immersive web strategies at work in the WB's *Dawson's desktop* experience, the producers creating the abc.go.com site for *Grey's Anatomy*, for example, understood that "Blogs penned in the name of their programs' characters are novel ways of feeding content to hungry viewers."[4] The site featured three flogs (fake blogs) created by the series' writers. The first two were in-character blogs, such as that for minor character Joe the bartender. *Grey Matter: From the Writers of Grey's Anatomy*, a third feature on the site, was billed as a blog, but it was more like the in-character flogs since the writers all stayed "in character" as fan-producers who felt inspired to offer their personal take on production developments. Although written by actual production team members in their own names, the writers recounted their professional and personal neuroses in a tone similar to that they created for the in-series voiceovers of main character Meredith Grey. In their chatty accounts of series developments and production decisions, the writers positioned themselves as fans who translated their passion for television into a career. Posting on a rotating basis, each writer used his/her initial post to relate his/her backstory and experiences in the media industry.[5]

These flogs were part of a larger campaign for *Grey's Anatomy* (US, ABC, 2005–) and a general one for the Thursday schedule into which the series was slotted. In its 2006–7 season ABC adopted the "Choose Thursdays" campaign to promote its female-centered Thursday lineup of *Ugly Betty*, *Grey's Anatomy*, and *Men in Trees*, all female-centered, protagonist-driven programs about women struggling with the blurred boundaries between private and professional life. In addition to the standard marketing campaigns, ABC continues to utilize post-network era strategies for offering viewers multiple ways to interact with its TV texts. Through its interactive and participatory features as well as its menu of content delivery choices—via TV, internet, DVD, or iTunes download—ABC offers viewers choices in ways to follow a show and its characters in an era, when, as we saw in chapter one, TV series are extended on the internet. The site for *Grey's Anatomy* (hereafter GA) is a testament to the impact viewer choice has had on televisual address. First, they have to choose whether to watch the series from all the timeslot's other choices across an immense channel spectrum. Then they have to choose to watch it on-air as-it-airs rather than in a timeshifted, downloaded or alternate format.

In this consumer choice-driven environment, networks have changed their marketing strategies: "With consumers suddenly able to access whatever they want whenever they want it and TV competing with everything from the Internet to iPods to cellphones, launching a successful show is only half the equation."[6] Networks also have to find alternate ways to sustain interest in their shows. ABC offers different levels of engagement for fans. It shapes the way it would like viewers to interact with GA, but it assumes that they will just pick and choose the most relevant aspects of the experience. Site visitors can listen to the Podcasts; find out about music used on the show; learn about the show's medical references; buy the magazine, soundtrack, or other items in the store. They also can watch or rewatch an episode for free on-site as streaming video or for a fee via downloadable ITunes file. In short, to whatever degree viewers desire, they can continue to engage with the TV text after the broadcast timeslot ends.

As already noted, they can also engage with creator Shonda Rhimes and the other series writers by reading the *Grey Matter* flogs and posting comments on linked message boards. The writers discuss their choices for character and story arcs and sometimes the professional and personal choices that led to them writing for GA. They speak directly to fans as if they were friends in the same way title character Meredith Grey does in the voiceovers that frame the weekly text. The writers' blogs and message board features are popular because they directly engage viewers, who, in turn, have a space in which to express their gratitude to the writers and their loyalty to the show. As one fan comments: "I love how all of the writers share their personal feelings with us. I mean, having a blog done by the freaking writers is incredible enough but to have insights into your lives and feelings is amazing!" (10/13/06). Fan preference for the writers' blogs, especially those from the series creator Shonda Rhimes, and their tendency to transform her into "a fantasised 'presence'" suggests something about the persistence of romantic notions of the author and may, as Hills has argued, point to the way media texts are reactivating the idea of the *auteur*, that is, of a series creator as the lone creative genius responsible for the finished product.[7]

At the same time, fan commentary and the writers' (and the network's) response to it suggests that it is misleading to think of the interaction in terms of a binary between all-powerful and savvy media producers and powerless and gullible fans. The remarks by both writers and fans on abc.go.com demonstrate that fans have been empowered in this era of media convergence. In his work on science fiction fandom, Alan McKee theorizes that "the distinction between the fan and the industry does not work as a simple binary," especially given the ways that the texts "fans are producing are indeed regarded as part of the real text."[8] ABC does position the blogs and fan commentary as part of the overall official GA text, a move that is indicative of the way networks have begun to view fan interaction as simultaneous rather than supplemental to TV programming and marketing decisions.

Judging by the number of posts to the comments sections linked to the *Grey Matter* blogs, they have become one of the most popular features on abc.go.com.

After thanking the writers for "another great episode," one fan describes how the blog "adds to the experience of watching the show." She continues, "I cannot tell you how much I look forward to reading the writers' feedback after the show airs—it is one of the true successes of GA!" (10/13/06). Its success has much to do with the way that blogging has evolved for many into their communication forum of choice as "bloggers recount everyday experiences, flag interesting stories from online publications, and exchange advice on familiar problems."[9] Blogging is characterized by immediacy and intimacy. It is a means through which fans can demonstrate "the 'timeliness' and responsiveness of their devotion."[10] In turn, they expect other fans as well as the creators of media texts to engage in a dialogue and offer an immediate response to concerns. Blogs register the blurred boundaries between private and professional, especially for a generation used to weblogs, LiveJournal, MySpace and other forms of user-generated commentary. Levy contends that the significance of the internet message board is in its emphasis on reciprocity:

> "If we learn something by reading the messages exchanged, we are also expected to provide information whenever it could be of use to someone else. The (symbolic) payback arises from the long-term reputation we develop in the virtual community."[11]

Mark Poster contends that virtual communities "derive some of their verisimilitude from being treated as if they were plain communities."[12] The GA website is a virtual space that allows viewers' interactions with each other, the show, and its creator/writers to take place 24/7 in ever more mobile formats.

The writers use the *Grey Matter* blogs to explain their intentions in the episode as well as to address viewer concerns and acknowledge viewer anxieties, as is evident from one of Rhimes' entries (2/09/07): "How is everyone? You still out there? Still good? Or are you yelling and screaming at your TV sets and cursing my name." She speaks both to how the writers seem as if they are always "on call" 24/7 and how fans "call them" on character inconsistency, demanding accountability. This emphasis on accountability hints at how TV programming has changed in response to fandom. Commenting on how GA is "not entirely playing by the rules of TV," Rhimes asks that viewers trust her. She concludes, "I should just stop writing and let you go ahead and yell at me now." The tone of the blog reflects the blurring of private and professional in the 24/7 workplace. The writers act as if they are responsible to viewers and assure them that they are checking the message boards continually, almost as if they are prepared to fire off a response any time of the day. In actuality, contributing a blog post a few times a season is a job requirement. Allan Heinberg explains, "Blogging is part of my new job description, because I now happen to have the best job in the whole history of jobs." Rhimes speaks even more informally, as if she were posting to MySpace: "Holy crap, am I glad it is my turn to blog again! I have missed it, let me tell you!" Most site visitors do not seem worried about whether or not these writers' blogs are carefully scripted or more off-the-cuff observations. The message board comments suggest that they are happy with the feature and feel validated by "how much the writers do care about the fans' ideas, thoughts, complaining," as one 10/13/06 post says. The same fan says that it is "rare to have writers who actually interact with the fans" and thanks the writers for taking the time to do it. A scan of the web for online commentary from various TV creators and writers indicates that it is not rare at all, as many are giving interviews and offering podcasts and vodcasts on official and unofficial sites.

The perception of the exclusivity of the feature is significant, though, as it does promote fan loyalty, just as ABC executives had hoped. Fans feel more dedicated to the show because they feel as if the writers are dedicated to them. "You are just so great to do these blogs for us fans," one comments after one of Rhimes' blogs. "I trust you and your writers completely" (9/19/06). In her 9/09/06 blog for the season three premiere episode, Rhimes draws on this already-established trust and asks fans to do her a favor and watch or TiVo the show in its new coveted, but high-pressure Thursday night timeslot: "Okay? So I don't burst a blood vessel in my brain from the stress?" In return for this favor,[13] she promises to give fans a sneak peek at the upcoming season: "I've noticed that a lot of you in the comments section and over on the message boards seem to be dissecting the promos for clues." Fans admit to recording the shows and then obsessing "over every last lock of hair, the outfits ... " (9/19/06). That is the kind of TiVo use that is most beneficial to a broadcast series.

Viewers are especially pleased when the writers tell them that they take their concerns seriously. After thanking Rhimes for considering fan response as well as ratings, one enthuses, "you listen to US. You read the comments and the MB" (9/19/06). Rhimes indicates how seriously she takes viewer feedback in her 2/16/07 blog for episode 3.17: "You all have some pretty strong feelings." Then she insists that she does personally read the forums: "I've been reading your comments. STRONG feelings. Which I respect." Here, she addresses one of the primary concerns of fans: the desire to be acknowledged both for the expertise on the text— knowing who the characters are and what they would logically do given their past behavior—and for the validity of their suggestions to show creators. Rhimes recognizes their expertise as well as their commitment to the show and its characters. She also uses the space as a way to manage their discontent with production decisions and hopefully retain them as loyal viewers. As she explains her decision-making process, she validates the importance of fans and their opinions of her and the show. In her 10/22/05 blog for episode 2.2 Rhimes confides that her whole staff is anxious when a show airs: "Because you all have a reaction. And we care about that." In addition to suggesting that fan response is paramount, she also addresses fans like trusted confidants and assumes that viewers know her as well as they do characters. They, in turn, address her as if she were a friend:

"Shonda, you have taken care of us for so long that now it is time for us to take care of you. Trust me, we all got your back and will all be planted in front of the tv watching" (9/19/06).

If they are not part of a Nielsen family, of course, their choice of *Grey's Anatomy* will not be counted.

When Allan Heinberg begins his 10/18/06 blog with, "You know Grey's Anatomy and its characters better than anyone, except maybe Shonda Rhimes," he reinforces Rhimes' position as *auteur* solely responsible for the "creative genius" of the series despite the fact that he and the other writers work collaboratively with her on episodes and that each of them has the main credit on one or more episodes. Fan comments indicate that the creator/writer has indeed become "a fantasised 'presence'," as if the text were created by an *auteur* and not generated collaboratively "according to formulaic industrial guidelines."[14] At the same time, the blogs actually make that collaboration more apparent as all the writers take their turns contributing both to them as well as to the development of the series-long story arcs. Heinberg speaks directly to the collaborative process. He recalls his anxiety about joining the writing staff: "Would the writers accept me? Would I be able to write in the voice of the show?" His candor impresses the fans and, consequently, they feel inspired to share their feelings. Heinberg encourages a blurring of the lines between the anxieties of the characters and writers and the writers and the fans. "'Who am I?' We ask that question all day every day in the Writers' Room—about the characters, about ourselves," Heinberg remarks. This kind of personal revelation by the writers appeals to fans, as this comment posted after Heinberg's blog confirms: "WOW!! Thanks for all the insight into what goes into each episode. I love that most of the writers seem to have as many insecurities as the characters!" (10/13/06). These exchanges are indicative, following Poster's logic, of the way "participants in these virtual communities express themselves with little inhibition and dialogues flourish and develop quickly."[15] Their comments also indicate that message board members "experience communications in cyberspace as if they were embodied social interactions."[16] Fans definitely feel as if the writers (and the characters) are going through the same experiences as they are, as is evident from the following post: "I thought maybe I was the only one who has been thru a day like that day ... It's comforting to know everyone goes through it" (10/13/06).

The idea that the fans are not that different from the writers takes on another dimension when several *Grey Matter* blogs reference the idea that the current writers used to be ordinary fans. As considerations of fandom and overflow become central to network strategies, it is not surprising that the writers emphasize their fan credentials. Heinberg positions himself in his 10/18/06 blog as equal to the fans, just a regular guy who somehow became a writer on GA: "I'm one of the new writers on Grey's Anatomy. Grey's-freaking-Anatomy, people. My favorite show on television. I've been a hardcore fan from the first moment of the first episode." They could be him, he implies to viewers, because like them he "read all the blogs. Listened to the podcasts. Devoured the DVD's, the bonus features, the commentary tracks." Then he establishes that he is a superfan, confiding, "between you and me? I've actually spent some serious time geekily compiling episode-by-episode Grey's soundtrack playlists on iTunes. Seriously. I'm that guy." The message board fan is *that* guy or *that* girl too. Conversely, then, *that* guy or girl could, in this new media sphere characterized by fluid boundaries between the amateur and the professional, someday translate his/her fandom into the basis for a fabulous job. Of course, in Heinberg's case, his work as a writer/producer on the hit shows *Sex and the City*, *The O.C.*, and *Party of Five* likely helped more than his fan credentials. When Marti Noxon, in her blog for episode 3.16, praises the GA production assistants and predicts, "assistants today—our bosses tomorrow," she also makes it seem as if it is possible to start out as a nobody and work your way up to writer or even show-runner (February 20, 2007). Like Heinberg, Noxon already has years of TV writing on her resume, including a long, and somewhat controversial, stint on *Buffy the Vampire Slayer*. Reinforcing the impression that there is a fluidity of the boundaries between committed fan and professional commentator, Blythe Robe, in her 2/22/07 blog, implies that writing for a TV show is a lot like hanging out with smart and funny classmates in a college dorm common room. Also indicating how the line between work life and personal life is definitely blurred, Noxon describes how Rhimes just invited her to "come hang out" at GA as a writer's "consultant," a title she admits is nebulous although it eventually involved her co-writing the episode.

The writers' blogs offer both a fantasy of mobility and a commentary on the changes in the mediasphere in which bloggers and superfans might find themselves contributing to the creation of the official TV text. After all, fan comments are part of the abc.go.com website and therefore ARE part of the official GA text. McKee has written about the reciprocity inherent in the fan-producer relationship, suggesting that the TV text becomes as much theirs as the producers'. The blog commentary certainly indicates that the line between the writers' creations and fan input is blurred. McKee contends that the boundaries of the TV text are no longer commonsensical. What counts as the official GA text is not clear. Is it only the on-air show or are the blogs included as well and, if so, what about the fan commentaries on the blogs? As McKee explains, canonicity is "a status granted to texts—of being real, of carrying authority—that is, finally, validated by *the fans themselves*—and not by the producers."[17] That validation is offered by fans, whose status is, in turn, validated in the blogs by the writers, as is the case with the way Heinberg begins his 10/18/06 blog: "So, here's the thing: you people terrify me," and then switches to praising the fans: "You're passionate, you're insightful, you're bravely outspoken." With this description he provides the profile that many would likely use to describe themselves. More importantly, he reiterates the message that they have influence: "And I don't know if you realize this, but the way you write about the show, debate it, love and/or hate it carries an enormous amount of weight in the Writer's Room." They matter so much, in fact, that he is intimidated by them: "All of which makes the experience of blogging here for the first time absolutely terrifying."

The appeal of Heinberg's blog can be attributed to the way he positions himself as a fan first and a writer second, or perhaps the way he points to the unstable boundary between the two positions. A good number of the posts encourage Heinberg and "welcome" him to "the family." Most envision the family of fans as a positive alternative to the offline families they cannot choose. Some recognize, however, that there is a surreal aspect to the online relationship that takes on a familial quality. As one fan comments to Heinberg, "You're terrified by us? I'M terrified by us ... lol. Shonda created this twilight zone kinda family. ... it's very strange and we're oddly dependent on people we've never met in our lives." Here she is speaking to what Jenkins terms, "the pose of intimacy," that is, the way people on the message board interact "as if they are confidants."[18] To some degree this interaction lowers "the barrier to cultural participation," as writers and fans are seemingly on an equal playing field.[19] At the same time, the writers are more empowered as the interaction is on their (and the network's) terms. The same fan addresses this complexity in the rest of her post:

> "When my GA buddy and I talk ... I find myself saying 'I'll have to ask Shonda ... maybe she'll explain that aspect' or she'll say 'well you remember when Shonda said it was always gonna be that way ... ' I think it's very terri- fying that we feel all y'all writers are like our buddies ... we can just pick up the phone and have a chat."

This participant is typical of those interacting in virtual spaces in which they com- municate "to each other as if they were in a physical common space, as if this space were inhabited by bodies."[20]

While fans like the effect of intimacy the blogs produce, they do express some anxiety about this mode of interaction. The writers seem as if they are responding to fan comments, but their address lacks immediacy as the writers/network decide when to post and the fans often just have to keep checking to see when a new blog appears. Several fans talk about how they have been doing so all summer and are thrilled that Rhimes finally posts pre-season three comments. Most feel grateful for any kind of interaction, as is evident in this typical posting: "Oh Shonda, thank you so much for posting. I, like many others, check the blog regularly, hoping against hope to hear from you again" (9/20/06). It is to the network's advantage not to update the blog in some specifically timed fashion as it makes viewers check it more often and each time they do, they are targets for more advertising or promotion for the series or other ABC or Disney content. The pacing does build anticipation, although it may also frustrate viewers. After she writes about how she is always willing to wait for a new blog from Rhimes, one fan adds as an afterthought, "Hell who am I kidding ... I have to wait ... I'm a slave to you writers" (10/13/06). Then she tempers the comment, adding, "just as u are slaves to our demands ... we're slaves to your genius" (10/13/06). These comments reflect the constant shifting of the line between producer and fan. As McKee asserts, "the distinction between the fan and the industry does not work as a simple binary."[21] The viewers have some degree of power in that if they choose not to watch the series, it is likely to get cancelled. On the other hand, even if they watch it religiously on-air as it airs, it may still get cancelled or, worse, the writers may take it in some frustrating direction.

Pursuing the idea that fans might be less empowered in this supposedly inter-active relationship, one comments after Heinberg's blog:

> "You're a fan? Really? You did all those things, like we do, not because you got hired by the show and needed desperately to catch up? But because you really did them, yourself? If so, we are incredibly blessed to have a fan writing the show. And if not? It was a great blog anyway. It had the requisite amount of squealing about how cool a job is this!"

Also comfortable with the performative element of the blog, a different post talks about the blog more theoretically:

> "God, this blog is interesting! I wish I could read a blog about writing this blog. I would ask you guys if writing about the themes of an episode is annoying or freeing? Do you use it to process what you got out of the writing or what you wanted the audience to get out of the episode?" (10/13/06).

Again the comments suggest an unsettling of the binary between powerless fans and powerful producers. Given that their comments are part of the official abc.go.com GA text and that the boundaries between where the fan comments end and the writers' choices for character and story arcs begin, it is clear that there is a grey area indeed in determining what constitutes the official *Grey's Anatomy* TV text and who is producing it.

Production worker blogs

Although they read like casual personal insights, the posts on *Grey Matter* were contractually obligated forms of expression and, as such, they fed into the network's attempt to control perception and circulation of its intellectual property and commentary upon it. These new forms of industrial self-fashioning are increas-ingly common, according to John Caldwell, as networks try to engage in brand management.[22] Given that it was equipped with a message board on which viewers posted comments in response to the flogs, the feature also catered to viewers' investment in the idea of themselves as an engaged audience that does not passively consume romantic fantasies. On one level, the *Grey Matter* flogs and related message boards become places in which a two-way communication opens up between viewers and production team members, an exchange that often goes beyond the kind of talking back viewers could engage in through fan mail. Yet, these kinds of interactions sometimes merely amplify viewers' voices rather than change the power dynamic of the television fan–television producer relationship. The dedicated website for a series functions as a feedback loop between fans and production team members, but also as a safety valve in which producers manage viewers' discontent and try to shape their perceptions of the show and its production process, as was the case in *Dawson's Chat*. A limited degree of fan–producer interaction was at least possible in those live cyber chats. Although not a one-to-one interaction, *Dawson's Chat* was structured so that the production team member had to address the questions the moderator selected from those coming in during the live chat, even if only to modify his/her pre-planned commentary to sound like an answer to the question asked. In contrast, *Grey Matter* did not offer any actual interaction between viewers and the production team as the writers just made posts and then at some time later viewers left comments.

Although her request didn't make sense from an industrial standpoint given that the majority of message board participants probably were not part of a "Nielsen family," Rhimes used *Grey Matter* to speak directly to viewers and urge them to watch the on-air broadcast rather than via some alternate delivery platform, so that the series would get the ratings it needed to be viewed as a hit. The flogs are particularly interesting as examples of how interactive spaces can be sites for public relations campaigns. The production workers turn to these kinds of new media spaces to keep viewers engaged, but also to lobby them.

Jesse Alexander's 2009 Twitter feed about *Day One*, the pilot for the long-arc serial the former *Heroes*, *Alias*, and *Lost* producer hoped to create for NBC, demonstrates how new media spaces can be platforms from which creators can also lobby potential fans before a series even premieres in the hopes that they would be a solidly organized group ready to rally against its cancellation, should the need arise. Alexander's Twitter feed links to his personal blog, *The Global Couch*, a space he utilized when he was co-executive producer of *Heroes* to explain and champion transmedia storytelling and comment on the circumstances that led to the 2007 Writers' Strike. Through the blog, he also interacted directly with those viewers posting comments on its message board. Even though it is a personal blog, Alexander is still speaking from a network employee position, so he has to counter problematic network comments or decisions in a very subtle way. Jonathan Gray suggests that these kinds of activities enable a "pre-creation" of textual meaning that becomes part of a series' interpretative frame.[23] Alexander's case is an especially interesting one as the paratexts he is creating are often a way to reframe the network information released about the series through official means.

As a member of the *Lost* and *Heroes* team, Alexander was involved in creating content for both story arcs and promotions. With the blurring of the lines between the two, it was no longer clear how to compensate writers and other production team members involved in the creation of immersive websites, mobisodes, flogs, podcasts, DVD featurettes, and the like. If the showrunner on such a series is not someone like Alexander who can keep all of these platforms in sync, the process becomes clunky or the careful balance between storytelling and promotion, between viewer-centered address and sponsor-centered address and activities, gets tilted too much in the favor of the sponsors and their promotions. All of these issues came to a head with the 2007–8 Writers' Strike. Maintaining his blog during the strike, Alexander offered carefully worded reports from the frontlines of the movement for writers to get compensation for content that the networks were labeling as promotion. He and the others who had worked on the *Alias* production team had created the original website for free, which unfortunately set a precedent. By the time Alexander was co-executive producer on *Heroes*, the participation in the creation of content for web and mobile platforms became a job requirement, but not one that changed the accepted compensation paradigms.

Although the strike was settled, NBC's ambivalence about online content and the transmedia storytelling approach to broadcast TV series continued to grow. By its third season, the *Heroes* multiplatform experience had been recognized with awards, but the series was no longer getting the ratings NBC expected of it. While Alexander continued to champion the transmedia approach on his blog, he did not post about the rash fall 2008 decision by NBC network executives to overhaul the *Heroes* production team in an attempt to reboot the series for the second half of the third season. Indicative of how the blog is still a mixed space of promotion and personal commentary, Alexander, like all savvy production workers with personal blogs, avoided talking about the issue or other controversial decisions made by the network of which he was still an employee, even if no longer on *Heroes*.

Network executives use the web as well to circulate their take on production and scheduling decisions and, more importantly, to feed press release materials to viewers who often circulate that information around the web as if it were insider insight. The continued circulation, especially on blogs that also blur the line between personal commentary and journalistic reportage, effaces that the information originated from a thinly veiled network press release.[24] Of course, a network cannot control how the information that it drops into the blogosphere is received. The gossip circulating about the shakeup at *Heroes* attributed the decision to an executive's kneejerk response to the critical *Entertainment Weekly* article that questioned whether *Heroes* could be saved from itself.[25] It asserted that the series could be fixed, but that it would never be a blockbuster again. After the shakeup, the magazine saw the treatment of the *Heroes* production team as further evidence of NBC's short-sightedness and its misunderstanding of how long-arc serials work. Instead of accepting the ratings dip as a part of the lifecycle of the long-arc serial format, the network executives assumed a new team would figure out the magic fix that would return the ratings to their previous heights. Any production team would have the same difficulty of balancing the desire of viewers for more multiplatform access points into the larger serial mystery with the needs of casual viewers for entry points into a series they have either never seen before or have only watched intermittently. Every Must-Click TV series, especially once it has banked two seasons, has to find ways to continue engaging loyal fans with complex content without excluding casual or even new viewers. While *Heroes* had been designed to strike that balance, it was not easy to achieve, especially with the constant pressure from the network to resolve storylines more quickly. As *Alias* had before it, *Heroes* redrew the lines between the good guys and the bad guys and downplayed the role of the series' mysterious organizations. The changes didn't bring in new viewers and did little to please the core fan base. The show never really recovered and was under threat of cancellation by 2010.

Gearing up for these kinds of challenges before the series had ever aired, Alexander began blogging during the pilot production of his upcoming NBC project *Day One* and then used his Twitter feed to offer continual updates. As with *Grey Matter* posts, Alexander sometimes used tweets to remind viewers that they would need to watch *Day One* episodes as they aired so that their choice would be registered and, thereby, impact NBC's decision to continue the series beyond its initial short-run episode order. The implied logic was that if viewers watched *Day One* as it aired, network executives would have no choice but to view the series as viable. With its acquisition of *Day One*, NBC seemed to signal that it was still willing to invest in long-arc series. The public perception of the series was that its central mystery was about the aftermath of a disaster, but during the 2009 Television Critics Association Summer Press Tour Angela Bromstad, the new NBC President of Primetime Entertainment, corrected columnists, saying testily: "It's an alien invasion, not a disaster." It was unclear whether it was a spoiler of the potential series' big reveal or a simple correction. Either way the comment added to the perception that NBC was tentative about the proposed long-arc serial. That tentativeness is a result of the network's cautious attitude toward long-arc serials and perhaps can be attributed as well to the aftershocks of a summer shakeup in NBC's executive power structure as Bromstad was part of a new executive team that was not the one that greenlit *Day One* and renewed *Heroes* for 2009. There were other indicators that NBC had lost faith in the continuing viability of the long-arc serial as a programming format. As Bromstad put it to the press tour, "*Heroes* was really successful for us, and it's a genre we cannot ignore," but, she added, "It does tend to be a little more of a narrow genre." The blogosphere was abuzz about her comments as she followed the potential spoiler with a declaration that *Day One* was being positioned more as a mini-series event rather than "an ongoing, returning show for a second season." Many bloggers said the executive's statements did not bode well for the long-term prognosis of *Day One*.

As Alexander had been offering fans updates on his potential new series via Twitter, he was able to counter her proclamations immediately. He did so by skillfully downplaying her statements—which must have irked him—and instead assured fans that if the initial episodes received high ratings, the series would be picked up and continue to get episode orders. He continued to lobby fans to view it that way even after it was announced in the fall that *Day One* would be a four-hour "event," rather than series.[26] Alexander insisted it was a great opportunity to showcase it and attract a broadcast audience so that it could then get a future episode order with the miniseries functioning as a backdoor pilot. Alexander's use of his blog and Twitter reflects an understanding of the kind of commentary and interaction enabled by each medium. He has the advantage of having an actual enthusiasm for new media and for the project on which he is working, which is not always the case for production workers required to use new media platforms to interact with viewers. A good example of the latter is the experiment FOX dubbed the "tweet-peat," which failed because the network did not understand the medium it was attempting to employ and enlisted cast and producer commentators who were unfamiliar with Twitter.[27]

FOX's tweet-peat

FOX decided to use a live Twitter feed to accompany a pre-premiere week repeat of the May season finale of long-arc serial/procedural hybrid *Fringe* and the pilot episode of musical-comedy series *Glee*, which had its initial airing in the slot after the *American Idol* finale in May 2009. Viewers were encouraged to be prepared to tweet questions to the series' Twitter feed during each simulcast and then the moderator would select some for the participants to address. Those answers and other comments by cast and producers would appear live on the bottom third of the broadcast viewer's television screen during the repeat. The tweet-peat event was imagined as a sort of live Q&A similar to *Dawson's Chat*, except everyone had to stick to 140 characters or less, as those are the parameters for a tweet.

At home viewers could not see the questions and so when a participant answered one, which was not all that often, the topic wasn't always clear. The bigger problem was that those participating seemed to have had done no pre-planning about what they might want to say about the episode. They ostensibly were watching the episodes along with the viewers, but had little to offer in relation to backstory about an episode or in the way of analysis or interpretation of the content. The resulting Twitter feeds were similar to those rambling and unenlightening production team episode commentaries now familiar from hastily produced DVD box sets with uninspired special features. In better DVD episode commentary, the designated production team and cast commentators actually offer some insight into the episode or the production process or, at least, some carefully managed revelations.

In both the *Fringe* and the *Glee* tweet-peats, the initial comments from the cast and production team members who were participating revealed that most of them had little familiarity with Twitter. The exception was Lea Michele (Rachel Berry) from *Glee*, who spent most of her tweets crowing about how she was the only one who could offer rapid-fire tweets. Of course, much like the immediate hostile reaction to the Aerie Girls interstitials running during the 2006 CW season premiere of *Veronica Mars*, almost every viewer wrote negative reviews of the tweet-peat experiment. Some pointed out how ill-suited a Twitter feed was for a television series as it made it impossible to concentrate on the action and took up far too much screen space. The posts on various message boards also revealed that the repeats attracted quite a few casual viewers who had not seen the episodes and were using the reruns to catch up with the series. FOX had clearly envisioned that those tuning in to the tweet-peats would be loyals who had seen them before, but just wanted the details fresh in their minds for the continuation of the storylines in the upcoming season.

If viewers were spontaneously tweeting about a series as it was happening, they would be offering short, snarky commentary similar to the rapid-fire posts on Dave Barry's real-time *24* blog. Someone would definitely have tweeted that Lea Michele was so busy offering meta-commentary on her own tweeting abilities that she didn't appear to be watching the episode at all. Her behavior was perfectly aligned with that of the spotlight-hungry character she plays on *Glee*. Given that the experiment was intended as a promotion disguised as viewer interaction, it is not surprising that viewer tweets did not appear on the screen. It would have made more sense for the network team to offer bursts of carefully worded, not off-the-cuff commentary. Or to share links to related content or to platforms with more detailed information. These are the typical strategies for a production work-er's or organization's use of Twitter, at least those that realize that the social utility works very effectively for sending out very specific, and carefully strategized sound-bites.[28]

FOX viewed Twitter as a space characterized by unedited interaction rather than one that is more often marked by the public performance of nonchalance—akin to the natural look that takes an actress two hours in a makeup chair to achieve. Alexander's tweet in response to Bromstad's comments about *Day One* did not represent his immediate reaction. Although he struck a casual tone, Alexander selected his 140 characters to convey a concise, targeted message that rallied fans without sounding hostile about the NBC executive's lack of support of his project. Alexander's actions exemplify the ways in which producers can use new media to counter the formerly one-way communications flow from networks about their series. They also demonstrate that Alexander's self-perception as a multi-platform content creator is increasingly in tension with the network's focus on the television platform and a traditional idea of the kinds of numbers that make a program viable.

Alexander's tweet about the initial *Day One* limited episode order was an intriguing one as he reminded viewers of their responsibility to watch TV on TV if they expect the series they choose to watch to be renewed. In doing so, he both empowered fans and put the responsibility for what's on TV on their shoulders—implying that networks air what the people say they want, which is measured by what they watch. The approach makes fans feel empowered to choose what stays on the network's schedule. The problem with the logic is that only Nielsen viewers need to be lobbied because the convoluted ratings measurement process is not a one-viewer, one-vote system, but a representative one in which the viewing preferences of a selection of supposedly representative viewers are measured.[29] The majority, if not all, of Alexander's Twitter followers, are probably not living in a Nielsen household. Whether they watch or don't watch will have no impact on the series' fate if it is determined by Nielsen's ratings alone. This reality is a source of frustration for producers as well as fans. Still, message boards for various ratings-challenged TV series are filled with similar pleas for people to watch episodes as they air and to rally their friends and family to do the same. The promise of these spaces is that viewers' opinions do matter. The comments of series' creators and production teams suggest that if enough viewers choose to watch TV on-air as-it-airs and then come together to advocate for its renewal, they will make a difference. Of course, even with all that effort there is no guarantee that a series will stay on the air, as viewers well know. Series can stay on the air with poor ratings and not get renewed even with decent ratings because of financial, scheduling, or even more subjective reasons known only to the network's executives. To whatever degree viewers can influence decisions, if they can at all, viewers are well aware that they do not get to make the decisions, and definitely have no final say about the fate of a TV series.

The logic of the TV choice argument makes it seem as if what is on TV is decided by viewers and reflects their tastes. Yet, as Eileen Meehan says, "television is not our fault," meaning that what gets on and stays on TV isn't really about what viewers choose to watch, but about what networks choose to schedule.[30] Connected to that scheduling decision are other related decisions, such as the desirability of the primetime block into which the series is slotted, all of which affects its potential to attract a sizeable audience. Beyond scheduling are a host of other economic factors that go into whether a series stays on the schedule or not. Different kinds of series also have different ratings goals, depending on production costs and financing deals. That said, no matter how minimal their production costs, low ratings are still worrisome to production teams as they are often used to make a case to cancel a show even if the decision is actually the result of considering those ratings alongside a bundle of more complicated scheduling, financing, promotion, and network branding issues.

Leno: back by popular demand or brought to you by Ford?

While all of those factors went into the creation of 2009's *The Jay Leno Show*, NBC's initial branding campaign suggested that the fall series was created in response to viewers' feedback about the kind of programming they want to see on television. In the on-air promotions NBC offered the following: *You said you wanted more comedy. We listened. The Jay Leno Show. New. This Fall.* NBC acted as if moving Leno and his familiar *Tonight Show* segments into primetime, adding some lackluster new bits, and calling it a new series was the kind of comedy viewers had in mind. If viewers were really polled, and that is unlikely, the request for "more comedy" meant new sitcoms as that broadcast TV format is the one in which comedy has been typically packaged in primetime, especially on NBC, the former home of blocks of Must-See sitcoms. The same specious claim that *The Jay Leno Show* was created in an attempt to cater to viewers' tastes was subtly embedded within the initial fall 2009 episodes. The show began like other talk shows with the announcement of Jay Leno followed by a few minutes in which he stood center stage as the audience finished applauding. The scripted performance of the audience's admiration for Leno was even more stage-managed than the typical talk show audience applause for the host. The difference was that the segment ended with the first few rows of the audience "spontaneously" coming over to the stage to surround Leno. They seemed to know that they were each allowed to shake his hand before returning, in a very orderly fashion, to their seats.

This audience performance of how Leno was "back by popular demand" shored up the claim that it was a groundswell of viewer support for Leno, and not a business decision, that brought him back to NBC. In contrast, Craig Ferguson, during the applause following his introduction as host of *The Late Late Show* on CBS, often cheekily admonishes the audience for clapping just because the warm-up comic has prepped them about when to applaud and the degree of enthusiasm they are expected to show. His audience loves Ferguson for the self-deprecating shtick that runs throughout the show, as it seems more "real," which, of course, is a key feature of his performance as late night underdog. Nevertheless, Ferguson's late night show and Leno's primetime show remain the same at their core because each is a promotional platform depicted as a space for friendly interaction. In this kind of talk show, the host chats with a guest in a friendly way and then tries to segue smoothly into a clip from the film or TV show, or, in the case of authors and musicians, a shot of the book or CD cover, that the person is there to plug. During the 10 p.m. show, Leno positions himself as more "real," by acknowledging this promotional element overtly and making guests participate in a bit he calls *Earn Your Plug.* There is a variety show element to what the guests have to do, although some clearly come up with the comedy bits themselves as another way to plug their projects.

In place of *Earn Your Plug* some guests participate in the *Green Car Challenge,* which ostensibly is a road race in a Ford electric car through an obstacle course, with current celebrities competing against the times of previous celebrities. The recurring feature is more significant as the way *The Jay Leno Show*'s fall 2009 presenting sponsor Ford and participating sponsor Omega timepieces earn their plugs too. Branded Omega timers appear in several places: most notably on the track's big board and as a bug on the right corner of the screen. Ford has its own advertising written into the branding and structure of the segment, which begins with a title card and an announcement of the sponsorship. Leno tells viewers that the track was built by Ford especially for his show. The segment features countless shots of the car, on display and in motion. Plastered on the back window of the brightly colored car is the familiar logo and slogan *Ford: Drive One.* Ford, of course, benefits by having its car associated in viewers' minds with movie star Drew Barrymore and the stars of NBC's *The Office,* among others. Leno even convinced Rush Limbaugh to participate. It was a sort of ironic plug from the conservative talk radio celebrity given that the whole segment more generally promotes the idea that Ford is creating a high-powered electric car and has risen to the "Green Car Challenge" implicitly proposed by former Vice President Al Gore, who is represented by a cardboard cut-out on the obstacle course. Through its innovative designs and developments, Ford proclaims itself a leader in green car innovations. In his comments before and after the celebrity runs the course, Leno earns his sponsors' money by explicitly mentioning Ford and Omega by name and, implicitly, by convincing his celebrity guest stars to associate themselves, albeit unofficially, with Ford's cars and Omega's timepieces. Despite the cynicism implied in the "earn your plug" concept, Leno is a sincere pitchperson in the end and an ideal one given he is a well-known collector of automobiles. *The Jay Leno Show* is a millennial update of the sponsor plugs that 1950s variety show hosts and their guests would integrate into skits and the *Green Car Challenge* is part of a multi-pronged and multiplatform branded entertainment campaign. A special ad card follows the segment and reinforces the message of the in-series segment and tells viewers where to find more information on the website. The card is a lead-in to Ford's regular 30-second spot, one of many that run throughout the show and across the prime-time schedule, more generally.

Despite the branded entertainment possibilities of this format and, hence, its appeal to advertisers, the 10 p.m. Leno experiment failed as a lead-in for local 11 p.m. newscasts. NBC affiliate stations that long had the number one newscast in their markets had slipped behind those of the other broadcast networks, thereby suffering reductions in both status and advertising rates. They calculated that for fall 2009 their revenue would be down by at least $22 million after declines in the standard 25–54-year-old news demographic, a drop of 25% on average, but almost 50% in some markets (48% in New York, followed by 47% in Philadelphia and 43% in Los Angeles). These affiliates began to complain much more loudly after the end of the November sweeps period during which network ratings determine the next quarter's advertising rates.[31] When Leno did not even fare well against reruns or during the holiday hiatus period, NBC affiliates began to talk of pre-empting his 10 p.m. show, thereby, undercutting its viability. Forced to act, NBC executives told the January 2010 Television Critics Association Winter Press Tour audience that it would be cancelling the 10 p.m. version of *The Jay Leno Show*, a proposal it officially confirmed the next week on Monday the 11th. As NBC wanted to retain Leno as a brand asset, it worked to offer him a half-hour, late-night version of his primetime show, a schedule change that it wanted to put into effect after NBC's Winter Olympics coverage concluded on February 28th. The new show would put Leno back at his old *Tonight Show* start time of 11.35 p.m. The move would make him the de facto main late night host even though he had been contractually obligated to step down in 2009 to make room for Conan O'Brien in a deal NBC struck with the two hosts back in 2004 to prevent O'Brien from leaving for a competing network show. In the proposed 2010 late night shift O'Brien, who had been helming the 11.35 p.m. show for only seven months, would host a show that would be called *The Tonight Show*, but would begin tomorrow at 12.05 a.m. after Leno had already offered NBC's first monologue of late night. Jimmy Fallon, O'Brien's 2009 successor at *Late Night*, would then be pushed back to 1.00 a.m. Rejecting this schedule shift and the implied demotion, O'Brien responded publicly on January 12th via a statement released through *PR Newswire* that was picked up by all the major print and online news sources.

To make his case, O'Brien employed NBC's own brand asset rationales and *It's about time* logic. Addressing the "People of Earth," he pointed to how the timeslot change would negatively impact *The Tonight Show* brand, which had been an 11.35 p.m. institution at NBC. He said he did not want to agree to "participate in" what he considered the "destruction" of "the greatest franchise in the history of broadcasting."[32] He added that, "*The Tonight Show* at 12:05 simply isn't *The Tonight Show.*" The Leno @ 10 p.m. fiasco had already proven that timeslots impact viewer expectations and O'Brien was subtly referencing Leno's inability to attract a prime-time audience and his failures as a lead-in both to the affiliate newscasts and NBC's late night line-up. O'Brien also explicitly recalled Leno's own ratings struggles when he first took over *The Tonight Show* from Johnny Carson in 1992. Of course, Leno replaced Carson when NBC was at the top of the ratings and did not have the kind of competition an 11.35 p.m. show has today. Not only does NBC now have to worry about CBS and ABC late night, but it also has to contend with Comedy Central and other cable network programming. In addition to an increase in their potential viewers' in-home entertainment options (e.g., DVDs, games, web and mobile content), late night hosts have to compete with DVR playback of earlier primetime programming, which, according to Nielsen Media Research, continues from primetime into the late night hour.[33] With all this competition, broadcast networks claim that they can only afford to keep shows that have good ratings from the outset, something O'Brien's *Tonight Show* lacked.

While a vocal new media fandom can generate embarrassing negative publicity for a network and its stars—which was certainly the case with anti-NBC and anti-Leno commentary that dominated Twitter during the scheduling controversy—networks still put much more stock in the ratings numbers given that the attention of a broadcast audience is still the commodity in which they traffic. The network continued to judge the performances of Leno and O'Brien by conventional broadcast metrics—the ratings they achieved, the lead-in audience they retained, and the lead-out audience they provided to the next show. Leno's failure to retain lead-in audiences from 9 p.m. affected NBC's standing more generally as it helped the standing of ABC and CBS, both of which experienced healthy ratings increases in fall 2009 because their dramas consistently beat Leno's uninspired show in the 10 p.m. slots. ABC's returning crime mystery procedural series *Castle* had an unexpected ratings surge and CBS posted top ratings for its 10 p.m. series, including the new hit *The Good Wife*.

While NBC's winter 2010 counterprogramming prospects for the unexpectedly open 10 p.m. slots were limited, NBC's development slate, which featured new series from *It is TV* powerhouse producers Jerry Bruckheimer and David E. Kelley, indicated that the network was adopting the traditional programming approach with which CBS had succeeded in the 2000s. As Jeff Gaspin said of the movement of Leno out of primetime and back into late night, "We now have the ability to start rebuilding NBC in a more traditional way … at a later date, after we have more strength, we can try new models again."[34] NBC did give long-arc serial maverick J. J. Abrams a spot on the 2010 pilot development roster, but his co-created series *Undercovers* about married spies leaned more toward quirky episodic procedural than long-arc mystery. That Abrams' co-creator is Josh Reims, a producer on ABC's *Brothers and Sisters* and *Dirty Sexy Money* as well as on Abrams' co-created WB college age melodrama *Felicity*, suggests that the new NBC pilot focuses as much on the love relationship as on missions. While Abrams', Orci's, and

Kurtzman's *Fringe* was having a critically acclaimed 2009–10 season over on FOX, the fact that its procedural elements were wrapped in a cult-style long-arc mystery made its third season renewal uncertain. Indeed, the final season of the decade was a do-or-die one for several of the series that made the first millennial decade such a strong one known for *It's not TV* series. The smartest move was the deal ABC made with the *Lost* production team to have 2009–10 be the long-arc serial's final season so that it could resolve its mysteries on its own terms. This contrasted to the messy way *The X-Files* ended in 2002 after FOX forced the production team to stretch out the serial mysteries over nine seasons, a much too extended time period, especially in the over 20 episodes per season era in which the series ran.

The question remains open as to whether broadcast networks will limit themselves in the future to programming they believe can generate overnight ratings numbers and leave the innovative, *It's not TV* series to others. My hunch is that network executives and their parent companies do not like to concede defeat on any level and so will keep trying to find that elusive, critically acclaimed, blockbuster ratings-generator, an original series that can prevail over those of HBO and FX at the Emmys, while bringing in the ratings numbers comparable to a predictable procedural. The broadcast TV lineup for the final season of the decade suggested as much given that the networks all offered micro-segmented schedules that featured a few atypical series scattered in among the more typical programming. Having the most successful long-arc serial on TV, ABC was most willing to continue in 2009 to take a risk on new *It's not TV* fare (i.e., *Flash Forward* and the miniseries *V*), but the support was tentative with both getting oddly split fall and spring runs. FOX kept its two new serial mysteries, Joss Whedon's *Dollhouse* and J. J. Abrams' *Fringe*, on its fall 2009 schedule despite their less-than-blockbuster performances in their freshman seasons, but the former was cancelled by December. The latter, while a critical success that was renewed, did not garner the ratings that would make it a sure thing for 2010.[35] If it or any of the other new or returning long-arc, series takes off as *Lost* did in its second fall after episodes became available on DVD and then on iTunes, it may spark others and the cycle will begin again. The networks are hedging their bets as the majority of their schedules look more like the one that has enabled CBS to crown itself *America's Most Watched Network*. These schedules suggest a return to what broadcast TV has done well in the past: variations on the family and workplace sitcoms alongside episodic ensemble dramas with medical, legal, and law enforcement or government agency settings.

No matter what the fate of the actual programs, the legacy of the long-arc serials of the 2000s is that every TV show now has online, if not on-mobile, extensions, which allow regular viewers beyond a dedicated fandom to spend more time following a broadcast TV series onto another platform and interacting with it there. The multiplatform approach works especially well with broadcast series that are hybrids of serial and episodic formats so that loyals can immerse themselves in a series mythology, but casuals can understand episodes without needing in-depth knowledge. One example is CBS's *Ghost Whisperer*, a paranormal procedural with some long-arc elements and a multiplatform address that is rarely mentioned on-air, but is well known to series loyals. On Fridays in fall 2009 *Ghost Whisperer*, an ABC-CBS coproduction that had been airing on CBS since 2005, was paired with the CBS-produced series *Medium*, which had been airing on NBC since 2005, but was cancelled in May 2009. While *Ghost Whisperer* had started out as a series intended to tap into the *for those who think young* demographic the WB had secured, it had never quite attracted those viewers and so it fit well with the always older-skewing *Medium*. The CW gave a prime Thursday slot to its paranormal procedural, *Supernatural*, although the series creator and the actors playing the network's ghost-hunting Hardy Boys were chafing to bring the multiplatform series to a close after five seasons. The CW now has a good multiplatform contender with its new 2009 series *Vampire Diaries*, from former *Dawson's Creek* creator Kevin Williamson. Also capitalizing on the viewer interest in adaptations of book series about vampire–human romances, HBO offered its own 2008 entrant *True Blood*, which the premium channel hoped would be one of the series that would re-establish its somewhat battered premium brand reputation. The series was especially significant as its transmedia marketing was created by some of the team which developed that of *The Blair Witch Project*, the feature film that inspired film and television production teams to consider new media's power as a platform for promotion disguised as content.

As noted in the introduction, the term "new media" is still a problematic one given that most "new media" is really some modification or hybridization of something that existed. Whatever terminology they use, most commentators agree that the last decade of the twentieth century and the first of the twenty-first was a period in which the strategies upon which U.S. broadcast TV and advertising industries have relied underwent modifications, if not a revolution of sorts. There have been several attempts to categorize these changes in relation to stages, such as the linear progression implied in the trio of terms, pre-network era, network era, and post-network era, or the trio of stages implied by the designators TVI, TVII, TVIII. These categories are certainly useful for distinguishing between different network practices, but, like all attempts at categorization, they are somewhat misleading as they imply that there are fixed divisions between the stages. The U.S. television industry does not really function in such clear-cut linear terms, especially given that practices might be widely adopted, but they are rarely formalized. Every season has a series that deviates from the supposed norm and, in so doing, either fails in the process or starts a new trend that then becomes the new standard, that is, until the cycle starts again. Add to that the fact that broadcast networks are still committed to behaviors that are supposed to be part of the previous stage that they left behind in the twentieth century.

In short, the broadcast television industry is more cyclical than linear. When one network makes an unexpectedly successful programming or scheduling decision, the rest try to copy it. The trend continues until another network, usually the one in last place, makes another programming or scheduling decision that succeeds in unexpected ways and the rest follow it. These decisions are not necessarily to do something new, as this book has hopefully demonstrated, but more often to revive some former practice, but implement it in a new way. ABC had success at the start of the decade with the revival of the primetime game show, for example, while CBS took a chance on the gamedoc, which is a variation on the game show crossed with the docudrama. NBC tried to win back its Thursday comedy by offering *30 Rock*'s variation on the 1950s reality (star) sitcom.[36] It should have tried harder to figure out what made a successful 1950s variety show work before reviving the category with *The Jay Leno Show*. People tuned in to the debut curious as to what kind of show might appear as unscripted comedy at 10 p.m. Clearly, Leno and his writers had no idea because they mostly imported the late-night show to the primetime spot. They missed an opportunity to invent a format more applicable to the new slot.

By sticking with broadcast fare that had already proven successful, CBS continued at the close of the decade to hold tightly onto the top Nielsen spots with its Monday night comedies and with its procedurals sprinkled liberally across its schedule. ABC even managed in 2009 to find a hit sitcom and a solid performer on which to build a foundation for a traditional Wednesday comedy night. As already noted, ABC, along with FOX, was still also investing in *It's not TV* series hoping to find or grow the next blockbuster or at least nurture a cult TV series, but was hedging its bets with new *It's just TV* entries in the procedural category. The CW is the only network that is still fully committed to the Must-Click multiplatform entertainment paradigm, which is hardly surprising since it is a netlet built on the foundations of the WB, which came of age alongside the World Wide Web, Napster, Friendster, and YouTube, not to mention emailing, downloading, MP3s, DVDs, and Bit Torrent. The problem is that the generation that also came of age during this time often chooses to access television content via alternate delivery platforms or devices and not by watching television series on-air as they air. The CW most embraces the idea that content consumed on any platform or device is still content that counts towards its numbers because it is dealing with the generation that everyone fears will never watch TV on TV. Many of them do not do so now, but it remains to be seen if that is really a generational or a situational practice, that is, a product of their currently mobile life stage in which entertainment content is more likely to be consumed alone on a laptop or a mobile device. Once they have their own homes, living room couches, and flat panel televisions that they do not have to share with parents, siblings, or housemates, they may watch TV on TV. Of course, they will be even more likely than today's viewers to access television programming on their own schedule via a DVR. With that future in mind, Nielsen Media Research changed its system to begin counting in the overnights, viewers watching that evening on DVR, and then offering a second calculation for viewers watching via DVR within seven days. That does little to account for the *It's not TV* viewers who are watching long-arc serials in extreme time-shifted blocks as saved content on a DVR or as purchased content on DVD or download. Whether a better measurement system can be found is yet to be seen, but it is unlikely that the firmly entrenched Nielsen company is going to be displaced, even though that is the outcome that many content producers hope will happen in time.[37]

It's about time. This book has been about broadcast TV in the first new millennial decade and the years leading up to it, focusing on the significant changes that this short period of time has brought. Network executives are fond of saying that television is not what it was two years ago. Television isn't what it was in 1996 when WB and UPN finished their first full seasons or in 1998 when *Dawson's desktop* appeared online. It isn't what it was in 1998 when the first *Seinfeld*-less NBC season began or in 2000 when CBS's gamedocs forever altered economic models. It isn't what it was in 2002 when *American Idol* and its branded entertainment deal arrived on FOX or in 2004 when ABC revived scripted broadcast TV with *Lost* and *Desperate Housewives*. It isn't what it was in 2005 when ABC achieved its blockbuster *Lost* ratings and made its game-changing deal with iTunes or in 2007 when most of the long-arc serials that copycatted *Lost* failed and the ABC series' own ratings dropped. This book also has shown that television is not that different from what it was two years ago, or two years before that, or, even fifty years before that. That continuity is often the result of the ways in which millennial broadcast television has revived many of the strategies that characterized midcentury broadcast television.

Given the cyclical rhythms of the industry, it may just be NBC's turn in the next decade to be the Must-See TV destination precisely because of new comedy blocks, its Jerry Bruckheimer procedural, and David E. Kelley drama. In the meantime the Twitter-sphere is buzzing about NBC's 2009–10 desperate schedule-shifting and late night debacle. The CoCos— fans in support of 2009's *Tonight Show* host Conan O'Brien—continue to tweet, blog, and offer real-time online commentary about O'Brien's and NBC's next steps. Production workers, fans, media theorists and reviewers are commenting on and analyzing the future of NBC and the fate of broadcast television more generally and contributing to online venues such as PopMatters and FlowTV.org and blogs such as TVSquad. The controversy and its implications for the future of network TV have been addressed in the online and print versions of *The New York Times*, *The Los Angeles Times*, *Chicago Tribune*, and *USA Today*, among countless other newspapers. Although obviously chagrined by O'Brien's ability to leverage online and print media to make his case directly to viewers, NBC has its PR machine churning out spin it hopes will circulate as fact.

NBC's Late Night Debacle demonstrated the power of new media platforms for enabling ongoing asynchronous access to and commentary on television content, but it also confirmed that the broadcast platform still matters as it reaches more people simultaneously than any other. During the two-week negotiations period, both Leno and O'Brien retained the upper hand by using the power of their broadcast television programs to tell their sides of the story directly to viewers, some of whom were also new media users who took sides via Twitter and message board posts and enabled the wider circulation of commentary and jokes about NBC's proposed late night schedule shift. Both NBC shows quickly saw a ratings boost from the previous week as people heard the buzz and tuned in to see what jokes Leno and O'Brien were making about each other and NBC. Twitter continued to be filled with real-time responses to the monologues and video clips appeared on sites across the web after the broadcasts. To experience the full comic impact of the increasingly pointed monologues offered by their hosts, more viewers began to tune in to the late night shows as they aired. While alternate delivery platforms are becoming more significant, the NBC controversy showed that daily coverage on broadcast television and the front pages of national and regional newspapers still carries significant weight.

The two-week controversy provided evidence that new media can gather viewers and drive tune-in, leading to an upsurge in ratings. NBC's late night competitors respectively mined the network's public controversy for ratings-boosting commentary, with CBS's Letterman dubbing the scheduling snafu NBC's Late Night Debacle and proposing a *Law & Order* spinoff, *Leno Victims Unit*. ABC's Jimmy Kimmel then hosted his entire late night show dressed as Jay Leno to mock the late night host's style and signature segments. When Leno countered with an invitation for Kimmel to appear on *The Jay Leno Show*'s 10@10 segment, Leno had a hard time maintaining the good sport persona given that Kimmel was refusing to play along and turned the segment into another opportunity for more comic skewering of Leno's behavior. Letterman continued his nightly Leno- and NBC-bashing and all the hosts, including Leno, saw upticks in their ratings. The problem is that web and mobile audiences that were adding to the ratings during the controversy are nomadic and, hence, unlikely to be those to be in the habit of becoming loyal on-air viewers. The 7.0 rating that Conan scored for his January 22nd farewell episode suggests that the on-air show had finally attracted the viewers, especially those in the elusive male 18–34 demographic, who were more likely to watch video clips posted online or access the show or excerpts from it on Hulu than to "tune in" at 11.35 p.m. during the regular run of the program. As that audience ages, it is unclear whether a majority will start to watch on-air programming or continue to watch broadcast television via alternate delivery platforms. Again, the question is whether viewing TV-off-TV is a generational preference or the product of a younger audience's living conditions and lifestyle. Since that is the question none of the networks know how to answer, it is not surprising that NBC is doing little to address it by reinstalling Leno for now in the hopes that after he settles back into his former role as host of *The Tonight Show*, he will command a broad general audience and return the NBC show to the number one position in the timeslot. If so, the spin will most certainly be that Jay Leno was brought back by popular demand. CBS immediately started spinning the Leno in primetime failure in contrast to its own programming successes, declaring that traditional broadcast TV has been brought back by popular demand.

The controversy demonstrated that broadcast television still has power, but its impact is more dramatic when it works in combination with new media. Networks and their advertisers have not yet found a way to measure just how dramatic the "broadcast airing" + "new media circulation" combination can be, but the next decade will necessarily see new methods of audience measurement, battles over compensation for multiplatform content, and revised advertising models and methods of rate determination. People will continue "to watch television," although what it means to follow a television program and through what devices content is accessed and how viewsers are measured will continue to evolve. One thing is certain. Right now, someone is inventing the new media device, social utility, or application that will bring change to the industry and some writer is creating the series that will start a new strain of programming and set the copycatting cycle in motion again.[38]

Notes

Introduction: It's network TV

1 The Big Four refers to ABC, NBC, CBS, and FOX. As the latter did not program more than fifteen hours a week, the FCC did not consider it a full-service network like the original Big Three. FOX has benefited from this categorization as it was then not subject to the Financing and Syndication rules (Fin-Syn) that said that a network could not produce and distribute content. Networks had to purchase content from "independent producers," sometimes actual independent production companies, but often from the television production company of a major Hollywood studio. Warner Brothers is one of the largest suppliers of television series. Twentieth Century FOX is also a large supplier and once the FOX network was formed and deemed exempt from the Fin-Syn rules, it could both produce and distribute content. That meant that FOX also could profit from "the back end," such as when a series was sold into syndication after a certain number of episodes (usually 100). In the past those profits would have gone to the independent production company, which was expected to deficit-finance a series, that is, to take a loss while it was in its first run on the Big Three in the hopes that it would make it to the point in which it could be sold into syndication. It is through syndication that production companies earn back their investments and stand to make huge profits. The Fin-Syn rules that prevented the Big Three from producing and distributing a series were repealed in 1995 after a long lobbying process by the Big Three, which complained that they were now at a disadvantage because of the growth of a huge channel spectrum filled with competitors, not to mention the Fin-Syn exempt FOX network. With the repeal of Fin-Syn, the television production divisions of Warner Brothers and Paramount feared that the networks would stop buying their series and, therefore, started to produce their own in-house. Those fears were a primary motivation for the creation of WB and UPN. They were often designated as netlets because they did not have the same hours of programming as the Big Three. This book often uses the term the Big Three to acknowledge that there is still a difference between the original three broadcast networks and FOX (such as that it still does not program 10 p.m.). As FOX is, of course, a large network and often included in the phrase the Big Four, especially when it is beating the other three in the ratings, this book distinguishes it from a netlet, the descriptor applied to the narrowcast networks WB and UPN, as well as the CW network that was formed when the two merged in 2006. For a concise history of how the Fin-Syn repeal allowed for several media conglomerates to own and control much of the programming and the other effects of vertical integration, see Jennifer Holt, "Vertical Vision: Deregulation, Industrial Economy and Prime-time Design," in *Quality Popular Television: Cult TV, the Industry and Fans*, ed. Mark Jancovich and James Lyons (London: BFI, 2003), 11–31. There is a growing body of work on the political impact of media conglomeration, see, for example, David Hesmondhalgh, *The Cultural Industries* (Thousand Oaks, CA: Sage, 2002) as well as Robert McChesney's

work: *The Political Economy of Media: Enduring Issues, Emerging Dilemmas* (New York: Monthly Review Press, 2008); *The Problem of the Media: U.S. Communication Politics in the Twenty-First Century* (New York: Monthly Review, 2004); and *Rich Media, Poor Democracy* (Chicago, IL: University of Chicago Press, 1999). On the creation of the WB and UPN and their merger into the CW, see, respectively, Bill Carter, "The Media Business: 2 Would-be Networks Get Set for Prime Time," *The New York Times* January 9, 1995, Section D and "With Focus on Youth, 2 Small TV Networks Unite," *The New York Times* January 25, 2006, C4. Susanne Daniels offers an anecdotal account of the rise and demise of the netlets, see Daniels and Cynthia Littleton, *Season Finale: the Unexpected Rise and Fall of the WB and UPN* (New York: Harper, 2007).

2 Although *The Jay Leno Show* started out strong in its debut and the weeks prior to the rollout of the bulk of the other network's season premieres, the series lost viewers over time and became more of a concern for NBC once network affiliates threatened to pre-empt it because of the losses they were experiencing because of the week lead-in to their local 11 p.m. newscasts. The cancellation and controversy over the show is discussed in the conclusion.

3 David Bauder, "Start with Jay Leno in Evaluating New TV Season," Associated Press (AP Wire) May 23, 2009. Michael Malone, "Affiliates Weigh Jay," *Broadcasting & Cable* December 15, 2008, 10.

4 The quality drama designator is a controversial term, with some critics pointing out that when it is used as an aesthetic description it effaces both the value assumptions that come with the designator and the ways in which "quality" is a marketing term connected to the attempt to appeal to the urban, upscale demographic preferred by advertisers. The first chapter uses Paul Rixon's description of the "quality drama series," as it focuses on the marketable features of such series. Rixon explains that the "quality drama" has come to designate series with "large ensemble casts in well-crafted multilayered narratives that explore a side of American society not found in more formulaic fare." See Rixon, "The Changing Face of American Television Programmes on British Screens," in Jancovich and Lyons 2003, 57–58. The classic discussion of the quality television designator is Jane Feuer, Paul Kerr, and Tise Vahimagi, *MTM: "Quality Television"* (London: BFI, 1984). There are countless books about television programs and their creators that leave the idea of the "quality programming" unexamined, usually those that are celebrating "the genius" of a particular writer/producer. In contrast, several recent articles have addressed how HBO, in particular, has used this marketing designator to distinguish its brand in the marketplace. A good example is Dana Polan's "Cable Watching: HBO, *The Sopranos*, and Discourses of Distinction," in *Cable Visions: Television Beyond Broadcasting*, ed. Sara Banet-Weiser, Cynthia Chris, and Anthony Freitas (New York: New York University Press, 2007), 261–83.

5 Media convergence is a topic of discussion in several recent studies. See Henry Jenkins, *Convergence Culture: Where Old and New Media Collide* (New York: New York University Press, 2006); Amanda Lotz, *The Television Will Be Revolutionized* (New York: New York University Press, 2007); Dan Harries, *The New Media Book* (London: British Film Institute, 2002), especially Jenkins, "Interactive Audiences?" 157–70; Harries, "Watching the Internet," 171–82; William Uricchio, "Old Media and New Media: Television," 219–30; see also John Thornton Caldwell, "Convergence Television: Aggregating Form and Repurposing Content in the Culture of Conglomeration," in *Television After TV: Essays on a Medium in Transition*, ed. Lynn Spigel and Jan Olsson (Durham, NC: Duke University Press, 2004), 41–74. In the same volume, see Spigel's "Introduction," 1–34; Lisa Parks, "Flexible Microcasting: Gender, Generation, and Television-Internet Convergence," 133–56; and Uricchio, "Television's Next Generation: Technology/Interface Culture/Flow," 163–82. For the impact of new media on the construction of entertainment content and platforms, see the essays in Noah Wardrip-Fruin and Pat Harrigan, eds., *First Person: New Media as Story, Performance and Game* (Cambridge, MA: MIT Press, 2004).

6 Overflow is a term coined by Will Brooker to describe the way a TV text is constructed to move viewers from the broadcast platform to the web so that their interaction with the text and, in turn, the network's and sponsors' chances to interact with them continue online. Through overflow, viewers' experiences of the series become entwined with web surfing. See "Living on Dawson's Creek: Teen Viewers, Cultural Convergence, and Television Overflow," *International Journal of Cultural Studies* 4, vol. 4 (2001): 456–72.

7 These issues are explored by Lisa Gitelman, *Always Already New Media, History, and the Data of Culture* (Cambridge, MA: MIT Press, 2006) and Jay David Bolter and Richard Grusin, *Remediation: Understanding New Media* (Cambridge, MA: MIT Press, 1999). See also William Boddy, *New Media and Popular Imagination: Launching Radio, Television, and Digital Media in the United States* (Oxford: Oxford University Press, 2004); David Thornburn and Henry Jenkins, eds. *Rethinking Media Change: The Aesthetics of Transition* (Cambridge, MA: MIT Press, 2004); Uricchio, "Historicizing Media in Transition," in Thornburn and Jenkins 2004, 23–38.

8 A comparison of midcentury and millennial television programming and industrial practices demonstrates that much of what seems new is a modification of something that already existed. I address the similarities, for instance, between *The Osbournes*, an MTV reality program about heavy metal star Ozzy Osbourne and his nuclear family, and *The Adventures of Ozzie and Harriet*, a long-running 1950s–1960s sitcom in which the Nelson family plays a fictionalized version of themselves. See Jennifer Gillan, "From Ozzie Nelson to Ozzy Osbourne: the Genesis and Development of the Reality (Star) Sitcom," *Understanding Reality Television*, ed. Su Holmes and Deborah Jermyn (London: Routledge, 2004), 54–70. Chapter four of this book looks at the revival of the reality (star) sitcom in relation to NBC's *30 Rock*, a cross between a reality (star) sitcom and the faux variety show sitcom like *The Jack Benny Show*. The chapter also considers how much of today's product integration can be traced to midcentury television in which sponsors played a major role in shaping content. *Ozzie and Harriet*, for instance, had deals with Hotpoint that set the standard for why so many sitcoms have kitchen and dinner scenes. Ozzie Nelson, *Ozzie* (Englewood Cliffs, NJ: Prentice Hall, 1973), 241–42. *Ozzie and Harriet* had opening credits that integrated Coca-Cola as well as interstitials that are similar to today's content wraps in which the series' stars appear in a hybrid advertisement in which they stay in character, but are really product spokespeople. NBC embraced the content wrap for many of its 2007–8 scripted series, including *Lipstick Jungle* in which the series' actresses appeared in-character during interstitials sponsored by Maybelline. Cosmetic company content wraps were already familiar from *America's Next Top Model* (ANTM). Chapter one of this book examines content wraps in relation to CW, the netlet on which ANTM currently airs. John Consoli offers a general discussion of the content wraps in "WB, CW, Toyota Pact for Marketing Campaign," *Mediaweek*, April 19, 2007. Available online www.mediaweek.com/mw/news/networktv/article_display.jsp?vnu_content_id=1003574108.

9 To put current industrial practices into historical context, see Boddy, *Fifties Television: The Industry and Its Critics* (Urbana, IL: University of Illinois Press, 1993); Michele Hilmes, *Hollywood and Broadcasting: From Radio to Cable* (Urbana, IL: University of Illinois Press, 1990); Spigel, *Make Room for TV: Television and the Family Ideal in Post War America* (Chicago, IL: University of Chicago Press, 1992); Douglas Gomery, *The Hollywood Studio System: A History* (Berkley, CA: University of California Press, 2005; expanded and revised from New York: St. Martin's, 1986); Gomery, *A History of Broadcasting in the United States* (Oxford: Blackwell, 2008); and Christopher Anderson, *Hollywood TV: The Studio System in the Fifties* (Austin, TX: University of Texas Press, 1994).

10 On the concept of viewsing, see Harries 2002, 172, 178, 181.

11 This practice is not new as much as it is now new media-enabled. The difference is that ordinary adult viewers are targeted with this content without having to send away for it (as would have been the case, for instance, for tie-in merchandise related to sitcoms like

Leave it to Beaver or *Gidget*). This content is now available at the click of a button for consumption by casual as well as loyal adult viewers. For details on the tie-ins and ancillary merchandise associated with midcentury teen-address television, see Moya Luckett, "Girl Watchers: Patty Duke and Teen TV," *The Revolution Wasn't Televised: Sixties Television and Social Conflict*, ed. Lynn Spigel and Michael Curtain (New York: Routledge, 1997), 95–116; Bill Osgerby, "'So Who's Got Time for Adults!' Femininity, Consumption, and the Development of Teen TV—from Gidget to Buffy," in *Teen TV: Genre, Consumption and Identity,* ed. Glyn Davis and Kay Dickinson (London: BFI, 2004), 71–86.

12 For a discussion of new media-enabled narrowcasting, see Parks 2004, 133–62.

13 Fans of *Star Trek*, for example, translated many of the fan practices in which they were engaged pre-internet to the web, which often changes the speed of circulation and the level of access, but not necessarily the content of their fan activities. Much has been written on *Star Trek* fandom as it exists both off- and online. See Camille Bacon-Smith, *Enterprising Women: Television Fandom and the Creation of Popular Myth* (Philadelphia, PA: University of Pennsylvania Press, 1992); Jenkins, *Textual Poachers: Television Fans and Participatory Culture* (New York: Routledge, 1992); John Tulloch and Henry Jenkins, *Science Fiction Audiences: Watching Star Trek and Doctor Who* (New York: Routledge, 1995); Stephen E. Whitfield and Gene Rodenberry, *The Making of Star Trek* (New York: Ballantine, 1968), 393–95; Jeffrey Sconce, "Star Trek, Heaven's Gate, and Textual Transcendence," in Roberta Pearson and Sara Gwenllian-Jones, *Cult Television* (Minneapolis, MN: University of Minnesota Press, 2004), 199–252; Pearson, "'Bright Particular Star': Patrick Stewart, Jean-Luc Picard, and Cult Television," in Pearson and Gwenllian-Jones, 2004, 61–80. On *Star Trek* and Race, see Daniel Bernardi, *Star Trek and History: Race-ing Toward a White Future* (New Brunswick, NJ: Rutgers University Press, 1998); Peter Chvany, "'Do We Look like Ferengi Capitalists to You?' *Star Trek*'s Klingon as Emergent Virtual American Ethnics," in *Hop on Pop: The Politics and Pleasures of Popular Culture,* ed. Henry Jenkins, Tara McPherson, and Jane Shattuc (Durham, NC: Duke University Press, 2003), 105–21. For an industry perspective on NBC's relationship to *Star Trek*, see Maire Messenger Davies and Roberta Pearson, "The Little Program That Could: the Relationship between NBC and *Star Trek*," in *NBC: America's Network*, ed. Michele Hilmes (Berkeley, CA: University of California Press, 2007), 209–23.

14 The change in attitudes toward fans has been charted in many studies and essays, see, for instance, Sharon Marie Ross, *Beyond the Box: Television and the Internet* (Oxford: Blackwell, 2008); Jenkins 2006; Derek Johnson, "Inviting Audiences In: the Spatial Reorganization of Production and Consumption in 'TV III,'" *New Review of Film and Television Studies* 5, no. 1 (April 2007), 61–80; Gwenllian-Jones and Pearson 2004: Gwenllian-Jones, "Web Wars: Resistance, Online Fandom and Studio Censorship," in Jancovich and Lyons 2003, 163–77; Cornel Sandvoss, *Fans: The Mirror of Consumption* (New York: Polity, 2005); Jonathan Gray, Cornel Sandvoss, and C. Lee Harrington, eds. *Fandom: Identities and Communities in a Mediated World* (New York: New York University Press, 2007).

15 For more on the clash between FOX and webmasters of fan sites for *The X-Files* and other series, see Amanda Howell, "The X-Files, X-Philes and X-Philia: Internet Fandom as Site of Convergence," *Media International Australia Incorporating Culture and Policy* 97 (November 2000).

16 The creation of the award-winning *Heroes* transmedia experience brought together Mark Warshaw, who had created the web presence for *Smallville* and innovated webisode, mobisode, and graphic novel content, with Jesse Alexander, who co-created content for the Alternate Reality Game, video game, and general web presence for *Alias* (and later worked on *Lost*). Prior to the finalized *Heroes Evolutions* web experience, the production team did create a more fan-centric site called *9th Wonders*, which borrowed a comic book aesthetic. It was displaced by, although eventually incorporated into, the larger *Evolutions* linked sites. The latter offered touch-points not only for fans with the series creative team and cast, but also for series sponsors with potential consumers.

17 Jenkins considers this concept of franchising and the blurred boundaries created by multiple points of entry. See "Quentin Tarantino's *Star Wars*? Digital Cinema, Media Convergence, and Participatory Culture," in Thornburn and Jenkins 2004, 281–311. Networks are now engaged in multiplatform self-promotion as well. Often networks and production workers use the internet to circulate "stealth advertising" in the form of informal "practitioner talk," as Caldwell details in *Production Culture: Industrial Reflexivity and Critical Practice in Film and Television* (Durham, NC: Duke University Press, 2008), 59.

18 Hills, "*Dawson's Creek*: 'Quality Teen TV' and 'Mainstream Cult'?" in Davis and Dickinson 2004, 54–67; Brooker 2001, 456–72; Jimmie L. Reeves, Mark C. Rodgers, and Michael Epstein, "Rewriting Popularity: The Cult *Files*," in *"Deny All Knowledge": Reading The X-Files,* ed. David Lavery, Angela Hague, and Marla Cartwright (Syracuse, NY: Syracuse University Press, 1996), 22–35. See also Gwenllian Jones and Pearson's introduction to *Cult Television* and Mark Jancovich and Nathan Hunt's discussion of how cult television developed as an economic category in "The Mainstream, Distinction, and Cult TV," on pp. 27–44.

19 Jenkins 2006, 293.

20 Jenkins 2006, 293 as well as chapter 3 "Searching for the Origami Unicorn: The Matrix and Transmedia Storytelling," 93–130.

21 A showrunner is the writer/producer (or sometimes a pair) in charge of "running the show," that is, of maintaining the continuity of its multiplatform elements and coordinating the production team to make sure everything runs efficiently. With a legion of producers on most shows, designating a showrunner is necessary.

22 Raymond Williams, *Television, Technology and Cultural Forms* (London: Fontana, 1974).

23 For discussion of the rise of the three network system, see Hilmes 1990; Hilmes, *Only Connect: A Cultural History of Broadcasting in the US*, 2nd edition (Belmont, CA: Wadsworth, 2006); Hilmes, ed. *The Television History Book* (London: BFI, 2004); Douglas Gomery 2008; Boddy 1993; Mark Alvey, "The Independents: Rethinking the Television Studio System," in Spigel and Curtain 1997, 138–58. Les Brown, *Television: The Business Behind the Box* (New York: Harcourt Brace Jovanovich, 1971); Ken Auletta, *Three Blind Mice: How the TV Networks Lost Their Way* (New York: Random House, 1992) offers a look at the decline of the three network system.

24 There have been many analyses of the applicability and limitations of Williams' concept of flow. See, for example, John Ellis, *Visible Fictions: Cinema, Television, Video* (London: Routledge, 1982); John Corner, *Critical Ideas in Television Studies* (Oxford: Clarendon, 1999), 60–69; Jane Feuer, "The Concept of Live Television: Ontology as Ideology," in *Regarding Television: Cultural Approaches—An Anthology*, ed. E. Ann Kaplan (Los Angeles, CA: American Film Institute, 1983), 12–22; John Fiske, *Television Culture* (London: Methuen, 1978); Jostein Gripsrud, "Television, Broadcasting, Flow: Key Metaphors in TV Theory," in *Television Studies Book*, ed. Christine Geraghty and David Lusted (London: Arnold, 1998).

25 The practice I term "network identity placement" is addressed in chapter two of this study in relation to FOX and chapter four in relation to NBC. Product integration is discussed throughout the book and the many trade articles that discuss the subject are cited in relation to particular examples.

26 Caldwell discusses media conglomerate repurposing of its texts across multiple platforms. See "Convergence Television: Aggregating from and Repurposing Content in the Culture of Conglomeration," in Spigel and Olsson 2004, 41–74.

27 Uricchio 2004 claims that the remote control, "signals a shift away from the programming-based notion of flow that Williams documented to a viewer-centered notion" (168). On the remote control more generally, see Louise Benjamin, "At the Touch of a Button: A Brief History of Remote Control Devices," in *The Remote Control in the New Age of Television*, ed. James Walker and Robert Bellamy, Jr. (Westport, CT: Praeger, 1993), 15–22, and in the same volume Bruce C. Klopfenstein, "From Gadget to Necessity: the Diffusion of Remote Control Technology," 23–40; Frederick Wasser, *Veni, Vidi, Video: The Hollywood Empire and*

the VCR (Austin, TX: University of Texas Press, 2001); Sean Cubitt, *Timeshift: On Video Culture* (New York: Routledge, 1991).

28 This capability is, of course, a source of great anxiety for networks and their advertisers. Joseph Ostrow, "PVRs a Real Fear Factor for TV's Ad Community," *Electronic Media* September 16, 2002, 9+; "Taking the Ads Out of Television," *The Economist* May 8, 1999, n.p. For the ways that viewers could create customized schedules, see John Markoff, "Two Makers Plan Introductions of Digital VCR," *New York Times* March 29, 1999, C1. For a discussion of the more long-term impact, see Joe Mandese, "DVR Threat Gets Downgraded," *Broadcasting & Cable* September 12, 2005, 20. See also Boddy, "Redefining the Home Screen: Technological Convergence as Trauma and Business Plan," in Thornburn and Jenkins 2004, 191–200.

29 Anne Friedberg offers a consideration of the multitasking made possible via the multiple windows of the web as well as the new cultural paradigms such behavior suggests. See "The Virtual Window," in Thornburn and Jenkins 2004, 337–53.

30 Mark Cotta Vaz, *Alias Declassified: The Official Companion* (New York: Bantam/Random House, 2002), 17.

31 Chapter three in this book discusses the ABC multiplatform approach and chapter four considers NBC's self-referential brand television.

32 The distinction between a sponsor's time franchise (e.g. *Texaco Star Theater*) and the participating or magazine-style sponsorship with which we are most familiar today is discussed in Boddy 1993, 160–62, 157–58. See also Erik Barnouw, *The Sponsor: Notes on a Modern Potentate* (New York: Oxford University Press, 1978). On early TV and sponsorship, see Nina C. Leibman, *Living Room Lectures: The Fifties Family in Film and Television* (Austin, TX: University of Texas Press, 1995); Lawrence R. Samuel, *Brought to You By: Postwar Television Advertising and the American Dream* (Austin, TX: University of Texas Press, 2001); Susan Murray, *Hitch Your Antenna to the Stars: Early Television and Broadcast Stardom* (New York: Routledge, 2005); Karal Ann Marling, *As Seen on TV: The Visual Culture of Everyday Life in the 1950s* (Cambridge, MA: Harvard University Press, 1994); James L. Baughman, *Same Time, Same Station: Creating American Television, 1948–1961* (Baltimore, MD: Johns Hopkins University Press, 2007); Gerard Jones, *Honey: I'm Home: Selling the American Dream* (New York: Grove, 1992); Jeff Kisseloff, *The Box: An Oral History of Television 1920–1961* (New York: Penguin, 1995).

33 Typically, sitcoms are closed-arc storylines in that they begin a story at the start of an hour and conclude it at the end of an hour. If Alan falls off a roof in CBS's sitcom *Two and a Half Men*, he is fine by the next episode and no one, not even his unsupportive mother, ever mentions the accident or his injuries again. There are serial elements to the series such as that the dedicated viewer knows about Alan's long-term conflicts with his mother, which have led to his lack of confidence and his clumsiness. The long-term "will-they-or-won't-they" Ross and Rachel romance in NBC's *Friends* is a common example of how seriality has become a facet of episodic series. Glen Creeber addresses the recent serial/series drama hybrids in *Serial Television: Big Drama on the Small Screen* (London: BFI, 2004).

34 For the impact DVD has on scheduling and flow, see Derek Kompare, "Publishing Flow: DVD Box Sets and the Reconception of Television," *Television and New Media* 7, no. 4 (2006), 335–60.

35 The declining appeal and ratings of *Heroes* was the "Fallen Heroes" cover story for *Entertainment Weekly*, October 31, 2008, 22–27. It claimed the show was "under siege," and "no longer a pop culture phenomenon." It was down that fall to an average of 9.4 million from 11.6 in 2007, which was itself down from its 2006 peak of 16 million viewers (23). "To hear series creator Tim Kring tell it, *Heroes* needs to be—or, at least, needs to be seen as—zeitgeist-tapping, blockbuster event television to remain viable" (24). The network wanted a blockbuster not cult series. Kring explained that he thought that the fact that his series had to create a full episode order, while others like *Lost* had a reduced order, made it

harder to keep the momentum. That same issue will be discussed in chapter three. This article, coupled with other press coverage, was rumored to have prompted the knee-jerk reaction from NBC Universal upper management which resulted in a November 2008 shakeup within the ranks of the *Heroes* production team. The foolish decision to sack some of the team led to more articles about NBC's problematic decision-making and its connection to the network's fourth place position.

36 On the history of the CBS–NBC rivalry, see Boddy 1993. For a discussion of CBS's purge of its rural sitcoms in favor of Norma Lear "quality" sitcoms, see Feuer, Kerr, and Vahimagi 1984, 152.

37 Tolan's comments were made at the 2009 Television Critics Association Summer Press Tour. They are reprinted in various sources, including on *Entertainment Weekly*'s blog from August 7, 2009, http://watching-tv.ew.com/2009/08/07/fx-nbc-producers-american-flag/. See also Brian Lowry, "Writers Lash Out at Network Choices," *Variety*, variety.com, August 14, 2009, www.variety.com/article/VR1118007291.html?categoryid=1682& cs = 1.

38 Reprinted on a *Los Angeles Times* blog post, "TCA Press Tour: Showrunners Blast NBC, Leno," latimes.com, August 7, 2009, http://latimesblogs.latimes.com/showtracker/2009/08/tca-press-tour-showrunners-blast-nbc-leno.html.

39 The increasing two-way flow of television programs as well as the impact of the global circulation of U.S. TV is discussed by several scholars. See, for example, Michael Curtin, "Media Capitals: Cultural Geographies of Global TV," in Spigel and Olsson 2004, 270–302; Lisa Parks and Shanti Kumar, eds. *Planet TV: A Global Television Reader* (New York: New York University Press, 2003); Denise D. Bielby and Lee Harrington, *Global TV: Exporting Television and Culture in the World Market* (New York: New York University Press, 2008) and "Global Television Distribution: Implications of TV 'Traveling' for Viewers, Fans, and Texts," *American Behavioral Scientist* 48, no. 7 (2005), 902–20; Albert Moran, *Copycat TV: Globalisation, Programme Formats and Cultural Identity* (Luton, U.K.: Luton University Press, 1998); John Sinclair, Elizabeth Jacka, and Stuart Cunningham, *New Patterns in Global Television: Peripheral Vision* (New York: Oxford University Press, 1996); Moran and Justin Malbon, *Understanding the Global TV Format* (Bristol: Intellect 2006); Moran and Michael Keane, eds. *Television across Asia: Television Industries, Program Formats, and Globalization* (London: RoutledgeCurzon, 2004); Timothy Havens, *Global Television Marketplace* (London: BFI, 2006).

40 On the problems with the U.K. broadcast of *24*, see Claire Cozens, "24 Sponsorship Deal Spells Trouble for BBC," *The Guardian* (U.K.) October 29, 2002. Available online www.guardian.co.uk/media/2002/oct/29/bbc.advertising?commentpage=1.

41 John-Paul Kelly analyzed these slogans in "Sky vs. Virgin: The Battle of the Brands," Television Without Borders conference, University of Reading [U.K.], June 27–29, 2008.

42 It did so through massive marketing. For an account, see John M. Higgins and Donna Petrozello, "HBO Reaching for the Stars," *Broadcasting & Cable* March 23, 1998, 28; Elizabeth Lesly Stevens, "Call It Home Buzz Office: HBO's Challenge—To Keep the High-Profile Programs Coming," *BusinessWeek* December 8, 1997, 77. For an update on its model, see Joe Flint, "HBO's Next Business Model," *Wall Street Journal* January 5, 2004, B1. For an overview, see Gary R. Edgerton, "A Brief History of HBO," in *The Essential HBO Reader*, ed. Gary R. Edgerton and Jeffrey P. Jones (Lexington, KY: The University Press of Kentucky, 2008), 1–20.

43 For the ways in which HBO uses assumptions about "quality TV" in an effort to distinguish its brand, see Deborah L. Jaramillo, "The Family Racket: AOL Time Warner, HBO, and *The Sopranos*, and the Construction of a Quality Brand," *Journal of Communication Studies* 26, no. 1 (2002), 59–75; Avi Santo, "Para-television and Discourses of Distinction: The Culture of Production at HBO," in *It's Not TV: Watching HBO in the Post-television Era*, ed. Marc Leverette, Brian L. Ott, and Cara Louise Buckley (New York: Routledge, 2008), 19–45. The anthology editors' introduction addresses the issue as well and most of the chapters at

least touch on the issue. See also A. J. Frutkin, "Enemy of the Safe," *Mediaweek* June 16, 2003, 1.

44 John M. Higgins, "Edgy Fare Drives FX," *Broadcasting & Cable* September 13, 2004, 4; Anthony Crupi, "Young Blood: FX Pulls in 18–49 Demo with Gritty Fare," *Mediaweek* January 16, 2006, 6.

45 Amanda Lotz proposes that the economic distinction is what *It's not TV* references in actuality, if not in popular perception. She discusses the distinction between HBO's subscription premium cable economic model and network television's model and how that impacts the content each can air. Lotz "If It Is Not TV, What Is It? The Case of U.S. Subscription Television," in Banet-Wiser, Chris, and Freitas 2007, 85–102.

46 See Lowry, August 14, 2009.

47 Paul Torre offers many insights about the international distribution of television texts. See "Block Booking Migrates to Television: The Rise and Fall of the International Output Deal," *Television & New Media* 10, no. 6 (November 2009), 501–20.

48 Likely in response to the success of *NCIS LA*, NBC is talking about developing an L.A. iteration of its *Law and Order* franchise for 2010.

49 The trades have discussed the impact of reality television's economic formats on broadcast structures. See Bill Carter, "Reality Shows Alter the Way TV Does Business," *New York Times* January 25, 2003, A1, Late edition. Chad Raphael analyzes the changes in detail in "The Political Economic Origins of Reali-TV," in Murray and Ouellette 2004, 119–36.

50 Gomery covers all these issues in "Talent Raids and Package Deals: NBC Loses Its Leadership in the 1950s," in Hilmes 2007, 153–68.

51 For more on the "reality (star) sitcom" programming category see Gillan 2004.

52 Chapter four analyzes this issue in detail. For more on Benny, see Gomery 2007, 154 and Susan Murray, *Hitch Your Antenna to the Stars: Early Television and Broadcast Stardom* (New York: Routledge, 2005).

53 Mashon, "NBC, J. Walter Thompson, and the Struggle for Control of Television Programming, 1946–58," in Hilmes 2007, 135–52.

54 Gomery 2007, 159–61.

55 Mashon discusses the change at NBC from full to participating sponsorship, 2007, 135–52. See Boddy 1993, 157–62.

56 As already noted, the strategy did not work. One problem was that Leno failed to provide a new format for the primetime slot. The format and cancellation of the show are discussed in detail in the conclusion.

57 "Size Does Matter," *Economist* May 23, 1998, 57.

58 Anderson 1994, 155.

59 On video display at the Disney Impact Summit, "Disney Channels Worldwide: Leadership and Influence in the Global Marketplace," Burbank, CA, August 10, 2009.

60 Richard Schickel, *The Disney Version: The Life, Times, Art and Commerce of Walt Disney*, 3rd edition (Chicago, IL: Ivan R. Dee, 1987), 23

61 Janet Wasko, *Understanding Disney: The Manufacture of Fantasy* (Malden, MA: Polity Press, 2001), 21.

62 Hugh Malcolm Beville, *Audience Ratings: Radio, Television, Cable*, Revised edition (Hillsdale, NJ: Lawrence Erlbaum Associates, 1998).

63 On the impact of and the possibility of revising ratings measurement, see Jon Gertner, "Our Ratings, Ourselves," *New York Times Magazine* April 10, 2005, 34+.

64 For a discussion of the role of lovemarks in marketing, see Kevin Roberts, *Lovemarks: The Future Beyond Brands* (New York: Power House Books, 2004). See also Marc Gobe, *Emotional Branding: The New Paradigm for Connecting Brands to People* (New York: Allworth Press, 2001). Jenkins 2006 details these new trends as well, see 20, 61–63, 68–70.

65 Boddy 2004, 3.

66 John Hagel III and Arthur G. Armstrong, *Net Gains: Expanding Markets through Virtual Communities* (Cambridge, MA: Harvard University Press, 1997).

67 Jenkins, "Why Fiske Still Matters," FlowTV 2, no. 6 (2005, June 10). Available online http://flowtv.org/?p=585.

68 Qtd. in Marshall Sella, "The Remote Controllers," *The New York Times Magazine* October 20, 2002, 68+.

69 Caldwell analyzes the rise of branding through channel idents and other means. "Critical Industrial Practice: Branding, Repurposing, and the Migratory Patterns of Industrial Texts," *Television & New Media* 7, no. 2 (May 2006), 99–134.

1 Fan tracking, targeting, and interaction from the web to the WB

1 Henry Jenkins, *Convergence Culture: Where Old and New Media Collide* (New York: New York University Press, 2006); Dan Harries, *The New Media Book* (London: British Film Institute, 2002), especially Jenkins, "Interactive Audiences?" 157–70; Harries, "Watching the Internet," 171–82; and William Uricchio, "Old Media and New Media: Television," 219–30. See also John Thornton Caldwell, "Convergence Television: Aggregating Form and Repurposing Content in the Culture of Conglomeration," in *Television After TV: Essays on a Medium in Transition*, ed. Lynn Spigel and Jan Olsson (Durham: Duke University Press, 2004), 41–74. In the same volume, see also Spigel's "Introduction," 1–34; Lisa Parks, "Flexible Microcasting: Gender, Generation, and Television-Internet Convergence," 133–56; and Uricchio, "Television's Next Generation: Technology/Interface Culture/Flow," 163–82.

2 Dana Boyd, "Why Youth Heart Social Network Sites: The Role of Networked Publics in Teenage Social Life," in *Youth, Identity, and Digital Media*, ed. David Buckingham (Cambridge: MIT Press, 2008), 119–42; Gitte Staid, "Mobile Identity: Youth, Identity, and Mobile Communication Media," in Buckingham 2008, 143–64; Sarah N. Gatson and Amanda Zweerink, *Interpersonal Culture on the Internet: Television, the Internet, and the Making of a Community* (Lewiston, NY: Edwin Mellen Press, 2004); Hiesun Cecilia Suhr, "Underpinning the Paradoxes in the Artistic Fields of MySpace: The Problematization of Values and Popularity in Convergence Culture," *New Media & Society* 11, no. 1 & 2 (2009), 179–98; Zizi Papacharissi, "The Virtual Geographies of Social Networks: a Comparative Analysis of Facebook, LinkedIn, and A SmallWorld," *New Media & Society* 11, no. 1 & 2 (2009), 199–220; Karen Mossberger, Caroline J. Tolbert, and Ramona S. McNeal, *Digital Citizenship: The Internet Society, and Participation* (Cambridge: MIT, 2008).

3 John Rodzvilla discusses the motivations for posting on online sites, *We've Got Blog: How Weblogs are Changing Our Culture* (Cambridge, MA: Perseus Publishing, 2002), 209–11.

4 Kurt Lindemann offers an analysis of how LiveJournal provides a way to circulate a desired self. "Live(s) Online: Narrative Performance, Presence, and Community in LiveJournal.com," *Text and Performance Quarterly* 25, no. 4 (October 2005), 354–72. Louisa Stein examines fannish investment in several series through the lens of the LiveJournal fan boards for *Gilmore Girls*, *Veronica Mars*, and *Supernatural*, exploring fan fiction forms in relation to the latter series. "Pushing at the Margins: Teenage Angst in Teen TV and Audience Response," in Ross and Stein 2008, 224–43.

5 Lindemann 2005, 355.

6 Caldwell 2008 discusses FOX's "shameless self-promotion" in the way it used parts of the franchise to promote the rest, including the "making-of" behind the scenes special. Promotion that looks like content is part of the new Electronic Press Kit (EPK), Caldwell says, which offers "predigested angles" on a media product (289–91).

7 Jimmie L. Reeves, Mark C. Rodgers, and Michael Epstein, "Rewriting Popularity: The Cult Files," in *"Deny All Knowledge": Reading The X-Files*, ed. David Lavery, Angela Hague, and Marla Cartwright (Syracuse, NY: Syracuse University Press, 1996), 22–35. Fans did congregate around the series and created commentary and analysis groups. See Susan J. Clerc,

"DDEB, GATB, MPPB, and Ratboy: *The X-Files'* Media Fandom, Online and Off," in *"Deny All Knowledge": Reading The X-Files,* ed. David Lavery, Angela Hague, and Marla Cartwright (Syracuse, NY: Syracuse University Press, 1996), 36–51; Rhiannon Bury, "Feminine Pleasures, Masculine Texts: Reading *The X-Files* on the DDEBRP," in *Cyberspaces of their Own: Female Fandoms Online* (New York: Peter Lang, 2005), 34–70; Bury, "Stories for Girls: Female Fans Reading *The X-Files*," *Popular Communication* 1 (2003), 217–42; Bury, "Waiting to X-Hale: A Study of Gender and Community on an All-Female *X-Files* Electronic Mailing List," *Convergence* 4 (1998), 59–83.

8 Patrice Flichy, *The Internet Imaginaire* (Cambridge: MIT Press, 2007) offers an overview of the history of Usenet. For specific fan discussions, see Matt Hills, *Fan Cultures* (New York: Routledge, 2002), 172–75. See also Nancy K. Baym, "Interpreting Soap Operas and Creating Community: Inside a Computer-Mediated Fan Culture," *Journal of Folklore Research* 30 (1999), 143–76, and Baym 1995, 51–52. While Clerc 1996 focuses on an *X-Files* group, Jenkins offers an account of a group for *Twin Peaks* in "'Do You Enjoy Making the Rest of Us Feel Stupid?': alt.tv.twinpeaks, the Trickster Author, and Viewer Mastery," in Lavery 1995, 51–69. Jenkins offers an account as well of MIT's *Star Trek* viewers in John Tulloch and Henry Jenkins, *Science Fiction Audiences: Watching Star Trek and Doctor Who* (New York: Routledge, 1995); Kurt Lancaster also examines these sites in *Interacting with Babylon 5: Fan Performances in a Media Universe* (Austin, TX: University of Texas Press, 2001).

9 Flichy 2007 offers a history of these developments. Sherry Turkle examines early online cultures in *The Second Self: Computers and the Human Spirit* (New York: Touchstone, 1984) and *Life on the Screen: Identity in the Age of the Internet* (New York: Simon and Schuster, 1995).

10 Qtd. in Marcus Errico, "FOX Fights 'Millennium' Fan Sites," *E! Online* November 16, 1996, www.eonline.com/News/Items/0,1,379,00.html. See also Laurent Belsie, "Web War: Hollywood Tangles with Fans' On-line Sites," *Christian Science Monitor* December 17, 1996, 1+; Amy Harmon, "Web Wars: Companies Get Tough on Rogues," *Los Angeles Times* November 12, 1996, A1+.

11 Henry Goldblatt, "TV's Most Lucrative Franchise: It's a Mystery," *Fortune* January 12, 1998, 114.

12 Kevin Johnson, "Show's Fan Sites Fight Off 'Demon' FOX," *USA Today* December 23, 1999, D4.

13 David Marshall with Susan Luckman and Sean Smith, "Promotional Desires: Popular Media's Presence on the Internet," *Media International Australia Incorporating Culture and Policy* 86 (February 1998), 64.

14 Brian Lowry, *The Truth Is Out There Official Guide to The X-Files* (New York: Harper, 1995), 139–40.

15 Amanda Howell, "The X-Files, X-Philes and X-Philia: Internet Fandom as Site of Convergence," *Media International Australia Incorporating Culture and Policy* 97 (November 2000), 145.

16 Lowry 1995, 239.

17 Howell 2000, 145.

18 See Errico 1996.

19 Goldblatt 1998, 114.

20 Anya Sacharow, "Log Off, Tune In (Television Networks' Use of the Web)," *Adweek* June 16, 1997, 58+.

21 Harmon 1996.

22 Ibid.

23 Holt 2003.

24 The lawsuit is covered in Horace Newcomb, ed. *Encyclopedia of Television* (New York: Routledge, 2004), 2605.

25 For more on Buffy Webmasters, see Amanda Zweerink and Sarah N. Gatson, "www.buffy. com: Cliques, Boundaries, and Hierarchies in an Internet Community," in *Fighting the Forces: What's at Stake in Buffy the Vampire Slayer,* ed. Rhonda, Wilcox, and Lavery (Lanham,

256 Notes

MD: Rowman & Littlefield, 2002), 239–51. In addition to the Wilcox and Lavery anthology, see Elana Levine and Lisa Parks, eds, *Undead TV: Essays on Buffy the Vampire* (Durham, NC: Duke University Press, 2007). See also Anne Bilson, *Buffy the Vampire Slayer*. BFI TV Classics series (London: BFI, 2005) and Wilcox, *Why Buffy Matters: The Art of Buffy the Vampire Slayer* (London: I.B. Tauris, 2005). *Slayage: An Online Journal of Buffy Studies* edited by Wilcox can be found at www.slayage.com. See also Geraldine Blousetin, "Fans with a Lot at Stake: Serious Play and Mimetic Excess in *Buffy the Vampire Slayer*," *European Journal of Cultural Studies* 54 (2002), 27–49. On the adult appeal of shows that are labeled teen TV, see Mary Celeste Kearney, "The Changing Face of Teen Television, or Why We All Love *Buffy*," in Levine and Parks 2007, 17–41.

26 For critical essays on the series, see the essays in Stacey Abbott, ed. *Reading "Angel": The TV Spin-off with a Soul* (London: I.B. Tauris, 2005). As it is a spinoff of *Buffy*, there are many articles that reference some crossover issues between the two series such as their representation of masculinities. See Dee Amy-Chinn and Milly Williamson, "The Vampire Spike in Text and Fandom: Unsettling Oppositions in *Buffy the Vampire Slayer*," *European Journal of Cultural Studies* 8 (2005), 275–88 and Allison McCracken, "At Stake: Angel's Body, Fantasy Masculinity, and Queer Desire in Teen Television," in Levine and Parks 2007, 116–44.

27 Harmon 1996.

28 IGN Film Force, "An Interview with Joss Whedon," filmforce.ign.com, June 23, 2003, 10, http://filmforce.ign.com/articles/425/425492p1.html.

29 Ibid. For comments on spoilers in relation to other series, see Jenkins, "Spoiling Survivor: The Anatomy of a Knowledge Community," in Jenkins 2006, 25–58. Jonathan Gray and Jason Mittell, "Speculation on Spoilers: *Lost* Fandom, Narrative Consumption, and Rethinking Textuality," *Particip@tions: Journal of Audience and Reception Studies* 4, no. 1 (2007), www.participations.org/Volume%204/Issue%201/4_01_graymittell.htm.

30 Howell 2000, 143–44.

31 For a discussion of 1990s fan activity in relation to a variety of TV series, see Victor J. Costello, *Interactivity and the "Cyber-fan": An Exploration of Audience Involvement within the Electronic Fan Culture of the Internet*, PhD diss., Univ. of Tennessee, 1999. Available online http://oai.sunsite.utk.edu/links/CostelloVictor.pdf. See also Costello and Barbara Moore, "Cultural Outlaws: An Examination of Audience Activity and Online Television Fandom," *Television and New Media* 8 (2007), 124–43.

32 On fan fiction and other fannish production, see Karen Hellekson and Kristina Busse, eds. *Fan Fiction and Fan Communities in the Age of the Internet: New Essays* (Jefferson, NC: McFarland, 2006); Louisa Stein, "This Dratted Thing: Fannish Storytelling Through New Media," in Hellekson and Busse 2006, 245–60; Kristen Pullen, "Everybody's Gotta Love Somebody, Sometime: Online Fan Community," in *Web Studies*, 2nd Edition, ed. David Gauntlett and Ross Horsley (London: Arnold, 2004), 80–91; Camille Bacon-Smith, *Enterprising Women: Television Fandom and the Creation of Popular Myth* (Philadelphia: Univ. of Pennsylvania Press, 1992); Nancy K. Baym, *Tune in, Log on: Soaps, Fandom, and Online Community* (Thousand Oaks, CA: Sage, 2000); and Jenkins 1992.

33 In *Fan Cultures* Hills systematically details the motivations for fan activity.

34 Sacharow 1997.

35 Ibid.

36 Mimi Chakraborty, "Homicide Fans on the Case," *The Times* [London] March 5, 1997, Features.

37 Sacharow 1997.

38 Bob Woods, "NBC Produces First Online Spinoff Series," *Newsbytes News Network*, February 11, 1997a. Available online www.newsbytes.com/HOMICIDE970211; Bob Woods "Homicide Web & TV Series Crossovers?" *Newsbytes News Network*, February 12, 1997b. Available online www.newsbytes.com/HOMICIDE970212.

39 Patti Hartigan, "'Homicide' Web Site Links Fans to Cyber Plot," *The Boston Globe* February 5, 1999, D14.

40 Chakraborty 1997.

41 Ibid.

42 Richard Helm, "TV Sets its Sites on Internet," *The Toronto Star* August 23, 1997, J10.

43 Ibid; Caldwell (2008) briefly discusses *Second Shift* in relation to its role as an experiment in using the web to brand a product as cutting edge (281–82).

44 Helm 1997.

45 Woods 1997a.

46 Hartigan 1999.

47 Alan Bash, "'Homicide' Spins Off Interactive Web Serial," *USA Today* February 11, 1997, 3D.

48 Sanctis qtd. in Helm 1997.

49 Hardin qtd. in Woods 1997b.

50 Woods 1997a.

51 Helm 1997.

52 Hartigan 1999.

53 Susan Karlin, "Tech-Shy TV Producer Extends Hit Shows to Web," *New York Times* October 5, 2000, G10.

54 Hartigan 1999.

55 Bash 1997.

56 Karlin 2000.

57 Ibid.

58 Ibid.

59 Ibid.

60 Bash 1997.

61 For an explanation of Fin-Syn, see introduction, note 1. See also Michael Freeman, "TV in Transition: Forging a Model for Profitability, Repurposing the First Step Toward Fiscal Viability," *Electronic Media* January 28, 2002, 1+; Diane Mermigas, "Finsyn Repeal Has Yet to Pay off," *Electronic Media* June 3, 2002, 30.

62 Bash 1997.

63 Karlin 2000.

64 Ibid.

65 Helm 1997.

66 Ibid.

67 Helm 1997.

68 Ibid.

69 Sacharow 1997.

70 Karlin 2000.

71 Ibid.

72 Ibid.

73 Press release, "Sony Pictures Digital Entertainment Teams with Channel 4 and Lineone to Launch Online Destination for Dawson's Creek," *PR Newswire* June 27, 2000. Available online www.prnewswire.co.uk/cgi/news/release?id=55601.

74 Brooker analyzes these details of the *Dawson's desktop* web presence. His essay is also significant as in it he theorizes overflow, which is central to the cross-platform address of many TV series. "Living on Dawson's Creek: Teen Viewers, Cultural Convergence, and Television Overflow," *International Journal of Cultural Studies* 4, vol. 4 (2001), 456–72. Jenkins 2006 comments on *Dawson's desktop* as well (115–18).

75 Sandra P. Angulo, "'Dawson's Creek' Fans Get an Online Sneak Preview of the Title Character's Screenplay-in-Progress," *Entertainment Weekly* December 8, 1998. Available online www.ew.com/ew/article/0,83981,00.html.

76 Jeff Jensen, "Columbia TriStar Teen TV Show Adds Interactive: Dawson's Online Walks a Fine Line between Editorial and Commerce," *Advertising Age* July 13, 1998a, 27.

77 Ibid.

78 Jeff Jensen, "Dep Touts Link to 'Dawson's Creek' Site: Haircare Brand Uses Web to Promote Relaunch," *Advertising Age* October 26, 1998b, 40.

79 Jenkins 2006, 279.

80 Jensen 1998a; Jensen 1998b.

81 Jensen 1998b.

82 "Columbia TriStar Interactive Opens a Window into the Private World of 'Dawson Leery,' with the Launch of Dawson's Desktop," *Business Wire* October 6, 1998. Available online www.thefreelibrary.com/Columbia+TriStar+Interactive+Opens+A+Woindow+Int+Private+World+of+ ... a053063143.

83 Ibid.

84 *Dawson's Chat*, June 8, 2000.

85 Ibid.

86 Ibid.

87 *Business Wire*, October 6, 1998.

88 *Dawson's Chat*, June 8, 2000.

89 *Business Wire*, October 6, 1998.

90 Brooker 2001, 457.

91 Williams 1974; Jenkins 1992.

92 Brooker, "Conclusion: Overflow," in *Audience Studies Reader*, ed. Will Brooker and Deborah Jermyn (New York: Routledge, 2003), 325.

93 Brooker 2001, 458.

94 Brooker 2003, 324.

95 Matt Hills, "*Dawson's Creek*: 'Quality Teen TV' and 'Mainstream Cult?'" in *Teen TV: Genre, Consumption and Identity,* ed. Glyn Davis and Kay Dickinson (London: BFI, 2004), 54–67.

96 Brooker 2001, 461.

97 Brooker 2001, 460.

98 This analysis is expanded in the conclusion in relation to *Grey's Anatomy's* blogs written by the writing team.

99 *Dawson's Chat*, June 8, 2000.

100 Ibid.

101 Ibid.

102 Ibid.

103 Ibid.

104 *Dawson's Chat*, October 12, 2000.

105 Ibid.

106 *Dawson's Chat*, October 26, 2000.

107 Their account of their internet-enabled active fan response is at odds with the account of viewers of *90210* offered in Graham E. McKinley, *Beverly Hills, 90210: Television, Gender, and Identity* (Philadelphia: University of Pennsylvania Press, 1997). McKinley's analysis of the consumer-oriented teen identities on display is important as many message board participants who post on "teen TV" sites express ambivalence about the impact of consumerism on their notions of their identities.

108 For a discussion of TWoP, see Marc Andrejevic, "Watching Television Without Pity: The Productivity of Online Fans," *Television and New Media* 9, no. 1 (2008), 24–46.

109 Bravo Press Release, "Bravo Announces First-ever Media Acquisition with TelevisionWithout Pity.com, the Online Destination for the Discerning TV 'Junkie,'" March 13, 2007, highlights available online http://featuresblogs.chicagotribune.com/entertainment_tv/2007/03/bravo_buys_twop.html. See also Josef Adalian, "Bravo Nabs Popular TV Website," *Variety*

March 13, 2007. Available online www.variety.com/article/VR1117961063.html? categoryid=14& cs=1.

110 "The Demise of Television Without Pity," October 28, 2008, captaintv.com, http://captintvblogspot.com/2008/10/demise-of-television-without-pity.html. See also Ryan, "Bravo Buys TWoP: Will the Snarky Site Lose its Bite?" *The Watcher* [blog], *Chicago Tribune* March 13, 2007. http://featuresblogs.chicagotribune.com/entertainment_tv/2007/03/bravo_buys_twop.html.

111 For a complete analysis of all its multiplatform content, see Cary M. Jones, "Twenty-first Century Superman: *Smallville* and New Media Mythmaking," *Jump Cut: A Review of Contemporary Media* 48 (Winter 2006). Available online www.ejumpcut.org/archive/jc48.2006/SmallvilleFans/index.html.

112 James Hibberd, "The WB's Supergirl Focuses on Branding," *Television Week* August 4, 2003, 19.

113 Tom Kapinos, Interview, *Dawson's desktop: Dawson's Chat Transcripts*, October 26, 2000.

114 Ibid.

115 Shippers and slashers are discussed in Melanie E. S. Kohnen, "The Adventures of a Repressed Farm Boy and the Billionaire Who Loves Him: Queer Spectatorship in *Smallville* Fandom," in Ross and Stein 2008, 207–23; Sharon Cumberland, "Private Uses of Cyberspace: Women, Desire, and Fan Culture," in *Rethinking Media Change: The Aesthetics of Transition*, ed. David Thorburn and Henry Jenkins (Cambridge, MA: MIT Press, 2004), 261–79. Often shippers and slashers create video mashups or montages, the tone of which is set by the music choice. Angelina I. Karpovich offers an interesting take on the role of music in fan videos, examining the way sound inflects the vidder's point of view on characters and relationships. "Reframing Fan Videos," in *Music, Sound and Multimedia: From the Live to the Virtual*, ed. Jamie Sexton (Edinburgh: Edinburgh University Press, 2007), 17–28.

116 It also has three types of young women with whom different consumer goods can be associated as was the case with the *Entertainment Weekly* coverage of "Women of the WB." See Bruce Fretts, "The Entertainers: the Women of the WB," December 25, 1998. Available online www.ew.com/ew/article/0,286245,00.html. See also Wayne Friedman, "Event-like Promos Build Loyal Young Core for WB," *Advertising Age* February 1, 1999, S1; Sara Teasdale, "The WB," *Advertising Age* June 28, 1999, 32; Jill Brooke, "Counterpunch: WB Network's Programming Success," *Adweek* March 30, 1998, 22–25; Tom Bierbaum, "The WB's Getting the Girls," *Variety* November 2–8, 1998, 30.

117 The series is obviously structured in season one to balance, as *The X-Files* did before it, monster-of-the-week stand-alone mysteries and a thread of mythology connected to the long-arc serial mystery running throughout the series.

118 As a DVD special feature, the team even did a featurette *Smallville Big Fans*. Some of the fans were shown tracking Chloe's Wall of Weird.

119 Personal Interview with Mark Warshaw. See also Kat Picson, "Chloe Chronicles: Behind the Scenes: An Interview with Web Producer Mark Warshaw," Kryptonsite.net, April 2003. Available online www.kryptonsite.com/chloechronicles.htm.

120 Qtd. in Paul Simpson, *Smallville: The Official Companion, Season 1* (London: Titan Books, 2004), 154–55.

121 For a perspective on the representation of cultural tensions in WB series of the time, see Murray Forman, "Freaks, Aliens, and the Social Other: Representations of Student Stratification in U.S. Television's First Post-Columbine Season," *The Velvet Light Trap* 53 (Spring 2004), 66–82.

122 *Smallville*'s representation of anxieties about masculinity is analyzed by Miranda Banks, "A Boy for All Planets: *Roswell, Smallville* and the Teen Male Melodrama," in Davis and Dickinson 2004, 17–28.

123 The Clark–Lex relationship is examined in relation to slash fiction in Kohnen 2008, 207–23; Stein, "'They Cavort, You Decide': Fan Discourses of Intentionality, Interpretation, Queerness

in Teen TV," *Spectator* 25 (2005), 11–22. See also Busse, "My Life is WIP on My LJ: Slashing the Slasher and the Reality of Celebrity and Internet Performances," in Hellekson and Busse 2006, 189–206; Gwenllian-Jones, "The Sex Lives of Cult Television Characters," *Screen* 43, no. 1 (2002), 79–90.

124 Friedman 1999, S1.

125 See Valerie Wee, "Selling Teen Culture: How American Multimedia Conglomerates Shaped Teen Television in the 1990s," in Davis and Dickinson 2004, 87–98; Fretts 1998.

126 Teasdale 1999.

127 Wee 2004, 87–98; Wee, "Teen Television and the WB Network," in Ross and Stein 2008, 43–60.

128 Friedman 1999.

129 BBC Press Release, "America Online Has Teamed up with Warner Bros. Television and the WB Television Network to Produce New Mini-dramas to Publicise Smallville," www.bbc.co. uk, April 29, 2003. Available online www.bbc.co.uk/cult/2003/04/29/4108.shtml.

130 TimeWarner Press Release, "America Online Offers Exclusive Access to Series of New Online Adventures Tied to the WB's Hit Series 'Smallville,'" April 14, 2004. Available online www.timewarner.com/corp/newsroom/pr/0,20812,670347,00.html.

131 Qtd. in BBC Press Release 2003.

132 TimeWarner 2004.

133 Ibid.

134 Ibid.

135 Ibid.

136 Michael Dolce, "Smallville Synergy: Five Questions with … Director of New Media for *Smallville* Mark Warshaw," *WizardUniverse.com,* October 6, 2003. Available online www. wizarduniverse.com/magazines/wizard/WZ20031006-five.cfm.

137 Ibid.

138 TimeWarner 2004.

139 Ibid.

140 Ibid.

141 Steve Fritz, "Smallville Goes Streaming With Green Arrow," newsarama.com, February 13, 2007. Available online http://forum.newsarama.com/showthread.php?t=101276.

142 T. L. Stanley, "Sprint and the CW Mobilize Supergirl for Mobisodes," *Brandweek* April 7, 2008, 8+.

143 Ibid.

144 John Consoli describes the content wrap strategy in "WB, CW, Toyota Pact for Marketing Campaign," *MediaWeek* April 19, 2007. Available online www.mediaweek.com/mw/news/ networktv/article_display.jsp?vnu_content_id=1003574108.

145 Ibid.

146 Ibid. See also Consoli, "CW Creates Content Wraps with Commercial Pods," *Mediaweek* May 22, 2006, 4; Consoli, "CW's Content Wraps May Keep DVR Viewer Interest," *Mediaweek* January 29, 2007, 4+.

147 Nat Ives, "The Media Business: Advertising—Addenda; Verizon and WB Join for Promotion," *New York Times* September 12, 2003, Section 4, New York edition.

148 Ibid.

149 Ibid.

150 Ibid. Jenkins 2006 discusses sponsorship as well in "Buying into American Idol" (58–92).

151 Ibid.

152 Qtd. in Simpson 2004, 154–55.

153 See, for example, Interview with Rob Thomas, televisionwithoutpity.com, March 9, 2005. Available online www.televisionwithoutpity.com/Shows/Veronica-Mars/Stories/The-Rob-Thomas-Interview.

154 Joss Whedon, "Joss Luvs Veronica," Whedonesque [blog], August 12, 2005. Available online www.whedoneque.com/comments/7502. Whedon appeared in the season two episode "Rat Saw God."

155 LiveJournal (2005) Veronica Mars Fashion Community. Available online www.community. livejournal.com/neptune_style; televisionwithoutpity.com; The CW Source. Available online http://weblogs.cw11.com/network/cwsource/2006/11/whats-the-deal-with-theaerie.html.

156 Jenkins 2006, 88.

157 Ibid, 81.

158 Hills 2002 and Jenkins 2006.

159 Jenkins 2006, 26–28.

160 Ibid, 53. He builds his analysis on an understanding of Pierre Lévy, *Collective Intelligence: Mankind's Emerging World in Cyberspace*, trans. Robert Bononno (Cambridge, MA: Perseus, 1997).

161 Jenkins 2006, 54.

162 Robert V. Kozinets, "E-tribalized Marketing? The Strategic Implications of Virtual Communities of Consumption," *European Management Journal* 17, no. 3 (June 1999), 254, 253.

163 See Jenkins 2006; Brooker 2001; Hills 2002; Gwenllian-Jones 2003.

164 See Stein's "Subject: 'Off-Topic: Oh My God U.S. Terrorism!' *Roswell* Fans Respond to 11 September," *European Journal of Cultural Studies* 5 (2002), 471–91; Sharon Marie Ross, *Beyond the Box: Television and the Internet* (Oxford: Blackwell, 2008); Susan Murray, "Saving Our So-Called Lives: Girl Fandom, Adolescent Subjectivity, and My So-Called Life," *Kids' Media Culture*, ed. Marsha Kinder (Durham: Duke University Press, 1999), 222; Jenkins 1992 and 2006.

165 Jenkins 2006, 79.

166 Murray 1999, 222.

167 Ibid, 223.

168 Ibid.

169 Don Slater, "Social Relationships and Identity Online and Offline," in Hill and Allen 2004, 600.

170 Judith Butler, *Bodies that Matter: On the Discursive Limits of Sex* (New York: Routledge, 1993) and *Gender Trouble* (New York: Routledge, 1990).

171 Susan Douglas, *Where the Girls Are: Growing Up Female with the Mass Media* (New York: Times, 1995).

172 Diablo Cody, "Women are from Venus, Veronica is from Mars," *City Pages* [Minneapolis/ St. Paul] October 13, 2004. Available online www.citypages.com.

173 Ibid.

174 Morley Safer, "The Look of Abercrombie & Fitch," *60 Minutes online* at cbs.com. November 24, 2004. Available online http://cbs.news.com/stories/2003/12/05/60Minutes/printable587099.shtml.

175 Thomas Frank, *The Conquest of Cool: Business Culture, Counterculture, and the Rise of Hip Consumerism* (Chicago, IL: University of Chicago Press, 1997), 32.

176 Ibid, 31.

177 Ibid, 26.

178 Ibid, 31.

179 Guerrero, "The Black Image in Protective Custody: Hollywood's Biracial Buddy Films of the Eighties," in *Black American Cinema*, ed. Manthia Diawara (New York: Routledge, 1993), 237–46.

180 Stein offers an insightful analysis of the role of a Second Life experience linked to *Gossip Girl*. See "Playing Dress-Up: Digital Fashion and Gamic Extensions of Televisual Experience in *Gossip Girl*'s Second Life," *Cinema Journal* 48, no. 3 (Spring 2009), 116–22.

181 Justin Wyatt, *High Concept: Movies and Marketing in Hollywood* (Austin, TX: University of Texas Press, 1994).

182 It is a display case for high fashion, as discussed by Ruth La Ferla, "Forget Gossip, Girl, the Buzz is All about the Clothes," *New York Times* July 8, 2008, A1.

183 Brooker 2001 talks about how *Dawson's Creek* used "signposting" to direct viewers to consume related products, especially those available at the local mall (468).

184 Aerie Tuesdays Press Release, "American Eagle Outfitters and the CW Network Announce Groundbreaking Partnership for Tuesday Nights," *PR Newswire*, September 14, 2008. See also American Eagle site, http://phx.corporate-ir.net/phoenix.zhtml?c=81256&p=irol-newsArticle&ID=905296&highlight. Sharon Edelson, "Aerie Partners with CW for Campaign," *Women's Wear Daily* September 14, 2006, 16, and "American Eagle Thinking Creative for Aerie," *Women's Wear Daily* January 12, 2007, 12.

185 Jenkins 2006, 57.

186 Ibid.

187 Jenkins 2006, 56–57.

188 For more on Alexandra Patsavas, see her own site at www.chopshoprecords.net as well as career summaries and interviews on various websites, including www.theocinsider.com/backstage/insidercommentary/archive/02.html, www.musicsupervisorguide.com/Articles.aspx?id=4, and www.ugo.com/channels/music/features/alexandrapatsavas/.

189 For a discussion of the tensions within the music industry in the era prior to the WB's emergence, see Keith Negus, *Producing Pop: Culture and Conflict in the Popular Music Industry* (London: Hodder Arnold, 1993).

190 Joanne Ostrow, "Web Shows and Entrée for Unsung Musicians," *Denver Post* February 13, 2000, H1.

191 T. L. Stanley, "Music Promos Will Flag WB's Dawson's Creek," *Brandweek* January 19, 1998, 5.

192 Ostrow 2000.

193 Ibid.

194 Eric Boehlert, "The Industry," *Rolling Stone* August 20, 1998, 31.

195 Ostrow 2000.

196 Richard Harrington, "'The O.C.': Tuned in to Bring Music to the Masses," *Washington Post* October 31, 2004, Y7.

197 Ibid.

198 Wener, "'The O.C.' Isn't Like Any O.C. He Knows," *Orange County Register* August 15, 2003, Music, 5.

199 Qtd. in Harrington 2004, Y7.

200 Ben Aslinger, "Rocking Prime Time: Gender, the WB, and Teen Culture," in Ross and Stein 2008, 78–91. Aslinger also addresses Patsavas' influence and the significance of the role of the music supervisor in television programming.

201 Wener 2003.

202 Maureen Ryan, "Sounds Good to Me: The Music of *The O.C.*," *The Watcher* [blog], *Chicago Tribune*, April 20, 2005. Available online http://featuresblogs.chicagotribune.com/entertainment_tv/the_oc/page/2/.

203 Ibid.

204 Ostrow 2000.

205 Ibid.

206 Ibid.

207 Mike Shields, "New Net, New Business," *MediaWeek* January 30, 2006, 5.

208 Roger Holland, "Down These Teen Streets a Girl Must Go," *PopMatters* May 29, 2007. Available online www.popmatters.com/pm/review/veronica-mars2.

209 Shaw, "'Gossip Girl' ' ... Psst ... Did You Hear?'" *Entertainment Weekly* November 20, 2007, 24.

2 Timeshifting, circumvention, and flow on FOX

1 For the impact DVD has on scheduling and flow, for instance, see Derek Kompare, "Publishing Flow: DVD Box Sets and the Reconception of Television," *Television and New Media* 7, no. 4 (2006), 335–60.

2 On material in between story segments see, for example, Brian Steinberg, "Newest TV Spinoffs: Situ-mercials", *Wall Street Journal* March 2, 2004, B11; T. L. Stanley, "Networks Bet Big on Mini Movies," *Advertising Age* August 9, 2004, 19.

3 On early TV and sponsorship, see Nina C. Leibman, *Living Room Lectures: The Fifties Family in Film and Television* (Austin, TX: University of Texas Press, 1995); William Boddy, *Fifties Television: The Industry and Its Critics* (Urbana, IL: University of Illinois Press, 1993); Erik Barnouw, *The Sponsor: Notes on a Modern Potentate* (New York: Oxford University Press, 1978); Lawrence R. Samuel, *Brought to You By: Postwar Television Advertising and the American Dream* (Austin, TX: University of Texas Press, 2001); Jeff Kisseloff, *The Box: An Oral History of Television 1920–1961* (New York: Penguin, 1995); Karal Ann Marling, *As Seen on TV: The Visual Culture of Everyday Life in the 1950s* (Cambridge, MA: Harvard University Press, 1994).

4 John Thornton Caldwell, *Televisuality: Style, Crisis, and Authority in American Television* (New Brunswick, NJ: Rutgers University Press, 1995), 117.

5 At the start of season one there is no breaking news crawl on the TVs as the episodes were filmed prior to 9/11. In season four the CTU, directed ineptly by Erin Driscoll, has flat screen TVs everywhere and they are sometimes tuned in to cable news, but they follow the old broadcast style of having blurry or fake identifiers. A TV in LA's Union Station, however, is clearly tuned to FOX News. By season six there is a definite brand distinction with the TVs inside CTU always tuned to FOX News and always in the background of shots.

6 Daniel M. Kimmel, *The Fourth Network: How FOX Broke the Rules and Reinvented Television* (Chicago, IL: Ivan R. Dee, 2004); Ben Bagdikian, *The Media Monopoly* (Boston, MA: Beacon Press, 1983); Auletta 1991.

7 Lowry's review appeared in *Variety* on January 11, 2006. Available online www.variety.com/review/VE1117929228.html?categoryId=32& cs = 1.

8 On FX repurposing, see "A Strong Start for '24' on FOX," *The New York Times* October 31, 2002, B1. FX also broadcast a Labor Day marathon—24 episodes for 24 hours—the month before *24* returned for season two. See "Re-Live the Longest Day of Jack Bauer's Life," *Market Wire*, August 2002. Available at bnet:the gotoplacefor management. In 2004 Big FOX added to its bottom line what would become three successful FX dramas, *The Shield*, *NipTuck*, and *Rescue Me*, which each premiered in nontraditional months, respectively, March, June, and July. This trio exemplifies the way that Big FOX challenged premium cable dominance through its short-run basic cable series with thirteen- to sixteen-episode seasons.

9 The technological line is also blurred between the phone as a communication and an entertainment device. Sponsors are also getting into the act. *24* sponsor Unilever, for example, created Degree deodorant commercials for Jack Bauer-level, ticking-clock scenario stress protection. By season six Unilever was producing commercial minisodes to crosspromote *24* and Degree even more effectively. For more on these new experiments in branded entertainment, see Steinberg, March 2, 2004; T. L. Stanley, August 9, 2004; Stuart Elliot, "A Sponsor and Its Show, Intertwined," *The New York Times* April 17, 2006, C8; David Hattenbach, "Beyond Integration: How to Make the Whole Brand Better Than its Parts," *Adweek* August 11, 2008, 13.

10 Soon others followed FOX's lead as David Frankel makes clear in, "Warner Spells Things Out at Global Summit: Challenges, Opportunities, Strategies Outlined as Video, TV, and Theatrical Converge," *Video Business Magazine* October 17, 2003. Gary Arnold, Best Buy Senior VP for Entertainment, says of Warner Brothers, which produces *The O.C.* for FOX and *Nip/Tuck* for FX, "They're trying to tie the DVD in to consumer excitement for the new TV Season." See also Josef Adalian, "FOX Out Front with *24* DVD," *Variety* July 15,

2002, 1; David Bianculli, "TV Lovers Want Their DVD," *New York Daily News* April 23, 2002, 35.

11 On changes to industry practices, see Caldwell, *Production Cultures* (Durham, NC: Duke University Press, 2008), in which he builds on many of his groundbreaking ideas from *Televisuality* (1995). See also Amanda Lotz, *The Television Will Be Revolutionized* (New York: New York University Press, 2007) and the essays in Lynn Spigel and Jan Olsson's *Television After TV: Essays on a Medium in Transition* (Durham, NC: Duke University Press, 2004).

12 Kellner, "September 11, the Media, and War Fever," *Television and New Media* 3, no. 2 (May 2002), 143.

13 Torture was outlawed in 1949 by the codes of the Geneva Convention.

14 Rebecca Dana, "Reinventing '24': Jack Bauer's Newest Nemesis Isn't a Terrorist—It's Public Opinion," *Wall Street Journal,* February 2, 2008. Available online http://online.wsj.com/public/article_print/SB120189888101136151.html.

15 Benedict Anderson, *Imagined Communities* (London: Verso, 1991); Homi K. Bhabha, "DissemiNation: Time, Narrative, and the Margins of the Modern," in *Nation and Narration*, ed. Bhabha (London: Routledge, 1991), 291–322; Lauren Berlant, *The Queen of America Goes to Washington City: Essays on Sex and Citizenship* (Durham, NC: Duke University Press, 1997) and *The Anatomy of National Fantasy: Hawthorne, Utopia, and Everyday Life* (Chicago, IL: University of Chicago, 1984).

16 Jamie Kellner, *Cable World Magazine*, April 29, 2002; Henry Jenkins, "Treating Viewers as Criminals," technologyreview.com, July 3, 2002.

17 Adalian, "Primetime Pickle," *Daily Variety* January 2, 2004, 1, qtd. Sandy Grushow, FOX Entertainment Group, as saying at the ending of the fall 2003 television season: "Anyone who says or believes that the network television business isn't under siege has their head firmly stuck in the sand." The anxieties continued well beyond 2001. See, for example, Bill Carter, "As Season Begins, Networks Struggle in Cable's Shadow," *New York Times* September 19, 2004, 1; Rob Owen, "The World of TV is in a State of Flux," *Pittsburgh Post-Gazette* January 22, 2004, B1; Anthony Boianco, et al., "The Vanishing Mass Market: New Technology. Product Proliferation. Fragmented Media. Get Ready: It's a Whole New World," *Business Week* July 12, 2004, 18.

18 Megan Mullen, *Television in the Multichannel Age* (Oxford: Blackwell, 2007), 150–71, 209–19; Lotz 2007, 85–102; Thomas Streeter, *Selling the Air: A Critique of the Policy of Commercial Broadcasting in the United States* (Chicago, IL: University of Chicago Press, 1996).

19 For a discussion of quality as a brand strategy on HBO, see Jaramillo 2002, 59–75.

20 Hills 2004, 54–67; David Lavery writes about how *24* is neither. "24: Jumping the Shark Every Minute," *FlowTV* September 8, 2006. Available online www.flowtv.org.

21 Qtd. in Carter, "For Fox TV, an Unusually Grim Autumn," *New York Times* November 20, 2006, C1.

22 MarketWire 2002.

23 MarketWire 2002.

24 Paul Woolf, "'So What Are You Saying? An Oil Consortium's Behind the Nuke?': *24*, Programme Sponsorship, SUVs and the 'War on Terror,'" in *Reading 24: TV Against the Clock,* ed. Steven Peacock (London: I.B. Tauris, 2007), 73–84; Karl Greenberg, "Inside Ford's Branded Entertainment Engine," *MediaPost News* October 16, 2006. Available online www.mediapost.com/publications/index.cfm?fa=Articles.showArticle&art_aid=49594; Claire Cozens, "24 Sponsorship Deal Spells Trouble for BBC," *The Guardian* [U.K.] October 29, 2002. Available online www.guardian.co.uk/media/2002/oct/29/bbc.advertising?commentpage=1; Marc Graser, "For Spies Opportunity with Bond, TV Sleuths," *Variety* November 4–10, 2002, 7.

25 Joanna Weiss, "From 'Starsky & Hutch' to 'Lost,' TV Moving Online," *Boston Globe* March 23, 2008, A1.

26 David Kronke, "Serial Thrillers: Now That Viewers Have Found 'Lost' There are Lots More Shows on the Way," *Toledo Blade* June 19, 2005, Arts 29, 30.

27 Qtd. in Kronke 2005.

28 Ibid.

29 This review by Doc Ezra appeared on needcoffeedotcom, a site that was awarded a 2006 Bloggie [for Best Kept-Secret Weblog], and can be found at www.needcoffee.com/html/dvd/24s1.htm.

30 Steven Horn, "24:1" [review], IGN Movies, September 17, 2002. Available online http://dvd.ign.com/articles/371/371265p1.html.

31 This season 3 DVD review by HTQ4 11/30/05 appeared on needcoffeedotcom and can be accessed at www.needcoffee.com/2005/11/30/24-season-3-dvd-review/.

32 Ibid.

33 Ibid.

34 From a KQEK review by Mark R. Hasan. Available online www.kqek.com/dvd_reviews/t2u/2192_24Season1.htm.

35 David Lambert, "*24*'s TV-on-DVD Success Leads to New DVD Concepts," October 22, 2003. Available online www.tvshowsondvd.com/news/24/764.

36 Qtd. in Kronke 2005.

37 Ibid.

38 Horn 2002.

39 DVD review March 13, 2007.

40 Goodman, "Jack's Back to Fight Terrorists Another Day in '24'—Sans Kim," *San Francisco Chronicle* January 7, 2005. Available online www.sfgate.com/cgi-bin/article.cgi?f=/c/a/2005/01/07/DDGIBALKFJ1.DTL.

41 Ibid.

42 Gilbert, "'24' Works Overtime to Open Season," *Boston Globe* January 14, 2006. Available online www.boston.com/ae/tv/articles/2006/01/14/24_works_overtime_to_open_season/.

43 Goodman, "Best Check Your Sanity at the Couch. '24' Takes 10 Minutes to Go Nuts," *San Francisco Chronicle* January 13, 2006. Available online http://articles.sfgate.com/2006-01-13/entertainment/17278525_1_polar-bear-moment-parallel-universe-hours.

44 Weiss 2008.

45 Ibid.

46 Ibid.

47 A scan of the shows for which message boards are available on the mega fan message board site TelevisionWithoutPity confirms how many cancelled shows still have active message boards, with all the posts still available from when the show was still running.

48 Brooker, "Living on Dawson's Creek: Teen Viewers, Cultural Convergence, and Television Overflow," *International Journal of Cultural Studies* 4, vol. 4 (2001), 457.

49 Ibid.

50 See also Jenkins, "Interactive Audiences?" in Harries 2002, 157–70.

51 Chapter one of this study considers how message boards become archives that register both immediate and delayed response to a program and enable it to continue not only after the on-air broadcast has ended, but long after the program has been cancelled. The information remains archived so that someone who is not actually checking the message boards while she watches and, in fact, is checking them long after the live discussion took place, can still find records of immediate fan response and measure it against other moments of fan response throughout the series.

52 Allen, "Multi-Panelled Narrative in *24*," in Peacock 2007, 36.

53 Rob White, "Against the Clock," *Sight and Sound* 12, no. 7 (July 2002), 7.

54 Jermyn, "Reasons to Split Up: Interactivity, Realism, and the Multiple Screen Image in *24*," in Peacock 2007, 57.

55 Chamberlin and Ruston, "*24* and Twenty-First Century Quality Television," in Peacock 2007, 17.

56 Ibid, 18.

57 Caldwell 1995, 20.

58 Peacock, "*24* and New Directions in Televisuality," in Peacock 2007, 18.

59 Lawson, "24, Which Returns this Weekend Brilliantly Broke the Rules of TV Drama by Emphasizing Structure Over Content. But Can the Producers Make the Gimmick Work Twice?" *Guardian* [U.K.] February 10, 2003. Available online www.guardian.co.uk/media/2003/feb/10/broadcasting.tvandradio1.

60 Allen 2007.

61 Chamberlain and Ruston 2007, 19.

62 See Woolf 2007, 73–84.

63 An episode of *Desperate Housewives* included a Buick LaCrosse featured in a car show presentation when one of the characters gets a job as a Buick spokesmodel. 2007 episodes of FX's *The Riches* and the pilot of NBC's *Quarterlife* featured car commercials smoothly integrated as part of their story arcs. USA's *Burn Notice* has countless lingering shots of a Cadillac, particularly of the logo, as the characters constantly drive the car down Miami streets and highways. See Greenberg, October 16, 2006.

64 Ibid.

65 Peacock 2007, 29.

66 Owen, "On the Set at '24': It's Not What It Seems," Scripps News Service April 13, 2007. Available online www.scrippsnews.com/node/21224.

67 Paul Miller, "Cisco Tele Presence," engadet.com October 2006. See also cisco.com for overview of Tele Presence system.

68 See Alan Nadel, *Containment Culture: American Narratives, Postmodernism, and the Atomic Age* (Durham, NC: Duke University Press, 1995) for the way a similar argument was made in the 1950s when Americans felt threatened by the launch of Sputnik. See also Susan Douglas, *Where the Girls Are: Growing Up Female with the Mass Media* (New York: Times, 1995).

69 Caldwell 1995, 117.

70 Ibid.

71 Allen 2007, 36.

72 Ibid.

73 Chamberlain and Ruston 2007, 17.

74 Ibid.

75 It was also the dominance of FOX in sports that led to the compressed time frame approach for *24*. Viewers were getting frustrated by the number of times *24* was preempted or put on hiatus because of sporting events. To avoid those interruptions, especially from the World's Series, FOX came up with the January uninterrupted season compressed winter/spring schedule.

76 Caldwell 1995, 13.

77 Ibid.

78 Ibid, 20.

79 Owen 2007.

80 Klinger, *Beyond the Multiplex: Cinema, New Technologies, and the Home* (Berkeley, CA: University of California Press, 2006), 72.

81 Kompare 2006, 340

82 Ibid, 339.

83 Jonathan Gray, "Television Pre-views and the Meaning of Hype," *International Journal of Cultural Studies* 11, no. 1 (March 2008), 33–49 discusses the way a TV series exists inside a pre-release flow of hype that shapes the text's meaning on other platforms before it ever exists as an on-air show.

84 24: Jolt gum is also available.

85 Jeff Gomez, a transmedia storyteller, distinguishes between transmedia storytelling and branded entertainment. See his various posts and interviews on his blog for Starlight Runner Entertainment. Available online http://starlightrunner.com/. For a discussion of transmedia storytelling see Jenkins' *Convergence Culture* (New York: New York University Press, 2006). He also offers multiple posts on *Confessions of an Aca-Fan: The Official Blog of Henry Jenkins*. See "Transmedia Storytelling 101," March 22, 2007. Available online www.henryjenkins.org/2007/03/transmedia_storytelling_101.html.

86 Klinger 2006, 72.

87 Ibid.

88 Ibid, 74.

89 Ibid, 72–73, 89.

90 Ibid, 73.

91 Ibid.

92 For a consideration of the roots of the "fair and balanced" brand promise, see Ken Auletta, "VOX FOX: How Roger Ailes and FOX News are Changing Cable News," *The New Yorker*, May 26, 2003, 58+. Robert Greenwald skewers FOX and its brand promise in his 2004 documentary *Outfoxed: Rupert Murdoch's War on Journalism*. As one former producer at FOX says, "There's no sense of integrity of having a line that can't be crossed." Al Franken satirizes the brand promise in *Lies and the Lying Liars Who Tell Them: A Fair and Balanced Look at the Right* (New York: Plume, 2004).

93 Erica Iacono, "Fox News Sets the Tone in Cable News Race," *PR Week* October 2, 2006. Available online www.brandrepublic.com/InDepth/Analysis/594889/Fox-News-sets-tone-cable-news-race/?DCMP=ILC-SEARCH.

94 Folkenflik, qtd. in Ibid.

95 Of course, the flag is also an unstable signifier as it might indicate that his position comes with a political agenda. In 2001, as Director, Division of Bacterial and Mycotic Diseases and a representative of the CDC, Cohen testified before the House Committee on Government Reform on the division's preparedness for bioterrorism. Available online www.hhs.gov/asl/testify/ t011030.html. In 2004, after the featurette was filmed, Cohen was promoted to Director, Coordinating Center for Infectious Diseases (CDIC), an organization with a $4 billion budget and 3000 staff members across the world.

96 Jim Rutenberg, "Fox Portrays a War of Good and Evil," *New York Times* December 3, 2001, C5, Late edition.

97 Waisbord, "Journalism, Risk, and Patriotism," in *Journalism after September 11*, ed. Barbie Zelizer and Stuart Allen (New York: Routledge, 2002), 208.

98 Jane Mayer, "Whatever it Takes; The Politics of the Man Behind '24'," *New Yorker*, February 19, 2007. Available online www.newyorker.com/reporting/2007/02/19/070219fa_fact_mayer.

99 On Bush's foreign policy and both its consistency and inconsistency with the foreign policy of earlier administrations, see Joseph S. Nye, Jr., *Soft Power: The Means to Success in World Politics* (New York: Public Affairs/Perseus, 2004); Walter Russell Mead, *Power, Terror, Peace, and War: America's Grand Strategy in a World at Risk* (New York: Knopf, 2004); Andrew J. Bacevich, *American Empire: The Realities and Consequences of U.S. Diplomacy* (Cambridge, MA: Harvard University Press, 2002).

100 Meehan, *Why Television is Not Our Fault: Television Programming, Viewers, and Who's Really in Control* (Lanham, MD: Rowman and Littlefield, 2005), 3–4.

101 www.cdcfoundation.org/cdc/eis.aspx.

102 Lewis, "Television and Public Opinion," in *A Companion to Television*, ed. Janet Wasko (Malden, MA: Blackwell, 2005), 445.

103 Ibid.

104 Meehan 2005, 67

105 Waisbord 2002, 209.

106 Waisbord 2005, 213.
107 Ibid.
108 Ibid, 209.
109 Meehan 2005, 3.
110 Waisbord 2005, 214. As of this writing, the fall 2001 anthrax attacks, which killed four people and infected seventeen others, have been traced to an academic researcher working for a government biodefense lab. He was reported to have committed suicide on August 1, 2008. A virologist who was labeled a person of interest by the FBI and the press sued and the cases were settled in his favor. Scott Shane, "Anthrax Evidence Called Mostly Circumstantial," *The New York Times* August 4, 2008. Available online www.nytimes.com/2008/08/04/us/04anthrax.html?_r=4&hp=&adxnnl=1&oref=slogin&adxnnlx=1217873109-RUiu5/r4VUllICqvE8ikueA&oref=slogin&oref=slogin.
111 Lewis 2005, 446.
112 Presidents have often had close relationships with Hollywood. Alessandra Stanley notes, "Officials in the Clinton Administration rubbed elbows with the cast of 'The West Wing'; his former press secretary Dee Dee Meyers worked as a consultant to the series." Both share what Stanley calls "colorful" "Oval Office deliberations," but what worries some about the power of *24* is that its scenarios are being used to justify policy decisions in the administration's War on Terror. See Stanley, "Bombers Strike, and America is in Turmoil. It's Just Another Day for Jack Bauer," *New York Times* January 12, 2007. Available online www.nytimes.com/2007/01/12/arts/television/12twen.html.
113 The short-lived *The Half Hour News Hour* premiered on FOX News on February 19, 2007.
114 See Judith Mayne, *Cinema and Spectatorship* (London: Routledge, 1993); Jackie Byers, *All That Heaven Allows: Re-Reading Gender in 1950s Melodrama* (Chapel Hill, NC: University of North Carolina Press, 1991); Laura Mulvey and Jon Halliday, eds. *Douglas Sirk* (Edinburgh: Edinburgh Film Festival, 1972); *Sirk on Sirk: Interviews with Jon Halliday* (New York: Viking Press, 1972); Laura Mulvey, "Notes on Sirk and Melodrama," *Movie* 24 (Winter 1977–78); E. Ann Kaplan, *Motherhood and Representation: The Mother in Popular Culture and Melodrama* (New York: Routledge, 1992); Lucy Fischer, "Three-Way Mirror: Imitation of Life," in *Imitation of Life: Douglas Sirk*, Director, ed. Lucy Fischer (New Brunswick, NJ: Rutgers University Press, 1991), 3–28; Jeremy Butler, "*Imitation of Life*: Style and the Domestic Melodrama," *Jump Cut* 32 (April 1987), 225–28; Marina Heung, "What's the Matter with Sarah Jane," *Cinema Journal* 26, no. 3 (Spring 1987), 21–43; Christine Gledhill, "Introduction—The Melodramatic Field: An Investigation," in *Home is Where the Heart is: Studies in Melodrama and the Women's Film*, ed. Gledhill (London: British Film Institute, 1987).
115 Susan Jeffords, *Hard Bodies; Hollywood Masculinity in the Reagan Era* (New Brunswick, NJ: Rutgers University Press, 1994); Michael Rogin, "'Make My Day': Spectacle as Amnesia in Imperial Politics," *Representations* 29 (Winter 1990), 99–124.
116 For a discussion of national narratives and motivated forgetting, see Berlant 1997 and 1984.
117 Mayer, February 19, 2007.
118 For the blurred lines of documentary and entertainment, see Stella Bruzzi, "Docusoaps," in *The Television Genre Book*, ed. Glen Creeber (London: BFI, 2001), 132–34 and *New Documentary: A Critical Introduction* (London: Routledge, 2000). See also Bill Nichols, *Blurred Boundaries: Questions of Meaning in Contemporary Culture* (Bloomington, IN: Indiana University Press, 1994), *Introduction to Documentary* (Bloomington, IN: Indiana University Press, 2001), and *Representing Reality* (Bloomington, IN: Indiana University Press, 1991).
119 On NBC's *The Biggest Loser* obesity does become dramatic in a beat-the-clock game show featuring ticking clocks and the rapidly changing numbers on digital scales. NBC followed FOX'S example and ran the show in uninterrupted format over consecutive weeks.
120 Mayer, February 19, 2007.
121 Ibid.
122 Ibid.

123 Dana, February 2, 2008.

124 Transcript from January 12, 2007, *Charlie Rose* Interview. PBS-TV.

125 Available online http://blogs.herald.com/dave_barrys_blog.html.

126 Meehan 2005, 2.

127 Ibid.

128 Lacono, October 2, 2006.

129 Michael Learnmonth, "Satire Hands a Right," *Variety* variety.com, November 20, 2006. Available online www.variety.com/article/VR1117954244.html?cs=1&s=h&p=0.

130 For an argument about the impact of declining presidential approval ratings on the popularity of *24*, see Dana, February 2, 2008. Dave Barry and the like attribute it to an overuse of the wooden dialogue generator. Dana says that showrunner Howard Gordon "wasn't prepared for how strong the associations had grown between '24' and the growing political maelstrom."

131 Eric Alterman notes in *What Liberal Media? The Truth about Bias and the News* (New York: Perseus Books, 2003) that most news content, even that from the supposedly liberal media, has become similarly sensationalized.

132 Jermyn 2007, 51.

133 Benjamin Svetkey, "American Idle," *Entertainment Weekly* ew.com, March 31, 2003. Available online www.ew.com/ew/article/0,438738,00.html.

134 Jermyn 2007, 52.

135 Ibid, 53.

136 John Gibson, FOX News' *The Big Story*, January 16, 2007.

137 Cal Thomas, "Aquarius Sunset," TownHall.com: Where Your Opinion Counts. January 30, 2007. www.towanhall.com. This blog site was originally established by The Heritage Foundation. Thomas is a panelist on FOX News Watch, a show that critiques the media. He was Vice president of the Moral Majority from 1980 to 1985. He has also partnered with Bob Beckel, a liberal with dubious liberal credentials, to pen some "fair and balanced accounts" of contemporary politics and host talk show debates.

138 *The O'Reilly Factor*, FOX News, September 13, 2006.

139 Stuart Herrington, "Sunday Forum: Two Problems with Torture," *Pittsburgh Post-Gazette*, October 21, 2007. Available online www.post.gazette.com/pg/07294/826876–35.stm.

140 Mayer, February 19, 2007. See also Amy Goodman, "Interview with Tony Lagouranis: Former U.S. Army Interrogator Describes the Harsh Techniques He Used in Iraq, Detainee Abuse by Marines and Navy Seals and Why 'Torture is the Worst Possible Thing We Could Do,'" DemocracyNow.org., November 15, 2005. Available online www.democracynow.org/2005/11/15/former_u_s_army_interrogator_describes.

141 Herrington 2007.

142 Ibid.

143 Slavoj Zizek, "The Message of the TV Series, That Torturers Can Retain Their Human Dignity If the Cause is Right, is a Profound Lie," *The Guardian* [U.K.] January 10, 2006. Available online www.guardian.co.uk/media/2006/jan/10/usnews.comment.

144 Mayer, February 19, 2007.

145 Ibid.

146 Irvine, "Why Torture Doesn't Work," November 22, 2005. Available online www.alternet.org/rights/28585/.

147 Herrington 2007.

148 Irvine, "Why Torture Doesn't Work," November 22, 2005. See the blog post on Irvine's comments, www.noquarterusa.net/blog/2007/11/04/torture-our-us-military-does-us-proud/. Also, see video www.humanrightsfirst.org/us_law/etn/elect08/media/.

149 The argument about the torturer's moral depravity is also made by Zizek, January 10, 2006.

150 Stanley, January 12, 2007.

151 Ibid.
152 Adam Green, "Normalizing Torture on '24'," *New York Times* May 22, 2005. Available online www.nytimes.com/2005/05/22/arts/television/22gree.html. See also, "Torture's Wider Use Brings New Concerns," *All Things Considered*, National Public Radio, March 13, 2007. Available online www.npr.org/templates/story/story.php?storyId=8286003.
153 Stanley, January 12, 2007.
154 Mayer, February 19, 2007.
155 Ibid.
156 Ibid.
157 On June 26, 1987 the following United Nations General Assembly Resolution took effect: Convention Against Torture and Other Cruel, Inhuman or Degrading Treatment or Punishment, G.A. res. 39/46, [annex. 39 U.N. GAOR Supp (No. 51) at 197, U.N. Doc. A/39/51 (1984)]. The following is quite clear: Article 2: No Exceptional Circumstances Warranting Torture; Article 4: Acts of Torture Are Criminal Offenses. It was ratified by the U.S. Senate in 1994.
158 Jon Wiener, "'24': Torture on TV," *The Nation* January 15, 2007. Available online www.the nation.com/blogs/notion/157437.
159 Qtd. in Colin Freeze, "What Would Jack Bauer Do?" *Globe and Mail* [Ontario] June 16, 2007, A9.
160 Herrington 2007.
161 Herrington 2007.
162 Fuchs, "24 Season Four: Body Snatchers," *PopMatters* December 16, 2005. Available online www.popmatters.com/tv/reviews/t/24-season-4-dvd.shtml.
163 Gilbert, January 14, 2006.
164 Elaine Scarry, "Citizenship in Emergency: Can Democracy Protect Us against Terrorism," *Boston Review* October/November 2002. http://bostonreview.net/BR27.5/scarry.html.
165 Mayer, February 19, 2007.
166 Ibid.
167 Ibid.
168 Ibid.
169 Ibid.
170 Herrington 2007.
171 Mayer, February 19, 2007.
172 Herrington 2007.
173 Jeff Beck, *CNN Headline News*, September 7, 2006.
174 The argument about the torturer's moral depravity is also made by Zizek 2006.
175 Douglas discusses a similar kind of composite character in relation to female sitcom stars since the 1960s in *Where the Girls Are* (1995).
176 For a perspective on the United States' role in peacekeeping and its representation of its own benevolent motivations in its international interventions, see Samantha Power, *A Problem from Hell: America in the Age of Genocide* (New York: Basic Books, 2002); Sherene Razack, *Dark Threats, White Knights: The Somalia Affair, Peacekeeping, and the New Imperialism* (Toronto: University of Toronto Press, 2004); Michael Ignatieff, "The Burden," *New York Times Magazine* January 5, 2003, 23; Ignatieff, "Why Are We in Iraq? (And Liberia? And Afghanistan?)," *New York Times Magazine* September 7, 2003, 38+. Many of these concerns had been anticipated by the authors and editors of *Cultures of United States Imperialism*, ed. Amy Kaplan and Donald Pease (Durham, NC: Duke University Press, 1994). See also Michael Hardt and Antonio Negri, *Empire* (New York: Harvard University Press, 2001). Cynthia Enloe points out the inconsistencies in the actions of American chivalric rescuers in *Bananas, Beaches, and Bases: Making Feminist Sense of International Politics* (Berkeley, CA: University of California Press, 1990), especially 145–56, and *The Morning After: Sexual Politics at the End of the Cold War* (Berkeley, CA: University of California Press, 1993).

177 For a variation of this heroic type, see James C. Collins and Jerry I. Porras, *Built to Last: Successful Habits of Visionary Companies* (New York: Harper Business, 1994), 112. Collins and Porras discuss a composite capitalist type, a visionary businessman who displays "both high ideals and pragmatic self-interest." The most successful visionary businessmen remain faithful to "core values" and can convey a core mission, "a sense of purpose beyond making money" (48). Collins and Porras theorize that all companies are profit-making enterprises, but a successful visionary company "explicitly speaks to ideals beyond profit and then emphasizes the importance of profit within the context of those ideals" (58).

178 See also Richard Slotkin, *Gunfighter Nation: The Myth of the Frontier in Twentieth-Century America* (New York: Athenaeum, 1992).

179 See Mayer, February 19, 2007; Dana, February 2, 2008.

180 In season four terrorist Dina Araz is given such a position as well. Her representation is ambivalent as she is both a cold-blooded murderer and a woman who is single-mindedly performing her duty and doing so with an extreme amount of dignity and grandeur. The representation seems to leave open a space for liberal viewers to see in her confirmation of Richard Heller's assertion that the War on Terror has created enemies of people who would have not otherwise been hostile to the United States. Upon closer examination the season really tilted much more to the right and reinforces the idea that many Muslim Americans are indeed sleeper cells and that liberal Americans should be careful in befriending them because they could end up aiding the terrorists or being killed by them, which is what happens on *24*.

181 February 26, 2007 post to Dave Barry's live blog for that evening's episode. Available online http:/blogs.herald.com/dave_barrys_blog/2007/02/24_4.html.

182 Dana, February 2, 2008.

183 Ibid.

184 Transcript from January 12, 2007, *Charlie Rose* Interview; also quoted in Noel Sheppard, "Kiefer Sutherland Discusses the Politics of '24' and His Own Socialist Leanings," *NewsBusters Exposing and Combating Liberal Media* January 26, 2007. Available online www.newsbusters.org.

185 In the star TV writer/producer era of Joss Whedon and J.J. Abrams, among others, there is a resurgence in auteurism. See Caldwell 2008.

186 Bob Andelman, Interview with David Fury, April 27, 2007. Available online www.mrmedia.com/2007/ … /fridays_with_mr_media_david_fury24.html.

187 Dana, February 2, 2008.

188 *Time* January 14, 2007. *Newsweek* January 12, 2007. Keith Olbermann, January 16, 2007.

189 Andelman 2007.

190 Ibid.

191 See Steve Silver, "*24*: Liberal or Conservative," *The New SteveSilver.net*. March 1, 2005. Available online www.steversilvernet/mt/archives/005702.html.

192 Andelman 2007.

3 Placeshifting, schedule-shifting, and the long-arc serial on ABC

1 Seth Schiesel offers an account of "location free TV," in "I Want My Moscow TV," *New York Times*, December 2, 2004, G1. Liane Cassavoy looks at Slingbox and other devices that enable a viewer to watch a home TV from any internet-connected computer. "First Look: Battle of the TV Place-Shifting Devices," *PC World*, December 2, 2006. Available online www.pcworld.com/article/128053/first_look_battle_of_the_tv_placeshifting_devices.html.

2 Bill Carter, "Will This Machine Change Television?" *New York Times*, July 5, 1999, C1; Paul Bond, "Weapon of Choice," *Hollywood Reporter*, March 19–25, 2002, 10+; "PVRs or DVRs: The Only Certainty is Growth," *Hollywood Reporter*, August 23–25, 2002, 8+; John Heinzel, "Will the PVR Fast-forward the TV Commercial's Demise," *Globe and Mail* [Ottowa]

December 13, 2002, B10; Steve McClellan, "Nilesen Wants to Know about PVRs," *Broadcasting & Cable* December 9, 2002, 22; Joseph Ostrow, "PVRs a Real Fear Factor for TV's Ad Community," *Electronic Media* September 16, 2002, 9+; Patti Summerfield, "PVRs Won't Kill the TV Ad," *Strategy* 1, vol. 2 (2002, October 21), 1; Louis Chunovic, "The PVR Revolution: Mere Myth or Nightmare to Come?" *Electronic Media* November 18, 2002, 8+.

3 The rise of HBO's original programming is covered in the introduction.

4 For more on the use of the professed literary quality of series positioned as a marketing hook, see Mark Jancovich and James Lyons, eds., *Quality Popular Television* (London: BFI, 2003), 2. See also Jason Jacobs "Issues of Judgment and Value in Television Studies," *International Journal of Cultural Studies* 4.4 (2001), 427–47.

5 Paul Rixon, "The Changing Face of American Television Programmes on British Screens," in Jancovich and Lyons 2003, 57–58. There are many descriptions of "quality TV" and critiques of the unexamined bourgeois value judgments implied by the many ways "quality" is defined and the uses to which the term has been put within the analysis of television programming. Rixon's definition is useful as it captures the international television buyer's perspective on American series as marketable commodities.

6 The assumption that there is a distinction between "quality TV" viewers and everyone else has been central to the long-standing competition between NBC and CBS. To differentiate itself in the marketplace, NBC executives claim its programming might be lower rated, but it is of higher quality than those series with which CBS is posting top ratings numbers. Responding recently to this NBC assertion, one CBS executive quipped that no matter how far at the bottom of the rankings NBC series fall, its executives make claims about its superiority.

7 For more on HBO's "quality" brand claim, see Dana Polan's "Cable Watching: HBO, *The Sopranos*, and Discourses of Distinction," in *Cable Visions: Television Beyond Broadcasting*, ed. Sara Banet-Weiser, Cynthia Chris, and Anthony Freitas (New York: New York University Press, 2007), 261–83; Mark C. Rogers, Michael Epstein, and Jimmie L. Reeves, "*The Sopranos* as HBO Brand Equity: The Arts and Commerce in the Age of Digital Reproduction," in *This Thing of Ours: Investigating The Sopranos*, ed. David Lavery (New York: Columbia University Press, 2002), 42–57; Deborah L. Jaramillo, "The Family Racket: AOL Time Warner, HBO, and *The Sopranos*, and the Construction of a Quality Brand," *Journal of Communication Studies* 26, no. 1 (2002), 59–75; Avi Santo, "Para-television and Discourses of Distinction: The Culture of Production at HBO," in Leverette, Ott, and Buckley 2008, 19–45; Marc Leverette, Brian L. Ott, and Cara Louise Buckley, eds. *It's Not TV: Watching HBO in the Post-television Era* (New York: Routledge, 2008).

8 For a discussion of the cultural values associated with different taste cultures, see Pierre Bourdieu, *Distinction: A Social Critique of the Judgment of Taste* (London: Routledge, 1984).

9 The story is recounted in Emily Nussbaum, "It's Not HBO. It's TV," *New York*, nymag.com, May 21, 2005. Available online http://nymag.com/metro/arts/tv/9190. Of course, Fontana reveled in the ways that HBO was not broadcast TV by producing as graphic content as he could imagine. See Bruce Fretts, "Nasty As He Wanna Be," *Entertainment Weekly*, ew.com, July 11, 1997. Available online www.ew.com/ew/article/0,288583,00.html; Andy Meisler, "Not Even Trying to Appeal to the Masses," *New York Times*, October 4, 1998, 2.45.

10 Alessandra Stanley addresses both the HBO exception and the fact that television in 2007 is no longer associated with "a sea of mediocrity," but instead with "pools and eddies of excellence." "You Are What You Watch," *New York Times*, September 23, 2007, 2.1.

11 Rick Kissell, "ABC, Eye Have Quite Some Night," *Variety*, variety.com, September 25, 2004. Available online www.variety.com/article/VR1117918069.html?categoryid=14&cs=1. See also Allison Romano, "ABC Happily 'Lost' and 'Desperate'," *Broadcasting & Cable* November 22, 2004, 8; Gary Levin, "ABC Has Four of Ten Top Shows," *USA Today* October 7, 2004, D4.

12 Since this chapter was originally written, Roberta Pearson's anthology *Reading Lost: Perspectives on a Hit Television Show* (London: I.B. Tauris, 2009) was published. Among its excellent essays, two are especially relevant to the discussion in this chapter, Derek Johnson's chapter on The Lost Experience ARG, and Paul Grainge's on the British scheduling of the series. Johnson, "The Fictional Institutions of Lost: World Building, Reality and the Economic Possibilities of Narrative Divergence," in Pearson 2009, 27–49; Grainge, "Lost Logos: Channel 4 and the Branding of American Event Television," in Pearson 2009, 119–38.

13 Eric Schmuckler and Marc Berman, "Serial Thrillers," *Mediaweek*, May 29, 2006, SR 14.

14 Schmuckler and Berman 2006, SR 14.

15 Michael Schneider, "NBC Opts to Air 'Day One' as a Miniseries: Move is Likely a Cost-cutting Measure," *Variety*, variety.com October 1, 2009. Available online www.variety.com/article/VR1118009437.html?categoryid=1236& cs = 1.

16 See chapter two on FOX.

17 Thomas K. Arnold, "'Lost' Makes Trek to No. 1 in DVD Sales," *The Hollywood Reporter*, September 14, 2006, 18.

18 Mark Cotta Vaz, *Alias Declassified: The Official Companion* (New York: Bantam/Random House, 2002), 17.

19 Ibid, 19.

20 Ibid, 19.

21 For a discussion of this print advertisement and others in relation to gender politics, see David Roger Coon, "One Step Forward and Two Steps Back: the Selling of *Charlie's Angels* and *Alias*," *Journal of Popular Film and Television* 33, no. 4 (Spring 2005), 2–11. For a variety of intriguing essays on the series, see Stacey Abbott and Simon Brown, eds. *Investigating Alias: Secrets and Spies* (London: I.B. Tauris, 2007). Sydney is representative of the composite television heroine who, in Susan Douglas' paradigm, must balance her power with sexiness in order to be deemed an acceptable character for mainstream U.S. TV. Her character like many others exploits "the tension between feminism and antifeminism" that Douglas says characterizes most of U.S. television's female heroes. *Where the Girls Are: Growing Up Female with the Mass Media* (New York: Times, 1995), 213.

22 Vaz 2002, 20.

23 Dan Snierson, "Secrets & Spies," *Entertainment Weekly*, March 8, 2002, 24+. See also Robert Levine, "Cracking the Code of 'Alias'," *New York Times*, nytimes.com, April 24, 2005. Available online www.nytimes.com/2004/04/25/arts/television-cracking-the-code-of-alias.html?; Snierson, "The Upside-Down Season", *Entertainment Weekly*, May 31, 2001, 64+.

24 Snierson 2002.

25 ABC would have to wait for *Grey's Anatomy*, another series whose premiere season focused on the dysfunctional family business dynamic, in 2005 and 2006 to generate a mainstream hit that also attracted the WB demographic to ABC.

26 Jeff Jensen, "Going … Going … Going … Gone: The Highs and Lows of 'Alias'—Creator J.J. Abrams tells us what he regrets and what he'd never change," *Entertainment Weekly*, April 14, 2006, 18.

27 Nikki Stafford and Robyn Burnett, *Uncovering Alias: An Unofficial Guide* (Ontario: ECW Press, 2004).

28 On time segmentation in different media, see John Hartley, "The Frequencies of Public Writing: Tomb, Tome, and Time as Technologies of the Public," in *Democracy and New Media*, ed. Henry Jenkins and David Thornburn (Cambridge: MIT Press, 2003), 254.

29 David Lavery and Robert J. Thompson, "David Chase, *The Sopranos*, and Television Creativity," in *This Thing of Ours: Investigating The Sopranos*, ed. David Lavery (New York: Columbia University Press, 2002), 18–31; Horace M. Newcomb, "This is Not Al Dente: The Sopranos and the New Meaning of Television," in *Television: The Critical View*, Seventh edition, ed. Horace Newcomb (New York: Oxford University Press, 2006), 561–78.

For accounts of the actualities of television production and its "authoring," see Jane M. Shattuc, "Television Production: Who Makes American TV?" in *A Companion to Television*, ed. Janet Wasko (Oxford: Blackwell, 2005), 142–54; Newcomb and Robert S. Alley, *The Producer's Medium* (New York: Oxford, 1983); Caldwell, "Industrial Auteur Theory (Above the Line/Creative)," 2008, 195–231.

30 The issue is discussed by Lorne Manly "The Laws of the Jungle," *New York Times*, September 18, 2005, 2.21.

31 Suzanne Ryan, "ABC Alters its Rollout of 'Lost' Episodes," *Boston Globe*, July 19, 2006, C2, Third edition.

32 As NBC has been particularly focused on this new annual scheduling, it is addressed in the analysis of NBC in the next chapter.

33 Janet Wasko discusses HBO's development of its VOD offerings. "The Future of Film Distribution and Exhibition," in Harries 2002, 200–201. For a perspective on networks' attempts to adopt some VOD strategies, see Anthony Crupi and John Consoli, "Nets Testing VOD Waters," *Mediaweek*, November 14, 2005, 5.

34 Disney-ABC Television Group, "Disney-ABC Television Group Takes ABC Primetime Online," Press Release, corporatedisney.go.com, April 10, 2006. Available online corporatedisney.go.com/news/corporate/2–6/2006_0410_abchitsshow.html. During this trial period *Alias* was streamed online as well, but as it was already in its fifth (and soon to be final) season, it was too late to generate the kinds of ratings bump online availability might provide for a series in its first or second season.

35 Jenkins considers the balancing act between a fan's fascination and frustration with a favorite television series in "*Star Trek* Rerun, Reread, Rewritten: Fan Writing as Textual Poaching," *Critical Studies in Mass Communication* 5, no. 2 (1988), 85–107.

36 Frank Ahrens, "With 'Lost Experience,' ABC Moves Beyond the Island," *The Washington Post*, May 13, 2006, D1.

37 James Poniewozik, "Why the Future of Television is Lost," *Time* October 2, 2006, 44+.

38 *Entertainment Weekly*, "Fall TV Preview: Fringe," *Entertainment Weekly*, September 18, 2009, 37.

39 Qtd. in Michael Ausiello "Finally, TV Gets Interesting," *Entertainment Weekly*, ew.com, October 23, 2009. Available online www.ew.com/ew/article/0,20314664,00.html.

40 John Ellis, "Scheduling: the Last Creative Act in Television?" *Media, Culture and Society* 22, no. 1 (2000), 36.

41 Ibid.

42 Carter, "ABC's Reality: 'We're Last: We Want to Get Out of Here,'" *New York Times*, April 28, 2003, C1, Late edition.

43 Carter, "Too Much 'Millionaire' Has Let the Network Grow Flabby in Prime Time," *New York Times*, February 5, 2001, C1, Late edition.

44 Ibid.

45 T.L. Stanley, "12 to Watch: Steve McPherson," *Electronic Media*, January 20, 2003, 51. Touchstone produced *My Wife and Kids*, *According to Jim*, and *8 Simple Rules* for ABC and *Scrubs* for NBC. It also produced *The Amazing Race* for CBS.

46 Carter, February 5, 2001, C1.

47 "Primetime Series: 2004–5," *Hollywood Reporter*, hollywoodreporter.com, May 27, 2005. Available online www.hollywoodreporter.com/hr/search/article_display.jsp?vnu_content_id=1000937471. *CSI* squeezed into second with 26.6 million viewers and *Desperate Housewives* finished fourth with 23.7; *Grey's Anatomy* was ninth with 18.5 and *Lost* was fourteenth with 16.0, *Extreme Makeover Home Edition* was fifteenth with 15.8.

48 "Primetime Series: 2005–6," *Hollywood Reporter*, hollywoodreporter.com, May 26, 2006. www.hollywoodreporter.com/hr/search/article_display.jsp?vnu_content_id=1002576393. *American Idol* competition show finished with 31.7 million viewers and its results show was second with 30.2 and *CSI* was third with 25.2 million. For ABC, *Desperate Housewives* finished

fourth with 22.2 million, *Grey's Anatomy* was fifth with 19.9 million, *Dancing with the Stars* was seventh with 18.6 million, and *Lost* was fourteenth with 15.5 million.

49 For the 2004–5 season *Survivor*'s two series finished with 20.97 and 19.67 million viewers in the 18–49 demographic, respectively. *The Apprentice*'s two series finished with 16.17 and 14.06 million viewers, respectively. Prestige series *Extreme Makeover Home Edition* had 15.86 compared with 11.54 million for *The Amazing Race*. ABC's other reality shows came in lower with *Wife Swap* at 9.34 and *Supernanny* at 9.03 million viewers and Bachelor and *Bachelorette slipping from previous highly rated seasons. See Hollywood Reporter, May 27, 2005.*

50 Carter, "Successes of Reality TV Put Networks in 'Survivor' Mode," *New York Times*, February 3, 2001, C1; Carter, "Thanks to 'Survivor,' CBS Gains on Thursday," *New York Times*, May 3, 2001, C1.

51 For a discussion of the prestige sponsorship for Sears and other companies with tie-ins with EMHE, see Jennifer Gillan, "*Extreme Makeover Home*(land) *Security Edition*," in *The Great American Makeover: Television, History, Nation*, ed. Dana Heller (New York: Palgrave, 2006), 191–207. For more on prestige sponsorships more generally, see William L. Bird, *"Better Living:" Advertising, Media, and the New Vocabulary of Business Leadership, 1935–1955* (Evanston, IL: Northwestern University Press, 1999). John McMurria positions EMHE as effacing the destructiveness of corporate supported neoliberalism. "Desperate Citizens and Good Samaritans: Neoliberalism and Makeover Reality TV," *Television & New Media* 9, no. 4 (July 2008), 305–22.

52 Carter, April 28, 2003, C1.

53 Carter, "Reality Shows Alter the Way TV Does Business," *New York Times*, January 25, 2003, A1, Late edition.

54 Chad Raphael examines the economic structure of the formats. "The Political Economic Origins of Reali-TV," in Murray and Ouellette 2004, 119–36, as does Ted Magder, "The End of TV 101: Reality Programs, Formats, and the New Business of Television," in Murray and Ouellette 2004, 137–56.

55 Carter, January 25, 2003, A1.

56 At the start of their 2003 seasons *The Bachelorette* was pulling in more than 17 million viewers compared with *Celebrity Mole*'s approximately 10 million. See Tim Goodman, "It's Time to Get Real about Reality TV," *San Francisco Chronicle*, January 20, 2003, D1, Final edition. Both *I'm a Celebrity* and a non-celebrity version of *The Mole* returned in 2009, with the latter considered a ratings failure, while the former once again generated controversy and enough traction in ratings that it is likely to live to see another cringe-worthy series run.

57 Goodman 2003, D1; Tom Shales, "All Too Real; With 'Reality' TV, the Networks Are Embarrassing Teary, Cringing Americans in Record Numbers and Those Are Just the Viewers," *The Washington Post*, January 13, 2003, C1.

58 Carter, February 3, 2001, C1.

59 Carter, January 25, 2003, A1.

60 Nancy Franklin, "Magical Mystery Tour: Forty-eight Castaways Win the Prime-Time Challenge," *New Yorker*, May 23, 2005, 92.

61 Poniewozik 2006.

62 David Segal, "Director J.J. Abrams, Running with the Shows," *The Washington Post*, May 5, 2006, C01. Final edition; Jeff Jensen, "When Steven King Met the 'Lost' Boys," *Entertainment Weekly*, December 1, 2006, 48.

63 *Nightline*, "Behind the Secrets of 'Lost,'" Jake Tapper's Interview with J.J. Abrams, Damon Lindelof and Carlton Cuse, *Nightline*, ABC-TV. Airdate, October 17, 2006; Joe Rhodes, "How 'Lost' Careered Into Being a Hit Show," *New York Times*, November 10, 2004, E1.

64 Fernandez, "'Lost' Takes an Odd Path to Diversity," *Los Angeles Times*, February 13, 2005.

65 Ibid.

66 Ibid.

67 Ibid.

68 Television Business International, "This Man Has the Lost Plot," Interview with Damon Lindelof. *Television Business International* 8 [London], August 1, 2006, 1.

69 Ibid.

70 *Nightline* 2006.

71 Laurie Ouellette and James Hay analyze the ways in which norms of behavior are enforced through these kinds of series. *Better Living Through Reality TV: Television and Post-Welfare Citizenship* (Malden, MA: Blackwell, 2008). While focusing on courtroom series, Ouellette also addresses the discipline function of unscripted programming. "Take Responsibility for Yourself: *Judge Judy* and the Neoliberal Citizen," in Murray and Ouellette 2004, 231–50. For a general overview of makeover programming categories, see Dana Heller, "Reading the Makeover," *Makeover Television: Realities Remodeled* (London: I.B. Tauris, 2007), 1–5. Caroline Dover and Annette Hill point out that reality programming categories activate meanings. "Mapping Genres: Broadcaster and Audience Perceptions of Makeover Television," in Heller 2007, 23–38.

72 Rick Kushman, "As Sitcoms Go Quiet, Engaging Dramas Capture Television's High Ground," *The Sacramento Bee*, December 26, 2004, C26.

73 Thelma Adams, "If We're Not Being Rescued, Let's All Start New Lives," *The New York Times*, September 19, 2004, 13.4.

74 Burnett, with Martin Dugard, *Survivor: the Ultimate Game* (New York: TV Books, 2000).

75 Burnett's description of the narrative dynamics of *Survivor* is quoted in Derek Foster, "'Jump in the Pool': The Competitive Culture of Survivor Fan Networks," in Holmes and Jermyn 2004, 275. For fan dynamics in relation to *Big Brother*, see Estella Tincknell and Parvati Raghuram, "*Big Brother*: Reconfiguring the 'Active' Audience of Cultural Studies," *European Journal of Cultural Studies* 5, no. 2 (2002), 199–215.

76 Burnett 2000.

77 Vaz 2002.

78 Olga Craig, "The Man Who Discovered 'Lost'—and Found Himself Out of a Job," *The Sunday Telegraph* [U.K.], August 14, 2005, 16. See also *Desperate Networks* (New York: Doubleday, 2006), the book from the *New York Times*' Bill Carter. His sources told him that *Lost* only stayed on the schedule because of a personal phone call from Braun to his replacement Steve McPherson. See also Interview with Lindelof. *Television Business International* 2006. See also Joseph Lee, "ABC's 'Desperate' Measures Pay Off," CNN/Money, cnn.com, October 13, 2004. Available online http://money.cnn.com/2004/10/13/news/fortune500/desperate_abc/index.htm.

79 Maureen Dowd, "From McBeal to McDreamy, Network Tries to Figure Out What Women Want," *Pittsburgh Post-Gazette*, May 18, 2006, B7.

80 James B. Stewart's anecdotal book *Disney War* (New York: Simon & Schuster, 2005) addresses this period.

81 Several articles examine the appeal of *Survivor* for viewers who like to speculate on outcomes. See, for example, Mary Beth Haralovich and Michael W. Trosset, "'Expect the Unexpected': Narrative Pleasure and Uncertainty Due to Chance in Survivor," in Murray and Ouellette 2004, 75–96; Foster 2004.

82 Mark Burnett, "What I Have Learned," *Esquire*, July 2001.

83 For a discussion of sponsors' anxieties, see Meg James, "TV: More Bang for More Bucks; Fall Shows' Costs and Effects Go Cinematic, but Some New Offerings Have Been Coolly Received," *Los Angeles Times*, October 2, 2006, C1. See also Stuart Elliott, "TV Networks Wonder How Much Lower Prices for Commercial Time Could Go," *New York Times*, September 25, 2001, C1, C16.

84 *Nightline* 2006.

85 Indicative of how fan tracking has become an activity hosted and framed by the network, the "Lost Book Club" existed virtually on the official website on abc.go.com. Accessed September 19, 2008.

86 Frank Ahrens, "'Lost' Fans Find a Niche on the Internet," *The Washington Post*, December 4, 2005, F7.

87 Jonathan Gray and Jason Mittell, "Speculation on Spoilers: *Lost* Fandom, Narrative Consumption and Textuality," Particip@tions 4, no. 1 (May 2007). Available online www. participations.org. Jenkins (2006) discusses spoilers as well in relation to *Survivor* (25–58).

88 On corporate uses of grassroots fan activities, see Simone Murray, "'Celebrating the Story as the Way it is': Cultural Studies, Corporate Media, and the Contested Utility of Fandom," *Continuum: The Journal of Media and Cultural Studies* 18, no. 1 (2004), 7–25. For the enlistment of audiences as free labor in the media industries, see Tiziana Terranova, "Producing Culture for the Digital Economy," *Social Text* 63, no. 18 (2000), 33–58.

89 Shelia Marikar, "'Lost' Producers Promise a Showdown Now, Answers Later," abc.news.com, May 21, 2007. Available online http://abcnews.go.com/Entertainment/story?id=3197096. On the internet-enabled storytelling of *Lost*, see Poniewozik 2006.

90 Gray considers the way a TV series now exists within a pre-release flow of hype that shapes the text's meaning before it ever exists as an on-air show. "Television Pre-views and the Meaning of Hype," *International Journal of Cultural Studies* 11, no. 1 (March 2008), 33–49. He builds his theory on the foundations of Gerard Genette, *Paratexts: Thresholds of Interpretation* (New York: Cambridge University Press, 1997).

91 Tom Lowry, "Network Finds a Marketing Paradise with 'Lost': Using Podcast, Interactive Games, Web Sites, and Good Old-fashioned Hype, ABC Has Turned a Cult-Style Show into a Cross-media Sensation," *BusinessWeek*, July 24, 2006. Available online www.businessweek. com/magazine/content/06_30/b3994072.htm.

92 The *Lost* "reading list" would include the work of Locke, Bentham, Rousseau, Hume, among others. Scott Colbourne suggests that by the end of the second season and into the Lost Experience launch, some viewers wanted to drop the course as it was getting too hard and too frustrating. "For people who are not doing the assigned homework and are overwhelmed by the pile of surreal mysteries, Abrams and his team will have to stop focusing on what is lost and find something: a good answer or two." See "Brave New Marketing? Lost Reconfigures TV: Even Your Favourite Show is Becoming Interactive," *The Globe and Mail* [U.K.] May 24, 2006, R1.

93 HBO took home a total of 34 Emmys in September 2004 and had 124 nominations.

94 Leslie Ryan, "Are Short-run Reality Series a Long-term Fix?" *Electronic Media* January 13, 2003, 1A+.

95 Ibid.

96 Ibid.

97 *Lost* would have to wait until 2009 to secure a lead actor Emmy, with Michael Emerson taking home the award. By then *Lost* had become a phenomenon but its genre amalgam status seemed to prevent it from taking home trophies, which were now going to AMC cable originals, the current home on the channel spectrum for "quality TV" series *Mad Men* and *Breaking Bad*.

98 Ellis 2000, 26.

99 As of this writing, ABC did not renew *Ugly Betty* at the end of the 2009–10 season.

100 Edward Wyatt, "Fewer Serials and Closure for 'Lost' on ABC's Horizon," *New York Times* January 15, 2007, E.11, Late edition; Gary Levin, "One Mystery Solved: 'Lost' to End in 2010," *USA Today* May 7, 2007, D.1. On the different needs of producers and networks in relation to end dates, see Poniewozik 2006.

101 *Desperate Housewives* had even more regular cast members than *Lost* and many series since these two have had increasingly large ensembles. See Bill Keveney, "TV Hits Maximum Occupancy," *USA Today* November 9, 2005, D1.

102 The press was fond of making literary and philosophical comparisons in its description of HBO series as Stephen Holden does in "Sympathetic Brutes in a Pop Masterpiece," *New York Times* June 6, 1999, 2.23.

103 Abrams is referencing the anthology series of the 1950s and 1960s.

104 Poniewozik, "The 100 Best TV Shows of All-TIME," *Time*, time.com, October 2007. Available online www.time.com/time/specials/2007/article/0,28804,1651341_1659192_1652600,00.html.
105 Robert Huesca and Brenda Dervin, "Hypertext and Journalism: Audiences Respond to Competing News Narratives," in Jenkins and Thornburn 2003, 282.
106 Ibid, 283.
107 All of this is enabled by what Matt Hills (2002) terms the hyperdiegesis (137).
108 George Landow, *Hypertext 2.0 The Convergence of Contemporary Critical Theory and Technology* (Baltimore, MD: Johns Hopkins University Press, 1997).
109 Gilbert, "'Lost' Sci-fi Gimmickry Will Trump Character," *Boston Globe* May 11, 2009, N1.
110 Terry Morrow, "Has 'Lost' Lost Sight of the Plot?" *Cincinnati Post* February 16, 2005, C4.
111 Jensen, "What to Do? Lessons from Cult TV Shows," *Entertainment Weekly* ew.com, April 11, 2005. Available online www.ew.com/ew/article/0,1046376,00.html.
112 Jensen, April 11, 2005.
113 Poniewozik 2007.
114 Morrow 2005, C4.
115 Jensen, April 11, 2005.
116 *Nightline* 2006.
117 Jensen, April 11, 2005.
118 Stephen Armstrong, "Lost Finds Its Way Back: Lost Returns to C4 Next Week for a Second Series and ABC Has Announced It Will Be Streamed. Is It Part of a New Genre of Drama?" *The Guardian* [U.K.] April 24, 2006, 3.
119 Jensen, April 11, 2005.
120 Jensen, April 11, 2005; Bill Keveney, "'Lost' Soul Mates; How the Men Behind the Mystery Keep the Hit Humming Along," *USA Today*, September 29, 2006, E1, Final edition.
121 Keveney, "'Lost' Wraps Around Space-Time Continuum," *USA Today* May 29, 2008, D8; Keveney, "'Lost' Beginning of the Adventure's End," *USA Today* January 25, 2008, D9.
122 Henrik Örenbring, "The Show Must Go On ... and On: Narrative and Seriality in *Alias*," in Abbott and Brown 2007, 18–23. Abrams speaks to the issue in DVD commentary for Phase One (2:13) and for Full Disclosure (3:11).
123 Toni Fitzgerald, "How ABC Fumbled Its Super Bowl Edge," *Media Life* January 29, 2003. *Alias* got a ratings boost to 17.4 million viewers after the 2003 Super Bowl, but that represented a significant loss of lead-in viewers. When *Survivor: the Australian Outback* was in the slot it pulled in 45 million in 2001. Of course, scheduling played a role as ABC had a long post-game show and *Alias* did not start until 11 p.m.
124 Jensen, April 11, 2005.
125 Hillary Robson, "Accusatory Glances: The Evolution and Dissolution of the *Alias* Fandom in Narrative History," in Abbott and Brown 2007, 151.
126 Marikar, May 21, 2007; Keveney, January 25, 2008, D9. For a discussion of why he and other producers were lobbying ABC for an end date, see Lindelof's 2006 interview with *Television Business International* 2006.
127 Johnson analyzes the ARG structure and its sponsorship in his essay in *Reading Lost* (2009), 27–49. Mittell offered an analysis of the ARG in "Lost in An Alternate Reality," FlowTV 4, vol. 7 (June 16, 2006). Available online http://flowtv.org/?p+165. To get a sense of the sponsors' perspectives on the experience, see PR Newswire, "Verizon Aggressively Leveraging Interactive Channels to Reach More Customers; Recent Sponsorship of ABC's 'The Lost Experience' Shows Verizon's Online Marketing Savviness," *PR Newswire* October 6, 2006. See also Ahrens 2006. On *Lost*'s marketing strategies in general, see Vinay Menon, "Who's Really Lost? Maybe the Viewers; Mad Marketing Genius Delivers Scary Shot of Reality to the Show's Most Passionate Viewers," *Toronto Star* October 19, 2005, F3.
128 "Chat Transcript with Alias Technical Consultant Rick Orci," *Deaddrop: Dedicated to Alternate Reality Gaming*, October 31, 2002. Available online http://deaddrop.us/?cat=6; Jesse

Alexander Blog post. Global Couch. February 2008, accessed February 15, 2008; Noah Robischon, "Secret Agent Fan: J. J. Abrams Declassifies an Online Companion to the Sexy Spy Series," *Entertainment Weekly* October 19, 2001, 85.

129 Robson 2007, 147–61.

130 Kurt Lancaster considers *Babylon 5* as a TV series that was built to offer viewers a transmedia experience. See *Interacting with Babylon 5: Fan Performances in a Media Universe* (Austin, TX: University of Texas Press, 2001).

131 Robischon 2001, 85.

132 Nicholas Maiese, "*Blair Witch* Casts its Spell," *Advertising Age* March 20, 2000, S8.

133 Marc Graser and Dade Hayes, "No Scratch from 'Witch' Itch," *Variety* February 28, 2000, 1.

134 J. P. Telotte, "*The Blair Witch Project* Project: Film and the Internet," *Film Quarterly* 54, no. 3 (2001), 33.

135 Graser and Hayes 2000, 1.

136 Telotte 2001, 34.

137 ABC Press Release, "'Lost' Game Lets Fans Hunt for Clues," abcnews.go.com, April 24, 2006. Available online http://abcnews.go.com/Entertainment/story?id=1881142.

138 Telotte 2001, 36.

139 *Nightline* 2006.

140 Ibid.

141 Telotte, 2001 35.

142 Tom Lowry, "Network Finds Marketing Paradise with *Lost*," *BusinessWeek* businessweek. com, July 24, 2006. Available online www.businessweek.com/magazine/content/06_30/b3994072.htm.

143 "The Beast," a marketing effort for Steven Spielberg's 2001 film *A.I.*, is often cited as the first major tie-in ARG. The movie's producers used the online platform to expand the appeal of the film. They got viewers engaged prior to seeing the film via "a murder mystery, with players tasked to figure out who killed a character connected to the 'A.I.' narrative. Players downloaded the game and a forum for discussion developed within the community." Evan Shamoon, "Unreality Show," *Hollywood Reporter* December 2007, S13+. See also Jenkins 2006, 123–27. Other shows on ABC were embracing new media as well. The series *Push, Nevada* also had an ARG.

144 The lines between feature film and television economies have been blurred, however, since a season of a broadcast television series has become something people can buy as a stand-alone product. Mike Benson of ABC marketing links the *Lost* sites to the BMW campaign saying both are hybrid forms of marketing and content. Cited in Ahrens 2006, D1.

145 See chapter one on the WB.

146 Örenbring, "Alternate Reality Gaming and Convergence Culture," *International Journal of Cultural Studies* 10, vol. 4 (2007), 448. See also Avery Vincent, "A Brief History of the Alias [v 1.0] Web Puzzle," www.unfiction.com, October 1, 2002. Available online www.unfiction.com/games/2002/01/01/alias/, accessed January 15, 2006.

147 Örenbring 2007, 450.

148 Ibid. See also Justin Kirby and Paul Marsden, eds. *Connected Marketing: The Viral, Buzz, and Word of Mouth Revolution* (Oxford, U.K.: Butterworth-Heinemann, 2005).

149 Stafford and Burnett 2004, 36–37.

150 Ibid, 37.

151 Vincent, October 1, 2002. Vincent's descriptions help give a feel for the flow of the web puzzle, which was found as a hidden site attached to the regular informational ABC.com site. This structure was similar to the *Dawson's Creek* site. Following the email address sydney.bristow@creditdauphine.com would lead viewers to creditdauphine.com:

> "Players were prompted to send email to analysis@creditdauphine.com that over the course of the game issued certain auto-responses that occasionally included hints and

clues leading mostly to documents that corresponded with events occurring within the television series. On that site was a link to the Find-Whatever faux search engine. All the links were mouse-overs except one—a little symbol that viewers had seen in the show: < 0 > Clicking on the symbol led to www.the-followersoframbaldi.org. This site did much to enrich the background of the fictional historical figure Milo Rambaldi, a key element in the Alias world. This site featured drawings of inventions by Rambaldi, links to other sites the followers found interesting (numerology, cryptology, etc.), a message board and a message submission form that opened chat bot named Alisha. At times Alisha could be given clues from the analysis emails and the show itself that prompted her to respond with information that gave the players documents and photos from the television show. One of those documents listed an FTP site that was accessible for about a day that had further information … "

152 Levy 1997; Jenkins 2006. See also Jennifer Buckendorff, "'Lost' in the Game: Fans 'Play' this Multilayered TV Series Like an Interactive Video Game," *The Seattle Times*, January 10, 2006, E1.

153 Shamoon 2007.

154 Shamoon 2007.

155 Avery 2002.

156 Ahrens 2006, D1.

157 Ibid; Maria Elena Fernandez, "More 'Lost' Than Ever; The Hit ABC Series Rolls Out a Game to Enhance the Viewer Experience. If You Can Find It, That is," *Los Angeles Times* May 5, 2006, E28.

158 Colbourne 2006, R1.

159 Bonnie Ruberg, "Q&A: Quizzing The Queen Bee of ARGS, Jane McGonigal," Gamasutra: the Art and Business of Making Games, www.gamaustra.com, www.gamasutra.com/php-bin/news_index.php?story=13182.

160 James 2006, C1

161 Ibid.

162 Qtd. in Stafford and Burnett 2004, 47.

163 Brooker 2003, 321–34.

164 Comic-Con attendees were targeted by in-storyworld advertisements such as that for Octagon Global Recruiting on behalf of the Dharma Initiative. The ad read, "Our national recruitment drive will commence in San Diego, California, July 24–27, 2008." This notification existed outside of the story world as well given the way fans were recruited as part of a TV series' "street team." In 2004 *Lost* was introduced at Comic-Con prior to its premiere so that the attendees would do the work of spreading the word about the series to ever-increasing circles of potential viewers.

165 Mittell 2006.

166 *PR Newswire* 2006.

167 Shamoon 2007.

168 Ibid.

169 Lowry 2006.

170 On how targeting fans has become a key industrial strategy, see Gwenllian-Jones 2003, 163–77. Johnson considers how that targeting requires fan management and a changing array of interactions among fans, producers, and media conglomerates. "Inviting Audiences In: the Spatial Reorganization of Production and Consumption in 'TV III'," *New Review of Film and Television Studies* 5, no. 1 (April 2007), 61–80.

171 "Chat Transcript with Alias Technical Consultant Rick Orci", October 31, 2002. Orci would go on to co-produce FOX's *Fringe*.

172 Alexander, "A Transmedia Studio on Every Desktop" [blog post], *The Global Couch*, January 21, 2008, www.globalcouch.blogspot.com, accessed February 15, 2008. Alexander offered his ideas about transmedia, particularly in relation to *Alias* and *Heroes*, as part of the

"Cult Media Panel," Futures of Entertainment 2, MIT Convergence Culture Consortium, November 7, 2007.

173 Alexander Blog post, Global Couch, February 2008, accessed February 15, 2008.

174 Andrew Wallenstein and Jesse Hiestand, "ABC, Unions Reach a Deal on Cell Phone TV Shows," Reuters, April 25, 2006.

175 James 2006.

176 Gray 2008.

177 Some media texts still exist on the web (Joss Whedon's *Wonder Woman*) even though they never existed in actuality, leaving fans to wonder what might have been or, perhaps, to take the paratextual buzz for evidence that such a text exists (e.g., message board queries such as, "Is there a J.J. Abrams *Superman*?").

178 See Gray 2008. These issues are discussed in more detail in chapter one, especially in relation to the cease and desist orders sent to fans creating sites for *Millennium*, the mythology series from *The X-Files*' Chris Carter.

179 This problem was especially significant in the 2006 season when so many long-arc serials failed on U.S. networks. Channel 4 in the U.K., for example, essentially paid $800,000 an episode for a cancelled series because NBC's *Kidnapped* was taken off the air so quickly. See George Winslow, "The World Turns to U.S. TV," *Broadcasting & Cable* January 8, 2007, 23.

180 Aaron O. Patrick, "The Race to Get TV Shows Overseas; U.S. Studios Hope to Beat Pirated Episodes on the Web; Now London Gets 'Lost' Fast," *Wall Street Journal* March 28, 2007, B1.

181 Ibid.

182 Lowry 2006.

183 Patrick 2007, B1.

184 Anne Sweeney, Co-Chair Disney Media Networks Group and President, Disney-ABC Television Group, discussed the imperative in her introductory remarks at the Disney Impact Summit, "Disney Channels Worldwide: Leadership and Influence in the Global Marketplace," Burbank, VA, August 10, 2009.

185 The multibillion-dollar long-term output deals common in the 1990s that obligated international buyers to buy one U.S. studio's film and TV output as a package, one often with more underperforming or unsuitable television series than hits, are discussed by Paul Torre, "Block Booking Migrates to Television: The Rise and Fall of the International Output Deal," *Television & New Media* 10, no. 6 (November 2009), 501–20. John-Paul Kelly discussed media conglomerate branding in the context of the battle between Sky and Virgin over the carriage of American content. "Sky vs. Virgin: The Battle of the Brands," *Television without Borders* conference, University of Reading [U.K.], June 28, 2008. This issue is also at the center of Grainge's 2009 chapter in Pearson's new *Reading Lost* anthology. Virgin could no longer carry *Lost* and *24* when Sky refused to renegotiate a package deal.

186 Rixon 2003, 48–61. Season one of *Prison Break* became the highest rated show in the history of France's M6 channel. Its reception was positively impacted by the broadcaster's scheduling and launch strategy, which involved the creation of a new theme song and a companion music video. See also Winslow 2007 below.

187 Channel 4 did not want to pay the approximately 1.9 million per episode asking price for the third and fourth seasons, according to Mimi Turner. "Sky One: Let's Get 'Lost'," *Hollywood Reporter* October 20–22, 2006, 54. See also George Winslow, "The World Turns to U.S. TV," *Broadcasting & Cable* January 8, 2007, 23.

188 Ibid.

189 Annette Hill and Ian Calcutt, "Vampire Hunters: The Scheduling and Reception of Buffy the Vampire Slayer and Angel," in Levine and Parks 2007, 62, 65.

190 Ibid, 62.

191 Ibid, 60–61.

192 Simone Murray, "Brand Loyalties: Rethinking Content Within Global Corporate Media," *Media, Culture, & Society* 27, no. 3 (2005), 416–33; Catherine Johnson, "Tele-branding in TVIII: the Network as Brand and the Programme as Brand," *New Review of Film and Television Studies* 5, no. 1 (2007), 5–24.

193 For Disney's larger brand building and management strategies, see Janet Wasko, *Understanding Disney: The Manufacture of Fantasy* (Malden, MA: Polity Press, 2001). Disney "magic" is also examined ideologically in Eric Smoodin, ed. *Disney Discourse: Producing the Magic Kingdom* (New York: Routledge, 1994). For accounts of midcentury brand building, see Christopher Anderson, "Disneyland," *Hollywood TV: The Studio System in the Fifties* (Austin, TX: University of Texas Press, 1994), 133–55 and Bill Cotter, *The Wonderful World of Disney Television: A Complete History* (New York: Hyperion, 1997).

194 Eric Covert, VP Creative Content and Production at Disney-ABC Television Group, detailed this strategy at the Disney Impact Summit, August 11, 2009. For specifics as to ABC's role, see Jim Benson and Anne Becker, "Synergy: Easy as ABC," *Broadcasting & Cable* October 10, 2005, 10.

195 The name change of Disney's television production studio in 2007 from Touchstone Television to ABC Television Studios reflects this attention to brand consolidation. See Nellie Andreeva, "Touchstone TV Rebranded to Fit Better with ABC Net," *Hollywood Reporter*, February 9–11, 2007, 66.

196 See Jenkins 2006 for a discussion of text messaging and *American Idol* (58–92).

197 Chapter one discusses how a similar dynamic characterizes *Smallville*'s webisodes.

4 Branding, synergy, and product integration on NBC

1 Michelle Hilmes has edited an excellent collection on the network's history from radio to the present. *NBC: America's Network* (Berkeley, CA: University of California Press, 2007). Specific articles are cited in notes below.

2 The era in which NBC dubbed its schedule Must-See TV is examined by Nancy San Martin, "'Must See TV': Programming Identity on NBC Thursdays," in Jancovich and Lyons 2003, 32–47; Amanda Lotz, "Must-See TV: NBC's Dominant Decades," in Hilmes 2007, 261–74. The challenges to that identity are discussed in Christopher Anderson's "Creating the Twenty-First-Century Television Network: NBC in the Age of Media Conglomerates," in Hilmes 2007, 275–90, and in Kevin Sandler's "Life Without *Friends*: NBC's Programming Strategies in an Age of Media Clutter," in Hilmes 2007, 291–307.

3 The trades were filled with commentaries about the displacement of sitcoms. Two representative articles are Bill Carter, "Reality Shows, Costs and Innovative Comedy Threaten a TV Staple," *New York Times* May 24, 2004, E1, Late edition; Richard Verrier, "No Time for Making New 'Friends' at NBC: Sitcom Writers Lament the Industry's Changes as the Network Plans to Devote 8 p.m. to Reality and Game Shows," *Los Angeles Times* November 7, 2006, C1.

4 On the impact of unscripted programming, see Paige Albiniak, "The Selling of Prime Time," *Broadcasting & Cable* September 16, 2002; Carter, "Reality Shows Alter the Way TV Does Business," *New York Times* January 25, 2003, A1, Late edition; Steve McClellan, "Idol Moments Ahead for Advertisers," *Broadcasting & Cable* January 5, 2004, 20; Jennifer Pendleton, "'Idol' a Standard for Integration," *Advertising Age* March 24, 2003, S2.

5 Silvio Waisbord, "Understanding the Global Popularity of Television Formats," *Television and New Media* 5, no. 4 (2004), 359–83.

6 Qtd. in Carter, "For Fox TV, an Unusually Grim Autumn," *New York Times* November 20, 2006, C1.

7 For a more nuanced discussion of the revolutionary and retrograde aspects of *Charlie's Angels*, see Douglas, *Where the Girls Are: Growing Up Female with the Mass Media* (New York: Times Books, 1994) and Elana Levine, *Wallowing in Sex: The New Sexual Culture of 1970s American Television* (Durham, NC: Duke University Press, 2007), 124–26.

8 Jenkins 2006 details the brand address strategies of *The Apprentice* and its extensive product placement (69–79).

9 Brian Steltcr, "Low Ratings End Show and a Product Placement," *New York Times*, nytimes. com, November 13, 2008. Available online www.nytimes.com/2008/11/14/business/ media/14/adco.html.

10 Ken Bensinger, "Carmakers Stretch Mileage of Product Placement Deals," *Los Angeles Times*, June 14, 2008, C1, C2. See also Claire Atkinson, "Ad Intrusion up, Say Consumers," *Advertising Age*, January 6, 2003, 1+; Erwin Ephron, "The Paradox of Product Placement," *Mediaweek*, June 2, 2003, 20; Carrie La Ferle and Steven M. Edwards, "Product Placement: How Brands Appear on Television," *Journal of Advertising* 35, no. 4 (2006), 65–86.

11 Roland Marchand, *Advertising and the American Dream: Making Way for Modernity, 1920–1940* (Berkeley, CA: University of California Press, 1985). See also Sut Jahlly, *The Codes of Advertising: Fetishism and the Political Economy of Meaning in the Consumer Society* (New York: Routledge, 1987).

12 Stuart Elliott, "And Now, a Commercial Break that Doesn't Seem Like One," *New York Times* March 21, 2007, C5; Elliot, "What Was Old is New as TV Revisits Branding," *New York Times* June 13, 2007, C5; Mike Flaherty, "AMC Introduces 'Mad-vertising': Blurbs Reference Products and Theme of 'Men,'" *Variety* August 22, 2008. Available online www.variety.com/ article/VR1117991021.html?categoryid+2526&cs+1.

13 "Idols" is an aptly named episode as the network is addicted to its *American Idol*-influenced product integrations. The omnipresence of these integrations in *The Office* makes even more sense as its principal cameraman came over from *The Survivor* team. The camerawork gives the show a docusoap feel. For more on the lucrative *American Idol* branded entertainment deals, see Catherine Applefeld Olson, "'Idol' Dealing," *Billboard* May 24, 2008, 54. Olson explains the history and motivation of the deals: "AT&T (formerly Cingular), Coca-Cola and Ford began their 'Idol' journey as sponsors for the show's first two seasons and it's no surprise they've held fast ever since. 'Idol' provides these companies some of the most highly integrated branding on TV. And that comes at a time when TV is struggling with the effectiveness of traditional spots due to the rise of commercial skipping digital video recorders."

14 Qtd. in Gail Schiller, "30 Rock Rolls Ads into Story Lines," *Hollywood Reporter* November 28, 2007, 9.

15 Maureen Ryan, "'Office' Promotions Pay Off in a Big Way," *The Watcher* [blog], *Chicago Tribune*, February 23, 2006. Available online http://featuresblogs.chicagotribune.com/ entertainment_tv/2006/02/office_workers_.html. Not only is the series downloaded in high numbers on iTunes and outselling *Desperate Housewives* on that platform, it also featured successful iPod product integration after Apple approached the show about an arrangement. While series creator Greg Daniels tells Ryan he can't reveal the numbers of iPods sold, just that it was "an awful lot," he does confirm that the NBC sales department was thrilled with the series as it skews young and affluent and, therefore, represents a desirable demographic for attracting advertisers. He worries that the on-air numbers do little to reflect the success of the series as the "Nielsen's ... don't measure college students very well."

16 Fey had already been linked to product placement in Emily Nussbaum's "What Tina Fey Would Do for a Soy Joy?" an article on product integration that appeared in *New York* magazine on October 13, 2008, 32+. An earlier version appeared on nymag.com on October 5, 2008.

17 Ozzie Nelson, *Ozzie* (Englewood Cliffs, NJ: Prentice Hall, 1973), 241–42. Mary Beth Haralovich looks at the set as a space of selling cultural concepts, particularly related to gender. "Sit-coms and Suburbs: Positioning the 1950s Homemaker," in *Private Screenings: Television and the Female Consumer*, ed. Lynn Spigel and Denise Mann (Minneapolis, MN: University of Minnesota Press, 1992), 116, 130–38.

18 Nina Leibman discuses scatter buys in the early 1960s. *Living Room Lectures: The Fifties Family in Film and Television* (Austin, TX: University of Texas Press, 1995). For more on "a participating sponsorship, with three, four, or as many as ten sponsors for a single series," see Boddy 1993, 158, 162.

19 Mark Graham, "Did 30 Rock's McFlurry Praise Cross the Line?" *New York* nymag.com, February 13, 2009. Available online http://nymag.com/daily/entertainment/2009/02/mcflurry_pepsuber.html.

20 Ibid. Follow-ups and responses are at http://nymag.com/entertainment/2009/02 and http://nymag.com/tags/mcflurrygate.

21 Fey's response to "McFlurrygate" is available on nymag.com, http://nymag.com/daily/entertainment/2009/02/vulture_exclusive_tina_fey_res.html.

22 Kristen Baldwin, "Tina Fey Responds to Alleged McDonald's Product Placement on '30 Rock,'" ew.com, February 13, 2009. http://hollywoodinsider.ew.com/2009/02/13/tina-fey-respons.

23 Brian Steinberg, "Behind the Scenes of the McFlurry-'30 Rock' Deal that Wasn't," *Advertising Age* adage.com, February 18, 2009. Available online http://adage.com/adages/post?article_id=134689.

24 Ibid.

25 Ibid.

26 Vince Waldron, *The Official Dick Van Dyke Show Book* (New York: Applause Theater Books, 2001), 167–68, 194–5.

27 All posts are from Steinberg 2009. Available online http://adage.com/adages/post?article_id=134689.

28 Ibid.

29 For more discussions of product integration, see Joe Mandese, "How Much is Product Placement Worth?" *Broadcasting & Cable* December 13, 2004, 18; Lawrence R. Samuel, "Advertising Disguised as Entertainment," *Television Quarterly* 34, no. 2 (2004), 51–55; Meg James, "Products are Stars in New Ad Strategy," *Los Angeles Times* December 2, 2004, C1+.

30 Some argue networks should not be engaged in this kind of "stealth advertising," especially as the only mention that it is advertising comes in the rapidly advancing final credits. I have noticed that my DVR never records the final moment when that line appears on *30 Rock*, which suggests it is set up so it folds into the next 30-minute block. See Meg James, "Probe of Stealth TV Ads Sought; An FCC official urges his agency to crack down on lax disclosure of fees for product placement," *Los Angeles Times* May 26, 2005, C1.

31 The references each includes make them the kind of series that do not circulate well in the international marketplace. That is fine for *The Office* as it is an American adaptation of the British original. *30 Rock* exemplifies the comedies that international program packagers have had a hard time selling as its humor and references are too local. This NBC series, like many of its others, is so filled with product placement that it would also run into regulatory problems. It is hardly a surprise that *30 Rock* aired in Germany to dismal ratings.

32 Cited in Schiller, November 28, 2007, 9.

33 Ibid. Also see Schiller, "Brands Take Buzz to Bank Through Free Integration," *Hollywood Reporter*, April 13, 2006, 1+.

34 Cited in Schiller, November 28, 2007, 9.

35 Cited in Schiller, "Primetime Placements on TV Jumped 30% in 2005," backstage.com, January 6, 2006. Available online www.backstage.com/bso/news_reviews/multimedia/article_display.jsp?vnu_contnet_id=100180699.

36 "Pitfalls in Commercial Techniques," *Television Magazine* 10 (November 1953), 36.

37 "The Fat Silhouette," *Time* December 26, 1955, 46.

38 Samuel, *Brought to You By: Postwar Television Advertising and the American Dream* (Austin, TX: University of Texas Press, 2001), 80–83.

39 Mann looks at Benny's role as radio and television pitchman and his use of irony. See "The Spectacularization of Everyday Life: Recycling Hollywood Stars and Fans in Early

Television Variety Shows," in Spigel and Mann 1992, 53–55. Benny's persona also is analyzed in Susan Murray, *Hitch Your Antenna to the Stars: Early Television and Broadcast Stardom* (New York: Routledge, 2005), 86–89, 26–27.

40 To counteract this perception, Benny always over-tipped, according to members of his production team interviewed for Kisseloff, *The Box: An Oral History of Television 1920–1961* (New York: Penguin, 1995).

41 Silverman's tenure at NBC was controversial as he was often critiqued for his emphasis on corporate synergy. See, for example, Mark Graham, "Ben Silverman's Fingerprints Found on 'Pepsuber' Sketchmercial, After All," *New York,* nymag.com, February 3, 2009. Available online http://nymag.com/daily/entertainment/2009/02/ben_silvermans_fingerprints_fo.html. The article highlights the product integration and crosspromotion that found its way into an SNL sketch. On leasing SNL sketches to advertisers, Silverman explained, "What we're doing is selling entertainment vehicles and marketing platforms. This is where programming is going. It's not just an ad for Pepsi, it's an ad for Saturday Night Live." From the start of his relationship with NBC, first as a packager of formats like *The Office* and later as co-Chairman, Silverman was a figure often in the press. See Charles Goldsmith, "American Agent Strikes Gold with British TV Programs," *Wall Street Journal* May 18, 2001, B1; Michael Wolff, "The Missing Link," *New York* June 4, 2001, 30; Michael Malone, "Silverman Searches Globe for Next Trend," *Broadcasting & Cable* November 14, 2005, 36; Josef Adalian, "Peacock Blindsided by Zucker's Zinger," *Variety* May 29, 2007, 1; Carter, "The Whole World is Watching, and Ben Silverman is Watching Back," *New York Times* September 17, 2006. Available online http://travel.nytimes.com/2006/09/17/arts/television/17cart.html. Most infamous was Matthew Belloni's November 8, 2007 *Esquire* story about his social life called "It's Ten O'Clock. Do You Know Where Your Network President Is?" Available online www.esquire.com/features/silverman1207—Esquire Magazine.

42 Mann (1992) writes about the purposeful contrast established on television variety shows between a Hollywood star's "aura" and a TV personality's perceived ordinariness (53–55).

43 Annette Hill, "Big Brother, the Real Audience," *Television & New Media* 3, no. 3 (August 2002), 323.

44 Qtd. in Donna Freydkin, "Morgan Just Keeps Climbing: Film, Book, Emmy Nomination," *Gannett News Service* July 22, 2009.

45 Marisa Guthrie, "Same Address, New Series for Tina Fey," *New York Daily News* October 8, 2006, 5.

46 Carter, "It's Easy to Find Tina Fey on TV, But Not Her Show," *New York Times* October 13, 2008, B6.

47 The role that the game show played in reviving ratings is discussed in Gary Levin, "Getting Shows Back on Track: 10 Questions and Answers," *USA Today* February 11, 2008, D3.

48 Steve Gorman, "Seinfeld Plugs Own Movie in '30 Rock' Guest Spot," *Reuters* October 3, 2007.

49 Commenting on the nbc.com Ask Tina Q&A blog space for the series. Fey and Jack McBrayer (Kenneth the Page) talked about how the appearance helped the series get some much needed attention and how grateful they were to Seinfeld.

50 Gorman 2007.

51 Andrew Hampp, "Promos Do Double Duty As Networks Fight DVR Dips," *TVWeek* June 2009. Available online www.tvweek.com/news/2009/06/promos_do_double_duty_as_netwo.php.

52 Rob Owen, "'30 Rock' Rolls with Smart Commentary," *Pittsburgh Post-Gazette* October 4, 2007.

53 Zalaznick qtd. in Bravo Press Release, "Bravo Announces First-ever Media Acquisition with TelevisionWithoutPity.com, the Online Destination for the Discerning TV 'Junkie,'" March 13, 2007. Highlights available online http://featuresblogs.chicagotribune.com/entertainment_tv/2007/03/bravo_buys_twop.html.

54 Bravo 2007.
55 On repurposing the archive of past series, see Jancovich and Hunt 2004, 37–39.
56 This long-standing brand tension between the two networks was discussed in the trades in the late 1960s. George Swisshelm, "Mass Numbers through Rube Show Could Hurt on Price Front," *Variety* October 29, 1969, 35, 52; Bill Greeley, "Gotham TV vs. Nat'l Rating: 'Sticks Nix Hicks Pix' Turnabout," *Variety* June 5, 1968, 23, 40. It is also historicized by several contemporary commentators. Two particularly interesting discussions are Victoria E. Johnson, *Primetime Television and the Struggle for U.S. Identity* (New York: New York University Press, 2008), 23, 120–27; Aniko Bodroghkozy, "Make it Relevant: How Youth Rebellion Captured Prime Time in 1970 and 1971," in *Groove Tube: Sixties Television and the Youth Rebellion* (Durham, NC: Duke University Press, 2001), 199–235.
57 "Alec Baldwin and Jeff Zucker Talk TV," money.cnn.com CNN.com. April 30, 2007. Available online http://money.cnn.com/2007/04/30/news/companies/zucker_baldwin.fortune/index.htm. On Zucker's controversial tenure, see David Teather, "Television: NBC to Leave Blood on the Studio Floor," *Guardian* [U.K.] October 20, 2006, 35.
58 After the initial novelty wore off, the *Leno Show* failed to bring in much of an audience from anywhere. As NBC had done before, it imported something meant for one space into another and seemed to make no effort to revise the format or come up with a better-suited new one.
59 *Office* webisodes are available at www.nbc.com/The_Office/video/webisodes/subtle-sexuality/#vid=1170161.
60 Anne Becker talks about how NBC had *Lazy Sunday* taken down from YouTube and then did not find a way to offer it on NBC's own site. "ABC's Digital Evangelists," *Broadcasting & Cable* March 27, 2006, 13.
61 See Gomery 2007.
62 Brian Stelter, "Can NBC Do for 'Quarterlife' What YouTube Could Not?" *New York Times* nytimes.com, December 24, 2007. Available online www.nytimes.com/2007/12/24/business/media/24quarter.html.
63 With Comcast brokering a deal with General Electric to take over majority share of NBC in the next decade, the possibilities for such deals with Comcast expand, while those with its competitors would likely cease.
64 See Gomery 2007.
65 Carter, "NBC Hired a Hit Maker: It's Still Waiting," May 17, 2009, BU.1.
66 Ibid.
67 Ibid.
68 Ibid.
69 Carter and Elliott, "A Roster That Leans on Comedy and 'The Apprentice'," *New York Times* May 16, 2005, C6, Late edition; Carter, "'The Office' Transfers to a New Cubicle," *New York Times* March 20, 2005, 2, 12, Late edition.
70 While winter 2010 saw the cancellation of *The Jay Leno Show*, which resulted in a shakeup in NBC's late night lineup, Fallon remained a brand asset for the network and the hope for attracting next-generation viewers. At the same Television Critics Association Winter Press Tour at which the Leno announcement set in motion NBC's late night debacle, the network also signaled that it was turning its attention back to franchising, not only with a *Law & Order*, Los Angeles edition (LOLA) on the development slate, but also with a new series from CBS's and Hollywood's star franchiser Jerry Bruckheimer of *CSI* and *Pirates of the Caribbean* fame.
71 Carter, May 17, 2009, BU.1.
72 Ibid.
73 Gary Whannel, *Fields of Vision: Television Sport in Cultural Transformation* (London: Routledge, 1992).
74 Ibid.

75 Rod Brookes, "Sport," *Television Genre Book*, ed. Glen Creenber (London: BFI, 2001), 87–89. See also Brookes, *Representing Sport* (London: Arnold, 2002).

76 Samuel 2001, 210, 81–82.

77 The conclusion discusses the January 2010 late-night shakeup through which O'Brien's seven-month tenure as *The Tonight Show* host ended after he refused to accept a schedule shift that pushed his show back to tomorrow at 12.35 a.m. to make room for Leno's return to 11.35 p.m. The shakeup came when NBC cancelled Jay Leno's 10 p.m. show, but did not want to lose him as a brand asset.

78 Leslie Torchin, "Location, Location, Location: The Destination of the Manhattan TV Tour," *Tourist Studies* 2, no. 3 (2002), 247–66.

79 Guthrie, October 8, 2006.

80 Some posts to the Gadgetwise *New York Times* blog on technology were following Obama's use of Twitter and the hiatus that he took from it after the election. Paul Boutin, "President Obama's New Twitter Feed," Gadgetwise: a *New York Times* blog, May 1, 2009. Available online http://gadgetwise.blogs.nytimes.com/2009/05/01/president-obamas-new-twitter-feed.

Conclusion

1 Meehan, "Why We Don't Count: The Commodity Audience," in *Logics of Television: Essays in Cultural Criticism*, ed. Patricia Mellencamp (Bloomington, IN: Indiana University Press, 1990), 117–37; Philip M. Napoli, *Audience Economics: Media Institutions and the Audience Marketplace* (New York: Columbia University Press, 2003); Harold Vogel, *Entertainment Industry Economics: A Guide for Financial Analysts*, Seventh edition (New York: Cambridge University Press, 2007).

2 Joe Mandese, "DVR Threat Gets Downgraded," *Broadcasting & Cable* September 12, 2005, 20. See also William Boddy, "Redefining the Home Screen: Technological Convergence as Trauma and Business Plan," in Thornburn and Jenkins 2004, 191–200.

3 Michael Malone, "Character Blogs Connect: TV-show Weblogs Provide Unique Marketing Opportunity and Draw Viewers," *Broadcasting & Cable* September 4, 2006, 10.

4 Ibid.

5 Caldwell comments upon various forms of industrial self-analysis throughout his book *Production Culture* (2008).

6 Betsy Streisand, "Learning her ABCs," *U.S. News & World Report* September 12, 2005, 54.

7 Matt Hills, *Fan Cultures* (New York: Routledge, 2002), 132.

8 Alan McKee, "How to Tell the Difference between Production and Consumption: A Case Study in Doctor Who Fandom," *Cult Television*, ed. Sara Gwenllian-Jones and Roberta E. Pearson (Minneapolis, MN: University of Minnesota Press, 2004), 177, 181.

9 Jenkins, "Blog This!" *Technology Review*, February 2002. Reprinted in *Fans, Bloggers, Gamers: Exploring Participatory Culture* (New York: New York University Press, 2006), 6, 179.

10 Jenkins, "Interactive Audiences?" in Harries 2002, 161.

11 Levy, *Cyberculture*, trans. Robert Bononno (Minneapolis, MN: University of Minnesota Press, 2001), 108–9.

12 Poster, "Postmodern Virtualities," in *The Television Studies Reader*, ed. Annette Hill and Robert Allen (New York: Routledge, 2004), 589. Originally published in *Arena Journal* (Melbourne, Australia), September 1994.

13 As I note later in this discussion, Rhimes' lobbying viewers to watch her show on-air as it airs is a typical one. Yet, only those viewers who are part of Nielsen families would actually count toward the still dominant measurement form of overnight ratings. Those watching on-air and then immediately commenting on the show online, however, have become increasingly important to production teams and their assessment of the success of episodes.

14 Hills 2002, 132, 133.
15 Poster 2004, 588.
16 Ibid, 589.
17 McKee 2004, 177.
18 Jenkins, "Blog This!" 2002, 180.
19 Ibid.
20 Poster 2004, 589.
21 McKee 2004, 177.
22 Caldwell 2008, 2.
23 Gray 2008, 34, 46.
24 Caldwell (2008) talks about stealth marketing in relation to the roles informal internet spaces and the trade press play in circulating "institutionalized storytelling" (59–62).
25 "Fallen Heroes," *Entertainment Weekly* October 31, 2008, 22–27.
26 Michael Schneider, "NBC Opts to Air 'Day One' as a Miniseries: Move is Likely a Cost-cutting Measure," *Variety* October 1, 2009.
27 Steven Levy, "Twitter: Is Brevity the Next Big Thing?" *Newsweek*. Available online www.newsweek.com/id/35289; Steve McClellan, "Nets Build Heat with Tweets," *Hollywood Reporter* August 18, 2009, 4; Maria Elena Fernandez, "Like It or Not, Two Fox Shows Are a-Twitter," *Bergen Record* September 2, 2009; Saul Hansell, "Advertisers Are Watching Your Every Tweet," *Bits: New York Times Blog* nytimes.com, July 16, 2009. http://bits.blogs.nytimes.com/2009/07/16/advertisers-are-watching-your-every-tweet.
28 FOX did a much better job with its use of iTunes to circulate tracks from each *Glee* episode and generate interest in the on-air series through the alternate platform. FOX also released a soundtrack midseason as well as DVD of the series' first half. Both strategies suggest *Glee* may become as representative of FOX's innovative windowing strategies as *24* had been before it.
29 Meehan 1990; Gertner 2005; Beville 1988.
30 Meehan 1990.
31 From a Harmelin Media study quoted in David Bauder, "Are Leno and O'Brien Going at It?" *Associated Press Newswire* January 13, 2010. Available online www.wthr.com/Global/story.asp?S=11818694. See also David Carr, "The Peacock's Feathers Go Gray," *New York Times* January 11, 2010, B1, B2.
32 The statement released through *PR Newswire* was available on *USA Today*'s website, among countless others. See www.usatoday.com/life/television/news/2010-01-13-conanstatement13_ST_N.htm.
33 Nielsen's presentation of its research findings is referenced in the following account of the company's national client meeting: Joe Mandese, "Nocturnal Transmissions: Nielsen Finds Prime-Time Creeping into Late Night," *Media Daily News*, www.mediapost.com, February 15, 2008. www.mediapost.com/publications/index.cfm?fa=Articles.showArticle&art_aid=76532.
34 Qtd. in Gary Levin, "What's Next for Conan as Curtain Comes Down?" *USA Today* January 22, 2010, 1.
35 As of this writing, *Dollhouse* was not renewed for 2010. *Fringe* is fast becoming the classic, critically acclaimed, ratings-challenged cult series, in part because of the stiff competition in its 2009 Thursday night spot. The series was renewed for a 2010–11 season.
36 I explore this programming category in Gillan 2004.
37 At present, Nielsen is championing its development of Anytime/Anywhere Media Measurement (A2/M2) to deal with the impact of alternate content delivery platforms. Its research suggests that DVR viewing can increase engagement with programming and advertising content, which is one of the points I make earlier in the book. For more on A2/M2, see http://en-us.nielsen.com/etc/medialib/nielsen_dotcom/en_us/documents/pdf/consumer_insight.Par.9919.File.dat/Consumer_Insight_Magazine_Issue1.pdf.

38 In December 2009 FOX was negotiating license fees for cable carriage of its broadcast networks and may be changing the future of "free" TV in the process. If broadcast TV is no longer free and basic cable has even more commercials than advertiser-supported "free" TV, then the economic structure of the industry and the distinctions between cable and broadcast television will change.

Selected Bibliography

Abercrombie, Nicholas, and Brian Longhurst. *Audiences: A Sociological Theory of Performance and Imagination.* London: Sage, 1998.

Agre, Phillip E., and Marc Rotenberg, eds. *Technology and Privacy.* Cambridge, MA: MIT Press, 1998.

Alexander, Jesse. Cult Media Panel. *Futures of Entertainment 2.* MIT Convergence Culture Consortium. November 18, 2007. Also available online: www.convergenceculture.org/weblog/2007/11/foe2_cult_media.php (accessed December 20, 2007).

Alvey, Mark. "The Independents: Rethinking the Television Studio System." In *The Revolution Wasn't Televised: Sixties Television and Social Conflict*, ed. Lynn Spigel and Michael Curtin, 139–58. New York: Routledge, 1997.

Anderson, Benedict. *Imagined Communities: Reflections on the Origin and Spread of Nationalism.* New York: Verso, 1983.

Anderson, Bonnie. *News Flash: Journalism, Infotainment and the Bottom-Line Business of Broadcast News.* San Francisco: Jossey-Bass, 2004.

Anderson, Christopher. "Creating the Twenty-first-Century Television Network: NBC in the Age of Media Conglomerates." In Hilmes 2007, 275–90.

———. *Hollywood TV: The Studio System in the Fifties.* Austin, TX: University of Texas Press, 1994.

Anderson, Chris. "The Long Tail," *Wired* 12, no. 10 (October 2004), available online: www.wired.com/wired/archive/12.10/tail_pr.html.

Andrejevic, Marc. *Reality TV: the Work of Being Watched.* Lanham, MD: Rowman and Littlefield, 2004.

———. "Watching Television Without Pity: The Productivity of Online Fans." *Television & New Media* 9, no. 1 (2008): 24–46.

Ang, Ien. *Desperately Seeking the Audience.* New York: Routledge, 1991.

Aslinger, Ben. "Rocking Prime Time: Gender, the WB, and Teen Culture." In Ross and Stein 2008, 78–91.

Aucoin, Don. "Why the Dr. is Out: Advertisers, Not Viewers, Dictate Which Shows Live and Which Die." *The Boston Globe* May 29, 1998, C1.

Auletta, Ken. *Three Blind Mice: How the TV Networks Lost Their Way.* New York: Random House, 1992.

Bacon-Smith, Camille. *Enterprising Women: Television Fandom and the Creation of Popular Myth.* Philadelphia, PA: University of Pennsylvania Press, 1992.

Bagdikian, Ben. *The New Media Monopoly.* Boston, MA: Beacon Press, 2004.

———. *Science Fiction Culture.* Philadelphia, PA: University of Pennsylvania Press, 2000.

Baym, Nancy K. "Interpreting Soap Operas and Creating Community: Inside a Computer-Mediated Fan Culture." *Journal of Folklore Research* 30 (1999): 143–76.

———. "Talking about Soaps: Communicative Practices in a Computer-mediated Fan Culture." In *Theorizing Fandom: Fans, Subculture and Identity*, ed. Cheryl Harris and Alison Alexander, 111–29. Cresskill, NJ: Hampton Press, 1998.

———. *Tune In, Log On: Soaps, Fandom, and Online Community*. Thousand Oaks, CA: Sage, 2000.

Becker, Ron. *Gay TV in Straight America*. New Brunswick, NJ: Rutgers University Press, 2006.

Bellamy, R. V. Jr., and J. R. Walker, eds. *Television and the Remote Control: Grazing on a Vast Wasteland*. New York: Guilford, 1996.

Benkler, Yochai. *The Wealth of Networks: How Social Production Transforms Markets and Freedom*. New Haven, CT: Yale University Press, 2007.

Bennett, James, and Tom Brown, eds. *Film and Television After DVD*. London: Routledge, 2008.

Bielby, Denise D., and Lee Harrington. *Global TV: Exporting Television and Culture in the World Market*. New York: New York University Press, 2008.

Bierbaum, Tom. "The WB's Getting the Girls." *Variety* November 2–8 (1998): 30.

Bird, Elizabeth S. *The Audience in Everyday Life: Living in a Media World*. New York: Routledge, 2003.

Bird, Rick. "A Tale of Two Networks." *Cincinnati Post* January 31, 2005, B1.

Bjarkman, Kim. "To Have and To Hold: The Video Collector's Relationship with an Ethereal Medium." *Television and the New Media* 5, no. 3 (2004): 217–46.

Boddy, William. *Fifties Television: The Industry and its Critics*. Urbana, IL: University of Illinois Press, 1990.

———. "Interactive Television and Advertising Form in Contemporary US Television." In Spigel and Olsson 2004, 113–32.

———. "New Media as Old Media: Television." In Harries 2002, 242–53.

———. *New Media and Popular Imagination: Launching Radio, Television, and Digital Media in the United States*. Oxford: Oxford University Press, 2004.

Bodroghkozy, Aniko. "Make it Relevant: How Youth Rebellion Captured Prime Time in 1970 and 1971." In *Groove Tube: Sixties Television and the Youth Rebellion*, 199–235. Durham, NC: Duke University Press, 2001.

Bolter, Jay David, and Richard Grusin. *Remediation: Understanding New Media*. Cambridge, MA: MIT Press, 1999.

Boyd, Dana. "Why Youth Heart Social Network Sites: The Role of Networked Publics in Teenage Social Life." In *Youth, Identity, and Digital Media*, ed. David Buckingham, 119–42. Cambridge, MA: MIT Press, 2008.

Broadcasting & Cable. "A Strategy for Stemming the Slide." *Broadcasting & Cable* May 20, 2002, 21.

Brooke, Jill. "Counterpunch: WB Network's Programming Success." *Adweek* March 30, 1998, 22–25.

Brooker, Will. "Living on Dawson's Creek: Teen Viewers, Cultural Convergence, and Television Overflow." *International Journal of Cultural Studies* 4, vol. 4 (2001): 456–72.

———. "Conclusion: Overflow." In *Audience Studies Reader*, ed. Will Brooker and Deborah Jermyn, 321–34. New York: Routledge, 2003.

———. *Using the Force: Creativity, Community and "Star Wars" Fans*. Revised edition. New York: Continuum International, 2003.

Brooks, Tim, and Earle Marsh. *The Complete Directory to Primetime Network and Cable TV Shows: 1946–Present*. 8th edition. New York: Ballantine, 2003.

Brower, Sue. "Fans as Tastemakers: Viewers for Quality Television." In *The Adoring Audience: Fan Culture and Popular Culture*, ed. Lisa A. Lewis, 163–84. London: Routledge, 1992.

Brown, Les. *Television the Business Behind the Box*. New York: Harcourt Brace Jovanovich, 1971.

Brunsdon, Charlotte. *Screen Tastes: Soap Opera to Satellite Dishes*. New York: Routledge, 1997.

——. "What is the 'Television' of Television Studies." In Newcomb 2006, 609–28.

Bruzzi, Stella. *New Documentary: A Critical Introduction*. London: Routledge, 2000.

Burr, Vivien. "Scholar/'shippers and Spikeaholics: Academic and Fan Identities at the Slayage Conference on *Buffy the Vampire Slayer*." *European Journal of Cultural Studies* 8 (2005): 375–83.

Bury, Rhiannon. *Cyberspaces of Their Own: Female Fandoms Online*. New York: Peter Lang, 2005.

——. "Stories for ~~Boys~~ Girls: Female Fans Reading *The X-Files*." *Popular Communication* 1 (2003): 217–42.

——. "Waiting to X-Hale: A Study of Gender and Community on an All-Female *X-Files* Electronic Mailing List." *Convergence* 4 (1998): 59–83.

Butler, Judith. *Bodies that Matter: On the Discursive Limits of Sex*. New York: Routledge, 1993.

——. *Gender Trouble*. New York: Routledge, 1990.

Caldwell, John Thornton. "Convergence Television: Aggregating form and Repurposing Content in the Culture of Conglomeration." In Spigel and Olsson 2004, 41–74.

——. "Critical Industrial Practice: Branding, Repurposing, and the Migratory Patterns of Industrial Texts." *Television & New Media* 7, no. 2 (May 2006): 99–134.

——. *Production Culture: Industrial Reflexivity and Critical Practice in Film and Television*. Durham, NC: Duke University Press, 2008.

——. *Televisuality: Style, Crisis, and Authority in American Television*. New Brunswick, NJ: Rutgers University Press, 1995.

——. "Welcome to the Viral Future of Cinema (Television)." *Cinema Journal* 45, no. 1 (Fall 2006): 90–97.

Campbell, Richard, and Caitlin Campbell. "Demons, Aliens, Teens and Television." *Television Quarterly* 34, no. 1 (Winter 2001): 56–64.

Carter, Bill. *Desperate Networks*. New York: Doubleday, 2006.

——. "The Media Business: 2 Would-be Networks Get Set for Prime Time." *The New York Times* January 9, 1995, D1.

——. "With Focus on Youth, 2 Small TV Networks Unite." *The New York Times* January 25, 2006, C4.

Castaneda, Maria. "The Complicated Transition to Broadcast Digital Television in the United States." *Television and New Media* 8, no. 2 (2007): 91–106.

Caughie, John. "Playing at Being American: Games and Tactics." In *Logics of Television: Essays in Cultural Criticism*, ed. Patricia Mellencamp, 44–58. London: BFI, 1990.

Caves, Richard E. *Creative Industries: Contracts between Art and Commerce*. Cambridge, MA: Harvard University Press, 2000.

Clerc, Susan J. " DDEB, GATB, MPPB, and Ratboy: *The X-Files*' Media Fandom, Online and Off." In *"Deny All Knowledge": Reading The X-Files*, ed. David Lavery, Angela Hague, and Marla Cartwright, 36–51. Syracuse, NY: Syracuse University Press, 1996.

Consalvo, Mia. "Cyber-slaying Media Fans: Code, Digital Poaching, and Corporate Control of the Internet." *Journal of Communication Inquiry* 27 (2003): 67–86.

Consoli, John. "CW's Content Wraps May Keep DVR Viewer Interest." *Mediaweek* January 29, 2007, 4+.

——. "CW Creates Content Wraps with Commercial Pods." *Mediaweek* May 22, 2006, 4.

Corner, John. *Critical Ideas in Television Studies*. Oxford: Oxford University Press, 1999.

———. "Performing the Real: Documentary Diversions." *Television and New Media* 3, no. 3 (2002): 255–69.

———. *Television Form and Public Address*. London: Hodder Arnold, 1995.

Costello, Victor J. Interactivity and the "Cyber-fan": An Exploration of Audience Involvement within the Electronic Fan Culture of the Internet. PhD diss., Univ. of Tennessee, 1999. Available online: http://oai.sunsite.utk.edu/links/CostelloVictor.pdf.

Costello, Victor, and Barbara Moore. "Cultural Outlaws: An Examination of Audience Activity and Online Television Fandom." *Television and New Media* 8 (2007): 124–43.

Couldry, Nick. *In the Place of Media Power: Pilgrims and Witnesses of the Media Age*. New York: Routledge, 2000.

———. *Media Rituals: A Critical Approach*. New York: Routledge, 2003.

Creeber, Glen. *Serial Television: Big Drama on the Small Screen*. London: BFI, 2004.

———, with John Tulloch and Toby Miller, eds. *The Television Genre Book*. London: BFI, 2001.

Crupi, Anthony, and John Consoli, "Nets Testing VOD Waters," *Mediaweek*, November 14, 2005, 5.

Cubitt, Sean. *Digital Aesthetics*. London: Sage, 1998.

———. *Simulation and Social Theory*. London: Sage, 2000.

Curtin, Michael. "Media Capitals: Cultural Geographies of Global TV." In Spigel and Olsson 2004, 270–302.

———. "On Edge: The Culture Industries in the Neo-Network Era." In *Making and Selling Culture*, ed. Richard Ohmann (with Gage Averill, Michael Curtain, David Shumway, and Elizabeth Traube), 181–202. Hanover, NH: Wesleyan University Press, 1996.

Dahlgren, Peter. *Television and the Public Sphere: Citizenship, Democracy and the Media*. Thousand Oaks, CA: Sage, 1995.

Daniels, Susanne, and Cynthia Littleton. *Season Finale: the Unexpected Rise and Fall of the WB and UPN*. New York: Harper, 2007.

Darley, Andrew. *Visual Digital Culture: Surface Play and Spectacle in New Media Genres*. London: Routledge, 2000.

Davis, Glyn, and Kay Dickinson, eds. *Teen TV: Genre, Consumption and Identity*. London: BFI, 2004.

De Certeau, Michel. *The Practice of Everyday Life*. Berkeley, CA: University of California Press, 1984.

Deery, June. "Reality TV as Advertisement." *Popular Communication* 2, no. 1 (2004): 1–19.

———. "TV.com: Participatory Viewing on the Web." *Journal of Popular Culture* 37 (2003): 161–83.

Doherty, Thomas. *Teenagers and Teenpics*. Philadelphia, PA: Temple University Press, 2002.

Donaton, Scott. *Madison and Vine: Why the Entertainment and Advertising Industries Must Converge to Survive*. New York: McGraw Hill, 2005.

Douglas, Susan. *Where the Girls Are: Growing Up Female with the Mass Media*. New York: Times, 1995.

Dovey, Jon. *Freakshow: First Person Media and Factual Television*. London: Pluto, 2000.

Dow, Bonnie. *Prime-Time Feminism: Television, Media Culture, and the Women's Movement Since 1970*. Philadelphia, PA: University of Pennsylvania Press, 1996.

Ellis, John. "Scheduling: the Last Creative Act in Television?" *Media, Culture and Society* 22, no. 1 (2000): 25–38.

———. *Seeing Things: Television in the Age of Uncertainty*. London: I.B. Tauris, 2000.

——. *Visible Fictions: Television, Cinema, Video*. Rev. edition. New York: Routledge, 1992.

Feuer, Jane. "The Concept of Live Television: Ontology as Ideology." In *Regarding Television: Critical Approaches—An Anthology*, ed. E. Ann Kaplan, 12–21. Los Angeles: The American Film Institute, 1983.

Feuer, Jane, Paul Kerr, and Tise Vahimagi. *MTM: "Quality Television."* London: BFI, 1984.

Finkle, Jim. "New Shows, New Marketing," *Broadcasting & Cable* February 21, 2005, 8.

Fiske, John. "Cultural Studies and Television." In *Channels of Discourse, Reassembled: Television and Contemporary Criticism*. 2nd edition, ed. Robert C. Allen. Chapel Hill, NC: University of North Carolina Press, 1992.

——. *Television Culture*. London: Routledge, 1989.

——. "The Cultural Economy of Fandom." In *The Adoring Audience: Fan Culture and Popular Culture*, ed. Lisa A. Lewis, 30–49. London: Routledge, 1992.

Flichy, Patrice. *The Internet Imaginaire*. Cambridge, MA: MIT Press, 2007.

Foster, Derek. "Community and Identity in the Electronic Village." In *Internet Culture*, ed. David Porter, 23–37. New York: Routledge, 1997.

——. "'Jump in the Pool,' The Competitive Culture of Survivor Fan Networks." In Holmes and Jermyn 2004, 270–89.

Frank, Thomas. *The Conquest of Cool: Business Culture, Counterculture, and the Rise of Hip Consumerism*. Chicago, IL: University of Chicago Press, 1997.

Friedberg, Anne. "The Virtual Window." In Thornburn and Jenkins 2004, 337–53.

Gatson, Sarah N., and Amanda Zweerink. *Interpersonal Culture on the Internet: Television, the Internet, and the Making of a Community*. Lewiston, NY: Edwin Mellen Press, 2004.

Geraghty, Christine. "Aesthetics and Quality Popular Television Drama." *International Journal of Cultural Studies* 6, no. 1 (2003): 25–45.

——. *Women and Soap Opera: A Study of Prime-time Soaps*. Cambridge: Polity, 1991.

Gertner, Jon. "Our Ratings, Ourselves." *New York Times Magazine* April 10, 2005, 34.

Gillan, Jennifer. "*Extreme Makeover Home*(land) *Security Edition*." In *The Great American Makeover: Television, History, Nation*, ed. Dana Heller, 191–207. New York: Palgrave, 2006.

——. "From Ozzie Nelson to Ozzy Osbourne: the Genesis and Development of the Reality (Star) Sitcom." In *Understanding Reality Television*, ed. Holmes and Jermyn, 54–70. London: Routledge, 2004.

Gitelman, Lisa. *Always Already New: Media, History and the Data of Culture*. Cambridge, MA: MIT Press, 2006.

Gitlin, Todd. *Inside Prime Time*. New York: Routledge, 1985.

Glynn, Kevin. *Tabloid Culture: Trash Taste, Popular Power, and the Transformation of American Television*. London: Duke University Press, 2000.

Gomery, Douglas. *A History of Broadcasting in the United States*. London: Blackwell, 2008.

——. "Talent Raids and Package Deals: NBC Loses Its Leadership in the 1950s." In Hilmes 2007, 153–68.

Gray, Herman. *Cultural Moves: African Americans and the Politics of Representation*. Berkeley, CA: University of California Press, 2005.

Gray, Jonathan. "Anti-Fandom and the Moral Text: *Television Without Pity* and Textual Dislike." *American Behavioral Scientist* 48, no. 7 (March 2005): 840–58.

——. "New Audiences, New Textualities: Anti-fans and Non-fans." *International Journal of Cultural Studies* 6, no. 1 (2003): 64–81.

——. "Television Pre-views and the Meaning of Hype." *International Journal of Cultural Studies* 11, no. 1 (2008): 33–49.

———. *Watching with The Simpsons*. London: Routledge, 2006.

Gray, Jonathan, and Jason Mittell. "Speculation on Spoilers: *Lost* Fandom, Narrative Consumption, and Rethinking Textuality." *Particip@tions: Journal of Audience and Reception Studies* 4, no. 1 (2007), available online: www.participations.org/Volume%204/Issue%201/4_01_graymittell.htm.

Gripsrud, Jostein. "Broadcast Television: The Chances of Its Survival in a Digital Age." In Spigel and Olsson 2004, 210–23.

Gwenllian-Jones, Sara. "Histories, Fictions and *Xena: Warrior Princess*." *Television and New Media* 1, no. 4 (2000): 403–18.

Gwenllian-Jones, and Roberta E. Pearson, eds. *Cult Television*. Minneapolis, MN: Minnesota University Press, 2004.

———. "The Sex Lives of Cult Television Characters." *Screen* 43, no. 1 (2002): 79–90.

———. "Web Wars: Resistance, Online Fandom and Studio Censorship." In Jancovich and Lyons 2003, 163–77.

Haggins, Bambi. *Laughing Mad: The Black Comic Persona in Post-Soul America*. New Brunswick: Rutgers University Press, 2007.

Haralovich, Mary Beth, and Michael W. Trosset. "'Expect the Unexpected': Narrative Pleasure and Uncertainty Due to Chance in *Survivor*." In Murray and Ouellette 2004, 75–96.

Harries, Dan, ed. *The New Media Book*. London: British Film Institute, 2002.

———. "Watching the Internet." In Harries 2002, 171–82.

Harrington, C. Lee, and Denise Bielby. "Global Television Distribution: Implications of TV 'Traveling' for Viewers, Fans, and Texts." *American Behavioral Scientist* 48, no. 7 (2005): 902–20.

———. *Soap Fans: Pursuing Pleasure and Making Meaning in Everyday Life*. Philadelphia, PA: Temple University Press, 1995.

Hartley, John. *The Uses of Television*. New York: Routledge, 1999.

Havens, Timothy. *Global Television Marketplace*. London: BFI, 2006.

Hellekson, Karen, and Kristina Busse, eds. *Fan Fiction and Fan Communities in the Age of the Internet: New Essays*. Jefferson, NC: McFarland, 2006.

Heller, Dana, ed. *Makeover Television: Realities Remodeled*. London: I.B. Tauris, 2007.

———. *The Great American Makeover: Television, History, Nation*. New York: Palgrave, 2006.

Herman, Edward S., and McChesney, Robert W. *The Global Media: The New Missionaries of Global Capitalism*. London: Cassell, 1997.

Hesmondhalgh, David. *The Cultural Industries*. Thousand Oaks, CA: Sage, 2002.

Hill, Annette. "Big Brother, the Real Audience." *Television & New Media* 3, no. 3 (August 2002): 323–40.

———. *Reality TV: Audiences and Popular Factual Television*. London: Routledge, 2005.

Hills, Matt. "*Dawson's Creek*: 'Quality Teen TV' and 'Mainstream Cult?'" In Davis and Dickinson 2004, 54–67.

———. *Fan Cultures*. New York: Routledge, 2002.

Hilmes, Michele. *Hollywood and Broadcasting: From Radio to Cable*. Urbana, IL: University of Illinois Press, 1990.

———, ed. *NBC: America's Network*. Berkeley, CA: University of California Press, 2007.

———. *Only Connect: A Cultural History of Broadcasting in the US*. 2nd edition. Belmont, CA: Wadsworth, 2006.

———. "Who We Are, Who We Are Not: Battle of the Global Paradigms." In Parks and Kumar 2003, 53–73.

Hilmes, Michele, and Jason Jacobs, eds. *The Television History Book*. London: BFI, 2004.

Holmes, Su. "'But this Time You Choose!': Approaching the Interactive Audience in Reality TV." *International Journal of Cultural Studies* 7, no. 2 (2004): 213–31.

——. "Reality Goes Pop! Reality TV, Popular Music, and Narratives of Stardom in *Pop Idol*." *Television & New Media* 5, no. 2 (2004): 147–72.

Holmes, Su, and Deborah Jermyn, eds. "Introduction: Understanding Reality TV." In *Understanding Reality Television*, ed. Holmes and Jermyn, 1–32. London: Routledge, 2004.

Holt, Jennifer. "Vertical Vision: Deregulation, Industrial Economy and Prime-time Design." In Jancovich and Lyons 2003, 11–31.

Holt, Jennifer, and Alisa Perren, eds. *Media Industries: History, Theory, and Method*. Malden, MA: Wiley-Blackwell, 2009.

Howell, Amanda. "The X-Files, X-Philes and X-Philia: Internet Fandom as Site of Convergence." *Media International Australia: Incorporating Culture and Policy* 97 (November 2000): 137–49.

Jancovich, Mark, and James Lyons, eds. *Quality Popular Television*. London: BFI, 2003.

Jancovich, Mark, and Nathan Hunt. "The Mainstream, Distinction, and Cult TV." In Gwenllian-Jones and Pearson 2004, 27–44.

Jaramillo, Deborah L. "The Family Racket: AOL-Time Warner, HBO, *The Sopranos*, and the Construction of a Quality Brand." *Journal of Communication Inquiry* 26, no. 1 (2002): 59–75.

Jenkins, Henry. *Convergence Culture: Where Old and New Media Collide*. New York: New York University Press, 2006.

Jenkins, Henry, and David Thornburn, eds. *Democracy and New Media*. Cambridge, MA: MIT Press, 2003.

——. "'Do You Enjoy Making the Rest of Us Feel Stupid?': alt.tv.twinpeaks, the Trickster Author, and Viewer Mastery." In Lavery 1995, 51–69.

——. "Interactive Audiences?" In Harries 2002, 157–70.

——. "Quentin Tarantino's *Star Wars*? Digital Cinema, Media Convergence, and Participatory Culture." In Thornburn and Jenkins 2004, 281–311.

——. "*Star Trek* Rerun, Reread, Rewritten: Fan Writing as Textual Poaching," *Critical Studies in Mass Communication* 5, no. 2 (1988): 85–107.

——. *Textual Poachers: Television Fans and Participatory Culture*. New York: Routledge, 1992.

——. "The Poachers and the Stormtroopers: Cultural Convergence in the Digital Age." Spring 1998. Available online: http://commons.somewhere.com/rre/1998/.

Johnson, Catherine. "Tele-branding in TVIII: the Network as Brand and the Programme as Brand." *New Review of Film and Television Studies* 5, no. 1 (2007): 5–24.

——. *Telefantasy*. London: BFI, 2005.

Johnson, Derek. "Inviting Audiences In: the Spatial Reorganization of Production and Consumption in 'TV III.'" *New Review of Film and Television Studies* 5, no. 1 (April 2007): 61–80.

Johnson, Victoria E. *Primetime Television and the Struggle for U.S. Identity*. New York: New York University Press, 2008.

Jones, Gerard. *Honey, I'm Home! Sitcoms: Selling the American Dream*. New York: Grove Weidenfeld, 1992.

Jones, Jeffrey. *Entertaining Politics: New Political Television and Civic Culture*. Lanham, MD: Rowman and Littlefield, 2005.

Karpovich, Angelina I. "Reframing Fan Videos." In *Music, Sound and Multimedia: From the Live to the Virtual*, ed. Jamie Sexton, 17–28. Edinburgh: Edinburgh University Press, 2007.

Kelly, Kieran. "Case Study: The Development of the Apple iPod." In Sexton 2007, 188–200.

Keply, Vance Jr., "From 'Frontal Lobes' to the 'Bob-and-Bob Show': NBC Management and Programming Strategies, 1949–65." In *Hollywood in the Age of Television*, ed. Tino Balio, 41–62. Boston, MA: Unwin Hyman, 1990.

Kilborn, Richard. "'How Real Can You Get': Recent Developments in 'Reality' Television." *European Journal of Communication* 9 (1994): 421–39.

Kinder, Marsha. *Playing with Power in Movies, Television, and Video Games: From Muppet Babies to Teenage Mutant Ninja Turtles*. Berkeley, CA: University of California Press, 1993.

Klein, Naomi. *No Logo*. New York: Picador, 2002.

Klinger, Barbara. *Beyond the Multiplex: Cinema, New Technologies, and the Home*. Berkeley, CA: University of California Press, 2006.

———. "Digressions at the Cinema: Reception and Mass Culture." *Cinema Journal* 28, no. 4 (1989): 3–19.

Kolko, Beth, Lisa Nakamura, and Gilbert B. Rodman, eds. *Race in Cyberspace*. New York: Routledge, 2000.

Kompare, Derek. "Publishing Flow: DVD Box Sets and the Reconception of Television." *Television and New Media* 7, no. 4 (2006): 335–60.

———. *Rerun Nation: How Repeats Invented American Television*. New York: Routledge, 2005.

Kozinets, Robert V. "E-tribalized Marketing? The Strategic Implications of Virtual Communities of Consumption." *European Management Journal* 17, no. 3 (June 1999): 252–64.

———. "How Online Communities Are Growing in Power." *Financial Times* November 9, 1998.

Kunz, William. *Culture Conglomerates: Consolidation in the Motion Picture and Television Industries*. Lanham, MD: Rowman and Littlefield, 1997.

Lancaster, Kurt, and Henry Jenkins. *Interacting with Babylon 5: Fan Performances in a Media Universe*. Austin, TX: University of Texas Press, 2001.

Landow, George. *Hypertext 2.0: The Convergence of Contemporary Critical Theory and Technology*. Baltimore, MD: Johns Hopkins University Press, 1997.

Lavery, David, Anglea Hague, and Marla Cartwright, eds. *"Deny All Knowledge": Reading The X-Files*. Syracuse, NY: Syracuse University Press, 1996.

Lessig, Lawrence. *Code and Other Laws of Cyberspace*. New York: Basic Books, 1999.

Leverette, Marc, Brian L. Ott, and Cara Louise Buckley, eds. *It's Not TV: Watching HBO in the Post-television Era*. New York: Routledge, 2008.

Levine, Elana. *Wallowing in Sex: The New Sexual Culture of 1970s American Television*. Durham, NC: Duke University Press, 2007.

Levine, Elana, and Lisa Parks, eds. *Undead TV: Essays on Buffy the Vampire Slayer*. Durham, NC: Duke University Press, 2007.

Lévy, Pierre. *Collective Intelligence: Mankind's Emerging World in Cyberspace*, trans. Robert Bononno. Cambridge, MA: Perseus, 1997.

———. *Cyberculture*, trans. Robert Bononno. Minneapolis, MN: University of Minnesota Press, 2001.

Lotz, Amanda. "How to Spend $9.3 Billion in Three Days: Examining the Upfront Buying Process in the Production of US Television Culture." *Media, Culture and Society* 29, no. 4 (2007): 549–67.

———. "Must-See TV: NBC's Dominant Decades." In Hilmes 2007, 261–74.

———. *Redesigning Women: Television after the Network Era*. Urbana, IL: University of Illinois Press, 2006.

———. *The Television Will Be Revolutionized*. New York: New York University Press, 2007.

Magder, Ted. "The End of TV 101: Reality Programs, Formats, and the New Business of Television." In Murray and Ouellette 2004, 137–56.

Mandese, Joe. "DVR Threat Gets Downgraded." *Broadcasting & Cable* September 12, 2005, 20.

Mann, Denise. "The Spectacularization of Everyday Life: Recycling Hollywood Stars and Fans in Early Television Variety Shows." In *Private Screenings: Television and the Female Consumer,* ed. Lynn Spigel and Denise Mann, 41–69. Minneapolis, MN: University of Minnesota Press, 1992.

Manovich, Lev. *The Language of New Media.* Cambridge, MA: MIT Press, 2001.

Mashon, Mike. "NBC, J. Walter Thompson, and the Struggle for Control of Television Programming, 1946–58." In Hilmes 2007, 135–52.

Mayer, Vicki, John Thornton Caldwell, and Miranda J. Banks, eds. *Production Studies: Cultural Studies of Media Industries.* New York: Routledge, 2009.

McAllister, Matthew. *The Commercialization of American Culture: New Advertising, Control, and Democracy.* Thousand Oaks, CA: Sage, 1996.

McCarthy, Anna. *Ambient Television: Visual Culture and Public Space.* Durham, NC: Duke University Press, 2001.

——. "The Rhythms of the Reception Area: Crisis, Capitalism, and the Waiting Room TV." In Spigel and Olsson 2004, 183–209.

McChesney, Robert W. *Rich Media, Poor Democracy.* New York: New Press, 2000.

——. *Telecommunications, Mass Media, and Democracy: The Battle for the Control of U.S. Broadcasting, 1928–35.* New York: Oxford University Press, 1993.

——. *The Political Economy of Media: Enduring Issues, Emerging Dilemmas.* New York: Monthly Review Press, 2008.

——. *The Problem of the Media: U.S. Communication Politics in the Twenty-First Century.* New York: Monthly Review, 2004.

McKee, Alan. "How to Tell the Difference between Production and Consumption: A Case Study in Doctor Who Fandom." In Gwenllian-Jones and Pearson 2004, 167–85.

Meehan, Eileen. *Why Television is Not Our Fault: Television Programming, Viewers, and Who's Really in Control.* Lanham, MD: Rowman and Littlefield, 2005.

——. "Why We Don't Count: The Commodity Audience." In *Logics of Television: Essays in Cultural Criticism,* ed. Patricia Mellencamp, 117–37. Bloomington, IN: Indiana University Press, 1990.

Miller, Toby, Nitin Govil, John McMurria, Richard Maxwell, and Tina Wang. *Global Hollywood 2.* London: BFI, 2005.

Mittell, Jason. "Generic Cycles: Innovation, Imitation, and Saturation." In Hilmes and Jacobs 2004, 44–49.

——. *Genre and Television: From Cop Shows to Cartoons in American Culture.* New York: Routledge, 2004.

——. "Narrative Complexity in Contemporary American Television." *The Velvet Light Trap* 58 (2006): 29–40.

——. "The Cultural Power of an Anti-Television Metaphor: Questioning the 'Plug-in Drug' and a TV-Free America." *Television and New Media* 1, no. 2 (2000): 215–38.

Moran, Albert. *Copycat TV: Globalisation, Programme Formats and Cultural Identity.* Luton, U.K.: Luton University Press, 1998.

Morse, Margaret. *Virtualities: Television, Media Art, and Cyberculture.* Bloomington, IN: Indiana University Press, 1998.

Mossberger, Karen, Caroline J. Tolbert, and Ramona S. McNeal. *Digital Citizenship: The Internet Society, and Participation.* Cambridge, MA: MIT Press, 2008.

Mullen, Megan. *Television in the Multichannel Age.* Oxford: Blackwell, 2007.

Murray, Janet H. *Hamlet on the Holodeck: The Future of Narrative in Cyberspace*. Cambridge, MA: MIT Press, 1997.

Murray, Simone. "Brand Loyalties: Rethinking Content within Global Corporate Media." *Media, Culture, Society* 27, no. 3 (2005): 415–35.

Murray, Susan. *Hitch Your Antenna to the Stars: Early Television and Broadcast Stardom*. New York: Routledge, 2005.

Murray, Susan, and Laurie Ouellette, eds. *Reality TV: Remaking Television Culture*. New York: New York University Press, 2004.

Napoli, Philip M. *Audience Economics: Media Institutions and the Audience Marketplace*. New York: Columbia University Press, 2003.

Negroponte, Nicholas. *Being Digital*. New York: Alfred Knopf, 1995.

Newcomb, Horace M., and Robert S. Alley. *The Producer's Medium*. New York: Oxford University Press, 1983.

——. "This is Not Al Dente: The Sopranos and the New Meaning of Television." In *Television: The Critical View*. 7th edition, ed. Horace Newcomb, 561–78. New York: Oxford University Press, 2006.

O'Regan, Tom, and Ben Goldsmith. "Emerging Global Ecologies of Production." In Harries 2002, 92–105.

Ouellette, Laurie, and James Hay. *Better Living Through Reality TV: Television and Post-Welfare Citizenship*. Malden, MA: Blackwell, 2008.

——. "Take Responsibility for Yourself: *Judge Judy* and the Neoliberal Citizen." In Murray and Ouellette 2004, 231–50.

Parks, Lisa. "Flexible Microcasting: Gender, Generation, and Television-Internet Convergence." In Spigel and Olsson 2004, 133–62.

Parks, Lisa, and Shanti Kumar, eds. *Planet TV: A Global Television Reader*. New York: New York University Press, 2003.

Poster, Mark. *The Second Media Age*. London: Blackwell, 1995.

——. *What's the Matter with the Internet?* Minneapolis, MN: University of Minneapolis Press 2001.

Raphael, Chad. "The Political Economic Origins of Reali-TV." In Murray and Ouellette 2004, 119–36.

Reeves, Jimmie L., Mark C. Rodgers, and Michael Epstein. "Rewriting Popularity: The Cult *Files*." In Lavery, Hague, and Cartwright 1996, 22–35.

Rixon, Paul. "The Changing Face of American Television Programmes on British Screens." In Jancovich and Lyons 2003, 48–61.

Rogers, Mark C., Michael Epstein, and Jimmie L. Reeves. "*The Sopranos* as HBO Brand Equity: The Art and Commerce in the Age of Digital Reproduction." In *This Thing of Ours: Investigating The Sopranos*, ed. David Lavery, 42–57. New York: Columbia University Press, 2002.

Roscoe, Jane. "*Big Brother* Australia: Performing the 'Real' Twenty-four-seven." *International Journal of Cultural Studies* 4, no. 4 (2001): 473–88.

Roscoe, Jane, and Craig Hight. *Faking It: Mock-documentary and the Subversion of Factuality*. Manchester: Manchester University Press, 2001.

Ross, Sharon Marie. *Beyond the Box: Television and the Internet*. Malden, MA: Blackwell, 2008.

Ross, Sharon Marie and Louisa Ellen Stein, eds. *Teen Television: Essays on Programming and Fandom*. Jefferson, NC and London: McFarland, 2008.

Samuel, Lawrence R. *Brought to You By: Postwar Television Advertising and The American Dream*. Austin, TX: University of Texas Press, 2001.

Sandler, Kevin. "Life Without *Friends*: NBC's Programming Strategies in an Age of Media Clutter." In Hilmes 2007, 291–307.

Sandvoss, Cornel. *Fans: The Mirror of Consumption*. New York: Polity, 2005.

San Martin, Nancy. "'Must See TV': Programming Identity on NBC Thursdays." In Jancovich and Lyons 2003, 32–47.

Santo, Avi. "Para-television and Discourses of Distinction: The Culture of Production at HBO." In Leverette, Ott, and Buckley 2008, 19–45.

Scannell, Paddy. "Big Brother as Media Event." *Television & New Media* 3, no. 3 (2002): 271–82.

———. "Public Service Broadcasting and Modern Life." *Media, Culture and Society* 11, no. 2 (1989): 135–66.

Schatz, Thomas. "The New Hollywood." In *Film Theory Goes to the Movies*, ed. Jim Collins, Hilary Radner, and Ava Preacher Collins, 8–36. London: Routledge, 1993.

Sconce, Jeffrey. "What If? Charting Television's New Textual Boundaries." In Spigel and Olsson 2004, 93–112.

Seiter, Ellen. *Television and New Media Audiences*. Oxford: Oxford University Press, 1999.

Sella, Marshall. "The Remote Controllers." *New York Times Magazine*, October 20, 2002, 68+

Shattuc, Jane M. "Television Production: Who Makes American TV?" In *A Companion to Television*, ed. Janet Wasko, 142–54. Oxford: Blackwell, 2005.

Sobchack, Vivian. *Meta-morphing: Visual Transformation and the Culture of Quick Changes*. Minneapolis, MN: University of Minnesota Press, 2000.

Spigel, Lynn. *Make Room for TV: Television and the Family Ideal in Postwar America*. Chicago, IL: University of Chicago Press, 1992.

Spigel, Lynn and Jan Olsson, eds. *Television After TV: Essays on a Medium in Transition*. Durham, NC: Duke University Press, 2004.

Staid, Gitte. "Mobile Identity: Youth, Identity, and Mobile Communication Media." In Buckingham 2008, 143–64.

Stein, Louisa. "Pushing at the Margins: Teenage Angst in Teen TV and Audience Response." In Ross and Stein 2008, 224–43.

———. "Subject: 'Off-Topic: Oh My God U.S. Terrorism!' *Roswell* Fans Respond to 11 September." *European Journal of Cultural Studies* 5 (2002): 471–91.

———. "'They Cavort, You Decide': Fan Discourses of Intentionality, Interpretation, Queerness in Teen TV." *Spectator* 25 (2005): 11–22.

———. "'This Dratted Thing': Fannish Storytelling Through New Media." In Hellekson and Busse 2006, 245–60.

Streeter, Thomas. *Selling the Air: A Critique of the Policy of Commercial Broadcasting in the United States*. Chicago, IL: University of Chicago Press, 1996.

Tapscott, Don. *Growing up Digital: The Rise of the Net Generation*. New York: McGraw-Hill, 1999.

Tasker, Yvonne, and Diane Negra. "In Focus: Postfeminism and Contemporary Media Studies." *Cinema Journal* 44 (2005): 107–10.

Telotte, J.P. "*The Blair Witch Project* Project: Film and the Internet." *Film Quarterly* 54, no. 3 (2001): 32–39.

Thornburn, David, and Henry Jenkins, eds. *Rethinking Media Change: The Aesthetics of Transition*. Cambridge, MA: MIT Press, 2004.

Tincknell, Estella, and Parvati Raghuram. "*Big Brother*: Reconfiguring the 'Active' Audience of Cultural Studies." *European Journal of Cultural Studies* 5, no. 2 (2002): 199–215.

Tinic, Serra. *On Location: Canada's Television Industry in a Global Market*. Toronto: University of Toronto Press, 2005.

Torre, Paul. "Block Booking Migrates to Television: The Rise and Fall of the International Output Deal." *Television & New Media* 10, no. 6 (November 2009): 501–20.

Tulloch, John, and Henry Jenkins. *Science Fiction Audiences: Watching Star Trek and Doctor Who.* New York: Routledge, 1995.

Tunstall, Jeremy. *The Media Were American: U.S. Mass Media in Decline.* New York: Oxford University Press, 2007.

Turkle, Sherry. *Life on the Screen: Identity in the Age of the Internet.* New York: Simon and Schuster, 1995.

Turow, Joseph. *Breaking Up America: Advertisers and the New Media World.* Chicago, IL: University of Chicago Press, 1997.

———. *Niche Envy: Marketing Discrimination in the Digital Age.* Cambridge, MA: MIT Press, 2006.

Uricchio, William. "Historicizing Media in Transition." In Thornburn and Jenkins 2004, 23–38.

———. "Old Media and New Media: Television." In Harries 2002, 219–30.

Vaidhyanathan, Siva. *Copyrights and Copywrongs: The Rise of Intellectual Property and How It Threatens Creativity.* New York: New York University Press, 2001.

Vogel, Harold. *Entertainment Industry Economics: A Guide for Financial Analysts*, 7th edition. New York: Cambridge University Press, 2007.

Waisbord, Silvio. "Understanding the Global Popularity of Television Formats." *Television and New Media* 5, no. 4 (2004): 359–83.

Wardrip-Fruin, Noah, and Pat Harrigan, eds. *First Person: New Media as Story, Performance and Game.* Cambridge, MA: MIT Press, 2004.

Wasko, Janet. *Hollywood in the Information Age: Beyond the Silver Screen.* Austin, TX: University of Texas Press, 1994.

———. *How Hollywood Works.* Thousand Oaks, CA: Sage, 2003.

———. "The Future of Film Distribution and Exhibition." In Harries 2002, 195–206.

———. *Understanding Disney: The Manufacture of Fantasy.* Malden, MA: Polity Press, 2001.

Wee, Valerie. "Selling Teen Culture: How American Multimedia Conglomeration Shaped Teen Television in the 1990s." In Davis and Dickinson 2004, 87–98.

———. "Teen Television and the WB Network." In Ross and Stein 2008, 43–60.

Weibel, Peter, and Timothy Druckrey, eds. *Net Condition: Art and Global Media.* Cambridge, MA: MIT Press, 2001.

Williams, Raymond. *Television: Technology and Cultural Form.* London: Fontana, 1974.

Wyatt, Justin. *High Concept: Movies and Marketing in Hollywood.* Austin, TX: University of Texas Press, 1994.

Van Zoonen, Liesbet. *Entertaining the Citizen: When Politics and Popular Culture Converge.* Lanham, MD: Rowman and Littlefield, 2005.

Zweerink, Amanda, and Sarah N. Gatson. "www.buffy.com: Cliques, Boundaries, and Hierarchies in an Internet Community." In *Fighting the Forces: What's at Stake in Buffy the Vampire Slayer*, ed. Rhonda Wilcox, and David Lavery. Lanham, MD: Rowman & Littlefield, 2002, 239–51.

Index

convergence in 65–66; text messaging and 65; web interface 66, 70–71
Gough, Alfred 50
Graser, Marc 163
Gray, Jonathan 231, 277n 90
Grey's Anatomy 24, 73, 144, 148, 157, 175, 223–30, 273n25
Grey Matter writers' flogs 223–30
Grushow, Sandy 81, 145
Guerrero, Edward 65
Gwenllian-Jones, Sara 59

The Half Hour News Hour 109, 117
Harper's Island 137
Hayek, Salma 188–89, 194–95, 197, 204, 209
Hayes, Dade 163
HBO (Home Box Office): *auteur* and 140; channel branding 10, 80, 135, 140; channel brand detachment 171; as competition for broadcast television 10–11, 80, 138, 142, 221, 240; compressed seasons on 80, 141; *It's not TV* tagline 10, 135–36, 138, 221; NBC and 221; premium channel 10,140, 142, 241; "quality" television and 21, 135, 156; revenue model 80, 140,142; scheduling 80, 140–42
Heinberg, Allan 225–30
Heritage Foundation 112, 113
Heroes: interlocking gear model and 4, 22–23; as multiplatform franchise and networked text 3–5, 22–23, 169; NBC and 6–7, 9, 22–24, 137, 232–33; NBC Universal logo and 24; Nissan sponsorship of 193; product integration 193; production team 136, 231–32, 249n16; ratings 7, 24, 137, 232–33; Sprint sponsorship of 6; transmedia marketing of 5–6,169
Heroes: Evolutions 3, 4, 22, 55, 169, 249n16
high concept, pre-sold property 65
Hills, Matt 3, 42, 57, 59, 224
Hill Street Blues 1, 9, 11
Hodges, Joseph 93–95
Holland, Roger 74
Hollywood studios, relationship to television 14–15, 31–33, 51, 81, 92, 143, 163, 181, 200–202
Homicide: Second Shift (*Homicide: Life on the Streets*) 35–39
Howell, Amanda 31
How I Met Your Mother 92
Hulu 23, 81, 85, 203, 207–8, 211, 221, 244

I'm a Celebrity … Get Me Out of Here (U.S.) 144, 146

Inside the X (*X-Files*) 30–31, 33–34, 39, 46
interactivity: immediate versus delayed 15, 86; simultaneous 86
intermediality 78
internet *see* World Wide Web
Inside the Obama White House (NBC News special) 217–20
international formats 145–46, 157, 175, 181–84, 209
interstitials 4, 27, 69–74, 193
iTunes (Apple) 52, 73, 75, 139, 176, 208, 222–27, 240; deal with Disney-ABC 22–25, 142–43, 172, 243

Jack Benny Program, The 196–98
JAG 11, 204
Jay Leno Show, The 1, 7, 8, 13, 17, 206, 210, 218, 236–44
Jenkins, Henry 3–4, 19, 40, 42, 57–59, 70, 166, 229, 274n35
Jermyn, Deborah 87, 115
Jimmy Kimmel Live! 168–69, 244
Joe Millionaire 145

Kapinos, Tom 44, 46
Kath 24, 184–88, 209–10
Katims, Jason 211
Katz, Evan 130
Kelley, David E. 239, 243
Kellner, Douglas 79
Kellner, Jamie 80
King, John 72
Klinger, Barbara 95, 101
Knight Rider 23, 89, 183
Kolb, Suzanne 46, 52
Kompare, Derek 95–96
Kurtzman, Alex 137, 240

laptop computer 26, 64, 66, 71, 81
Late Night with Jimmy Fallon 7, 13, 206–7, 210, 215–18, 238, 286n70; beta testing of 206, 218; repurposing of 206, 215; short form content 206–7, 215–17; *see also 7th Floor West*
Late Show with David Letterman 13, 218, 244
Late, Late Show with Craig Ferguson 237
Law 12, 210, 244, 286n70
Lawson, Mark 88
lean-forward TV 85
Levy, Pierre 58,166, 225
Lewis, Justin 106–8
LG mobile 97